How to Do
Everything
with
iMovie™ 2

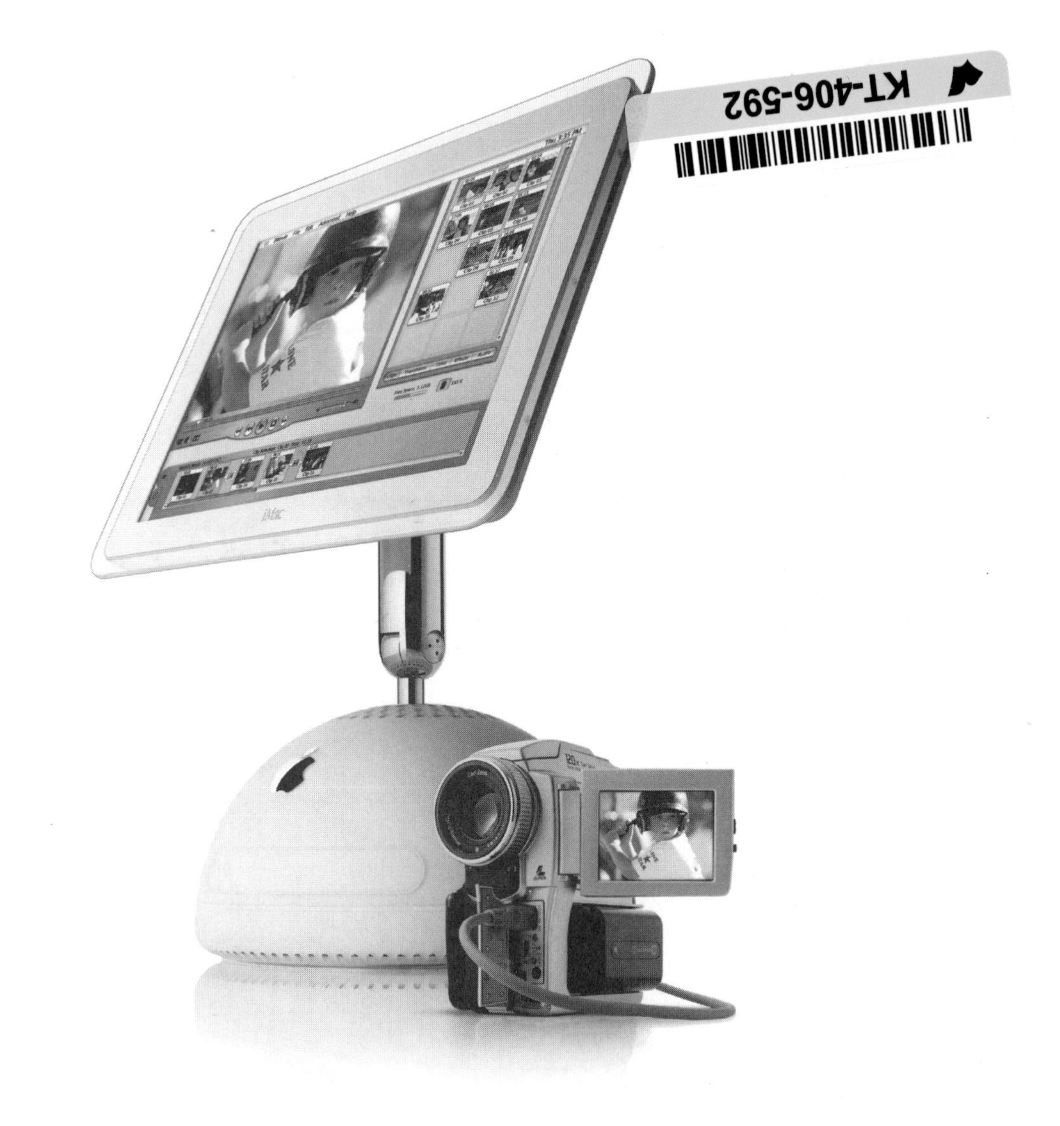

How to Do *Everything* with iMovie™ 2

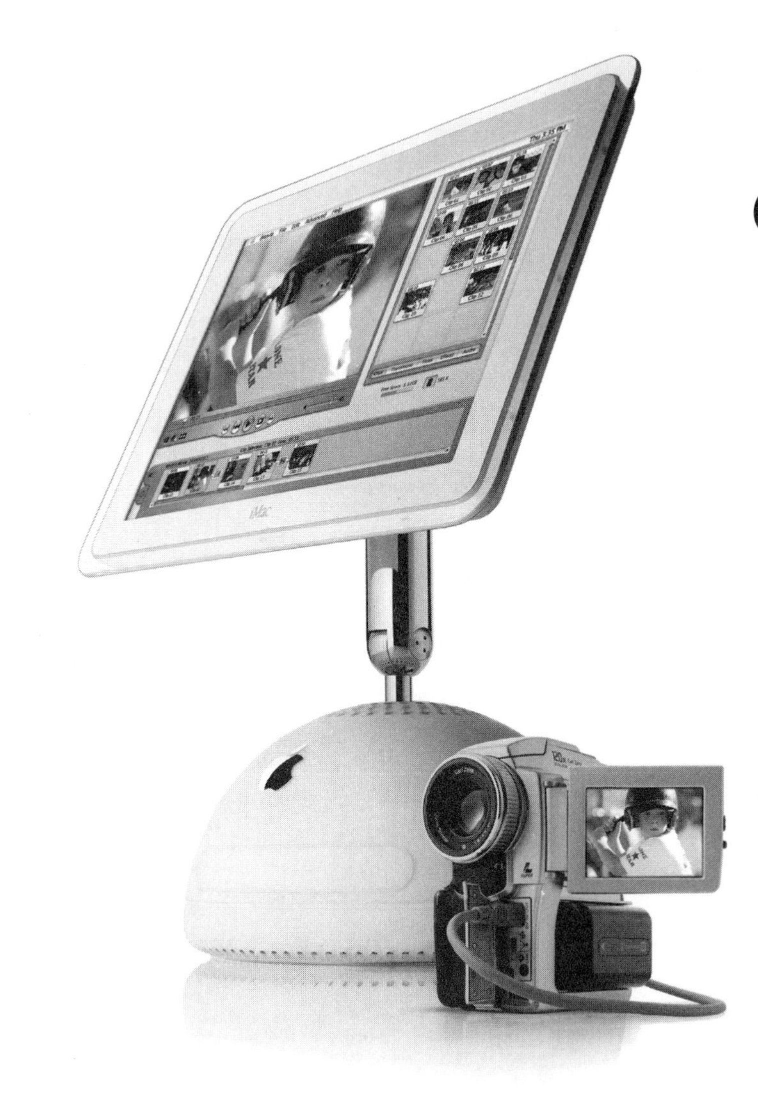

Tony Reveaux
Gene Steinberg

McGraw-Hill/Osborne

New York Chicago San Francisco Lisbon
London Madrid Mexico City Milan New Delhi
San Juan Seoul Singapore Sydney Toronto

McGraw-Hill/Osborne
2600 Tenth Street
Berkeley, California 94710
U.S.A.

To arrange bulk purchase discounts for sales promotions, premiums, or fund-raisers, please contact **McGraw-Hill/**Osborne at the above address. For information on translations or book distributors outside the U.S.A., please see the International Contact Information page immediately following the index of this book.

How to Do Everything with iMovie™ 2

1234567890 FGR FGR 0198765432

ISBN 0-07-222267-0

Publisher	Brandon A. Nordin
Vice President & Associate Publisher	Scott Rogers
Acquisitions Editor	Marjorie McAneny
Senior Project Editor	Betsy Manini
Acquisitions Coordinator	Tana Diminyatz
Technical Editor	Amy Hoy
Production and Editorial Services	Anzai! Inc.
Illustration Supervisor	Lyssa Wald
Cover Designer	Will Voss

This book was composed with Corel VENTURA™ Publisher.

Dedication

For my parents, Edward C. and Marion Reveaux.

——Tony Reveaux

To my family, who made it possible for me to realize the impossible dream.

——Gene Steinberg

About the Authors

Tony Reveaux is a San Francisco-based writer and consultant who has produced multimedia exhibitions for theaters and museums, and contributed to dozens of technology and art publications, is a senior writer for *Film/Tape World,* and has written *Cool Mac Clip Art Plus!*. Tony has an MFA in Filmmaking, and has taught film and media studies at the University of California at Santa Cruz, the San Francisco Art Institute and the San Francisco State University Multimedia Studies Center.

Award-winning technology journalist and Osborne author **Gene Steinberg** has been an Apple computer expert since the introduction of the Macintosh in 1984. He is a columnist for Gannett News and *USA Today* and a contributing editor for CNET and ZDNet. Gene has written hundreds of articles and more than two dozen books on computers and the Internet, including *Mac OS 9: The Complete Reference* (McGraw-Hill/Osborne, 2000), and *Upgrading & Troubleshooting Your Mac: Mac OS X Edition* (McGraw-Hill/Osborne, 2001). In his spare time, Gene and his teenaged son, Grayson, are developing a science fiction adventure series, *Attack of the Rockoids* (www.rockoids.com).

At a Glance

Contents

Acknowledgments

My thanks to the patience and enlightened momentum of all of Osborne's word herders in Berkeley, headed by Acquisitions Editor Marjorie McAneny, channeled by Acquisitions Coordinator Tana Diminyatz and Senior Project Editor Betsy Manini, and fine-tuned by Technical Editor Amy Hoy. Special thanks to Ottawa's Tom Anzai and his team who produced this book and managed the exceptionally heavy graphic traffic that it demanded. And, to my agent, Margot Maley Hutchinson.

I only wish that all of my filmmaking students had enjoyed the opportunity to have *How to Do Everything with iMovie 2* and Apple's iMovie 2 to learn with. They taught me how to teach. And, as always, I wish to express my appreciation for the chance to work with members of the film and video production community, whose toughness and professionalism are matched only by their fairness and generosity.

——Tony Reveaux

Books cannot be written in a vacuum, and were it not for the help of Osborne/ McGraw-Hill's supremely talented editorial staff, this book would never have been possible. I would also like to give special thanks to my friend and agent, Sharon Jarvis, who has always been there with sage advice to help me get over the rough spots and to make this all happen.

Deserving of special praise are the miracle workers at Apple Computer who created iMovie 2 and empowered budding filmmakers around the world to greater heights of creativity.

I must give my sincere thanks to my little nuclear family—my brilliant son (and sometimes co-author), Grayson, and my beautiful wife and business partner, Barbara—for tolerating the long hours I spent glued to my computer keyboard to finish this book on schedule.

——Gene Steinberg

Introduction

Right out of the box, with every Macintosh, comes a filmmaker's dream. Apple's iMovie lets you start editing digital video even before you pick up a camcorder. With *How to Do Everything with iMovie™ 2,* we want to help you choose that camcorder and know how to use it to make the movies that have been in your mind. The good paradox about iMovie 2 is that it is so transparently easy to use that it opens up the great potentials of ideas and possibilities of experience we see in movies and television. We all bring some of that with us into even the most humble home movie we may put together.

The book starts up where you will end up, with examples of finished short digital videos. Scenes from the iMovie Tutorial are there, because that will help you to begin cutting even before you are shooting. Since we want you to be well prepared, you'll find everything you need to know about setting up your Macintosh to support your productions.

From writing a script, to framing through the lens of your camcorder, to recording sound, the whole production process is explained. Time-saving tips and economical examples will help you keep the home in home movie. At the same time, we never lose sight of the practices of professional media making, to better understand where those big movies came from, and where you can go if you want to advance to intermediate videomaking, or further into joining independent and commercial production.

By the time you arrive at Part III, Editing with iMovie 2, you will probably have a few cassettes worth of raw video footage with which to build a movie—or several movies. As you begin to organize your images into sequences, and the sequences into scenes, you will quickly learn to work on the Shelf, clicking and dragging your clips and making video magic. You've been recording sound tracks with every scene you have shot, and as you advance to editing audio on the Timeline, the voices and noises on the track become choices and not chances. When you see—and hear—how easy it is to add sound effects from the built-in library, you will have a Roadrunner of a time animating your family antics.

Writing a book of this sort is not a one-way street. We want to learn from you as much as you learn from us. So if you have comments and questions about iMovie and movie-making in general, we'd love to hear from you.

Tony Reveaux
tonyrv@attbi.com

Gene Steinberg
gene@macnightowl.com
www.macnightowl.com
www.rockoids.com

Part I Getting Started

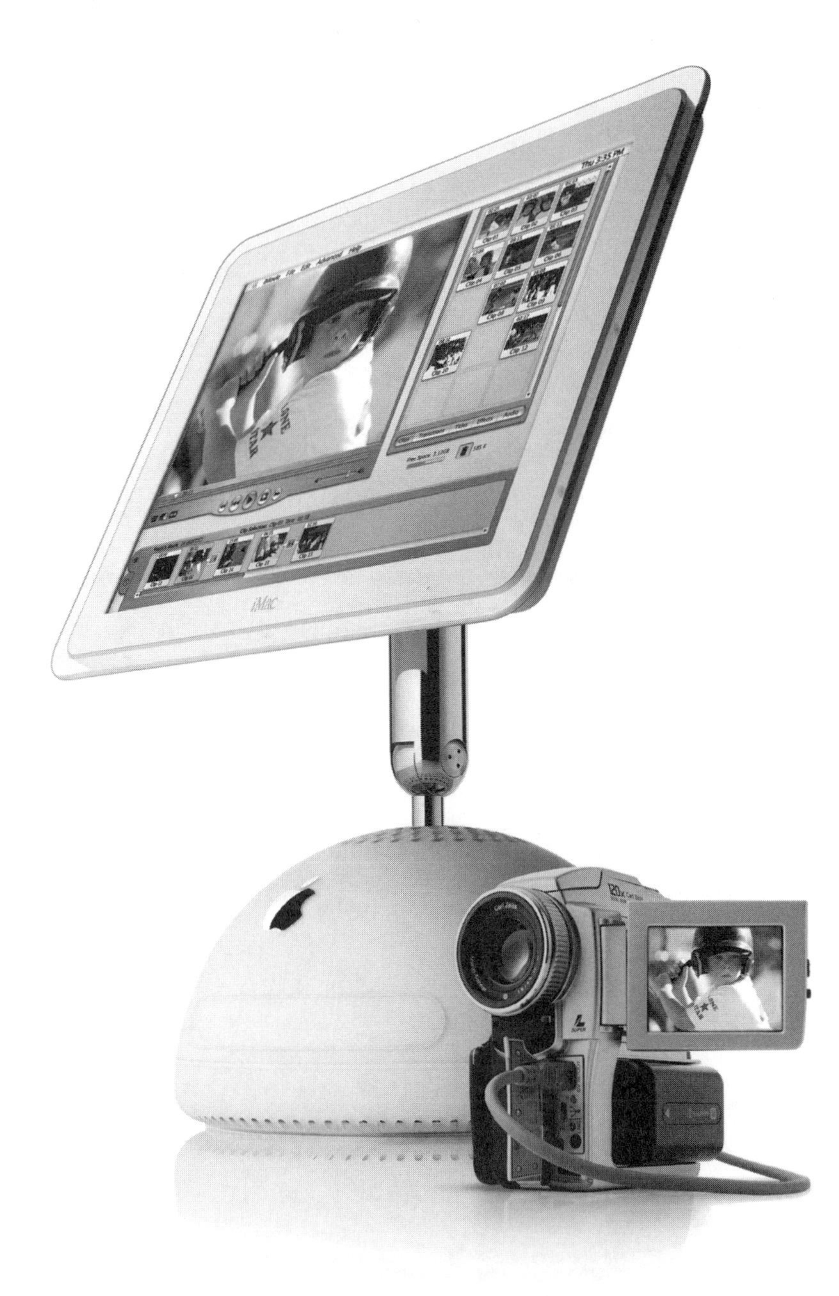

Chapter 1

Making iMovies that Work for You

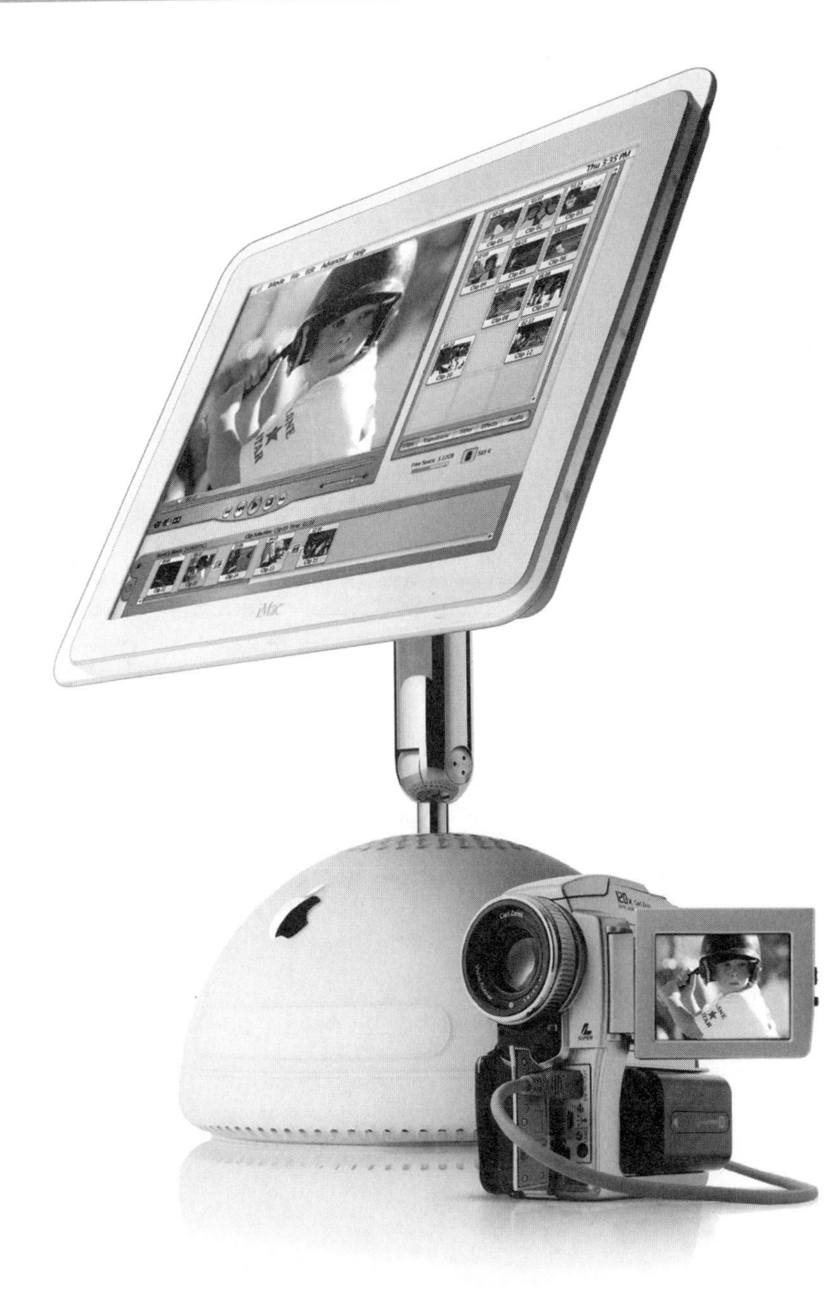

How to...

- Discover opportunities for making movies
- Make home movies a part of your family life
- Create an educational video
- Improve your game
- Make a rehearsal video

A World of Movies with iMovie 2

What is iMovie 2? It may be easier to say what it isn't. This friendly digital video editing software program is both so simple and yet so complete, that almost anything you may point your camera at can be recorded, creatively designed and edited, and turned out as a finished movie. This is why iMovie 2 is the beginner's best buddy and the professional's ready resource.

With iMovie 2 on your Mac, and a camcorder in your hand, all the pieces are in place.

In this book, you'll learn how to put your footage into the computer, and then use iMovie 2 like a TV to look it all over. Editing your videos is as easy as click and drag and cut and paste.

You can erase the pieces you don't need and try out different arrangements of your shots and scenes—as many times as you want. Put in transitions, like fade-in and fade-out, just like you see at the theater. Next, you can add and edit sound, music, and your voice. Titles are as simple as typing in "My First Movie."

In this chapter we'll look at just some of the opportunities and possibilities awaiting you, your camcorder, and iMovie. Each person reading this will think of many more. The frames on these pages are just rough black-and-white shadows of the bright streams of living color and sound you will start making the first time you press the button.

TIP *For a free iMovie Film Festival, go to Apple's iMovie Gallery at http://www.apple.com/imovie/gallery/. There you can view dozens of videos made with iMovie, as well as check out an invitation to submit your own movie to share with the world.*

Home Movies

Life happens. iMovie 2 plays it back. Compared to everything else in your life, your family will always be the most important. You care about what you do together. In snapshots, souvenirs, and stories, you recount and relive the moments, the episodes, and the memories of being yourself as well as part of a group.

Home movies, however imperfectly, capture the very stuff of life. Compared to those early 8mm cameras, today's easy-to-use camcorders can be ready to pick up in a minute to catch that familiar, important, or funny instant before it goes away.

But it's not just the camera that has made the big difference between good home movies and not-so-good ones. It's that most home movies were never edited. iMovie 2 was made for home movies. In Part III: Editing with iMovie, we will show you how easy it is, and how you can make almost any kind of movie at home, or anywhere.

The iMovie 2 Home Movie Tutorial

The home movie pictures we show here are included in Apple's iMovie tutorial (see the progression of pictures that make up Figure 1-1). We'll be using these clips in this book to show you how to edit your home videos. They are a perfect

FIGURE 1-1 Two kids make a great splash when they wash the dog—after they catch him, that is. © Apple Computer

example of how a home movie can happen. A boy and a girl are given the job of getting the family dog into the tub for a soak. Their actions, and the things they do as they work and play, are full of fun and joy. But, if you watch them in the exact order they were captured by your camcorder, it won't necessarily make for good viewing. That's the same reason that watching family videos can often be a chore, rather than an entertaining experience. But as you edit using iMovie 2, you will bring these scattered clips of wet pet and laughter together into a rhythm that can be watched like a song.

NOTE *Don't have a copy of the Apple iMovie tutorial? You get these files if you bought a new Mac with any version of iMovie installed, or have the CD version at hand.*

Here are some of the kinds of home movies you can make:

- **All about your baby** Everyone wants to see the baby, and you—and he or she—will have these images for all time. All right, the kids usually don't want to see themselves as babies, but the rest of the family will love it.
- **Your child's story** A home movie can be ongoing, like a diary, growing along through the years with your child as he grows from toddler to adolescence and beyond.
- **Birthdays, graduations, and weddings** Save every event and occasion to reflect upon who's who and who was there.
- **Family reunions** Every gathering is a one-of-a-kind event. Your production will ensure that everyone will be remembered—those who are new and those who are gone.
- **Pets** They are part of the family, too, and every one of them is a star. Animals have the innate ability to upstage anyone in a home movie.

Travel

Every trip is a voyage of visual discovery. Along with our memories, we bring back snapshots and souvenirs that help us to remember. They also provide a way to share the experience with others. A good travel video will capture the high points of your destination—local color, events and activities, and your personal favorite moments.

Don't forget you and your traveling companions. Here's where you can show what you did, why it was so much fun, and where you got that tan and your brilliant smile (or look of terror) when that roller coaster was running at full speed.

NOTE *Before you leave on that once-in-a-lifetime trip, make sure that someone else knows the basics of how to hold a shot with your camcorder so that you won't be absent from all the scenes. A fast rehearsal before you depart is a great idea.*

An Online Travelogue Guide

You'll always find a nice collection of travel videos on Apple's iMovie Gallery site. You can use these just to see the sites, or to get some neat ideas on what to do when you reach your vacation spot.

Here are some of the kinds of travel videos that your friends would like to see:

- **Getting there** From start to finish—sailing on the cruise ship, riding the horse-drawn carriage, or traveling on the steam railway—the journey is always an adventure.
- **People-oriented** Unify your video by following the point of view of your child visiting a farm for the first time, or your mother experiencing a homecoming to the old country.

TIP *You can really make your child feel part of the production if you make him or her the narrator. Watching the sights unfold from a child's point of view makes the movie all the more inventive, and it helps keep the kids from getting bored.*

- **Destination-driven** Make an event the centerpiece of your travel video, such as going to the Airstream trailer convention or attending the performance of *Aida* at the pyramids in Egypt.
- **Your hometown** Make a travelogue of you and your family "visiting" your hometown. You'll have this to send to distant relatives and to take with you on visits, where your movie will answer a thousand questions.

Documentaries

A documentary video is one that reports a truth about the world. With a realistic approach, it tells us about something that already exists and has a history, even if it is a short one. As a documentary videomaker, you are as much an eyewitness as you are a story-teller.

But that doesn't mean your film should be a carbon copy of what is in front of the camera. Your point of view and your personal style will become as much a part of your documentary as the subject matter. Two people making documentaries of the same subject may come away with two very different presentations.

After making home movies, making documentaries can be the best way for you to learn video. After you choose a subject, find out everything about it. Where is it? How did it get there? What happens at this place? Who does it? And, how is it done?

Weir Fishing on Nantucket Sound

This short video, shown in Figure 1-2, shows you the work of the few remaining weir fishermen setting and fishing their traps for squid and mackerel. You are introduced to the art of this most ancient and conservation-oriented fishery starting from an underwater scene, and traveling up to the boat where the men are raising the nets, and then moving to the decks where the day's catch is sorted.

FIGURE 1-2 *Weir Fishing on Nantucket Sound* brings you into the salt water, sun, and wind of fishing with nets. © Mooncusser Films.

Director Christopher Seufert, in describing how the documentary was made, says, "It was shot on a Canon XL1. We used a Hitachi boom-mounted Hi-8 for some of the underwater footage and the rest was shot by a diver with an underwater housing."

A whole world is out there waiting for you to make a documentary video:

- **Something old** Bring history alive by documenting something such as what printing is like in a letterpress shop, a tour of a Civil War fort, or the yarns told by a quiltmaking group.
- **Something new** Show and explain what is happening in current and innovative events such as solar panels being installed at the school, the opening of a recycling plant, or the painting of a public mural.
- **Show a process** Your video can capture and convey to others how things work, such as the day of a drawbridge operator, the rounds of a horse veterinarian, or how a baker designs and makes a wedding cake.

Sports

Take your camcorder to where the action is, and get the action back in spades. Your team will gain points by studying your videos of practice sessions. With iMovie 2, you can edit to the play, and highlight the action with slow motion and freeze frame. You can identify actions and players with titles. Now that editing is so easy (and videotape is recyclable) you can shoot freely and end up with the most crucial and exciting highlights on your computer or TV screen.

Here are some of the game plans for making sport of iMovie 2:

- **Practice makes perfect** Set your camcorder on a tripod, take the remote control, and gain extra perspective on your own performances. Practice your tennis serve, analyze your golf swing, jump your horse, get a long view of your diving, and enjoy a private replay to advance and improve.
- **Make game videos** You will really be the complete soccer mom when you show your player child scenes from the big game that he couldn't see from the sidelines.
- **Mark trails** Make survey videos of the different park trails available to help your hiking group plan tour schedules.
- **Finish to the frame** Posting your camcorder at the race's finish line will provide much more exciting and exact records of whose nose crossed first.

Dramatic Stories

Mention movies and television and you think of the stories they can tell. The narrative flow of one scene after another, like sentences in a conversation, makes a story even if it wasn't intended to be one. You can see that even when you play back the raw footage of a home movie.

Dramatic videos are given a structure and continuity in the shooting and in the editing, so that the stories they tell can be understood and appreciated for what they have to say. In Chapter 4 you will learn about the different ways you can plan a production by developing your concept, visualizing with storyboards, and writing scripts. You may find enjoyable ways to tell short and simple stories by improvising and acting out with friends.

Halo Promo, a Romantic Interlude in Paris

The attractions and closeness, and then the misunderstandings and withdrawal, are seen between a man and a woman in French filmmaker Laurent King's romantic urban interlude, as shown in Figure 1-3. The couple are seen together in dim

FIGURE 1-3 *Halo Promo*. © Laurent King

interiors, walking in the streets, inside a car, and on a riverboat on the Seine. Most of the scenes are at night, illuminated by their mutual awareness as well as by the city lights. All this is told without dialogue. Without a language barrier, King has made it even easier for his iMovie to be shown on Web sites all over the world.

NOTE

Halo Promo was shot on 16mm Fuji film, transferred to video, and then edited and compressed in iMovie. "The secret of the night photography," says King, "is to light evenly throughout the foreground so the background doesn't go black." To see his video in full color and with all its subtle details, go to Apple's iMovie Gallery.

There are as many ways to tell a story as there are stories. You can do it one movie at a time:

- **A child may lead** Children's play often acts out adventures and episodes. Follow children with your camcorder and edit their character and charm into the screen.
- **Poetry in motion** Let a reading of a favorite poem or essay be your narrative sound track. Find and shoot visual associations to the words and your thoughts. Edit with the images that may be landscapes, windows, clouds, streets, faces, colors, and textures.
- **Act it out** Work on a play with a drama class at your high school or college. With one camera, you can capture every key line, shot, and action throughout the process of the rehearsals. Edit in iMovie 2 and you and the class will have a roughly lit but completely cinematic version of the play. A video is also a good instructional tool for getting a sense of how the play looks to the audience; this can help the rehearsal process, keeping the action fluid, and making the performance as professional as possible.

Education and Training

iMovie 2 has been at the head of the class for many teachers in K-12 and middle schools. iMovie 2 is so easy to use that there are many reports of even third-graders making movies on Macs. In high school classrooms iMovie 2 has supported science experiments and drama rehearsals. Video can be a powerful tool for teaching, guidance, and instruction. Wherever we need to pass on structured information to other people, a simple video can be more effective than dozens of booklets and handouts.

Here are some of the ways that short videos can help pave the way to improved understanding:

- **Training school crossing guards** If new guards can actually see traffic and pedestrian situations that illustrate the safety regulations they must enforce, their training will be less abstract, more specific, and better connected to the real world.
- **Pet care** Seeing is much more effective than lectures or manuals. When children and adults watch others relate to animals one-on-one, they will be more confident themselves when checking their pet's health, administering medication, grooming, and training.
- **Factory floor safety training** All the charts on the wall won't do as well as a simple video to demonstrate to workers the exact procedures for using health and safety fixtures such as degreasers and eyewash fountains.
- **Customer relations sales training** With video as a non-judgmental mirror, salespeople can rehearse introductions, and service familiarization, closings, and follow-ups. Videos can help them answer the question, "How did I do?"

Music and Entertainment

MTV has shown how a wide variety of creative visualizations can complement music and its performance. Music, dance, and motion pictures go together as partners in rhythm. Your movies may have supportive background music, or the music may be the very subject of the piece. Every kind of live entertainment—rock or classical music, dance concerts, stage musicals, theater, opera, poetry reading, or stand-up comedy—can be made into your videos.

Sound editing in iMovie 2 can be as easy, flexible, and economical as cutting the images. You can edit the sound that was recorded in the shot, change it around, or place it under another shot. But you are not limited to the sound that is on the track of the footage. You can add music from a live performance or from a CD, and even combine them.

CAUTION *We should mention, of course, that we assume you are making these movies for your own or your family's use and amusement. Otherwise, you have to observe copyright restrictions on rerecorded material and not distribute videos containing that material without permission.*

Shooting the Band

In the music video you see in Figure 1-4, the song drives a vision, and the camera, too, is one of the performers. The music video has become the ideal medium to showcase a group, demonstrating not just vocal and instrumental skills, but performing skills as well. You see the singer and the three musicians performing, with camera angles and framing giving them brief but compelling presence. To accent the action, their images are often altered with additions and overlays of graphic textures.

Black-and-white flashes, streaks, and film patterns rhythmically intercut the footage to enrich and enliven the experience, and contribute to the beat of the music. According to director Christopher Seufert, "The band One-Handed Molly was shot entirely on consumer Hi-8, hence our use of the black-and-white effect."

FIGURE 1-4 Here is One-Handed Molly performing their piece, *Hourglass*. © Mooncusser Films.

Your videos can be records of your performances or of others':

- **Make a rehearsal video** Your camcorder can be your best—and most forgiving—critic. Set it on a tripod, activate it for continuous recording, and then go ahead and practice your song, lines for a play, or dance movements. You can replay the session for analysis, and edit your best tries to keep—until better ones come along.
- **Make a cinepoem** Choose a favorite song or piece of music and use it as the channel for a dream-like visual continuity. Shoot images of shapes, textures, and colors that appeal to you. Edit them to the music using effects and transitions like fades, wipes, and dissolves.
- **Make a dance performance video** A modern dance duo can be shot in stages, from long shots showing the action on the full stage, to closer shots of the two dancers. They can take turns using the camera as they dance. Now you can edit it with a variety of scale that can include cutting back and forth between the two dancers.

Experimental Videos

Film and video both started out as someone's experiment, and you, too, can try out your ideas and experiments in what you record and how you use the digital equipment that makes the images and sounds possible. iMovie 2 is part of what Apple calls the digital hub. This is not an object nor a product. It is the multi-directional connectivity between different devices with diverse media that share a common digital code.

When you connect your camcorder to your Mac with a FireWire cable to import footage from the videotape to iMovie 2, and then add music to your soundtrack from a CD that you inserted, you see the digital hub at work. The digital hub also allows for more ways and directions for information to go back and forth. Experimental video can be another way of saying "think different." Here's an example of how the tools of digital video can be repurposed and expanded in a creative and enlightening way.

The Telephone, an Experimental Video Tour Installation

Canadian artist Janet Cardiff took a new look at the traditional museum exhibition audiotour where the visitor is issued a tape player with a pre-recorded informational program that guides him from point to point. For the San Francisco Museum of Modern Art's *010101: Art in Technological Times* show, she presented *The Telephone*, an experimental video tour installation.

At the beginning of the tour you are issued a DV camcorder with the LCD viewer opened out and a pair of audio headphones to monitor the videotape's stereo soundtrack, as shown in Figure 1-5. You press the playback button on the

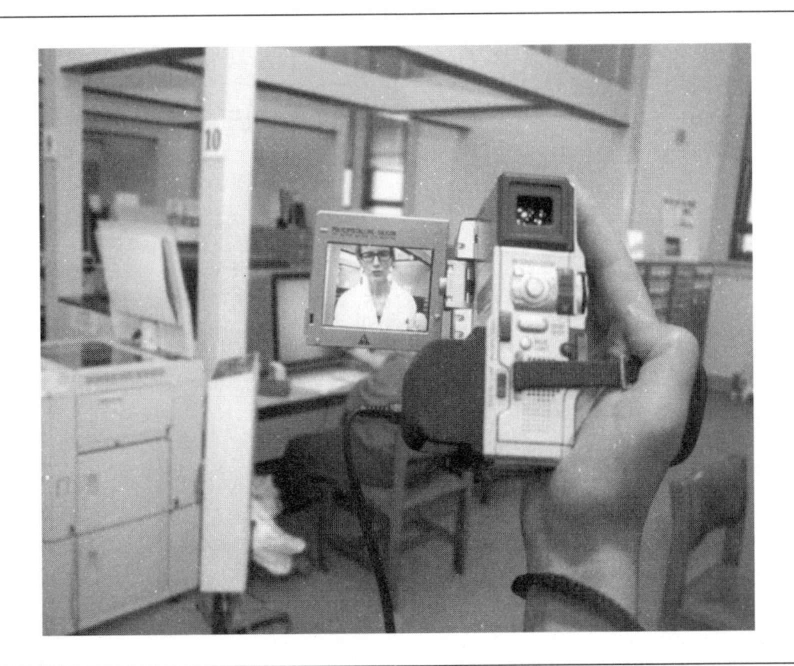

FIGURE 1-5 Janet Cardiff's video installations may use the camcorder as a display and playback device.

camcorder, and listen to the artist's voice on the soundtrack as she gives you directions for walking through the building. Here are just a few of the stations you would encounter on this tour:

1. You are led to the main stairway balcony. There you hear the full acoustic mass of the cavernous lobby space resonate with a gospel singer's voice.
2. You are directed to a certain painting on the wall, and told to hold up the viewer so it matches. The woman in the painting has been changed to a different person.
3. In the viewer you are shown a door with an Employees Only sign on it, and are asked to find it.
4. You find and reach the door. You are instructed to open it and go up the stairway. For the exhibition, the Museum has left it unlocked.
5. As you climb the empty stairwell, you are "overtaken" by a running man seen briefly as an image on the viewer, but heard thoroughly and realistically in your headphones as a moving stereo sound.

6. Having reached the top floor, you are asked to go to a certain window. In the distance you can see San Francisco's Corona Peaks.

7. The final image in the viewer is a reverse angle shot, taken by the artist from Corona Peaks, looking at the Museum in the city's skyline.

Experimental art is the ability to think different, which starts by looking different. Cardiff looked at the camcorder and saw all of its capabilities, which can go well beyond just shooting videotape. Expand your talents and skills by making videos with iMovie 2 and explore the digital hub.

The Closing Scene

In this first chapter, we have explored the scope and range of opportunities awaiting you for making videos with iMovie 2. This is just the tip of the digital iceberg. With every step you take, more alternatives and choices will appear.

In the next chapter, you'll learn about the hardware foundations of your Macintosh and its peripherals, to make sure that you are fully prepared to support and produce digital video with everything optimized to the fullest.

Chapter 2

Setting Up Your DV Studio

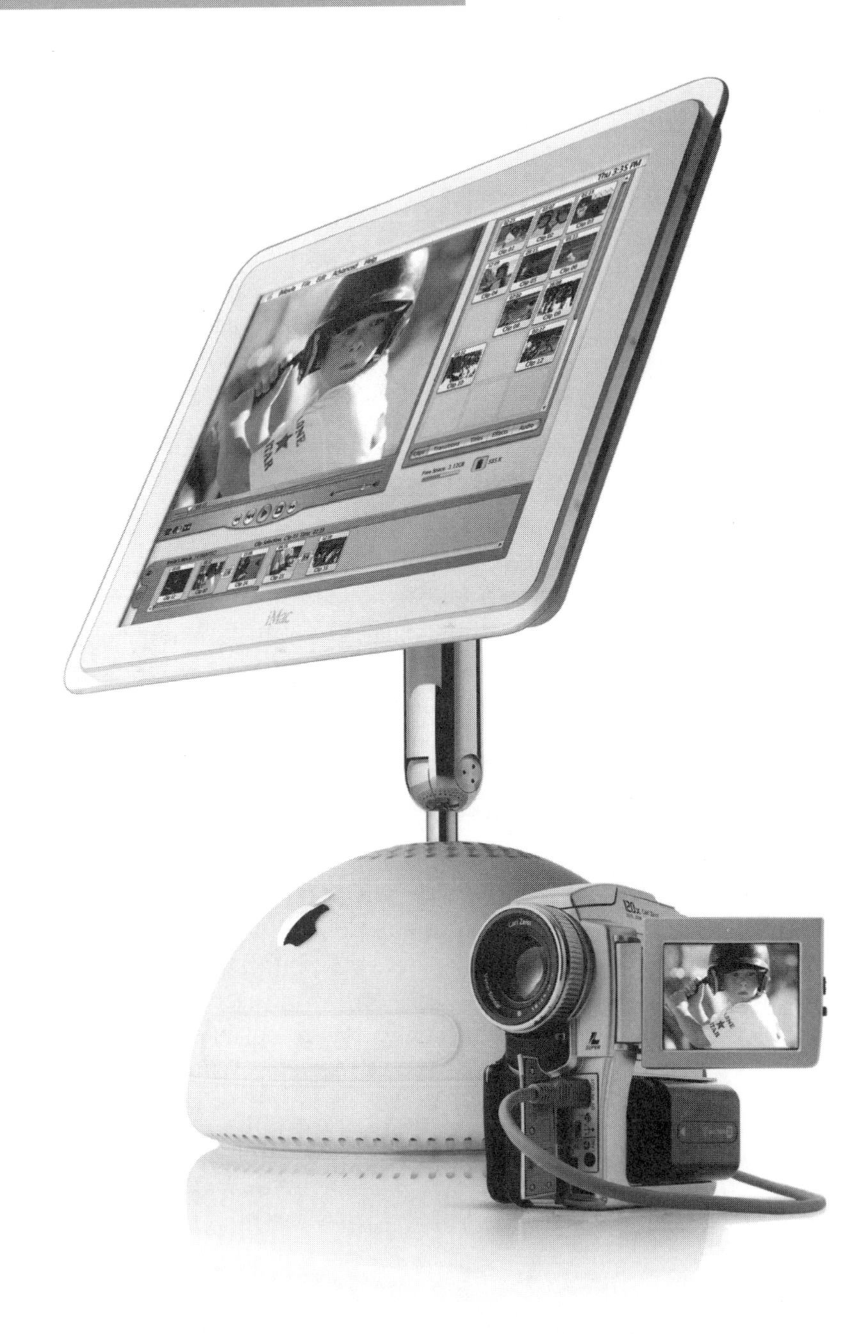

How to…

- Prepare your Mac for production
- Choose the memory you need
- Connect your Mac for multimedia
- Expand your desktop with more monitors
- Turn your Mac into a TV set

Optimizing Your FireWire Mac for iMovie 2

All new Apple computers you buy today share a single feature, one that has earned the company an Emmy Award. Did we say an Emmy? Yes indeed. Whether it's the sexy iBook or PowerBook G4, the iMac or the powerful Power Mac G4, they all have something in common—a high-speed port that enables them to communicate with just about any digital camcorder on the market, plus hundreds of other peripherals.

We're talking about FireWire.

You'll also find FireWire on lots of vintage Macs. The list is pretty big, so all we can do is suggest that you look at the specs for your model, and if you see the telltale connection port that's oval at one end, flat on the other, you'll know FireWire is present.

There is one more element to our equation, that clever, ultra-smooth multimedia application that is the focus of this book: iMovie 2. With iMovie 2 at hand, all you need to complete your DV (digital video) studio is a DV camcorder, and you're ready to start planning for the day you can shout, "Action!"

Even Older Macs Aren't Obsolete

All right, what about those older desktop Macs. Maybe you have the original beige G3 desktop or minitower, or perhaps a vintage Power Mac 9600 that's been outfitted with a G3 or G4 processor upgrade and still runs full-time doing its thing. Well, don't feel left out. Any Mac with a PCI slot is eligible for FireWire, courtesy of an upgrade card. Best of all, the cards often cost less than $50. They come from such makers as Belkin and Keyspan, and are readily available from your favorite computer emporium. If you have an older PowerBook with a PC card slot, you can get a FireWire CardBus adapter and get with the program.

TIP *Another option to consider is a PCI combo card—one offering both FireWire and USB. The net advantage is that you can also use some of those nice USB input devices, such as Apple's own Pro Keyboard and Pro Mouse.*

To be perfectly fair, you don't need FireWire to use iMovie 2. You can still edit the pictures and movies on your Mac's hard drive. But without FireWire, it's half a loaf.

And One More Thing…

That's what Apple's Steve Jobs is wont to say at the end of a Macworld Expo keynote when he's ready to introduce a new, unexpected product. But when equipping your ideal Mac editing station, there are actually two more things to think about (all right, we admit it, the title was a bit misleading).

First is RAM. It's cheap, and destined to remain so for a while. iMovie 2 will thrive on lots of RAM, and, if you've made the leap to Mac OS X, you'll find that much, much more RAM will enable you to get the best possible performance from Apple's gorgeous Unix-based operating system. Since more memory is better than less, try to find a dealer who will provide a free RAM upgrade as part of the price.

NOTE *Dealers will also exact a small installation service charge for the free RAM, and sometimes the service charge is not much less than the cost of the RAM itself. But when the dealer installs your RAM, he's responsible for testing your computer to make sure it works fine before he gives it back to you.*

The second additional item is processor speed. Now, iMovie 2 will work fine on any Mac with a G3 processor, but if you have an older beige or Blue and White G3, consider a processor upgrade—more likely to the G4 level. While it won't get you all the performance of a real G4 (which has faster hard drives, faster optical drives, and speedier system busses), it'll be close enough for jazz.

But even a regular iMac with FireWire (see Figure 2-1) has plenty of punch for producing an iMovie 2 project.

FIGURE 2-1 These are iMac DV Special Edition systems, complete with FireWire, big hard drives and, of course, iMovie 2.

Why Apple Is Using FireWire

FireWire is one of the fastest peripheral standards ever developed, which makes it great for use with multimedia peripherals such as video camcorders and other high-speed devices like the latest hard disk drives and printers. FireWire is like Universal Serial Bus (USB) in many ways, and the two technologies coexist on Macintosh systems. While USB is great for lower-speed input devices such as keyboards, mice, and joysticks, FireWire is aimed at higher-speed multimedia peripherals such as video camcorders, music synthesizers, and hard disks.

Both I/O technologies offer incredible convenience through their "hot plug" capability, so you don't have to turn off or restart the computer when you attatch a new peripheral. For additional ease of use, they also feature automatic configuration—no device IDs or terminators—and simple-to-use cables. USB can support up to 127 devices per computer; and FireWire, up to 63 devices. Both technologies provide their own bus power, enabling connecting peripherals to be even simpler. And both technologies are cross-platform industry standards. In addition to offering new FireWire devices, third-party peripheral manufacturers have announced products that convert older analog video equipment for use over FireWire. This means you don't need to buy new video gear until you're ready; even your original camcorder from a decade ago will work great over FireWire.

Finally, FireWire is a peer-to-peer technology, which means you can connect other Macintosh systems on the same FireWire bus, using "Target" mode. This enables a whole new world of shared peripherals. What's more, two or more computers can share the same FireWire video camera or scanner when they are "daisy chained" on the FireWire bus.

FireWire is the future of computer I/O technology. Together, FireWire and USB radically simplify I/O connections. The age of SCSI, dedicated serial and modem ports, Apple Desktop Bus (ADB), and analog video is fast coming to a close. New Apple products no longer support them. USB and FireWire bring new ease of use. Attaching a hard disk to your computer is now as easy as plugging in a telephone. By including built-in FireWire, all Power Macintosh computers are now professional audio/video systems. As we move into the future, FireWire will allow for interoperation with new digital consumer electronics devices such as televisions, VCRs, and set-top boxes. In fact, manufacturers of all these devices have already announced support for FireWire as their interface of choice.

An Overview of Analog and Digital Media

You are going to make iMovies! Your accomplished projects will be turned into digital media documents. So let's start at the beginning. The films and the television programs that we all see influence and shape the "look" of what we want to create as videographers. Most of the public media that we watch still comes from analog origins, such as regular film.

When you make your iMovies, you may actually include analog sources in your project, as you will discover in Chapter 15. You'll also want to check out Chapter 16, where you will learn how to deliver your digital iMovie to an analog VHS tape that can be watched on a regular home TV.

TIP

If you are one of the millions who have embraced the snazzy DVD video format by buying one or more players (or a Mac with a DVD drive), you'll be pleased to know that you can also make your own DVDs out of an iMovie 2 video. All you need is a Power Mac or flat-panel iMac with SuperDrive and iDVD software. We'll show you how easy it is in Chapter 18.

But let's continue with our introduction. Chapter 3 outlines the similarities and differences between film and video. Your understanding of analog and digital media will help you be a better iMovie-maker. In fact, your understanding will become increasingly necessary as you go on to intermediate, advanced, and professional levels of videography.

An Overview of Analog Media

Film-based photographs and movies, radio and television broadcasts, VHS videotapes, LP (long playing) vinyl records, and audiotapes are examples of analog media. Analog is a continuously variable signal, often represented by sinuous waveforms. Analog circuits are much harder to design and analyze than digital ones because the designer must take into account effects such as gain, resistance and capacitance, and interference between signals. It's not just a set of binary numbers, as in digital.

In this area of the digital lifestyle, you might be surprised to know that there are still some technicians, critics, and collectors who remain unconvinced that digital is the same or better quality than analog. As they see it, 35mm motion picture film has more depth and character than digital projection, and LPs played through tube amplifiers reveal more warmth and richness than can be produced by CDs.

NOTE

It's not an illusion that LPs can deliver an apparent image of spaciousness and richness. Engineers have long known that some of the distortions evident in this music delivery format do, in fact, impart that sort of illusion, even though it may not even exist on the master tape. In addition, some tube amplifiers can alter the frequency response of a signal in such a way as to make music "bloom"—seem warmer and richer.

An Overview of Digital Media

Audio CDs, CD-ROMs, DVDs, streaming video, digital television, and MP3 files are examples of digital media. Even Hollywood movies are being produced in digital format. And all that digital information can be managed with a personal computer. Apple's Digital Hub is the secret tool—teamed with your computer, it enables the moving, sharing, and displaying of different kinds of digital information.

Let's get a little technical. Digital data is stored or transmitted as a sequence of discrete symbols from a finite set, including magnitudes, letters, and symbols, which are expressed in bits and bytes of binary form—that is, using only the two digits 0 and 1. Most digital components function correctly within a range of parameters, but such variations can corrupt the output of an analog circuit. Digital data can be applied at different levels of both "lossless" and "lossy" compression. Digital visual media comes down to pixels, as revealed in Figures 2-2 and 2-3.

"Lossless" compression shrinks data to a smaller size, but without sacrificing content, and, when expanded to its original form, all data is intact. An example of "lossless" compression is a file you might compress with Aladdin's StuffIt software so that it can fit on a disk or transfer over the Internet in a shorter amount of time. When the file is finally decoded or expanded, it is in the exact shape it was in when it was compressed. Nothing is lost.

FIGURE 2-2 Digital images can combine drawn and photographed sources.

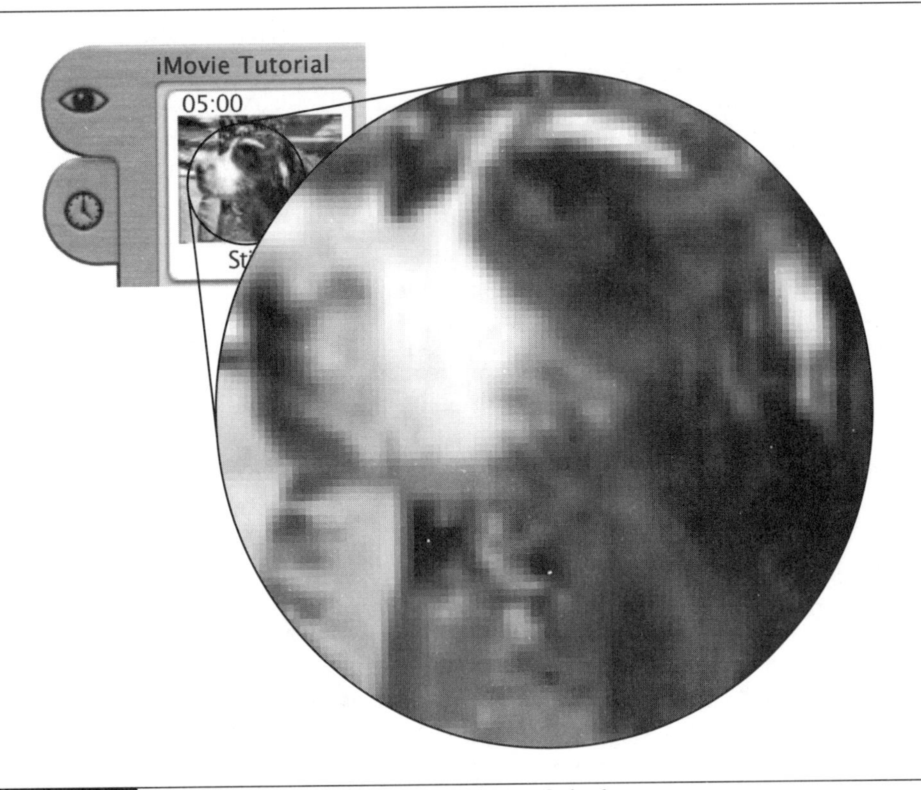

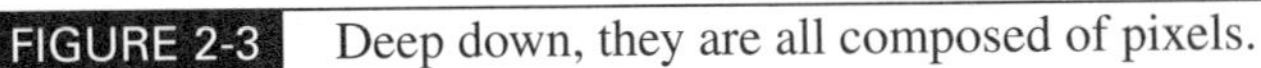

FIGURE 2-3 Deep down, they are all composed of pixels.

"Lossy" compression is a technique in which repeated or redundant data is discarded. Sometimes, data that may not be noticeable by its absence is also discarded. More than 90% compression is achieved in DVDs, for example, and a lot of clever methods are used to shrink a movie with minimal loss in quality. For one thing, the encoding software analyzes a film frame by frame to see what changes. If you have a scene with a moving figure on a static background, only the information that changes in that figure from frame to frame needs to be retained. The rest can be thrown out.

NOTE *The ever-popular MP3 music format also uses a form of lossy compression, in which portions of the musical spectrum you're not likely to hear (perhaps because it is "masked" by other musical tones) are discarded. A high-bit rate produces sound almost indistinguishable from that of a regular CD, but as you decrease the bit rate, more data must be discarded, and you will begin to hear a real difference.*

How Big-Screen Production Is Moving to Digital

Our motion picture industry, which has for four generations formed the fundamental images of our entertainment, has been undergoing a slow but sure change from analog to digital. Probably nobody understands digital filmmaking, from exposure to exhibition, better than George Lucas, famed not only as the creator of all those *Star Wars* epochs, but as the founder of Industrial Light and Magic, one of the premiere special effects operations.

"The whole process of editing is to manipulate the images, and the acting and the performance," Lucas says. "The fact that we can now manipulate things in the frame, as opposed to just manipulating frames gives us a better way of improving the performances and getting the story told, and the characters developed the way we want them."

NOTE *As a point of reference, a single frame of film contains over 12 million pixels of information. Film runs at 24 frames-per-second. NTSC video, the North American video standard, runs at 30 frames-per-second.*

With *Star Wars: Episode I— The Phantom Menace,* few frames were produced without some level of digital production in the special effects, combining both live action and animation, plus full animation, in the post-production process. As part of its premiere, a milestone was reached when *Episode I* was exhibited in four theaters with digital projection systems. Instead of arriving as reels of film, the entire film was delivered in the form of a portable hard disk.

With *Star Wars: Episode II—Attack of the Clones*, Lucas is reaching his goal of the all-digital production. The picture was shot completely digital, including exterior locations. Over time, Lucas foresees more theaters hosting digital projection, eventually replacing film.

The digital version of *Star Wars: Episode I— The Phantom Menace* was the best-selling DVD of all that went on sale in the fall of 2001. And Lucas considers the DVD version an integral part of the production of the movie, providing his director's cut of the feature as well as taking advantage of DVD's encyclopedic interactive digital technology to present the totality of the studio's conception and production. A menu screen from this DVD is shown in Figure 2-4.

TIP *Star Wars: Episode I—The Phantom Menace DVD is highly recommended as an informative revelation of many basic and advanced production techniques and processes.*

FIGURE 2-4 *Star Wars: Episode I—The Phantom Menace* DVD will give you hours of interactive access to all the of the film's digital layers of concepts, design and production. ©1999 Lucasfilm Ltd. & TM. All rights reserved.

The Digital Hub Expands the Media

"With so much digital content readily available, and with a growing number of devices that can capture even more digital content, you'll be able to use your Mac as a 'Digital Hub,' not only to enjoy all of this digital content but also to create your own," said Apple CEO Steve Jobs at Macworld 2001 San Francisco. Jobs, of course, is referring to the whole spectrum of digital media, from CDs and DVDs, to scanners, digital cameras, and camcorders.

This prediction becomes increasingly true every day as more ingenious devices, applications, accessories, and solutions for sight, sound, and communications become available. What do they have in common? They all share the same digital language. iMovie 2 is a resourceful and versatile part of the digital hub, capable of wearing many hats and taking many roles in helping you to make your media messages.

NOTE *Steve Jobs expanded the vision of the digital hub during his keynote at Macworld 2002 in San Francisco by introducing iPhoto, an application that manages your digital photo library. It's also interesting to note that Apple truly set the standard with this vision, as other PC makers quickly picked up the digital hub theme as part of their own product promotions.*

iMovie 2 for Mac OS 9 or Mac OS X?

Even though Mac OS X began shipping free of charge on new Macs in May 1991, many of you will no doubt avoid switching to the new operating system and stay with some version of Mac OS 9 (except to get the lay of the land) until all or most of your favorite applications make the transition. Fortunately, iMovie 2 looks nearly the same in either operating system and the same instructions apply.

NOTE

To be perfectly fair, past the interface, there are tremendous differences between Mac OS 9 and Mac OS X. The latter, because of its Unix heritage, is far more reliable, relatively free of system instabilities, and capable of far better multitasking.

While iMovie 2 comes on all new Macs and is part of the Mac OS X bundle, don't despair if you don't have a copy. Just visit Apple's iMovie Web site, at http://www.apple.com/imovie, to order a downloadable version.

System Requirements for iMovie 2 in Mac OS 9.1

Here are the basic requirements for getting up to speed with iMovie 2 under the traditional or Classic Mac OS:

- A Macintosh computer with a 300MHz or faster PowerPC G3 or G4 processor and built-in FireWire port
- At least 64MB of RAM (128MB recommended)
- A CD or DVD drive
- 200MB of available (unused) hard disk space (2GB recommended)
- A monitor that supports 800×600 pixel resolution and thousands of colors (1024×768 pixel resolution and millions of colors recommended)
- Mac OS 9.1 or later
- QuickTime 4.1.2 or later (QuickTime 5.x is free from Apple)
- FireWire 2.4 or later (FireWire Support and Enabler extensions)

Introducing iMovie 2 and Mac OS X

Mac OS X is a powerful new platform that evolved from the Unix-based NeXTSTEP system and raises the sophistication of the Macintosh desktop with its Aqua user interface. Mac OS X is still a great work in progress, and more updates will be coming your way. Every week sees more applications, utilities, plug-ins, and drivers being released in Mac OS X native versions.

If you have a new Mac, Mac OS X is already there, but your computer probably boots under Mac OS 9.x. All it takes is a trip to the Startup Disk Control Panel, a switch of the system versions, and a restart to switch over.

Best of all, with Mac OS X 10.1, iMovie 2 is part of the standard installation—no trips to Apple's Web site, no special installations. And, as you can see in Figure 2-5, Apple's new Aqua look for iMovie 2 was already crafted in its Mac OS 9 version, for seamless switching from one to the other.

NOTE *If you haven't updated your Mac OS X installation to version 10.1 or later, we highly recommend you take this step. Check with Apple's Web site (http://www.apple.com/macosx) for the latest low-cost upgrade policy. Older versions of Mac OS X are slow and bug-prone and were meant for early adopters rather than mainstream use.*

FIGURE 2-5 Is this iMovie 2 for Mac OS 9 or iMovie 2 for Mac OS X? You can't tell the difference without a scorecard.

System Requirements for iMovie 2 in Mac OS X

If you don't have Mac OS X installed, just what do you need to get with the program? Aside from the upgrade kit for the new operating system, of course, here are our recommendations for the minimum Mac OS X platform for iMovie 2:

NOTE *Our requirements are a mite stiffer than Apple's for Mac OS X, because you will be using a powerful video editing application and you'll want to get the best possible performance.*

- A Macintosh computer with a 300Mhz or faster PowerPC G3 or G4 processor and built-in FireWire port

CAUTION *You can easily add a FireWire card to desktop Macs with PCI slots. We do not, however, recommend installing Mac OS X on an older Mac (one that originally came with a 601, 603 or 604 PowerPC chip), with a G3 upgrade card. While such systems often do work, if you use the third party software to allow for an "unsupported" installation of the operating system, Apple won't give you any support. Feel free to ignore our advice if you must, but proceed with care.*

- At least 128MB of RAM (256MB or better is recommended)
- A CD or DVD drive
- 200MB of available (unused) hard disk space (2GB recommended)
- A monitor that supports 800×600 pixel resolution and thousands of colors (1024×768 pixel resolution and millions of colors recommended)

When you upgrade to Mac OS X, and use native software, you'll enjoy a number of robust operating system features that will make for a more pleasant and productive video editing experience:

- **Protected memory** Instead of having to restart every time an application crashes, only the program that is in trouble will have to shut down. Your desktop and other active programs will remain untouched, each protected within its own memory address space.

NOTE *The exception to this rule occurs if you're using older Mac software, designed to run in the Classic environment, where Mac OS 9.x runs within Mac OS X. If such an application crashes, you'll need to also restart Classic to be free of unstable performance in that mode.*

- **Preemptive multitasking** Your Mac's processor power will be more rationally and efficiently distributed under Mac OS X, favoring the program in progress, so it isn't forced to compete with other background activities. This means that the QuickTime movie you are running is less likely to suffer speed variations.
- **Symmetric multiprocessing** Have a Mac with two brains? Mac OS X efficiently allocates tasks to each processor. Applications that multithread, or perform more than a single function at a time, such as iMovie 2 and Apple's DVD authoring software, iDVD 2, will benefit from speedier rendering of complicated productions.
- **Advanced virtual memory** Until Mac OS X, virtual memory was always a mixed blessing. Although it allowed programs to work with less built-in memory, by moving unused data to your hard drive in a "swap file," multimedia software in particular would stop and stutter if you didn't have enough real RAM installed. Some programs wouldn't run at all, and you often had to switch virtual memory off and on as needed (a restart is required each time). Memory management, virtual and RAM, is dynamic under Mac OS X. The operating system allocates the amount of memory a program needs, and performance is much better under a heavy load.

NOTE *Having superior virtual memory isn't a free ride. To make a program do its thing, it's better to have lots of real RAM than to force the operating system to resort to a slower moving hard drive's virtual memory file when you run out of memory.*

Choosing Memory and Storage

Though low-cost, third-party processor upgrades are readily available for many Macs (including the iMac and older PowerBooks), many of you will just stick with the microprocessor that came with the model of your Mac. Processor power and speed is expressed in megahertz (MHz) or gigahertz (GHz). Memory and storage, on the other hand, are readily expandable. When you work with iMovie 2 you work with digital video, and DV requires lots of memory and storage for the management of large amounts of audiovisual data.

Using Apple System Profiler to Sort Things Out

Apple System Profiler is an application that provides a systems report that displays a reality check of your CPU, system version, memory, storage, and device connections, plus the applications you've installed. We've shown the Mac OS X version in Figure 2-6, and it reveals the whole 'Brady Bunch' of everything in, on, and connected to your computer system.

Where's it located? Under Mac OS X, it's in your Utilities folder. For Mac OS 9.x, check your Apple menu.

Apple System Profiler

System Profile | Devices and Volumes | Frameworks | Extensions | Applications

Serial number: XB205076M8H

▼ Software overview

Mac OS overview — System: Mac OS X 10.1.3 (5Q45)

Note: No startup disk was selected.

▼ Memory overview

▶ Built-in memory: 768 MB PC133 CL3

L2 cache: 256K

L3 cache: 2 MB

▼ Hardware overview

Machine ID: 406 — Processor info: PowerPC G4

Model name: Power Mac G4 — Machine 1000 MHz

Keyboard type: Apple Pro Keyboard — Processors: 2

▼ Network overview

Ethernet Where: built-in — Flags: Multicast, Simplex, Running, b6, Broadcast, Up

Address: 00.03.93.86.14.aa — IP Address: 192.168.0.10

Broadcast address: 192.168.0.255 — net mask: 255.255.255.0

Ethernet Where: built-in — Flags: Multicast, Running, PointToPoint, Up

Address: 00.00.00.00.00.00 — IP Address: 172.163.1.170

Broadcast address: Not available — net mask: 255.255.0.0

▼ Production information

ROM revision:

Boot ROM version: 4.33f2

Serial number: XB205076-M8H-ff11-3-5

Software bundle: Not applicable

Sales order number: M8667LL/A

FIGURE 2-6 The Mac OS X and Mac OS 9 versions of Apple System Profiler are quite similar, so we're showing only the 10.1 version here.

Apple System Profiler can be a great tool to help you diagnose a system problem. Perhaps you've hooked up a FireWire drive to store your captured movie clips, but it's not working. Apple System Profiler is the tool that'll reveal whether your Mac really sees the device. Perhaps that FireWire plug in the back of your G4 got jostled out, or the scanner power was not turned on. This handy application is a good place to start your troubleshooting by confirming system configurations and the devices that are recognized.

TIP

If you have a fairly recent Mac, Apple System Profiler will even show your computer's serial number, so you don't have to poke around the back or bottom to see what it is. This is a boon for those of you who need Apple technical support. The first question they ask, after your name and phone number is, of course, the computer's serial number.

About This Computer (or About This Mac)

If you want a fast overview of your Mac's RAM and operating system setup, take a gander at the About This Computer window (see Figure 2-7) in your Classic Mac OS's Apple menu. The corresponding version for Mac OS X, called About This Mac, is shown in Figure 2-8.

FIGURE 2-7 About This Computer tells you the basics about system versions and memory.

FIGURE 2-8 Under Mac OS X, it's called About This Mac.

With About This Computer displayed, you'll not only see the system version and RAM allotment, but whether virtual memory is on and how much of a bite of RAM your open applications are using. The Mac OS X version, About This Mac, just shows system version, RAM allotment, and what sort of processors your Mac is equipped with.

TIP *If you want to learn more from the Mac OS X About This Mac screen, click on the system version. The display will change to the build number (information Apple's software engineers use to track the development process). If you have a recent Mac, a second click will reveal the computer's serial number (if not, it will return you to the first About This Mac screen).*

A Few Words about RAM

With a memory-intensive multimedia program like iMovie 2, you can never have too much RAM (random access memory). This is where the data that is being worked on by the currently operating application is, along with your operating system resources, temporarily stored. Your computer comes with a minimum amount of RAM, and you can increase that total by adding RAM chips, or modules, as noted in Table 2-1.

If 64MB is the minimum and 128MB is recommended, then you should bite the bytes and go for more. With additional RAM around, more memory can be allocated to iMovie 2 to make it work more efficiently with larger projects. Judge the amount that you need by the work that you do. As you become more ambitious

Memory	
RAM Slots:	1, SO-DIMM
Min - Max RAM:	64 MB–320MB
RAM Sizes:	32, 64, 128, 256MB
Install in Groups of:	1

TABLE 2-1 iBook (FireWire) Memory

and accomplished, your movies will probably get longer and the files larger. Add RAM to support the level and pace of your advancing workflow.

To determine how much RAM your particular machine can accept, and for more valuable technical information, go to Apple's Spec Database at http://www.info.apple.com/applespec/applespec.taf. Table 2-1 shows the memory specifications for a first generation iBook with FireWire, just as an example.

NOTE *The configuration table tells you that this iBook can host as much as 320MB of RAM, so when you go shopping for more, you'll know what RAM module sizes to ask for.*

A Short Course on Virtual Memory

Apple's virtual memory is an internal system workaround to use drive space as a substitute for RAM when there isn't enough memory available for the demands of an active application. Under the Classic Mac OS, iMovie 2 will run smoother and faster when virtual memory is turned off. However, when you turn off virtual memory, you sharply increase memory needs for applications and the OS. Add more RAM to avoid this situation in the first place. To adjust virtual memory, follow these steps:

1. From the Apple menu, choose Control Panels.
2. Select Memory, which brings up the Control Panel shown in Figure 2-9.
3. Click the Default button. This will optimize virtual memory at one megabyte above installed RAM and set your Mac's disk cache (speeding up access to frequently used data) at 32K per MB of RAM (up to 8096K).
4. If you are running into performance problems with virtual memory, such as stuttering sound or dropped frames, switch virtual memory off. Just click the off button in the Virtual Memory category.
5. Restart your Mac to set your changes (the Memory Control Panel will close as your Mac's desktop clears).

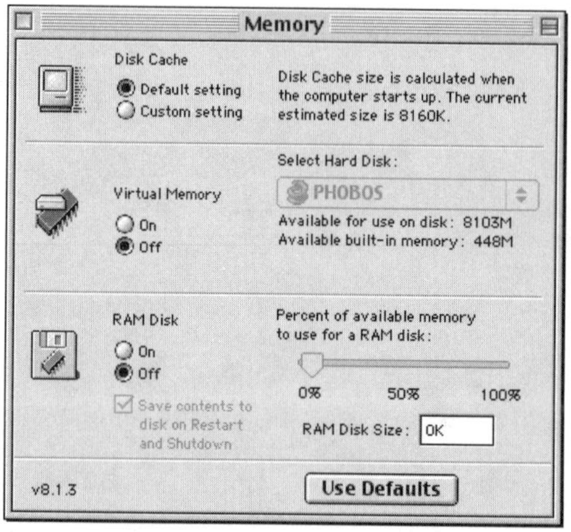

FIGURE 2-9 At the Memory Control Panel, you can adjust virtual memory for better iMovie 2 performance.

Under Mac OS X, virtual memory is present full time, but the advanced memory management provides the benefits with fewer possibilities for poor performance. However, there is no substitute for real RAM, and it doesn't hurt to buy all your Mac can handle. Since a hard drive is much slower than RAM, performance takes a hit whenever the operating system needs to go to the drive to swap data.

Optimizing Classic Mac OS System Memory

Though we may hope that our Mac whirls through its paces like a well-run merry-go-round, the scene may be more like a game of musical chairs with the Marx Brothers. Processing power and memory are continually being bargained for and fought over by applications and operations, particularly under the Classic Mac OS. Everything you can do to level the playing field will help iMovie 2.

Adjusting Application Memory Memory is like the "fuel" for the program's "engine." Each application requires a minimum amount of RAM to run without crashing and burning, and additional amounts of RAM are needed as the demands increase for the work you are asking the application to do. Here is how to allocate the RAM for iMovie 2:

1. Quit iMovie 2, if it's already running.
2. Go to the Finder and select the iMovie icon.
3. Choose Get Info from the Finder's File menu, or type COMMAND+I.

4. Select Memory from the Show pop-up menu, which produces the screen shown in Figure 2-10.
5. In the Preferred category, enter the amount of memory (in kilobytes) that you want to allocate for iMovie 2. You should increase memory in 5000KB (5MB) increments, up to a maximum of 50MB.

CAUTION *You cannot allocate more memory than you Mac has and expect it to run properly. Before you allocate memory to an application, check the About This Computer box to see how much memory is normally available after startup. Allow about 10MB for overhead, to accommodate expansion of system memory for some programs, and you will see how much is available for your running applications.*

6. Click the close box of the Get Info screen.

NOTE *If you're using Mac OS X, feel lucky that the Unix-based operating system will sort this all out and that you don't have to bother with such niceties, so long as you have plenty of RAM around to deliver the maximum possible performance.*

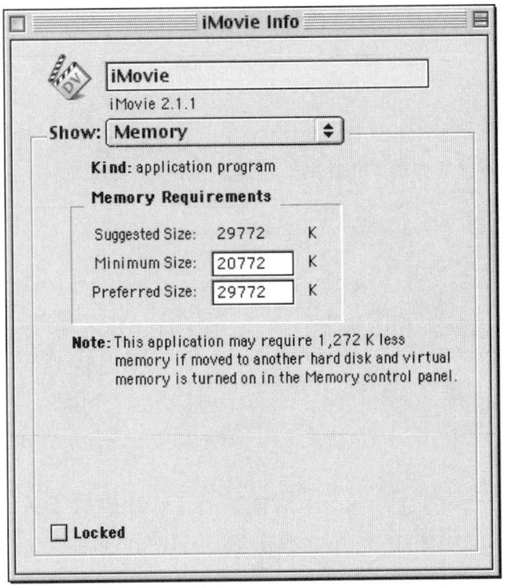

FIGURE 2-10 Set memory for a Classic application here.

Make an iMovie Set of Extensions Under your Classic Mac OS, Apple includes a convenient Control Panel, Extensions Manager, which enables you to activate or deactivate your extensions. While the standard software that comes with Mac OS 9.x will not hobble iMovie 2 in any way, if you've added lots of goodies to your Mac, now's the time to consider setting up a lean, mean set so that iMovie 2 can strut its stuff.

The biggest reason to do this is that any extension that uses a lot of system resources may just make iMovie 2 run slower or use more system memory, in which case there will be less for you to add to iMovie 2 via Get Info.

Here's how to create our special iMovie 2 set:

NOTE *The reason we are having you make up a special Extensions Manager set is so that you can easily switch between the set you optimized for iMovie 2 and the set you normally use, without having to go through the bother of reconfiguring everything over and over again.*

1. Choose Control Panels from the Apple menu and select Extensions Manager (see Figure 2-11).
2. Choose the Mac OS 9.x Base Set from the Selected Set pop-up menu.
3. Click the Duplicate Set button.
4. Give your new set a namc (iMovic 2 Sct will do just fine).
5. Click OK.
6. Under Control Panels and Extensions add only the items for third party software you must run (and we hope the list will be small).
7. Once you've selected the extensions you want, click Restart and let your Mac go through its normal restart process.

TIP *A fast way to switch sets is just to restart. As soon as you see the Happy Mac icon, hold down the spacebar, which will bring up Extensions Manager. Switch the Selected Set to the one you want and click Continue. Your Mac's startup process will continue with the set that you need for that work session.*

NOTE *Here's another argument in favor of switching over to Mac OS X: no extensions to configure or fret over. Although there are such things as "kernel extensions," which are largely drivers for your video card and peripherals, the odd behavior and system crashes wrought by too many extensions, or extensions that conflict with one another, is a thing of the past.*

Extensions Manager

Selected Set: Mac OS 9.2.1 Base

On/Off	Name	Size	Version	Package
☒	**System Folder**	720K	-	-
☒	Classic Support UI	708K	1.3.1	Mac OS 9....
☒	MacTCP DNR	4K	1.0	Mac OS 9....
☒	ProxyApp	8K	1.0	Mac OS 9....
⊟	**Control Panels**	32.2 MB	-	-
☒	Appearance	624K	1.1.4	Mac OS 9....
☒	Apple Menu Options	76K	1.1.9	Mac OS 9....
☒	AppleTalk	212K	1.1	Mac OS 9....
☒	ColorSync	112K	3.0.3	ColorSync...
☒	Date & Time	144K	8.3.3	Mac OS 9....
☒	Energy Saver	148K	3.0.5	Mac OS 9....
☒	File Exchange	596K	3.0.5	Mac OS 9....
☒	File Sharing	520K	9.0.2	Mac OS 9....
☒	General Controls	48K	8.0.2	Mac OS 9....
☒	Internet	268K	1.0.2	Mac OS 9....
☒	Keyboard	88K	8.6	Mac OS 9....
☒	Launcher	64K	3.1.3	Mac OS 9....
☒	Location Manager	372K	2.0.1	Mac OS 9....
☒	Memory	84K	8.1.3	Mac OS 9....
☒	Monitors	112K	8.6.3	Mac OS 9....
☒	Mouse	60K	8.1.1	Mac OS 9....
☒	Numbers	16K	7.1	Mac OS 9....

Changes take effect on restart — Restart — Revert — Duplicate Set...

Show Item Information

FIGURE 2-11 Get ready to lean out your System Folder from here.

Defragmenting (Optimizing) Your Hard Drive Sometimes called "defragging," optimizing or defragmenting a hard drive will reorder the files, and put all elements of a file together for the best possible performance. When data is written to a drive, it's divided into little pieces, and those little pieces may be spread out all across the drive.

While a small amount of defragmentation doesn't hurt performance, if you copy and remove lots of big files, the end result is that little bits of files are scattered all over the drive, and it takes longer for the read/write heads of your hard drive to find them. When you optimize, the data is rewritten, in contiguous pieces, so the drive spends less time assembling the file and you get a little faster performance.

To be perfectly blunt, you shouldn't have to do this very often, unless you write and delete lots of files to your Mac's drive. Some folks go for years and never optimize their drives. But for heavy-duty files, such as videos and huge graphic files, optimizing your drive every few weeks will ensure maximum performance.

Third-party packages like Norton Utilities (or the SystemWorks version, which includes extra utilities) from Symantec, PlusOptimizer from Alsoft, or TechTool Pro, can do the job for you.

In every case, optimizing is a matter of following these steps:

1. Restart your Mac from the startup CD provided with your disk utility software, holding down the "C" key at startup to boot from the CD.

CAUTION *In order to perform a proper optimization, you must start from another drive or the CD that includes your disk maintenance software. If you have a new Mac and an older version of the software, you'll need to contact the publisher about a version that works with your Mac. Should you be using Mac OS X, make sure the disk maintenance software you use is compatible (even if it's not native to the new OS).*

2. After restarting, locate and launch your disk maintenance software and run its optimizing process.

NOTE *If you have several drives connected to your Mac, or they are very large with lots of files on them, the process may take an hour or two, so be patient. All of these utilities display progress bars so you can monitor what's happening.*

3. When the optimizing process is complete, restart your Mac.
4. If you are using the Classic Mac OS, you'll want to rebuild your desktop. This is done by holding down the COMMAND+OPTION keys as soon as the last extension icons are visible.
5. Keep the keys held down till you see the message asking if you want to rebuild the desktop. OK the message and let the process continue.

NOTE *Why rebuild the desktop under Mac OS 9.x? The process updates the databases used by the Mac Finder to track document and application icons and links. A bloated or corrupted desktop database can hurt performance and, in rare circumstances, result in system crashes.*

What Type of Drives Do You Need for Video?

Digital video demands a great deal of storage space, as you can see in Table 2-2. To make digital movies, you need to decide where to park the imported raw footage from your camcorder. Then you need enough space to store outtakes and rough cuts, and room for the constant card-shuffling of frames and files that is the editing process.

Running Time	Disk Space
1 minute	228MB
5 minutes	1GB
15 minutes	3.5GB
30 minutes	7GB
60 minutes	13GB

TABLE 2-2 Imported digital video storage, both audio and video streams

Fortunately, the price of storage media has dropped greatly in the past few years, helping to make working with a multimedia program like iMovie 2 even more affordable. In this section, we'll take a look at storage media, and the sort of devices you'll want to use for your regular video projects.

It seems not that long ago that a 1GB hard drive could cost close to a thousand dollars (in fact one of your humble authors bought a lowly 100MB drive for that figure back in 1989). Today, you can get a 100GB hard drive for less than $350. Seems like huge amount of storage space, but when you are working with digital video, that real estate gets occupied very fast. The best way to provide more storage is, first of all, to choose the largest capacity hard drive available for your Mac when you buy it.

Some Macs come in several configurations with various processor and hard drive options. If you opt for Apple's "build-to-order" service, which is also available from many authorized dealers, you can choose a different capacity.

You can, however, simply buy a second drive. If you have a minitower with an empty drive bay, you can easily add a second storage device for additional space or as a convenient backup in case something happens to your main drive.

CAUTION *All recent Macs come with ATA-based hard drives (rather than SCSI, as in the old days). This drive standard allows you to add a second or "slave" drive, so long as your Mac's hardware supports the feature. If you're unsure, check the products specs for your make or model, or ask your dealer. If a second internal won't work in your minitower, you'll either have to consider buying an expansion card that adds drive connections (such as a high-speed SCSI card or ATA card) or you'll have to go external.*

If another internal drive is out of the question, because there's no room or there's no compatibility, you'll have to consider the external route. While external drives are more costly, there's plenty of variety. Your Mac's FireWire port, for example, can be used not just for your camcorder, but to add extra storages and other peripherals, all daisy-chained, one next to the other.

What's more, FireWire is hot-pluggable, which means you can add a new device just by attaching it to your Mac and waiting a few seconds for it to be detected.

Mass-Storage Devices and FireWire

Mass-storage devices will be the type of peripherals most radically transformed by the adoption of FireWire. Ease of use will take on new meaning as you mount external hard disk drives with the simplicity of connecting a single plug. FireWire eliminates all the complexity and restrictions associated with using SCSI mass-storage devices. FireWire can further simplify these peripherals by providing the DC power required to drive the device, rather than requiring you to plug it into an AC outlet; this feature, however, is only useful for smaller storage devices. Larger drives still sport separate power supplies.

FireWire-based mass-storage devices communicate with the computer in an asynchronous mode using the Serial Bus Protocol-2 (SBP-2). This protocol enables high-speed data transfers and should scale up as FireWire itself and FireWire hard disks get faster. Mass-storage devices on FireWire will include hard disk drives, magneto-optical drives, high-capacity removable drives, tape drives, and CD/DVD products, including both read-only and read/write drives.

NOTE

Don't get the wrong idea. You may still have to install special drivers for your new storage device, although both Mac OS 9.1 and later, and Mac OS X can handle just about any FireWire drive we've thrown at them. In addition, before removing a drive, make sure you dismount it, by dragging the icon to the trash. Otherwise you risk a possible crash or drive directory damage, even under Mac OS X.

What kind of drive should you pick? Look for a rotation speed of at least 7200 rpm for good performance. You may also want to make sure you have a FireWire drive using the latest technology, such as the "Oxford" chip set, for good performance. Look for drive specs that allow for at least 8MB of sustained throughput (you want at least twice what you need for video capture), a specification most products can handle.

NOTE

What about SCSI? Well, we're not dismissing this older technology. The fastest SCSI drive out there is capable of faster sustained performance than any FireWire device, but it's much more expensive, and the complexities of termination and setting proper ID numbers can be annoying. If you decide to go SCSI, don't depend on an older Mac's standard SCSI port, which is too slow. Get a high speed SCSI card, supporting Ultra160 or LVD standards.

If you're working in the field, perhaps with one of those elegant iBooks or the Titanium PowerBook G4, look for a portable drive, such as LaCie's PocketDrive series as seen in Figure 2-12, which can store up to four hours of uncompressed digital video.

FIGURE 2-12 "Honey, I shrunk the drive!" LaCie 48GB PocketDrive FireWire/USB external hard drive.

NOTE *Where does USB figure into all this? While fast enough for a small backup drive, such as a Zip or SuperDisk, or even a scanner, it's not nearly fast enough for video capture. This could change as the new, faster USB 2.0 standard comes into wider use, but for now FireWire or the fastest SCSI drives are the way to go.*

The Ins and Outs of Video Connections

As you go about your creative ways, producing, editing, duplicating and exhibiting your movies, you will be making a lot of important connections. You can connect analog to digital—and vice-versa—with some flexibility.

Converting Analog to Digital

If you need to bring in video from an older camcorder, VCR or TV, look for a camcorder with analog to digital conversion with "pass through." This will enable you to convert your analog video/audio to a digital signal that can either be recorded to tape or passed directly through the FireWire interface to your Mac.

NOTE *Pass through means that you don't need an intermediate (and sometimes somewhat costly) conversion device in between the analog device and your camcorder. The DV in/out port takes an RCA-style video-in and audio-in ports. The plugs are usually color coded: yellow = video; white = left-channel audio; red = right-channel audio.*

Analog-to-digital YUV video converter

With this type of converter you can use existing analog camcorders, TVs, and VCRs with a FireWire-based Macintosh system. Instead of taking up a PCI slot, it handles analog-to-digital conversion through a small external box connected to a FireWire port on the computer. The resulting video files are QuickTime movies in the raw video format—they are not DV, MPEG, M-JPEG, or Sorenson format until you choose to convert them to a specific format using QuickTime.

Analog-to-DV converter

This converts incoming analog audio and video to a decompressed digital stream before sending it to your Macintosh system over FireWire. The conversion happens in real time and essentially makes all analog audio/video products appear to the computer as DV devices with high-quality video streams. It also allows for the export of DV video to analog video.

To grab the output from your VCR or TV, set it to video mode. You can watch the movie on the TV through the VCR, record to VHS, or record the broadcast with the camcorder. Some camcorders and some VCRs and TVs have S-Video ports, which will accept an S-Video cable plug. S-Video provides a cleaner and better quality video transfer than RCA, but you need additional audio cables to capture the sound.

TIP

If your camcorder doesn't have a pass through device, don't despair. Check with your Apple or consumer electronics dealer for other options. One flexible device, the $399 Formac Studio, has a variety of conversion options and can be used as the intermediary between an analog camcorder or other analog video source and your Mac, without the need of a DV camcorder.

About FireWire

Apple's FireWire (IEEE 1394) also known by Sony as i.Link DV Interface, is one of the fastest peripheral standards. It's maximum speed is 400Mbps, which is a rate fast enough to support full-frame, full-motion video. Hot-pluggable, FireWire is a key technology for digital video professionals, and FireWire devices can be daisy-chained together to link as many as 63 devices simultaneously.

NOTE *Most FireWire cables for Macintosh, such as those that are meant to connect a Mac to a camcorder, are in the 4-pin-to-6-pin configuration. Cables designed to connect a storage device or scanner are usually 6-pin at both ends. Does it matter? Usually no, except where a storage device derives power from the FireWire port (both LaCie and SmartDisk have such drives), in which case 6-pin is the only way to go. The 4-pin variation doesn't supply power.*

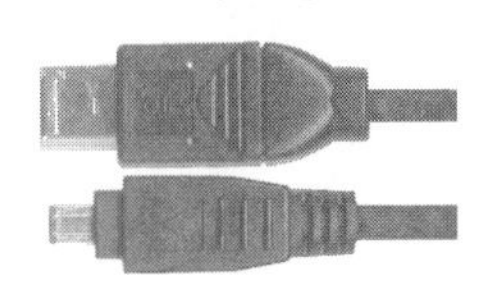

About USB

USB (Universal Serial Bus) is another hot-pluggable technology, but the original standard, the one adopted in Macs, works at a mere 12 Mbps, too slow for digital video, but fast enough for a variety of peripherals. You can daisy chain up to 127 USB devices by attaching peripherals through interconnected external hubs. USB peripherals include printers, scanners, digital cameras, graphics tablets, Zip drives, hard disk drives, magneto optical drives, CD-RW drives, joysticks, game controllers, keyboards, mice, and Palm OS-based handheld devices.

NOTE *If you get a USB hub to expand your USB chain, make sure that it is a powered model, with separate AC adapter. Bus-powered hubs can support peripherals such as keyboards and mice, but are unable to supply sufficient AC power for motor-driven units like scanners and printers.*

About PCI

PCI (Peripheral Component Interconnect) is a standard for connecting peripherals to a personal computer. Found in Mac minitowers like G4s, the ports are configured in the form of internal slots that receive a component as a pluggable card. Technically speaking, PCI typically runs at 33MHz or 66MHz and carries 32 bits at a time over a 124-pin connector or 64 bits over a 188-pin connector. It hosts peripherals like video cards, video tuners, graphic accelerators, format adapter cards, digitizer cards and compression cards.

NOTE *What about AGP? The Accelerated Graphics Port, standard issue on the Power Mac G4 and the Cube, provides speedier graphics performance, but is already filled with a graphic card. Unless you want to replace that card with a faster model (such as an NVIDIA GeForce3 or ATI Radeon 8500, both of which really only excel at 3D graphics), this isn't a matter to be concerned about.*

Adding More Monitors

One of the miracles of the Mac (and one only recently discovered on the Windows platform) is its native ability to add and even daisy-chain up to six monitors and manage them all with the simplest drag-and-drop configuration. For each additional monitor you must install another PCI video card, which will be ranked in terms of how large a monitor it can support and at what maximum resolution.

There are also "two-headed" graphic cards, such as the AGP-based NVIDIA GeForce4 MX, which enable you to connect two monitors to the same card. It comes with Apple's top-of-the-line G4's, where it supports one digital (using Apple's ADC connector) and one analog display.

NOTE *An iMac or iBook with FireWire can support a second display under Video Mirroring. The image reflects the current internal screen on other computers or different displays. This mode can be very useful serving as a screen repeater for conference and classroom environments. Under the Classic Mac OS, go to the Control Strip to turn Video Mirroring on or off.*

How do you configure two monitors on your Mac?

Once you've got the proper graphic cards and connections made, turn on both monitors and then boot your Mac.

When the startup process is complete, follow these steps:

NOTE *We're describing the process under Mac OS 9.x here, but you can achieve the same result by doing essentially the same thing with the Display preference panel in Mac OS X's System Preferences application.*

1. Choose Control Panels from the Apple menu, and choose Monitors from the submenu.
2. Now click the Arrange icon in the Monitors Control Panel (see Figure 2-13) and the screen will show you the current monitor configuration.
3. Once you've confirmed that all your connected displays are present and accounted for, you can you can easily change the desktop arrangement by moving one monitor icon to the left or to the right.

TIP *You can also mirror, or have both monitors display the same image, by dragging one monitor icon atop another. To stop mirroring or duplication, drag the monitor icons apart.*

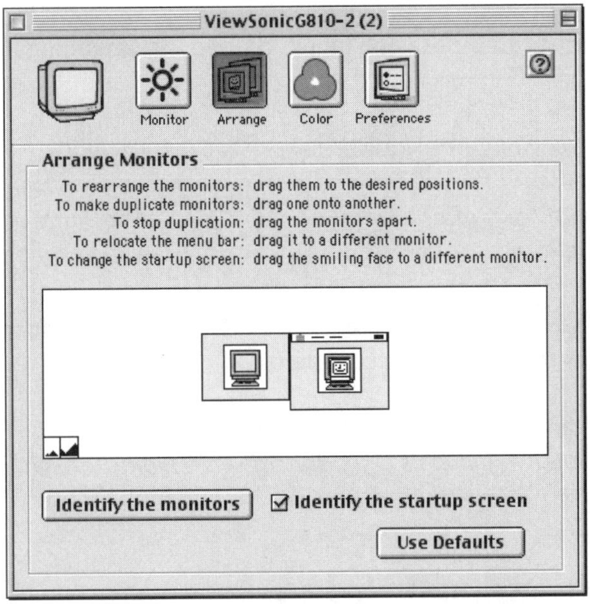

FIGURE 2-13 Manage your expanded desktop with this Monitors Control Panel.

4. To move the menu bar from one screen to another, just drag the menu bar from one monitor icon to the other. The results will be almost instantaneous.
5. If you want to use a different monitor as the default during startup, drag the smiling Apple face from one monitor icon to the other. The change will be in effect the next time you boot your Mac.
6. When you are finished configuring, click the Close box to dismiss the Monitors Control Panel.

You gain the following advantages in a multiple monitor setup:

- See the whole image on a larger "display" monitor, uncluttered by your menu bar and system messages, which you can display on a smaller "data" monitor

- Expand your desktop and show a panoramic view of your work area
- Run a clip at full-size in one monitor while you are doing the actual editing on the other

TIP *The advanced multitasking of Mac OS X is a perfect vehicle for using multiple monitors. You'll be able to view movie clips and edit at the same time without skipping a frame. Trying to do heavy-duty tasks under Mac OS 9 is apt to result in dropped frames or stuttering sound.*

- If you have a TV card installed (see next section), you can use the smaller monitor as the broadcast feed window.

TIP *If your camcorder has a 2 1/2-inch or 3 1/2-inch color LCD viewfinder screen, you can use it as a small additional monitor to check your work—just export your video or use the TV output on some video cards.*

Bringing in Broadcast Video

Your digital studio can expand to the broadcast world by adding a TV tuner card or external media unit that can accept signals from broadcast or cable TV.

One example is ATI's XCLAIM TV USB Edition, a combo TV tuner and video capture card that can even work on a first generation iMac and enable you to use iMovie 2 to edit your clips. Now we should point out that there are no miracles here. USB, being much slower than FireWire, isn't going to deliver a full-frame, full-motion video stream and audio. But you'll get adequate quality, probably no worse than a VHS deck.

ATI's packaging is highly useful, however. The built-in tuner handles 125 cable channels and 70 broadcast channels, and you have nifty features like picture-in-picture (see Figure 2-14), which actually displays four channels at once, although not in full motion (bandwidth limits, remember?).

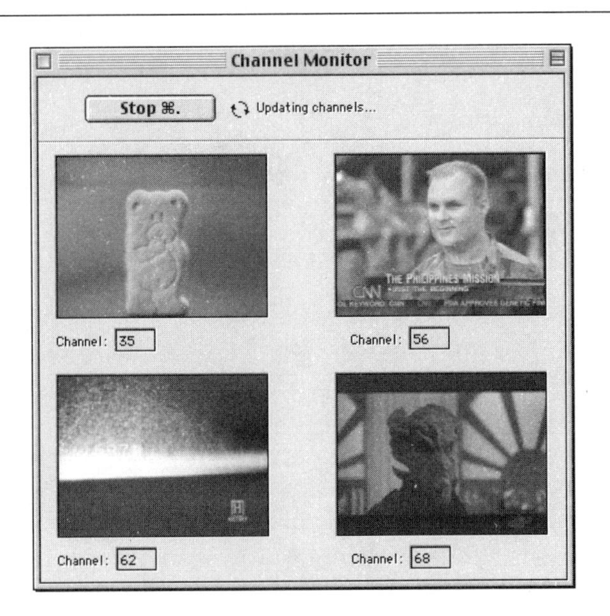

FIGURE 2-14 Within the limits of the USB standard, ATI's XCLAIM TV USB Edition can do such miracles as provide four channels of video in a single window.

The Closing Scene

Your FireWire Macintosh has the native ability to support and produce digital video. To get the most out of iMovie 2 you need to set up your Mac to be the best "launching pad" it can be to provide speed and efficiency to match the pace of your progress. Once your Mac is set up in the ways we suggest, you'll be better prepared to enter the exciting world of movie making, using Apple's marvelous desktop video editing program, iMovie 2.

In Chapter 3, we'll move from Mac to camcorder, and you'll learn about the wide range of products available and how to select the one that meets your needs and your budget.

Chapter 3

Looking at Camcorders

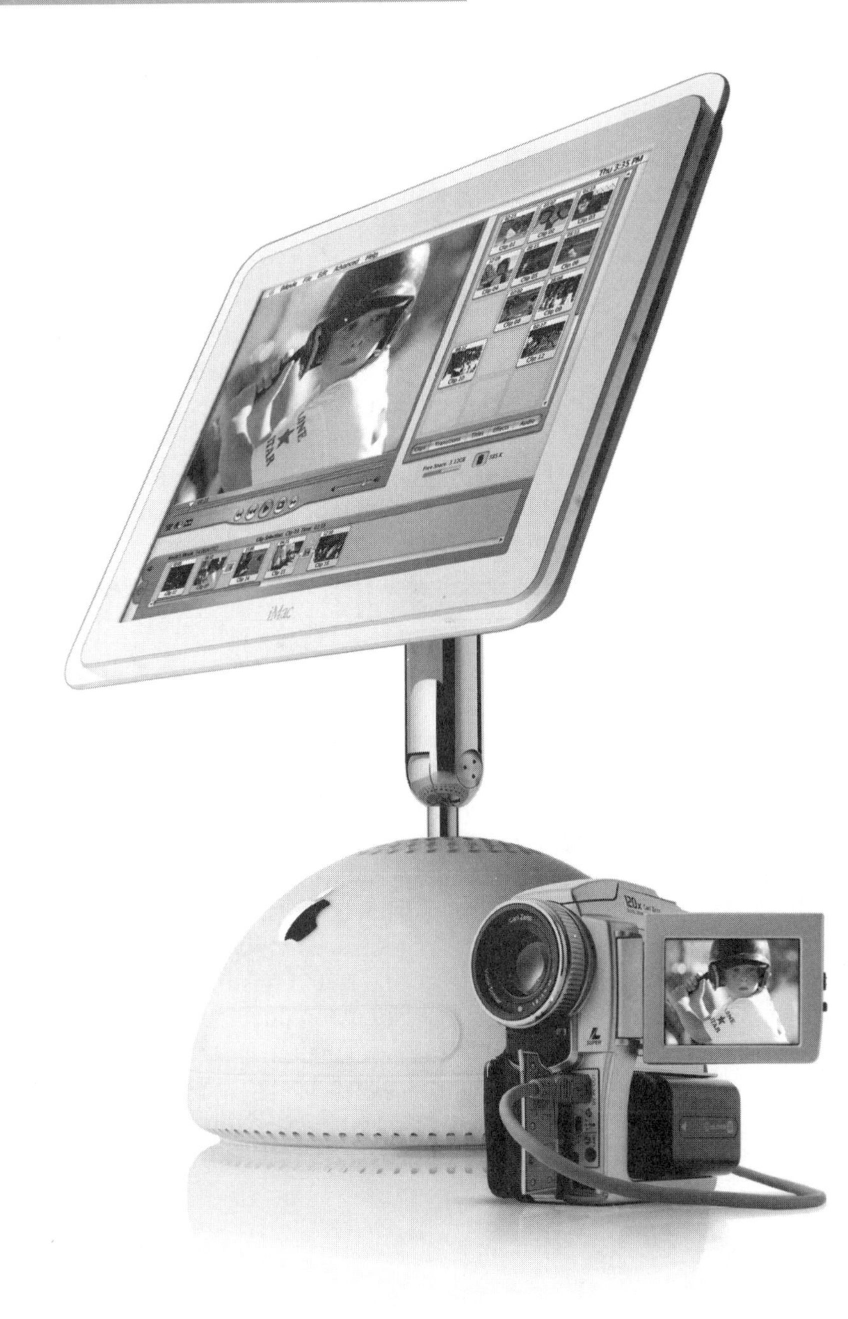

How to...

- Discover how video is different from film
- Learn about DV tape formats
- Learn what features to look for in a camcorder
- Consider different DV formats
- Choose a DV camcorder to match your needs

Looking at Camcorders

A powerful Mac system and iMovie 2 form only part of the equation when it comes to setting up a complete desktop video workstation on your Mac. You also need equipment for shooting your video productions. In the old days, when budding filmmakers wanted to capture family events or corporate gatherings, they bought cameras that used 8mm film.

Today, the camcorder is king. Take a combination of VCR and video camera technology, add some incredible technology to make the package small and convenient, and you have one of the most popular consumer electronics products.

But before we show you how to pick the right camcorder for your needs, perhaps a little history is in order.

How Films Are Made

Until video was invented and developed, the major method of capturing visual motion with sound was with motion pictures, or film (see Figure 3-1). We still may refer to the action of image capture as "filming" a scene, although it is more common to see that replaced with "shooting" a scene. We may call the videos that we make "movies" as well as "videos." As in "iMovie," the word "movie" evokes a fully realized and deliverable audiovisual concept. It takes knowledge, care, and attention to shoot, edit, and finish a good scene in video, but producing the same scene in film is much more complex and time-consuming.

In Part II you will discover all the steps that go into producing DV with iMovie 2. But right now, movies are the forefront of this discussion..

We all go to the movies, so as a matter of perspective, here is some background on 35mm and 16mm film, which are in current use, and on Super-8 film, used primarily for amateur and industrial applications (see Figure 3-2).

FIGURE 3-1 35mm prints of feature-length films often come to the theater on reels like these.

FIGURE 3-2 Tony's film, *Peace March,* was shot in 8mm and blown up to 16mm for editing and finishing.

35mm and 16mm Film

Table 3-1 shows two of the popular film formats.

Film Gauge	Frame area	12 minutes of running time at 24 frames-per-second	Main Applications
35mm	½ in. sq.	1,000 ft.	Theatrical features, commercials
16mm	⅛ in. sq.	400 ft.	Documentaries, independents

TABLE 3-1 Comparison of Two Popular Film Formats

NOTE *Yes, we are aware of 70mm and so on, but we wanted to concentrate on the norm rather than the high-cost exceptions.*

Super-8mm Film

Until home video took over, first 8mm film, and then a wider, bolder version, Super-8mm film, were for years the reigning home movie formats. In essence, 8mm was simply 16mm split down the middle. Super-8 kept the same gauge as 8mm, but increased the frame area by reducing the size of the sprocket holes that go down one side of the film strip.

In an era where a one-hour tape seems brief, it may come as a surprise to discover that Super-8 50-foot cartridges yielded about 2½ minutes of running time. And instant gratification, the ability to see the fruits of your labors as you can do today with a camcorder, wasn't possible. After shooting, you had drop off an exposed Super-8 cartridge at the same drugstore or camera store that serviced your snapshots, and it would take about a week for you to get back a spool of processed reversal film. It was ready to edit or to bring directly to show with your Super-8 home movie projector. Since editing such material required sitting down and actually cutting and then splicing with some sort of adhesive tape, few bothered—thus the indelibly amateurish reputation of home movies.

Super-8 was also used for industrial, commercial, and scientific applications. Just as 16mm, and MiniDV are sometimes blown up to 35mm, 8mm could be blown up to 16mm. Lest we forget, the format was also silent, which meant that audio had to be added later on during a conversion to a more sophisticated film format. Near the end of the Super-8 era, some synchronous sound-on-film systems were produced. This film format used magnetic striping for the sound track, and the cameras included a microphone input and a sound recording head. The projectors had magnetic sound playback heads to read the tracks. The systems were complex and expensive, and the striped original stock yielded finished footage that was all but impossible to edit because of the sound separation between film frame and recorded signal necessary for correct synchronization of sound and picture in your projector.

Kodak's K40 Kodacolor, the standard Super-8 color film, is still in limited manufacture, but Super-8 is all but extinct, used mostly by hobbyists and experimental filmmakers.

NOTE *Here's an important historical tidbit: Abraham Zapruder, with his Bell & Howell 8mm camera, captured 26 seconds of horrific imagery of the 1963 assassination of President John F. Kennedy in Dallas. This piece of a home movie has become one of the most widely seen films in the world, and has been translated into almost every medium of communication.*

A Moment of Respect, Please Super-8 is the noble ancestor and archetype of the camcorder you hold in your hand and the home video you made with iMovie. Hour-long camera runs, synchronous sound, instant playback, and sophisticated editing in iMovie—we could only dream of such things back then in the days of those famous Kodak moments.

The High Cost of Film Production

Film production costs, even for 16mm—which is about one-fourth the cost of 35mm (see Figure 3-3) have risen greatly in the last decade. Film has certain photographic advantages over video in many cases, particularly in the sharpness and lifelike feel of the completed movie, but completing production is a multi-step, many-layered, and

FIGURE 3-3 **A vintage Mitchell 35mm camera on a tripod**

labor-intensive procedure. Here is an idea of what the workflow is like in producing a 16mm, 55-minute documentary for television. What follows is a very abbreviated outline of the process:

1. **Exposure** Principal photography is done on location. Raw stock (unexposed film) is loaded into the camera, usually from a pre-loaded 1,000-foot film magazine, and the scene is shot.
2. **Recording** Sound is recorded on a separate portable tape deck, with a wireless link to the camera for 'sound sync'—synchronized sound and picture.
3. **Development** All the exposed film, now the "original," is taken to a commercial film lab. There the photochemical process of development and processing is completed. This is also where prints are made. Prints are copies of the original that are printed on to the kind of film stock that can be edited and projected. Dailies are quick and economical prints struck from the originals and are delivered to the studio for their review the next day. For reels that are confirmed, "one-light workprints," dubs from the original film, are struck for editing. The original film is stored in the lab's vault, where it is preserved for later uses.

NOTE *It's worth mentioning that improper storage of vintage movies over the years has resulted in the loss of a valuable heritage. Even comparatively recent films, such as 1978's Superman starring Christopher Reeve, suffered from some noticeable color shift over the years. Untold millions of dollars have been spent restoring old films to as close to their original condition as possible. Some of these restored films are even being offered in DVD versions, so you can enjoy the fruits of this labor.*

4. **Sound dubbing** The sync tapes are recorded to larger work reels for editing in the sound studio.
5. **Editing** Even for low-budget documentaries, most post-production today is done digitally on an editing station like an Avid, or with Apple's Final Cut Pro. As an alternative to cutting and splicing work prints of the original film by hand, editing is done with videotape copies of the original reels. The tape is edited in the digital editing station, where selected sequences are recorded on to hard disks. The camera sound, recorded digitally, is enhanced by sound effects, music, and additional dialogue. Once the sound

components are assembled, they are edited with the film clips into a professional, finished production.

NOTE *In the final, or post-production, process, even dialog may be redone. In a process called ADR (automatic dialog replacement) the actors dub their original dialog with a "cleaned" version free of background noise and, perhaps, the occasional stumble that happens even when experienced performers are involved.*

6. **Matching and mastering** When the final cut is laid out to a video master, a film editor must do the actual matching, a process of locating all those parts and pieces of original film and cutting them to match the sequences from the video master. They are cut in A/B rolls, where picture alternates with lengths of black film, A roll opposite to B roll, so that the splices won't show and titles and transitions are smooth. Depending on how much color correction or special effects are needed—and what the budget will allow—the finishing process may go through different steps to create both a positive master and a negative master, from which the prints are struck. There will be some trial prints, and then, finally, the release prints. When all of the film editing is done digitally, many of those steps can be skipped. If the film is going straight to television, the lab can set the timing for a TV print so that it will best match the narrower light values of broadcasting. Other release prints can be destined for theatrical exhibition, such as at a film festival.

NOTE *A video tap, or video assist, is a monitoring system in which a video camera is attached to a film camera through a video-in jack to permit the director and the DP (director of photography) to view the camera input on a monitor. After each shot, tape playback from the recorder and playback unit can reveal how well the action went. These "instant dailies" are not always reliable for confirming photography, but they certainly can catch a lot of flubs on the set.*

In all, film production and the post-production process are swiftly becoming more digital and less analog, and one studio's movie may be completed with a different mix of the two than another's next door. More independent, documentary, and industrial producers have been leaving film altogether and shooting in video. With digital projection, the movie goes straight out to a hard disk—or satellite uplink—instead of to a release tape.

Table 3-2 shows some of the key differences between film and tape, which impact strongly on the quality of the finished product.

Film	Videotape
Greater resolution	More homogenous
More depth of field	More consistent field of focus
Greater color subtlety	Brighter color
Realistic shadow detail	Thin shadow detail
Warmer character	Corner-to-corner consistency
Softer	Harder
Smooth swish-pans	Swish-, or blur-pans break up
Cumulative artifacts	Dropouts

TABLE 3-2 Film and Videotape Appearance Comparisons

NOTE *Sometimes the editing process also results in different versions of the same film. There will be the theatrical version that may garner a PG-13 or R rating because of adult languages and situations, and a sanitized version more suitable for viewing on commercial television. In some cases, there may be a third version, a so-called "director's cut," which contains scenes that may have been left out of the original version. This alternate edition can often be found in the DVD version of a movie or in a special re-release.*

How Video Cameras Work

A camcorder is a combination TV camera and videotape recorder in one portable unit. A point-and-shoot compact camcorder and a television studio camera, like the one shown in Figure 3-4, have many basic electronic principles in common, and they have some principles in common at the photographic end of the equation as well.

Motion picture and still cameras receive light through their lenses. The light is then focused on the frames of the silver halide photosensitive film where it etches the image, which is revealed after the film is developed.

Your DV camcorder also receives light through the same kinds of lenses, but the light does not etch film—something very different happens. Inside the camera there is an electronic sensor called a CCD (charged-coupled device), which is a grid of photo diodes. These diodes change the photons (of light) that strike them into electrons. Capacitors store and distribute the electrons into series of voltages that express the image information such as brightness, contrast and color. The voltage is converted to a number by an A/D (analog-to-digital) converter, and the

FIGURE 3-4 **From the 1950s, a studio television camera on a pedestal dolly.**

series of numbers is stored and processed by a microprocessor within your camera. A similar A/D process goes on with the sound input from the microphone, and that digital data is added to the picture information for synchronous sound. Once you record image and sound on magnetic tape, playback can be almost immediate. Just rewind, press Play, and enjoy.

NOTE *More chromatically-advanced cameras actually have three CCDs: one each for red, blue, and green. This provides a form of color separation that yields greater qualities of resolution, color luminance, fidelity, and rendering. These cameras are sometimes called three-chip cameras.*

What to Look for in a DV Camcorder

The very first thing you should look for is that, above all, it is a FireWire-compatible camcorder, because you want to be able to connect it directly to your Mac without having to buy a separate, outboard adapter.

You then want to determine what format to use. There are several different types of videotape out there, many for specialized professional applications, like Beta-SP and HD (high definition) video, but the two that are in the ballpark of affordable and doable digital video are Digital8 and MiniDV, which is also known as DV.

How Many Colors?

How many possible shades of gray, or colors, are needed to accurately translate to video what our eyes can see in the original image? Our eyes see an almost infinite number of shades. This would be impossible for a video system to handle. As with most computers and digital still cameras, 256 shades is the number required. So our black and white signal has a total possibility of 256 shades, as do the R-Y (red-yellow) and the B-Y (blue-yellow) components. In computer terms, this is called 8-bit quantization (although 256 shades is equally accurate).

The video signal is now represented by three strings of numbers, one for Y, one for R-Y and one for B-Y. The Y component numbers appear 13.5 million times a second, while the B and R numbers appear 3.375 million times a second each. Each time a number appears it has a value between 0 and 255 (in a computer "0" is a number, so there are a total 256 numbers).

NOTE *Why go digital at all? Well, in addition to the presence of a FireWire port for easy transfer to your Mac, you want to be able to edit your videos in iMovie. Besides, the picture quality on even the most inexpensive camcorders is just stunning. Pictures are much sharper, and colors are much better than those in movies made with analog camcorders in VHS, Super-VHS, 8mm, and Hi8 formats.*

MiniDV

MiniDV is the most popular digital video format for camcorders. The MiniDV cartridges are very compact and easily stored. In addition to the camcorder itself, you can play back MiniDV tapes on video tape recorders (VTRs) that support the DV, DVCAM, and DVCPRO formats. DV in the highest speed, or SP mode, appears to be the universal tape format because it will play back in any of these VTRs. This camera design has changed the face of home video, with some new MiniDV units so small you can cover them with your hand, like the Canon Elura seen in Figure 3-5.

NOTE *Prevent Recording: Like other video formats, the standard and mini-DV cassettes have record-prevention tabs. These tabs are similar to those found in the 8mm and Hi-8 format. The tabs are movable—unlike the break-off tabs of the VHS cassette. In contrast to an 8mm cassette, however, a DV cassette displays an open hole to prevent recording, while a closed hole allows recording.*

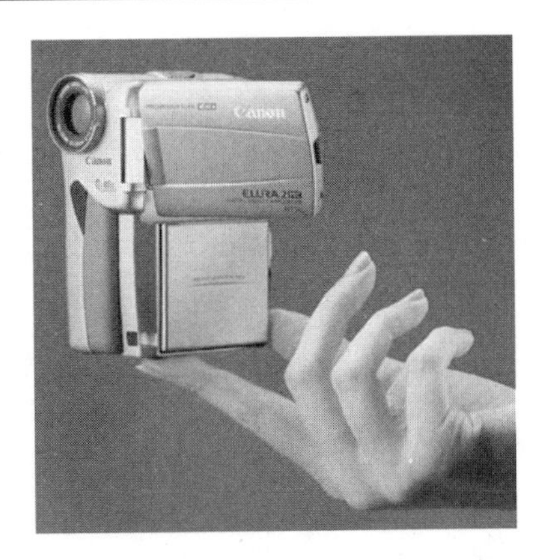

FIGURE 3-5 The Canon Elura puts the mini in MiniDV.

Digital8

Developed by Sony, Digital8 is a hybrid technology. It uses the same camera body frame and drive configuration that was used for its line of analog 8mm and Hi8 cartridges, but packs the electronics on board to record and play back digital signals to and from the very same tape. In digital recording, you won't get the same length of running time as in analog. A Hi8MP cartridge (see Figure 3-6), for example, will deliver 30 minutes on analog Hi8, or 15 minutes recording in Digital8. But overall, Digital8 cameras and tapes are much less expensive than MiniDV systems. Hi8's low shooting cost is about $6/hr using Fuji M221MP, vs. $12-24/hr with the various DV tapes available.

FIGURE 3-6 One advantage of Hi8 format is the low shooting cost.

If you have a trove of legacy analog 8mm and/or Hi8 cartridges, you're in luck. A Digital8 camcorder can play back this vintage material, and you can easily import their signals directly into your digital domain. Or, you can just record over them in the name of recycling.

CAUTION *Though 8mm tape will work just fine, Sony recommends using only the highest quality of Hi8 for Digital8 videomaking.*

NOTE *Which to use? That's up to you. If you need backwards compatibility with 8mm or Hi8 video, and want to save a few dollars, Sony's Digital8 is the way to go. If you want the highest image quality (and in the end the difference isn't drastic), consider MiniDV. Sony, by the way, offers products in both formats.*

Table 3-3 briefly lists the various digital videotape formats and media, so you can see the advantages and disadvantages in terms of recording time.

Format	Tape Type	Tape Speed	Maximum Load	Usage
Digital8 8mm/Hi8	ME (metal evaporate), MP (metal particle) (uses Video8, Hi8 tapes)	28.6 mm/sec (estimated)	60 min.	Consumer Cameras
MiniDV/DV	ME (metal evaporate)	18.81 mm/sec	80/120 min. (SP/LP)	Prosumer/ low-end industrial

TABLE 3-3 DV Videotape Formats and Their Applications

CAUTION *Videographers in the field in different parts of the U.S. report that it may not always be easy to find MiniDV cartridges for sale at small and medium-size camera and electronics stores. So stock up before you hit the road.*

A Survey of Camcorder Features

There are more than a dozen manufacturers of camcorders, some with common alliances under the hood (meaning that lenses and electronics may have been manufactured by some of the same companies), and new models are being introduced somewhere in the world every week. There is not always a consistent combination of features in certain camcorders. New features are always being

Digital Video Cassette Design (Smaller is Better)

At the heart of the digital video format is a new cassette. In fact, there are two cassettes sizes. Currently, the first has a capacity to record up to four and a half hours (4h30min) of video, while the latter can record a maximum of one hour of video. The cassette that is the main focus of our attention here is the second one, and it is called the mini-DV cassette (mini DVC). As its name implies, it is small—2.6×1.9×0.5 inches (66×48×12.2 mm). In comparison, an 8mm cassette is 3.7×2.5×0.6 inches (95×62.5×15 mm). A VHS cassette is 7.4×4.1×.98 inches (188×104×25 mm). The mini-DV cassette takes up less than half the overall space (43.4%) of an 8mm cassette. The mini-DV cassette was designed for use in smaller, portable equipment such as camcorders, and the larger version, DV standard cassette, was designed for digital video VCRs and broadcast equipment.

The tape inside the cassette for VHS is ½ inch (12.7 mm) wide; 8mm tape, as its name implies, is 8 mm (or slightly less than ⅓ inch) wide; while DV tape is 6.35 mm (¼ inch) wide.

The tape cassette housing itself protects the tape until it is pulled into the record/play mechanism. The DV cassette uses a reel lock system to prevent tape sagging and other tape damage. The tape is therefore not only protected within a robust shell, but the tape also is wound neatly within the cassette for best alignment during both recording and playback. The locking tape door opens to expose the tape only when the cassette is in the machine, minimizing the entry of dust.

introduced, and others migrate to other model levels. The cost continues to drop for higher and higher technologies.

Here is a review of many of the different features you will find in the latest products. They reflect the incredible diversity and flexibility of these marvelous products. But even the lowest cost model can get you near-broadcast quality in many instances, so it's often a matter of just which features you want to pack on.

Eyepiece Viewfinder You frame your shots and confirm focus through the viewfinder, same as with a regular camera. So the eyepiece viewfinder should fit comfortably against your face. Some of the better camcorders may have a diopter adjustment there so you can compensate for not using your glasses.

Also be sure the camcorder has a swivel finder that can go from flush to the camcorder body to raising up at an angle to allow you to hold the camcorder lower on your body or for tripod use.

- **Color** Most camcorders from mid-range up have a color viewfinder, enabling you to monitor all the values in the shot (see Figure 3-7). Color LCD viewers are useful as an outboard video monitor, so you can view your work in progress.
- **Black and white** It may be the lower-price camcorders that shave costs this way, but many videographers prefer a black-and-white viewfinder. It has a brighter image, and is sharp and right to the point for definitive composition.

LCD Viewer An LCD (liquid crystal display) viewer is a miniature flat-panel display that doubles as a viewfinder and a field monitor, and, in the studio, an ancillary editing monitor. Depending upon the cost of the camcorder, they are usually $2\frac{1}{2}$ inches or $3\frac{1}{2}$ inches diagonal, and you want one that has full flexibility. Swiveled facing forward, it can act as a mirror when you film yourself. You are less likely to jostle the camcorder in a tripod set-up if you use the LCD instead of the eyepiece viewfinder. But you should first set up your shot with the eyepiece viewfinder for convenience.

FIGURE 3-7 On this Sony DCR-TRV530 Digital8 camcorder the eyepiece viewfinder is swiveled up and the LCD viewfinder is swiveled forward. There is a manual focus ring on the lens and an accessory shoe on top (useful for add-on lighting or mics).

Lens All camcorders now have zoom lenses with variable focal lengths that substitute for a bag full of fixed lenses. The greater the zoom range—from wide angle to telephoto—the better, but more glass makes the camcorder that much heavier. A shorter zoom range, however, often means a more compact model. You get what you pay for, and a more expensive camcorder usually has a better quality lens, like a Zeiss. A motorized zoom lens system adds even more weight to the unit, drains battery power, and its smoothness in motion can be matched by your increasing skill with a manual zoom. But fewer and fewer camcorders are made with manual zoom.

NOTE *While the name Zeiss may not be quite as well known as the name McDonalds, its parent company, Carl Zeiss, is a world-famous manufacturer of high quality lenses for cameras, eyeglasses, telescopes, and even many of the projection systems used in planetariums, such as New York's Hayden Planetarium.*

Here are two additional zoom features you'll want to be on the lookout for:

- **Digital zoom** This might be all right on a very high-end camcorder, but it takes strong electronics to keep a digital zoom stable and unjaggy. The more you zoom in, the worse it gets.
- **Optical zoom** You should choose an optical zoom, and find as good a quality lens as you can afford.

NOTE *Most camcorders now have combined optical and digital zoom features. For maximum quality, you'll want the widest optical zoom range, but you'll want digital zoom to enhance your shooting capabilities for extreme conditions.*

Manual Override Don't get a camcorder without it. A camcorder's light sensor-activated automatic exposure system gets better with every model generation, but you want to be able to adjust and lock down the lens diaphragm for many reasons in a specific setting. We'll discuss this topic in more detail in Chapters 6 and 7. A ring control override is more stable than sliders. In other cameras, like some of the Canons, it is a menu selection.

Image Stabilizer The modern camcorder is full of small miracles, and this is certainly one of them. It will never replace a tripod for motionless framing, but it does give you the freedom to shake the camera a bit as your shoot and not have that motion hurt the finished picture. You don't have to keep your hand in a vice, as it were. Over time, once you learn the limits of your camcorder, you will learn how to "dance with it" and not push it beyond its means.

NOTE *Just remember that the more you use such features as the image stabilizer and zoom lens, the more power is drawn by the camcorder, which means less time between battery replacements or recharge sessions.*

Here's a brief description at the two types of image stabilizers available:

- **Digital image stabilizer** Again, the better quality the camcorder, the more likely its digital image stabilizer is cleaner and more stable, and won't lose too much of the frame in compensating for motion.
- **Optical image stabilizer** The optical image stabilizer is a more high-end feature, and involves a fluid-dampened suspension prism compensation system that does not compromise the received frame area.

Still Camera Mode This is a beautiful feature, which enables your camcorder to do double-duty: first, to capture moving pictures and, second, to capture still pictures. As you will see in Chapter 13, it's easy—and sharp and clean—to extract a frame for a still. Some camcorders come with media storage formats like Memory Sticks, which would be most useful if you worked with other cameras or devices that used them as well.

NOTE *We don't want to pretend that a camcorder with a still picture feature can necessarily replace a separate digital camera or even a film camera. Within its limits, however, it can capture neat still shots for your movie, or a casual picture just for fun.*

16:9 Widescreen TV Effect This is a recording mode that actuates an internal iris mask that crops the image horizontally from the "normal" 4:3 aspect ratio (ratio of width to length) to a 16:9 aspect ratio. This brings the effect more in line with the ratio of a standard film and the aspect ratio used by HDTV (high definition television). Thus far, iMovie 2 does not support 16:9, but you could make a graphic mask to superimpose over your wide footage to simulate 16:9.

Built-In Speaker This may seem like a small thing, but not all camcorders come with this feature, and then you must rely on monitoring the sound with headphones through the camcorder's headphone jack. With a built-in speaker you can review the scenes completely and comfortably through playback on the LCD viewer. Don't expect vivid stereo sound, but just being able to hear voices clearly in the field is a boon to videographers. It's also great for family videos, especially if your camcorder as a built-in color LCD. You'll save a trip to the TV to attach your camcorder (assuming your TV has convenient input jacks for a camcorder, of course).

Accessory Shoe An accessory shoe is a powered bracket mounted on the top, or sometimes on the side, of the camcorder body. Depending on the model, the accessory shoe can support a photo light or a microphone or even both.

Remote Control A good remote control is worth its weight in gold and not just for couch potatoes. First of all, it replaces the old cable release for actuation from a distance, enabling you to run the camcorder without having to poke at a button and thus risk jiggling a fixed-down setup. You can take a group shot and include yourself. It can act like a VCR's remote control while you watch playback. With many of the advanced features in some models, such as seen in Figure 3-8, it controls in-camera editing and effects. Perhaps you'll get the best use of a remote control when you have your camera installed as an animation stand, or when you need to put distance between you and your subject in wildlife videography.

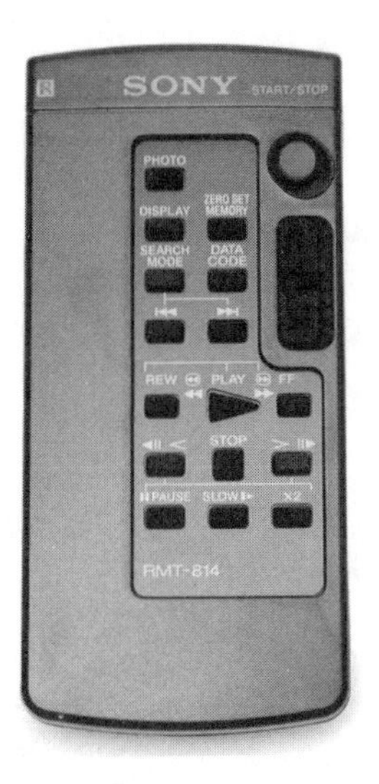

FIGURE 3-8 The wireless remote control of the Sony DCR-TRV230 will work at distances up to 16 feet. It can start and stop recordings, zoom the lens and manage playback functions.

Analog Line-In For the complete DV studio, don't forego this feature. These inputs allow you to connect a VHS player or TV to your camcorder. You can view this analog video on your LCD viewer, digitize it to DV, and then bring it into iMovie.

TIP *Some of Sony's camcorders, such as the DCR-PC110, include an analog-to-digital pass-through feature that enables direct conversion of analog sources to digital without re-recording the material first. This is a great way to import analog views directly to your Mac via iMovie 2, using the digital camcorder as intermediary.*

How to Choose Your DV Camcorder

Here are the three basic camera paths to becoming an iMovie videographer:

- You already have your own DV camcorder
- You inherited a DV camcorder or have one you can borrow
- You are ready to buy a new DV camcorder

If you already have a DV camcorder, naturally you want to be able to go ahead and make digital movies with iMovie 2. You'll want to review the features that we discussed above, so you can make sure that your camcorder has the right features, particularly a FireWire port. If it doesn't, or if you are ready to buy a camcorder anyway, then use the feature list as a guide. If you are buying a used DV camcorder, the same guidelines apply.

The first thing you must look for, of course, is a camcorder that is within your price range. Then you need to confirm the Macintosh FireWire compatibility of any model you may consider. Apple is the best source for that information, which is updated on their Web site at http://www.apple.com/imovie/shoot.html for Supported Camcorders.

NOTE *Not all camcorder makers label their FireWire ports with that name. Many call it by its technical name, IEEE 1394, while Sony simply calls it i.Link. But FireWire still is, by any other name, FireWire.*

What level of DV videography do you want to pursue? Take the time for the opportunity to look within yourself to see what you really like to do and want to accomplish, and out to the world to see what you want to engage with and capture in video. There are roughly four levels of DV moviemaking to choose a camcorder for:

Recreational Use Without iMovie 2 available, you probably wouldn't be here. You would be back among the point-and-shoot tribe who don't arrange their snapshots into albums anymore than they would edit their tapes. You want to be able to bring back attractive movies from vacations, weddings, and sports, but you don't have the time to make it a committed hobby.

There are Digital8 and MiniDV camcorders available for under $600 that are more than adequate for delivering high-quality video images, like those shown in Figure 3-9. They may have more controls than you think you need, but they include automatic focus and exposure and are easy to use. Your DV studio may not expand beyond your camcorder, Macintosh and iMovie 2, so you probably won't need such frills as analog-in.

FIGURE 3-9 Canon's Z Series of MiniDV camcorders are ergonomic, easy to use and moderately-priced, making them ideal for the recreational videographer.

Intermediate Use At this stage you will want all the DV tools at your disposal, even if you don't get around to using every single one. You want to make movies that can move through the digital hub. You want to integrate analog material, send QuickTime movies over the Web, and accomplish finished works that are of good enough image quality to be presented to audiences beyond friends and family. For under $800, you can get a fully featured Digital8 or MiniDV camcorder that can deliver just about everything in the book.

Advanced The meridian for the advanced user is the fully featured, three-chip MiniDV camcorder, like the GL1 shown in Figure 3-10, which can range from. $1,200 to $2,000. You depend upon DV in your profession or business, such as corporate communications, real estate, medical and scientific, or you're a serious video artist. With this level of camcorder, you can confidently produce footage that is clean and sharp enough to go out to duplication, multimedia, and broadcast.

Professional At the professional level, your camcorder is your living, because you are a video maker. Favored by the "indies," the independent video feature-length and commercial producers, the Canon XL1S (see Figure 3-11) and the Sony DCR-VX2000 DV are no longer really camcorders, they are full-size production camera systems costing between $2,500 and $4,000. They have high-resolution imaging CCDs, interchangeable lenses and microphones, PCM digital stereo audio, and very sophisticated image control and monitoring at all levels of production.

FIGURE 3-10 The Canon GL1 three-chip MiniDV camcorder.

FIGURE 3-11 This Canon XL1S camcorder offers solid professional performance, sufficient for heavy-duty advanced and professional use.

Next Wave

What's next in camcorders? Probably the technology will forgo linear videotape altogether. We'll probably see non-linear media like the DVDs that are replacing CDs in our Macintosh minitowers. One notable example of this technology is the Hitachi DZ-MV100ADO (see Figure 3-12), already available at many consumer electronic shops for under $1,000. It is a digital camcorder that records JPEG images and full-motion MPEG2 video onto an 8 cm DVD-RAM disc with nearly 3 gigabytes (GB) total capacity (double-sided). Powered alternately by a lithium-ion battery or AC adapter, the DVDCAM can record up to 1 hour per side of standard video or 30 minutes per side of fine video. This means that in the field, you can go from one point to the other for review, or even meaningful rough edits. The digital hub just added another spoke.

FIGURE 3-12 Hitachi DZ-MV100ADO DVDCAM

The Closing Scene

Camcorders were once the province of high-budget videographers, but today's consumer-level camcorders can deliver extraordinary quality, with plenty of extra features to fit the needs of even professional users. If you check the specs carefully, and consult the product reviews in such magazines as *Sound & Vision,* you'll find one that suits your needs.

In the next chapter, you'll learn the next phase of planning your video project, writing your script.

Part II

Creating iMovies

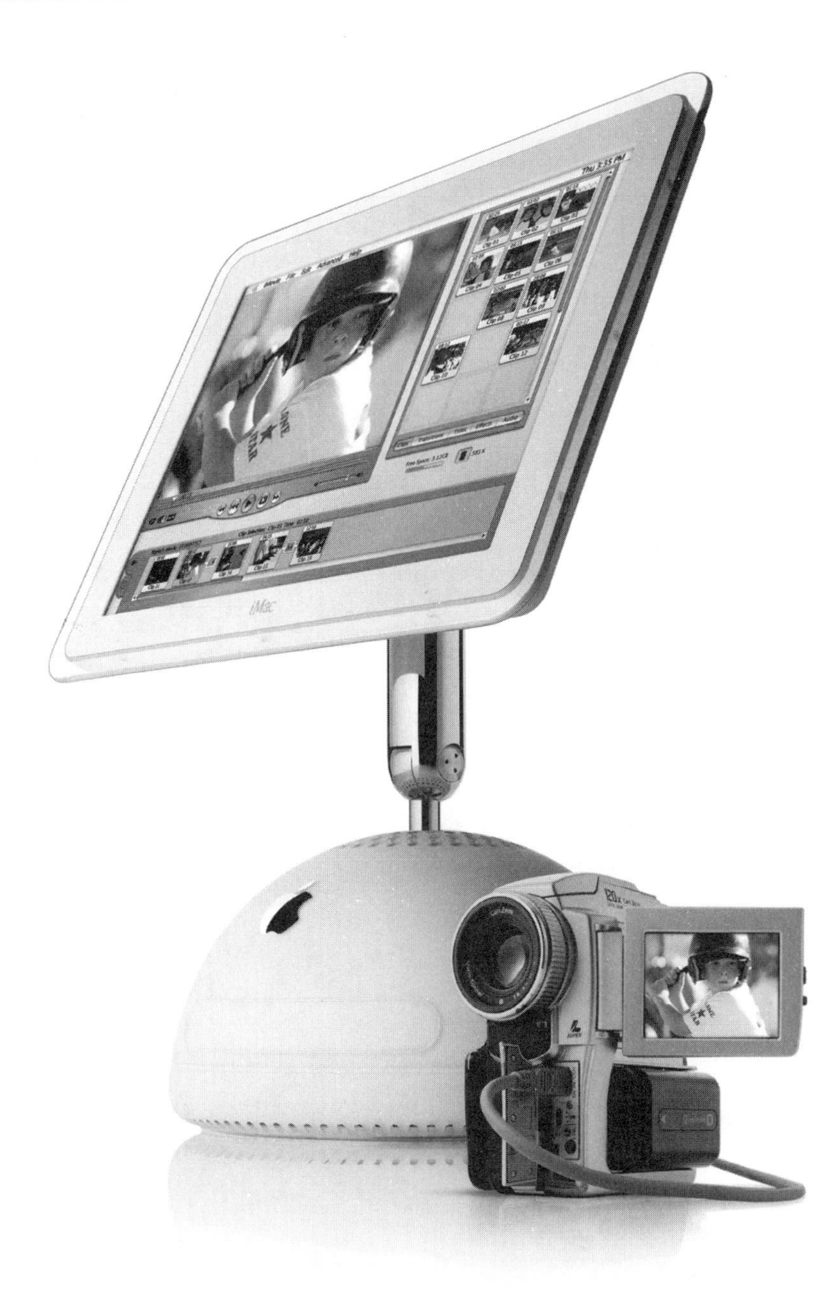

Chapter 4

Planning, Plotting, and Producing

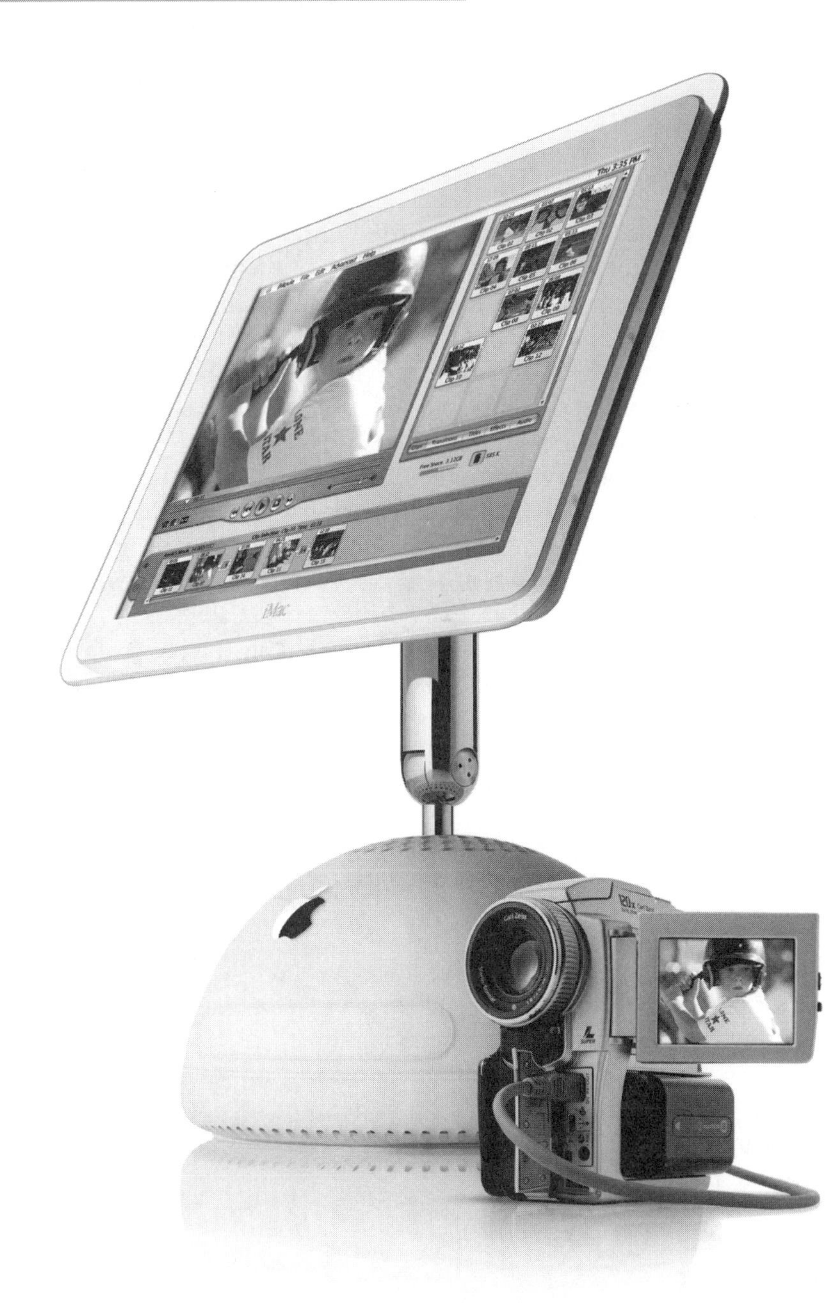

How to…

- Develop your concept
- Write a treatment
- Scout locations
- Audition and cast actors
- Make a storyboard

Now we're ready to get down to the nitty-gritty. In previous chapters, you discovered many of the types of projects you can create with iMovie, projects that evoke visions of excitement and adventure. You learned, also, how to set up your FireWire-equipped Mac for optimum moviemaking performance, how to optimize memory, storage capacity, connectivity, and display. You learned how to deal with the often diverse and contradictory needs of analog, digital, film, and video in the multimedia world.

After you've examined our review of the types of camcorders available, and have acquired one, you're ready to make a movie for just a few dollars' worth of tape. For make-it-up-as-you-go-along moviemaking, such as capturing a family event or just shooting whatever suits your fancy, even a recreational-level camcorder is more than adequate.

But if you want to tell a story, you have to consider taking a more professional approach to your moviemaking. To get the most out of your ideas, equipment, budget, crew, actors, and everybody's precious time you may need to do some degree of planning. We call that "preproduction." In this chapter we will suggest and illustrate some ideas that can help you make the best-laid plans for all of your moviemaking.

Start with a Concept

Some concepts can be as brief as a dynamic three-second title introduction, as momentary as a real-time recording of a sudden event, or as ongoing as a series of scenes that track a child as he or she is growing up.

A video sketch can get you started in moviemaking, or you may find that it is what you really like the best and just want to do more. A conceptual outline can help you work out an idea to see what kind of a movie might be in there, and where to take it.

First you should write a treatment, which is an extended summary of your movie, covering plot and characters. In the film and TV industries, a treatment helps coalesce the ideas for your project, and it is often used to sell it to a studio.

Progressing from a treatment to a screenplay to a shooting script is a constructive evolution that can be just as helpful, and even necessary, for a just-for-fun, ten-minute movie project as it is for a Hollywood feature. You are free to find and use what will work for you.

NOTE *We should mention that some very famous film directors, such as Stephen Spielberg, actually got their start making home movies. This doesn't guarantee that your home movie will earn you a Hollywood job or set you on a lifetime career path in that direction, but it does sometimes happen.*

Make a Video Sketch

There's no better place to start with your camcorder than a video sketch. It's just you and your camcorder, hand-held, simply recording your visual explorations without the obligation of documentation or deadline.

Where should you go? It's up to you. Perhaps a farmers' market, a crafts museum, an old neighborhood, or even your backyard. Any of these opportunities will give you the chance to become familiar with all the features and settings of your camcorder. Framing, focusing, zooming, filming while walking—try it all out here. Get accustomed to your camera's features and learn its quirks. For example, if your camcorder has (as just about all do) an image stabilizer, try to see just how effective it is in regular use, and whether there's too much shaking in your pictures when you pan or move to keep up with your subject.

When you bring that footage into iMovie, you will be able to review the results at your leisure and make further discoveries in editing. You may discover themes in your videography, such as the different nationalities at the market, or the colors and forms of the produce. You may discover that by intercutting two faces from the totem pole at the museum, you have created an animated character.

NOTE *What do we mean by intercutting? In iMovie, take two frames from the first face shot, and add it to two frames from the second face shot. Duplicate that four-frame edit about 20 times. When you play that series back, the face appears to undergo an animated metamorphosis.*

The more video sketches you make, the more accomplished a videographer you will become. Your eye will become more perceptive, and you will start creating sequences, portraits, reviews, and stories from what you capture with your camcorder.

Making an Outline

If you are thinking about making a movie of any kind, great or small, creating a simple outline will help to illuminate the entire concept and to reveal the means necessary to make it happen. The outline is also the basis for a treatment.

An outline can take any form that is comfortable for you, but it should include these elements:

- The concept, idea, or issue that is inspiring this project
- Estimated total running time when your movie is finished
- Who it is about and what their levels of involvement are
- Where it will take place
- When it did, or will, happen
- The events and actions that are driving the story
- What locations are proposed, and if permissions are needed to shoot in those locations

CAUTION *Getting permission to shoot in a public space is an important point. As you know, movie studios often have to go through a local government or business owner to get permission to shoot in a particular location. For casual shots, this seldom represents a problem but, if you actually plan to have actors and scenery in a public space, it's essential and may be required by local ordinance.*

- Costumes, props, or vehicles
- Camera, lighting, and sound support
- Production time estimate
- Rough budget estimate
- Distribution and exhibition targets

Writing a Treatment

A treatment is a complete, condensed visual narrative of a film story, as if told by a person watching it develop from beginning to end. A treatment answers that question "What is your movie about?"

A treatment for a feature can go on for more than three pages, but the general opinion is that, if it can't be told in one page, then it's a movie with a problem. Your five-minute movie has equal rights to that one page.

The exercise of writing that page will go a long way to help you clarify your concept and provide an arm's-length objectivity that will triumph over a waving-your-hands-in the-air approach.

Even if you are recruiting volunteer help for your production from among your friends, class, or club, handing out copies of the treatment will speed things up. Treatments are also key documents for permissions and grant proposals, and are the basis for developing your concept into a real screenplay.

Storyboard Your Production

One of the easiest, cheapest, and yet most effective film planning exercises for the visualization process is the storyboard. A storyboard is a form of a comic strip, or picture script. Figure 4-1 is an example of a storyboard for a television show. It is a sequence of numbered frames with a sketch, title or transition inside each frame. It may have lines of text at the bottom of the frame for location, action, or dialog references.

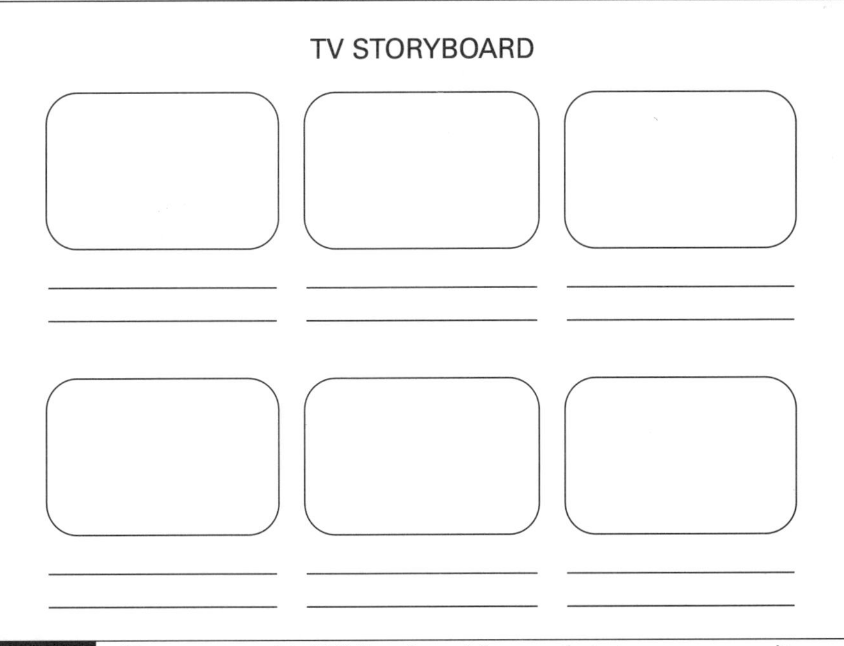

FIGURE 4-1 You can copy this TV Storyboard form and start up your own sitcom.

A storyboard can be drawn quickly in the form of crude stick figures, rendered with a high degree of detail, or illustrated, as seen in Figures 4-2. In the golden age of the Hollywood studios, professional artists created photo-realistically drawn storyboards that featured likenesses of the stars playing in the picture. They are now treasured as collectibles.

The form of your storyboard can be whatever is most practical for you. Here are some of the configurations that storyboards can take:

- Use printed storyboard page forms, available at art stores and online from industry supply houses.
- Create your own form page and make photocopies.
- Use 3×5 index cards and anchor them on a bulletin board. Change shot and scene order simply by moving them to different positions. Cards may be the easiest to photograph for an animatic.

NOTE *Is this film industry lingo getting to you? Just hang in there. We'll explain what this means in the next section.*

The video clips and imported images that are displayed on iMovie's Shelf are a form of storyboarding. Many short pieces and sequences can be arranged there and in the Clip Viewer without ever leaving iMovie.

Make an Animatic from Your Storyboard

Now that you have developed a swift, flexible, and expressive storyboard system, you can put it into motion as an animatic. An animatic is a rough, step-by-step animated sequence photographed directly from the frames of a storyboard. Studios like Lucasfilm, that must plan far ahead for big budget scenes, may produce animatics in detailed 3D animations with sound. You can see them in action at http://www.starwars.com/episode-i/feature/19980920/.

This iMovie animatic can serve as a cheap and easy early-bird rehearsal for your production. See Chapter 13 for details on photographing flat art and animation techniques.

Start with a Silent Animatic

Here's how to use an animatic to organize your production:

1. Shoot each full frame, with the sound recording turned off on your camcorder (assuming such an option is available, of course).
2. Make sure that the storyboard frame number is included in each shot.

FIGURE 4-2 This is a sample storyboard, depicting scenes for a proposed movie. © Tom Pankratz, Gambit Films.

3. Time the duration of each shot to match the scene's estimated playing time. A wristwatch is fine, or you can just check the running time display in your camcorder for a rough approximation.
4. Now import the completed animatic as a new project in iMovie.

NOTE *We cover the subject of importing and editing your clips in the three chapters that comprise Part IV. You'll want to refer to those chapters for the cold, hard facts about editing your movies.*

5. Preview the animatic to test your concepts of how the continuity should flow.
6. As needed, edit your animatic to match proposed changes.
7. When you're done, you can export it back to your camcorder or save it as a QuickTime movie for viewing on your Mac whenever you want.

Making a VO (Voice Over) Animatic

Voiceovers make your story start to come alive, with spoken dialog illustrating the action. It can be done as simply as you or one of the actors speaking into the mike for all the parts and lines. VO animatics can be useful when you're blocking out the narrative, which includes the process of setting up the positioning for the actors and scenery in your movie.

To make your VO animatic, first produce a silent version, as we described in the previous section. The next step is to record your voiceover portion. Chapter 12 covers the subject of adding sound to your iMovie 2 projects in full detail.

TIP *You can go even further with a VO and have all the actors read their own lines. This is worth the effort for the planning stage of a movie. Now the action and continuity becomes much more three-dimensional. It will give you valuable insights for editing your scripts.*

Making a Soundtrack Animatic

Music—or its absence—is an important part of every movie. You can start simply by recording in a track of background music that matches the moods you want to achieve in the finished film. If music and sound effects are of pivotal importance in the story, here is a good place to try them out.

NOTE *Using existing music was, in fact, done in the early talkies. For example, Tchaikovsky's Swan Lake is the opening theme in the famous horror movie Dracula. Otherwise the movie had no background music at all; that is, until Universal released an updated version with the proper mood music to propel this classic film. If you want to use commercial music in your production, you'll have to get permission from the copyright holder. We cover this subject on more detail in Chapter 12.*

If you've had original music composed and performed for your film, adding it to your animatic will help you to see how well it will work in the final production. You can combine music and sound effects with a VO and you will have an animatic that comes close to the full movie experience.

Writing a Screenplay

The heart and soul of a movie, at least until the director and producers make their own changes, of course, is the screenplay.

A screenplay for a full-length commercial feature film is 125 to 150 pages in length for a production that will take 6 to 12 months to complete. Also known as a film script or video script, a screenplay is written as a fully developed story containing scene descriptions and character dialogue. It describes the action sequences, transitions, and continuity. Figure 4-3 illustrates a sample script from the same production as shown back in Figure 4-2, showing the basics of a typical screenplay.

Professional scripts have to follow a special, industry-standard formula for layout, with specific, rigid setups for how dialog and action descriptions are separated. There are even standards for the amount of space used to indent a specific passage in the script.

The industry also demands the use of accepted terms and sequences. Some, as favored by broadcast television in a three-camera production (such as used in sitcoms since the days of *I Love Lucy*), are double column with dialogue on one side and camera directions on the other.

A screenplay is continuous. It follows the form and flow of the proposed finished film. The screenplay is also the basis for the shooting script, which is discontinuous, meaning that scenes are usually shot out of sequence for efficiency and to make better use of expensive locations and specially designed scenery.

```
EXT. MOVIE THEATER - NIGHT

   A stream of people wait in line for a movie.

   Above, A marquee reads: TITANIC

   Scooter and Rachel, looking like they haven't slept in
   days stand in line.

   Rachel HIDES something under her long overcoat.

TICKET COUNTER

   Scooter and Rachel approach the ticket counter. Scooter
   makes eye contact with

   THE TELLER

   who hands Scooter two tickets and a box of RAISINETS. The
   teller gives a knowing nod.

INT. THEATER LOBBY - NIGHT

   Scooter and Rachel sneak up a hallway.

INT. PROJECTIONIST ROOM - NIGHT

   LOUIS, a heavy set man in his early 30s, devours a box of
   Raisinets. He stands next to a huge movie projector.

   Louis spills the remaining Raisinets into his mouth.

   He tosses the EMPTY BOX into the trash and walks to the

   TABLE

   Louis grabs a reel marked TITANIC.

EXT. PROJECTIONIST ROOM - NIGHT

   A hand turns the doorknob.

INT. PROJECTIONIST ROOM - NIGHT

   A door CREAKS open. Louis swings around and sees

   A HAND

   in the doorway shaking a fresh box of Raisinets.

   Louis heads towards the door - the Raisinets calling him
   like the Pied Piper.
```

FIGURE 4-3 Here's a sample page of a formatted screenplay for a short production, as seen in the storyboard in Figure 4-2.

NOTE *The magic of the film is that all the discontinuous scenes are finally edited into a cohesive whole that gives the production its rhythm and pace. Quite often the film editors are the unsung heroes of the industry, taking huge amounts of film and tape, cutting them down, and assembling them a sensible, coherent sequence.*

A typical screenplay incorporates the following elements:

- An opening, or establishing, shot that begins a scene
- Description of an interior or exterior location
- Establishment of the time of day
- Identification or description of a location
- Description of the look of a character
- Description the character's actions in the screenplay
- A character's dialogue
- A description of a scene's action, such as "a door opens"
- Key scene elements like "TABLE" or "A HAND" that suggest a close-up or insert shot

NOTE *It's fair to say that a script usually gives a film director just a rough idea of the look of a scene and its essential action. It's up to the director to bring these sparse descriptions to life with tight, believable performances from the actors.*

You don't need to follow these exact forms of screenplays to come up with a form of continuity that works for you and your crew. Always tailor the planning to the size and nature of your production.

If you want to pursue professional-level script writing, you might consider taking a class or, at the start, just reading some books on the subject to get a feel for proper screenwriting techniques.

TIP *One book that serves as a useful introduction is The Complete Book of Scriptwriting by J. Michael Straczynski, from Writer's Digest Books. Straczynski is the prolific writer of hundreds of scripts for such TV programs as Murder, She Wrote and Walker Texas Ranger, but is most famous as the creator, executive producer, and head writer of Babylon 5.*

Once you've grasped the basics of screenwriting, you'll want to move on to software that enables you to roll your own. A scriptwriting application automatically sets up the proper formatting to give your script the proper look and feel, so you don't have to mess with tabs and cells to make your word process follow the proper form.

- Script Werx (http://www.ScriptWerx.com) is an economical program that customizes Microsoft Word so you can easily create video scripts and screenplays.
- Final Draft (http://www.finaldraft.com/support/) is an advanced, multi-column scriptwriting software package that is regularly used in the film and TV industries.
- Movie Magic Screenwriter 2000 (http://www.screenplay.com) is the prime competitor of Final Draft in the industry, providing a similar set of features for experienced, as well as budding, scriptwriters.

NOTE *As of the time this book was written, both Final Draft and Movie Magic Screenwriter 2000 were available in Mac OS X versions.*

Writing a Shooting Script

The final stage of preproduction planning is the shooting script. The shooting script accounts for all the elements of the project, fleshing out the scenes first sketched in

About Our Sample Scripts

Figures 4-2 and 4-3 come from the same sequence of *Self Distribution*, a short video by Tom Pankratz of Gambit Films in San Francisco. As you look over these illustrations, you'll see how a storyboard, a screenplay, and a shooting schedule relate to each other in the creative and production processes. The film itself was shot in DV, edited in Final Cut Pro, Apple's professional video editing application, and then transferred to DVD.

This bright and funny short shows how a pair of independent filmmakers are denied their chance to have their film shown by the crass and commercially minded theater owner. As a result, they take matters into their own hands. Luring the projectionist away from the booth with his favorite candy, they thread up their film in the projector and see their title roll on the big silver screen.

your screenplay. When it includes a timetable for shoots and locations and the full list of the elements needed (such as props and extras), as shown in Figure 4-4, the shooting script can be called a shooting schedule.

The shooting script is also used as the basis for the final editing of the film. Only the essential elements of the story will remain. Unlike the screenplay, the shooting script is discontinuous. Many elements of the story are shot out of sequence. This is done for many reasons, such as the availability of locations, expensive scenery, or a specific performer needed for the production.

As you can see, above, the shooting script is the production assembly line for the film. Shots are taken based on the location and the camera position and setup. This is the most practical way to work, as each setup involves camera(s), lights, microphones, props, and the characters prepared in a specific set of costume and makeup. Scenery, such as the stairs in Figure 4-5, are all brought into the planning of where the action goes and where a camera might be placed.

NOTE *In rare situations, such as the live version of Fail Safe shown on TV in recent years, a drama may be shot in sequence, like a play. But even TV dramas are generally shot out of sequence, just like a regular movie.*

You probably won't need to prepare a shooting script as complete as the one we're illustrating here, but you should think ahead as much as you can. Avoid wasted time and effort by checking your shooting script to make sure that you haven't missed anything that's crucial to your production.

Each shot is numbered. The Shot List will go on to the editing room for identification and matching as the production is assembled into its final form. We will be covering camera shots and shooting in Chapter 6.

Scouting Your Locations

Perhaps one of commercial cinema's qualities that is most deceptive to the independent filmmaker is the seeming ease and freedom of locations. A chase sequence will go through a department store, a telephone switch room, or a power plant, as if they were wide open to anyone.

Matching real locations with the ones specified in the screenplay is a far more complex and difficult process than you may realize. The first part of the process is the scouting—finding suitable locations and bringing back the information so that the director and producers can choose which ones to use.

SELF DISTRIBUTION
Shooting Schedule
June 23-24, 2000

Time	Activity	Scene.set up.shot	Description
10:30PM	Crafty Call, Producer/Director Call		
11:00PM	Crew Call, Actor Call		
11:15 - 12:00	Light for EXT Theatre		
12:00 - 12:50	**Shoot EXT Theatre, EXT Ticket Booth, INT Ticket Booth**		
		3.1.1	WS of line in front of theatre (if possible)
		3.1.2	MS of Marquee
		3.2.1	MS Scooter/Rachel in line
		3.2.2	MCU Rachel's bulging coat
		4.3.1	CU Tickets and Candy on counter
		4.3.2	MS OTS Teller gives a nod
		4.4.1	MS OTS Scooter and Rachel nod
12:50 - 1:10	Light for INT Lobby		
1:10 - 1:30	**Shoot INT Lobby**		
	TBD	5.5.1	CU Employees Only Sign
	TBD	5.5.2	FS Scooter and Rachel go through Employees Only Door
		5.6.1	FS Scooter and Rachel sneak up hallway
1:30 - 2:30	Light for INT Projection Room		
2:30 - 3:30	**Shoot INT Projection Room**		
		6.7.1	MS Louis downs candy, hits box, trashes box, turns to table
		8.7.2	MS 2SH Rachel steps toward Scooter, both look out at accomplishment
		6.8.1	ECU slo mo Louis taps box, swallows last raisinette
		8.9.1	MS door creaks open, raisinettes shake
		8.9.2	CU Raisinettes pull out out of doorframe
		8.9.3	MS Louis at table, notices noise, walks to door, XTs, Scooter and Rachel burst in, Scooter XT CR, Rachel stops at table
	if time	8.10.1	Inserts - see box
3:30 - 4:10	DINNER		
4:10 - 6:00	**Shoot INT Projection Room**		
		8.11.1	MS Louis at table, notices noise, walks to door, XTs frame
		8.11.2	CU Louis notices noise
		8.11.3	MS single to 2SH Rachel pulls out reel, opens it, hands it to Scooter
		8.12.1	FS Rachel puts Titanic reel on floor, kicks it, pulls out her reel, opens it, hands it to Scooter
6:00 - 6:20	Light for EXT Projection Room		
6:20 - 6:45	**Shoot EXT Projection Room**		
		8.12.2	CU Louis opens door a crack, peers out, walks toward camera
		8.12.3	ECU Hand on doorknob
6:45 - 7:15	Light for INT Office		
7:15 - 8:00	**Shoot INT Office**		
		2.13.1	MS 2SH Scooter and Rachel in office, hear whole diatribe
		2.14.1	Rachel's reactions
		2.15.1	Scooter's reactions
8:00 - 8:45	Light for INT Theatre		
8:45 - 9:30	**Shoot INT Theatre**		
	if time	9.16.1	FS 2SH Rachel and Scooter's faces in window, beam of light
		9.17.1	WS 2SH Rachel and Scooter's faces in window, beam of light

VO
Marvin
Receptionist

INSERTS
ECU box in trash
ECU Titanic Reel
ECU Rachel's Hand on Reel
ECU reel on floor scoots to cam
ECU Scooter - reel into camera
ECU hand on switch
ECU hand threads film
ECU Film through projector

TO BE SHOT: CITY SCAPE / BUILDINGS / DOOR SLAM

FIGURE 4-4 This is the shooting schedule for *Self Distribution*. © Tom Pankratz, Gambit Films.

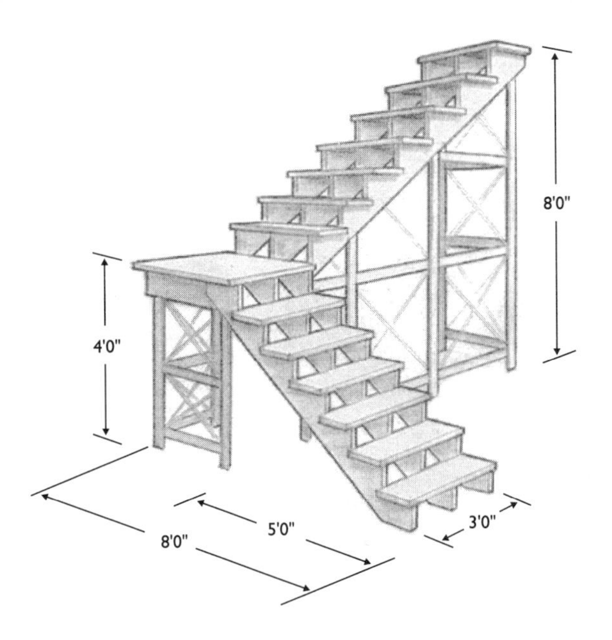

FIGURE 4-5 This cellar stairs unit is an example of the hundreds of pieces of scenery that are available for rental. © IDF Studio Scenery.

Location scouts use various media to investigate suitable places:

- **Maps** The more detailed the better

TIP *A valuable online source of maps and driving directions is Microsoft's Expedia Web site. Just point your browser to: http://www.expedia.com/pub/agent.dll?qscr=over&rfrr=-357. Another may be a local Chamber of Commerce at the location itself, or a travel bureau if you're in a foreign country.*

- **Photo prints** Often stapled together to make a panorama

TIP *An easy way to make a panorama is stitching software, which can do all the work on scanned photos from a simple interface. One likely candidate is Corel PHOTO-PAINT 10, part of the Corel Graphics Suite 10 for Macintosh, which is compatible with both Mac OS 9 and X.*

- **Feature and detail photos** Taken of your prospective location
- **A video of the location** Taken showing suitable places for shots
- **Related information** To determine changes in the landscape due to weather, tides, and to consult train schedules to make sure that a rolling freight doesn't wreck an expensive shoot.

After you've found a suitable location, one of the personnel connected with the project must secure the location and confirm the details needed to gain access. This is usually the job of the assistant producer or assistant director.

Here is a list of the details you need to confirm before moving your equipment and personnel to the location:

- **Permissions** While there's no problem making casual shots from most locations, if you plan on moving in actors, directors, and equipment, you need to work with the local authorities to secure permission to use a specific location.

CAUTION *Don't take this process lightly. Shooting a film in a public space without permission may run afoul of local laws.*

NOTE *If you're scouting an exterior location, you can determine things like ground conditions, power and water sources, natural light patterns, and seasonal effects for more efficient planning of shots.*

- **Determine and mark shooting angles** Block off bad camera areas.
- **Hire and schedule local security** These may include park rangers and store guards or off duty police.

NOTE *Local residents may also be ideal candidates to hire as extras for your project. It makes them feel part of the production and helps ensure a smoother reception when your crew rolls in.*

As you can see, scouting and securing a location is a complicated undertaking, and one that's not always successful. For casual, amateur shots, no problem, but for a full production it may be difficult and costly. If family and friends can provide suitable locations for you, that's often the best way to go. In the end, your camcorder may be the best scouting aid of all, because it'll give you an idea of how the locations will play out in your production.

Here are some key things to do if you find some suitable locales for your production:

1. Shoot a video report showing different camera angles and suitable spots for specific scenes. You'll also want to shoot at different times of the day, pointing the camera in different places, so you can see how natural lighting and the position of the sun or, perhaps, cloudy surroundings might impact your shoot.
2. Once you've taken your footage, import it into iMovie (as we explain in Part IV of this book), so you can edit key angle sequences and panoramas and get a sense of how your location will look in the finished movie.
3. Choose frames for stills to output to a color printer for planning prints.

Audition and Cast Your Actors

The actors, and anyone else who is filmed and appears in a shot, are considered part of the "front of the camera" activity, or the "talent." All of the actors are probably friends and acquaintances, but if you need to recruit additional performers, try local theater groups and acting classes. Even if there's no money involved, many up-and-coming performers might welcome the experience and the chance to show their talents. It looks good on resumes too.

Don't Play with Guns

We are all used to seeing guns in film and in TV shows. Lazy screenwriters who can't articulate a good conflict motivation in expressive words put a pistol in the character's hand instead. This is a convention that could spell trouble for any independent producer who is careless with props.

This is particularly true in today's sensitive climate, in light of the tragic events of September 11, 2001.

Unless you are rehearsing and producing in a completely private and secured space, do not display a gun, or any other weapon. Do not enact an assault or simulate a suicide.

Someone a block away who can't know that "It's only a toy gun!" will dial 911, and you may frame some unannounced atmosphere in the form of a SWAT team. You've seen this happen in comedy films, of course (such as one of the films in the popular *Lethal Weapon* series), but it can happen in real life, too. Just be careful.

The language of light does not treat all faces equally. Only a screen test and tryout will reveal if the candidate has the right "look," the right voice, and the right appeal for your production.

Setting Up a Screen Test First do a close-up screen test. Here's how it can be done economically:

1. Put your camcorder on a tripod for comfort and also to get a consistent shot of actor and scene.
2. Rotate the LCD screen of your camcorder, so it faces the actor like a mirror. He/she can take care of keeping in the frame, and will be provided with feedback for details and nuance.
3. Light the face with the very same sources—daylight and/or artificial—that will be used in the production.
4. Use the same kind of microphone that will be rigged in the production.

NOTE *This is particularly important, since different microphones have different sonic characters that might impact how the performer will sound in the finished production. What sounds good on one mike might not on another. Use the actual script for the spoken lines by the proposed character.*

5. Identify the test with a slate or card, and a voice cue.

Consider an Action Test The tryout, or action test demands fewer conditions than the screen test, but is more challenging for both the candidate and the director.

The tryout reveals how the candidate acts and moves in space within the screen frame. It's remarkable how different a person's movements may seem in daily life and then on the screen—perfectly normal in front of you, but then, perhaps, either fluidly expressive, or all abrupt and jerky in the rushes on the screen.

Here's how to conduct a tryout test:

1. Frame as a medium shot or a medium-long shot. This will enable you to see all or most of the performer's body plus some of the background scene.
2. Choose an action and lines within a scene from the actual script
3. Put least one other character on stage, even if it's a stand-in. See how the candidate's actions relates to another human body.

4. Choose a scene that includes many different actions, such as crossing the stage slowly and striding; sitting down and standing up; turning and moving shoulders; or even some sort of body contact, such as shaking hands with or even embracing another character.
5. If a principal or lead role is already chosen, and the tryout is for a supporting role, then you must test with the principal.
6. If you are including "atmosphere" in your production, such as groups or crowds of extras, you should test them also. If you don't, you may find out too late how one or two of your extras are noticeably out of character.
7. Identify the test with a slate or card, and a voice cue.

Develop a Production Schedule

The sample page from a Movie Magic's Scheduler software, shown in Figure 4-6, displays many more elements than your production will typically have to deal with. But it lists a range of concerns that every producer must consider. You have to think of everything and then provide for it.

Movie Magic Scheduler and Movie Magic Budgeter are examples of film production software that can be used not only by the studios, but even many small independent producers. These programs are easily configured to include the categories you need for your production (quickly set via a pop-up menu).

TIP *If you don't want to invest in extra software, you can use the spreadsheet component of AppleWorks or even Microsoft Excel to set up the information you need to have at hand for scheduling your production.*

As you see, there are many elements—a complicated To Do List—which you have to manage to make even a small movie. From actors to props to extras, scenes, and production personnel, it can be a complicated undertaking, especially if only a handful of people are involved. The more you organize your needs in advance, the easier it will be to film your movie as quickly as possible, with as few glitches as possible.

TIP *Don't assume that having all the elements in place will make this production a cakewalk. Many things can go wrong and give the budding producer and director migraines—temperamental performers, illness, broken props, scheduling mishaps, and bad weather. The watchword is to prepare yourself as much as possible for things that can go wrong.*

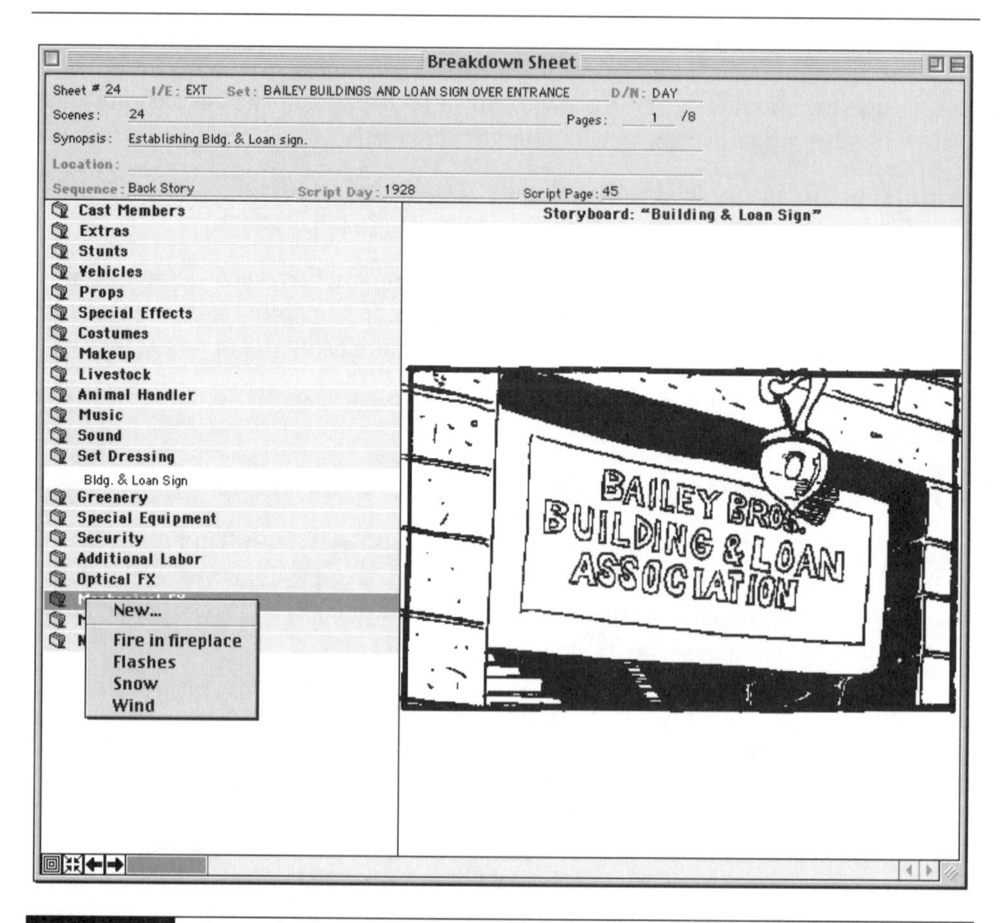

FIGURE 4-6 A sample sheet from a production using Movie Magic Scheduling © CreativePlanet Inc.

Secure Releases

The role of the media today is much more dynamically loaded than it was even ten years ago. The inexpensive hand-held camcorder, with its color and synchronous sound, now routinely goes places that only a shoulder-mounted 16mm or network video news camera went before.

Watch television any day and you will see images that truly originated on a camcorder, sometimes one not much more expensive than the one you own.

With this simplicity, however, comes greater responsibility. The right of individual identity is highly valued. On top of that, ours is a very litigious society, where lawsuits are filed at the drop of a hat, and sometimes for what seems to be the most trivial reasons.

Many videomakers have had unsigned appearances come back to haunt them. Someone, like the friendly carriage driver who appeared in that five-second reaction shot without giving you signed permission, is persuaded that he can sue you—and your distributor—for his likeness being used without his permission. And some do win.

The best defense is a signed release form, in which you get permission to use the individual in your production. We've included a public domain general release form in Figure 4-7. As a general release, it does not include any further special levels of participation, such as a speaking role versus a non-speaking role, stunt work, or any other talent premiums, such as dancing or musicianship. Feel free to copy it for your use.

GENERAL MEDIA RELEASE FORM

I hereby give____________________the absolute right and permission to copyright and/or publish non-commercial motion picture film, live television, videotape, or audio recording of me for any legal, ethical manner that the producer(s)__________________see fit. I also grant the right to include my possessions and/or background objects that may appear in the final product.

I hereby state that I am 18 years or older.

____

I understand and fully agree to the terms and conditions of this release.

DATE:______________________

NAME:______________________(signature)

ADDRESS:____

PARENT OR GUARDIAN:______________________(signature)

ADDRESS:____

WITNESS:______________________(signature)

ADDRESS:____

NOTE: Parent or Guardian's signature required ONLY if person is under 18 years of age

FIGURE 4-7 General Media Release Form

Take This to Heart

If your footage may ever appear in any public or commercial venue, you, as a producer/director, are best advised to get a release for everyone who appears in front of the camera, however briefly, including your relatives and even your close friends. You should receive from each a completed and signed copy of the form, and don't use their likeness in your completed production without that form.

Even in an informal, improvisational, and collegial production group, this simple transaction can provide a bond of collaborative understanding. It helps to make it all more "real." It also helps to keep you out of a potential legal wrangle should someone later on decide he really didn't want to be in your production after all.

The Closing Scene

In this chapter, we've shown you how to use the very same techniques the professionals use for preproduction and for making your shoot go as smoothly as possible.

In our next chapter, you'll learn the techniques the professionals use to get the best possible footage from your camcorder.

Chapter 5 Supporting and Moving Your Camera

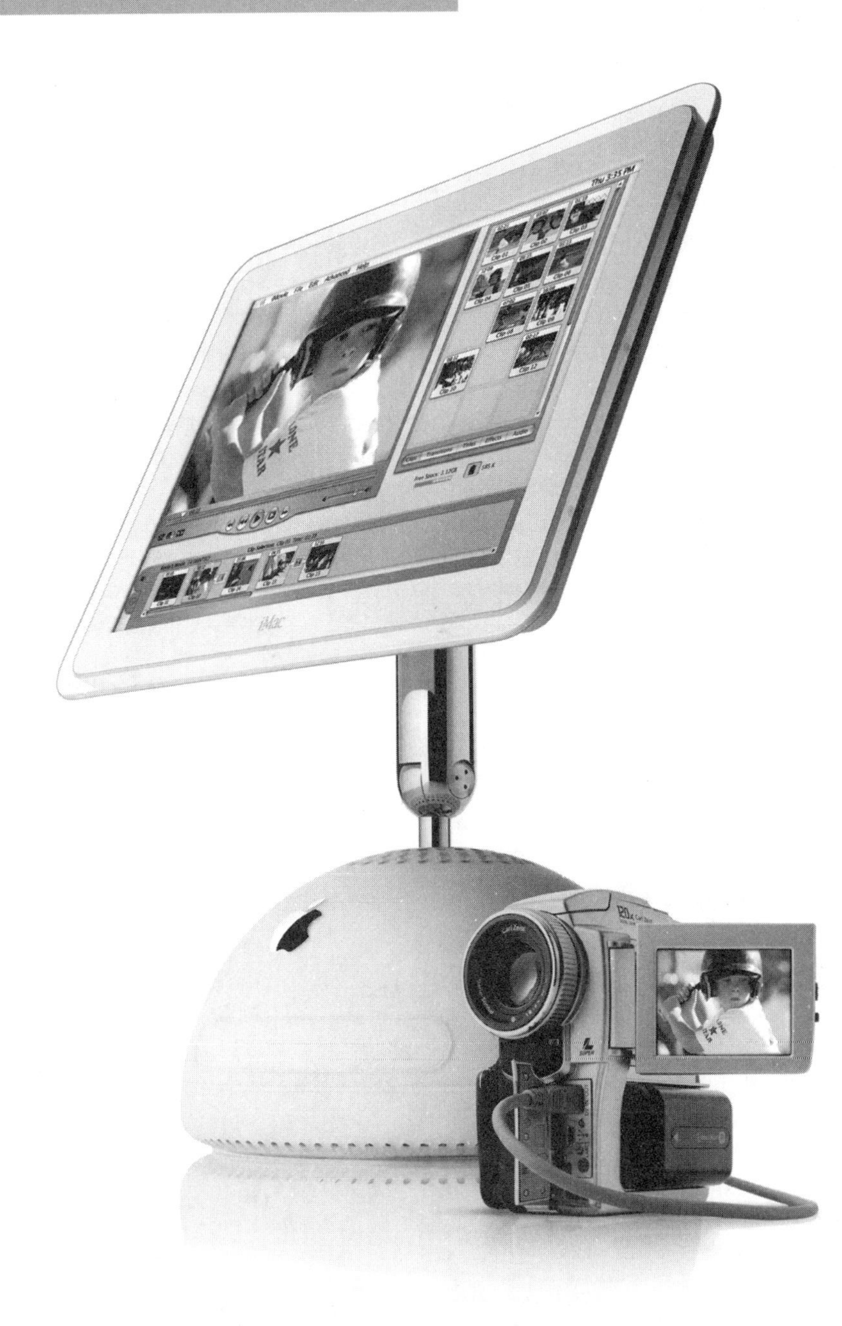

How to...

- Hold your camcorder
- Use a tripod
- Use a monopod
- Make dolly and tracking shots
- Improvise camera supports

On the screen, the virtual "camera eye" floats, flies and hovers as if it were a spirit-driven entity unaccountable to the laws of gravity. Your visual imagination is just as good. Your camcorder, however, will need a little help.

The first support systems for the camcorder are your hands and your body, and we will coach you in making the most of handheld videography. The tripod is the Rock of Gibraltar of professional-looking movies of every kind, and you will see how and why in this chapter. You'll also discover how you can make good effects with smaller accessories such as a monopod.

Since improvisation is always the independent videomaker's most valuable accessory, we'll pass on some of the tips we've seen. The same goes for moving camera support, where anything that rolls may go. Some of these accessories may be what you are planning on buying anyway, but it's nice to know how far you can stretch the boundaries.

NOTE *We are not suggesting you should go out and spend a bundle on every single tool you need. It's sometimes cost effective to rent items that you require only occasionally.*

The Handheld Camcorder

The consumer camcorder was designed for the human hand to hold. The styles may differ, from Sony's "box-with-buttons" solution to Canon's Z Series "atomic ray gun" ergonomics. It is with the professional-level systems such as the ten-pound Canon XL-1S that these cameras become too large and heavy to hold with one hand.

Just as a new flat-panel iMac with G4 processor has far more computing power and versatility than the tennis-court-size supercomputers of the 1950s, your camcorder packs more audiovisual automation inside its case than a community television station of the same era. Auto focus, auto-exposure, image stabilization, and internal microphones make handheld strategies possible and easy because they can take care of all these functions automatically while you are moving.

This power and freedom is both a blessing and a handicap. Moving your lens from one angle to another is as easy as pointing your finger. But later, when you see that shot displayed on the screen, it may be so visually unsettling as to be unusable. Unsteady, wobbly, and wandering camera movement is what gave "home movies" its bad name.

Free Handheld Movement

You can go quite far with handheld camerawork. You just need to work with it and hone your skills as a videographer. Approach shooting with your camcorder as you would a sport, and practice your skills as you would practice to perfect your golf swing or tennis stroke. Like a dancer, you will be partnering with your camera. Here are some stages and directions that can help you gain great footage:

TIP *The image stabilizer helps to make handheld shooting possible. But all image stabilizers are not equally as effective in all camcorders. You will need to test and practice to see how far or fast you can go with your camcorder before it begins to lose its stability assistance.*

- **Know your controls** It will be hard to feel completely at ease with your camcorder as long as its controls remain a puzzle. Making video sketches will help to bring you up to speed.
- **Review every play** Because videotape can be recorded and played back over and over again, you don't even have to do "dry runs." Try a shot, rewind, and look at the results right there in your LCD viewer.
- **Get your grip** Hold your camcorder with both hands, until you find the grip that suits you best with the form factor of that model. Some camcorders have a hand strap—usually for the right hand—that can give you snug support like a baseball glove.

NOTE *If you're a lefty like one of your humble authors, you may need to work a bit harder to make a camcorder that's designed for a right-handed universe feel comfortable, but the effort will pay off in superior shots.*

- **Practice with both viewers** Try different positions and movements viewing through the eyepiece, and then from the LCD viewer. You will have more accurate focus and framing through the eyepiece, but more freedom to move around using the LCD viewer. In both positions, hold your arms against your body for more support and stability.

NOTE *In very bright sunlight the image in the LCD viewer may be too washed out, and the eyepiece may be easier to see through. The watchword is "experiment"—just do what works best for you. In the end, the quality of the finished picture is all that counts.*

- **Waist level viewing** The LCD viewer enables you to hold the camcorder comfortably at waist level. You will appear less conspicuous when doing candid camera work.
- **The human tripod** To make a "human tripod," kneel down on one leg and support the camcorder with your elbow on your high knee. This will support a good and stable low shot.
- **The café table view** An easy stability position is available when you are sitting at a table or standing at a railing. Keep your hands stable by resting your elbows on the table or railing.
- **Smooth body follow shots** For doing a standing pan, or horizontal rotational shot, such as following a running horse or a cyclist, first stand facing the end point of the shot, where the subject is going. Keeping your feet placed firmly, twist your body, to the left or the right, to the start point of the action. As the subject moves, relax your body and it will do a natural return to match the end point.
- **Improvisational support** Always and everywhere, look for objects and surfaces, like furniture and walls, that you can lean against for "pick me up" added stability.

TIP *Some camcorders have a recording button with a* START/STOP *feature, which enables them to keep running after just one touch, unattended. This can be convenient, but it's easy to jar the camera when you go back to push the button again to stop the recording at the end of the shot. Practice smooth finger-squeezes to keep the camera steady.*

Using a Tripod for Stability

Only when the camera is fixed or engaged in a naturalistic movement can it disappear from the screen. Even in a good handheld straight shot, if the edges of the frame are moving, the shot will be distracting to the audience. For an

Some Hard Won Advice on Hand-held Videos

Shooting hand-held video is a continual struggle of fighting physics and trying to repeal the law of gravity. While taking advantage of the fluid freedom of the lens' continual three-dimensional movement in space, you are still trying to come back with images that are reasonably sharp and readable.

You can better your chances of battling the blur by using as wide-angle a focal length as you can. Set lens focus at 5-7 feet. Another way is to address the shutter speed. Set the shutter speed to 1 over the focal length, or the closest available setting on your camera. For instance, if you are using a 500 mm lens, set at 1/500 sec.; a 200 mm lens, set at 1/250 sec.; and a 50 mm lens, set at 1/60 sec.

Another factor is ambient light level. The brighter the light the better. The more cloudy and overcast it is, or if you are working in shadow, then you are not going to be able to stop down the lens to help sharpness and definition. Here is where a good built-in image stabilizer can help, or the conditions may push you towards moving from hand-held to a tripod.

establishing shot or a landscape view, a fixed camera permits the clarity of direct reality.

The tripod is the workhorse of camera support, and the principles of their design have remained unchanged since the hardy wooden-legged model with the heavy Mitchell 35mm camera. The three legs are collapsible. This classic model stands as low as waist-height, and high as shoulder-height.

A good tripod should be light enough to be carried, with a mounted camera, by one person. When erected, it should be sturdy enough to hold the camera steady without shaking. Today there are quality tripods made of carbon fiber that are ultra-light yet extremely strong.

Every camcorder has a threaded socket at the bottom of the grip or the case, called a tripod socket, or receptacle. This is an international standard that will receive the screw bolt of most support accessories.

TIP

You don't have to spend an arm and a leg on a tripod either. Even consumer electronics shops have them (sometimes even the electronics section at a K-Mart or Wal-Mart or large supermarket). In the end, you want to make sure that what you buy is rock stable when set up at your location.

Tripods Come in Different Sizes

In this section, we'll describe the various types of tripods available. While it's nice to have several at hand, take a look at the following and see which model meets most of your needs. You can always buy another type later as your needs (and budget) expand:

- **Pocket, or tabletop tripod** Inexpensive, light and versatile, it is the ideal companion for your camcorder. Like the tabletop model in Figure 5-1, most will collapse into a compact package under eight inches and erect to over two feet. Serving as a grip extension or a mini-monopod, these are also handy to brace against vertical surfaces or even your own body.
- **Standard** As shown in Figure 5-2, these models collapse to under three feet and will erect to over five feet. Meant for the hobbyist photographer, they may not be as solid and stable as the professional, but they can be a good value. Some compact models can fit in a daypack or overnighter and be ready at a moment's notice.

FIGURE 5-1 Tabletop, or junior tripod, compact and convenient for a low-angle shot.

TIP *If you pick a standard model, see if the dealer will let you try it out to see just how rock stable it is. If it wobbles back and forth at the slightest breeze or bump, choose a different model.*

- **Professional** There is a wide range of heights and strengths here, but they are very stable and strong, and are able to support a camera load of at least ten pounds and up to 35 pounds. They are fully adjustable in every way and may accept different camera heads. Quality tripods are taller than the less expensive models. They achieve the proper height without the extension of the center arm, or post, because a tripod is most stable at the point where the tops of its legs meet.

FIGURE 5-2 A good standard tripod with a video head will support most of your dramatic needs.

What Makes a Motion Picture Tripod Different from a Still Photography Tripod?

A good question, as the politicians say. The moviemaker must be able to pan the camera, which is to rotate it horizontally. The tripod head, on which the camera is mounted, must therefore be able to swivel and must have a control arm. Unlike the tripod used with a still camera, which also has a head that can swivel, but does not necessarily support panning, the movie tripod must have the stability to support shake-free filming while the camera is panned.

These are the main types of movie tripod heads:

- **Friction head** Most tripod heads, and all the inexpensive ones, are friction heads. They have two disks that rotate against each other with variable pressure for a fast or slow pan.
- **Fluid head** These are very expensive professional heads with sealed fluid-dampening assemblies. Most commercial 35mm filmmakers and television studios use them.
- **Geared head** An older style head, but very stable. Used in applications like scientific media making as well as professional film.
- **Ball head** While it does not always support panning, a ball-and-socket joint is very direct and efficient for quick positioning.

Tripod Features

In addition to the head of the tripod, there are other features you may want to consider in looking for the one that meets your needs. These include:

- **Two-way pan head** Two control handles. One adjusts the east-west, and the other the north-south, level axes of the pan head.
- **Bubble level** This works like a carpenter's level, so you can get the pan head level as you adjust the tripod legs.
- **Center post** Raised and lowered by a geared crank, the center post supports the tripod head and enables you to make minute height adjustments for the camera.
- **Reversible center post** Enables you to turn the post and head upside down, providing very stable low-angle shots, and can take floor shots for inserts. It makes it easy to set up the tripod up as a copy stand for flat copy and object photography.

Tripods Must Mind Their Feet

Minding their feet isn't something confined to how children conduct themselves. Unlike the still photo tripod, the movie tripod must brace against the rotational movement of panning. The traditional tripod has spiked feet that can engage in rocky soil. Most professional movie tripods are stabilized with a ground spreader where the tripod feet are clamped into its sockets. This insures the maximum amount of rigidity, particularly on rough terrain.

A moderately priced standard tripod has built-in spreader struts. You can improvise an instant spreader with pieces of rope tied between the feet. A piece of scrap carpet can serve as a ground pad and receive the foot spikes. If you are shooting in someone else's home, a carpet ground pad is a good idea anyway.

TIP *A camera clamp is another inexpensive but valuable item for your camcorder kit bag. They come in different configurations, but the kind that is like a big C-clamp with a camera head, or just a camera screw, can provide a way out for many mounting challenges. These clamps can make it easy to mount the camcorder on a baby buggy or a bike for a moving shot, or a high location for photographing wildlife.*

Using a Monopod for Mobility

The inexpensive monopod can be one of the most valuable tools for supporting your camcorder. Essentially, a monopod is one leg of a telescoping tripod, with a camera head at the top. You may find so many uses for it, it may not ever leave your camera.

Here are some of the most important features of the monopod, and some ways you can use them to best advantage:

- **Mobility** The fact that you can pick up your camera and monopod and walk or run from shot to shot gives you tremendous flexibility in covering an event or a sport.
- **Extended grip** Fully collapsed, the tubular section acts as a big pistol grip for your camcorder.
- **Added support** When you use the monopod for vertical support when you make most of the static shots you would ordinarily do hand held, you get near-tripod quality images. For longer takes, you should use your tripod.
- **Strap support** Add the bracing of the camera's shoulder strap over your neck or over your shoulder, lean the camera and monopod somewhat ahead to give tension to the strap, and gain even more stability for longer takes.

- **Belt support** While using the shoulder strap, collapse the monopod to a length that will enable you to secure the foot in your belt or in the change pocket of your jeans. You will have a very strong moving support configuration.
- **Ground shots** Hold the fully-extended monopod down to ground level with the camcorder at a level angle. You can do static or moving low-level shots, such as a "dog's-eye" view sequence.
- **High angle shots** With your monopod fully extended, and using your remote control for recording, you can take privileged and even dramatic shots high over a crowd in a political demonstration or sporting event.

Moving the Camcorder

Some of the most natural-looking shots and sequences that we take for granted in film and television can be, behind the scenes, complicated to produce. Consider the common scene in which the camera follows, from the side, two characters talking as they walk along a street. Or the shot in which the camera leads and then follows a character as she walks through a museum.

To get those shots and make them look good, the camera must travel along with the characters, but so smoothly that the viewer can concentrate on the dialog and the action without distraction.

You could shoot the first scene with a pan from a fixed tripod. But you would lose the constant frame, and would have to zoom to frame and focus as they come near, and go further away. With your camcorder braced with a strap and a monopod, you could probably get by with a follow shot in the museum scene. But in leading her, you would have to walk backwards.

Tracking Systems

Setting up for a tracking shot is a labor-intensive task, but commercial filmmakers learned a long time ago that is the only way to ensure a smooth, seamless, and unobtrusive moving shot. Tracking is used instead of a dolly or handheld when the frame must remain precise throughout the shot. When the camera is further away from the action, a wheeled dolly can often be used. Track dollies may be a wheeled camera tripod mount, or larger systems with crew riding on the dollies.

Track systems have become much more modular and lightweight. You can rent systems that are compatible with a camcorder and are easy to set up. The Microdolly Track System weighs only 10 pounds and fits into a soft case bag 34 inches long. It can be set up with 13 feet of track on almost any surface in less than two minutes. Some high-production weddings have been shot with a track as the only way to truly capture that walk down the aisle.

The Handyman's Camcorder

Your camcorder mounted on the end of a monopod can serve as a visual reporter for inspecting hard-to-reach areas you need to search for roof leaks or construction defects, or even that missing ring that your child tossed into the air last night. Perhaps you have a crawl space, an attic, or a gap behind a big appliance that you can't get to, but you need to see what is—or isn't—there.

Insert the camera into the space and use the remote control to record. Withdraw the unit, and then review the footage to see if the cat is really there or how far the water has risen or where that lost engagement ring landed. In some situations where the LCD viewer is not too far away to see, your camcorder can become a periscope for those high shelves.

Dollying

When the camera moves forward along a path, it gives the screen the most heightened realism of unfolding space, like what we experience when we walk. A dolly shot can provide this kind of smooth, unbroken course. This is where the camera—and often lights—are mounted on a wheeled cart, called a dolly, which is either self-propelled with an electric motor or, more likely, is pushed by grips, or stagehands. In the industry, dollies come in a large variety of configurations. They can range from a minimal, three-wheel walkalong, to *Star Wars*-like vehicles that have lights and camera mounted and elevated on a powered crane and can carry the cameraman, assistant cameraman or focus puller, and grip-driver.

As an independent videomaker you can always rent a lightweight portable wheeled dolly system for a day or two. There are compact professional models that can fold up and will fit in the trunk of your car. But for the improvising, low-budget videomaker, there are other cheaper, if somewhat rougher, alternatives:

- **Wheelchair** With the camera mounted on a tripod that is tied down to the frame of the chair, the camera operator sits in the wheelchair that is pushed by another crew member. And people will open doors for you. Tracking, leading, and following shots can be achieved with fair stability. The wheelchair folds up to carry in the trunk of your car.
- **Baby buggy** Multiple-wheel buggies are best. The camera is clamped to the push bar of the buggy or is mounted on a tripod that is tied down to the buggy frame. The camera operator pushes the buggy, guiding the shot through the LCD viewer. The buggy is not as smooth or steady as a wheelchair, but some people will smile at your camera. Most baby buggies fold up for travel.

- **Electric golf cart** The full-size electric-powered golf cart is close to being an all-terrain dolly. It can travel over hard surfaces, ground cover, and grass lawns. With its pneumatic tires and considerable weight, it provides good stability. The golf cart can carry the camera operator, the grip-driver, and often a third crew member, as well as lights and other equipment.

The Crane's-Eye View

That birds-eye view that you see in so many films and TV shows where the camera looks down on, and then follows the action, is usually shot with a crane. A full, or true aerial shot, is reserved for those taken from a camera mounted in an airplane or helicopter. It is hard to find an action picture today that doesn't have the obligatory helicopter sequence swooping six feet over the landscape and between large buildings.

Crane shots have been a pivotal part of moviemaking since the turn of the century. Today's motion picture support technology has developed a large variety of camera cranes. They range from the camcorder clamped to a reinforced microphone boom to the towering behemoth that is towed by a tractor trailer and can reach heights of over three stories.

Motion picture camera cranes must meld the predictable precision of aerospace devices with the industrial strength of construction machinery. The telephone lineman's aerial bucket and the camera crane share in common much of the same hydraulic and electromechanical systems. The difference is that the camera on the crane must be raised, extended, panned and tilted without so much as a bump or a shudder.

Chapman/Leonard, Pegasus, Titan, Akela, Triangle, and Jimmy Jibs—they can look like a 70-foot long slender girder, a Ground Zero grabber, or they can sport the struts and guy wires of a huge grounded TV antenna. They are really modular systems more than standard models, and each production company that rents them makes up it's own unique size and range combination of pedestal, dolly, stage, or location crane that will suit its scenes. The director of photography often must communicate with the crane camera through radio and a remote video tap. Here are some of the equipment you would see on the crane lot:

- **Jib arms and booms** A horizontal camera support mounted on an adjustable vertical column or extendable arm.

- **Stage cranes** Few cranes are ever really fixed—they are supported on wheeled pedestals. But these cranes move quickly from one static location to another, and are used like giant tripods.
- **Mobile cranes** They may be mounted on a camera truck or a tracked dolly, and they are meant to be active in full arm articulation while their support is moving, even if sometimes in a chase scene. This is the rig you would use for one of those extended gymnastic tracking shots.
- **Ridable cranes** These may support one cameraman at the end of the arm, a two person riding platform, or a crew on a mobile crane. For a 35mm camera and a camera operator, the arm must have an end support of at least 550 pounds.
- **Remote cranes** Like the Louma crane, Skycam system, and OConnor's Digi-Head, a digitally controlled robotic camera support head, these cranes support the camera at the arm end, and the camera operator controls it all remotely. This kind of system has gained much ground in the digital age. They tend to be used for lightweight but very extendable studio cranes where supporting and stabilizing an operator at a great height is too demanding.

Steadicam

There are many scenes that you will see in commercial films, such as some key shots in *The Shining* and *The Fugitive,* which were made, not by a dolly or tracking system, but by a Steadicam. This camera stabilization system combines the image steadiness of a dolly with the freedom of movement of a hand-held shot. The cinematic skills of the Steadicam operator combine with the stamina of a weight lifter and the moves of a martial arts expert.

As you see in Figure 5-3, the Steadicam distributes the mass of the camera and places the center of gravity (CG) of the camera system within reach of the operator. By manipulating the camera at its CG, the operator is free to perform ultra-smooth camera moves—360-degree pans, follow shots, etc.—while standing, walking, jumping, or running. Since there are no tracks or dolly, the camera can "see" the floor and the ground.

FIGURE 5-3 Steadicam Operator/Instructor Kevin Braband moves the lens through three-dimensional space.

Low Budget but Steady Supports

There are two low-budget support alternatives to consider. For under $500, the Steadicam JR can handle video cameras with weights up to four pounds. The biggest operational difference between the JR and the full Steadicam is that the JR does not have a mechanical articulated arm to support the weight of the rig. Instead, you must use your own arm. The JR, like all Steadicams, requires practice—and stamina—to produce high-quality shots.

For under $400, The Glidecam 2000 Pro is only 14 inches tall but will support any video camera weighing up to 6 pounds. Its offset handle grip is attached to a free-floating gimbal, which enables your hand to move up and down, and side to side, thereby isolating your hands from unwanted motions from the camera.

You and Your Camcorder as a Steadicam

You and your camcorder, with its audiovisual automation, can make a virtual Steadicam. As you gain more skill and confidence with your camcorder, you will learn to move, like a dancer, around your own personal center of gravity. You will be able to achieve continuous compound movements with acceptable stability.

Sometimes this is the only way you could ever complete a scene in an environment where tracks, dollies and crew would be too obtrusive. Examples could be:

- **Corporate communications** You follow a worker through the steps of his assembly task across the factory floor.
- **Education** Recording a nursery school with the kids engaged in interactive gameplaying, or filming a music class with students rehearsing their instruments.
- **Dramatic** Following and tracking a character as he or she walks from the balcony, down a hall, and up a narrow flight of stairs.

Consider the Differences

There is every reason to make your camcorder footage look as professional as possible, using the tools and techniques of the film and video industries. But there are some differences that are in your favor.

For theatrical motion pictures, the finished product is a projected image the size of a basketball court. The slightest out-of-frame camera jiggle will make the audience feel like the room is shaking. Your iMovie will be presented on a television screen and your computer monitor. That lesser scale of display is much more forgiving, and will absorb a lot of your bumps and wobbles.

Video, and especially camcorder video with its smaller lenses, does not have the clarity and depth of film. There is less visual information. Which is all to say that you shouldn't hesitate in making the best movies you can if you don't have access to support equipment. You can get away with a lot more production slips than your Hollywood counterparts.

The Closing Scene

In this chapter, your skills as a videographer were posed for growth as you learned how to stabilize and move your camera for maximum impact. With time and practice, your photographic skills will improve as will the quality of your work.

With this background, you'll want to move to the next chapter, as you learn how to take the right shot, from close-up to wide-angle, for the right occasion, and how to get the most out of the tools of the trade.

Chapter 6

Capturing the Shot

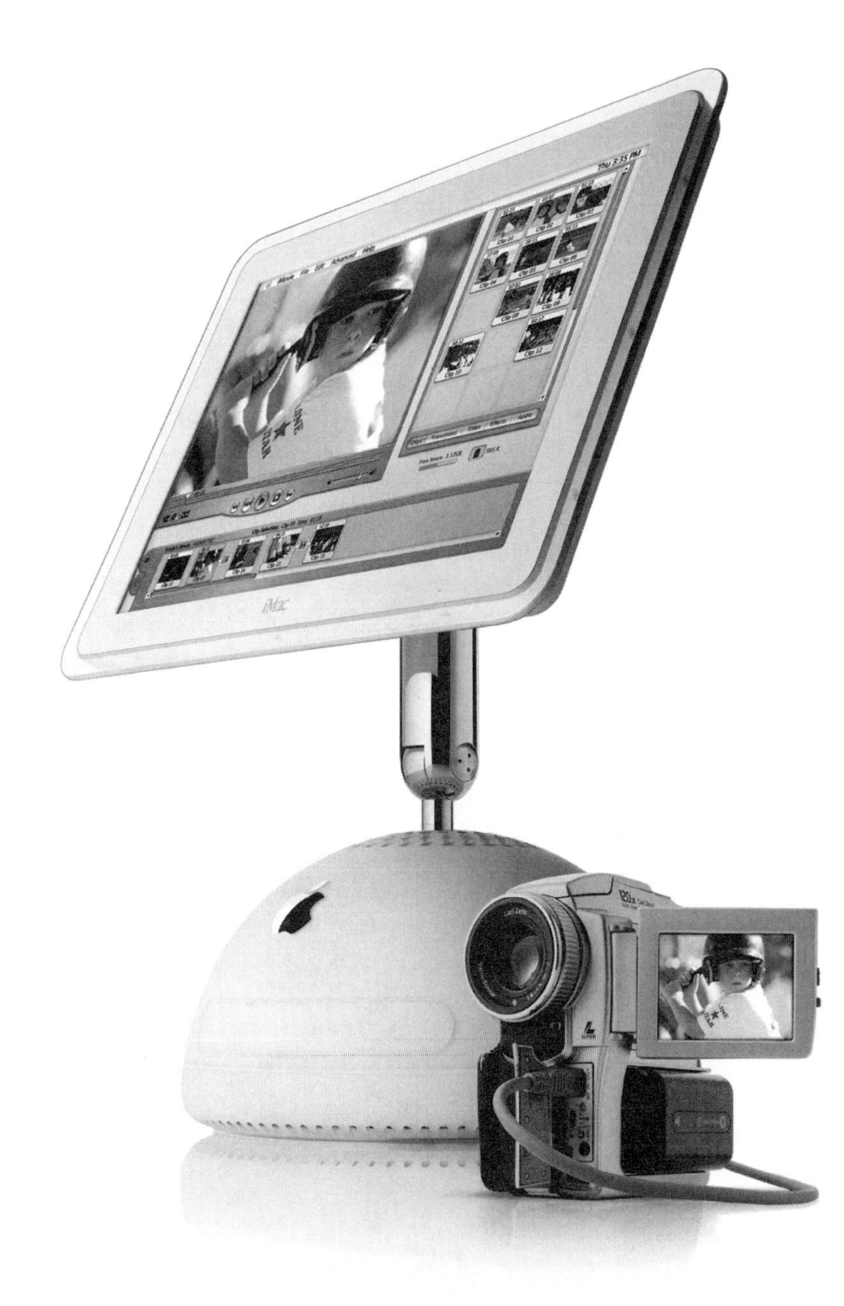

How to...

- Identify the different camera shots
- Frame the shot for the right action
- Use manual focus
- Use panning for descriptive motion
- Make meaningful zooms

When you are shooting scenes with your camcorder, your editing work has already begun—yes, even before you actually import your clips into iMovie 2. You are looking at the world and selecting some images and actions, but not others. You are making important decisions that will impact your final production.

The more movies you make, the more guided your intuition will be and the more precise your planning will become in the shots you choose and how you make them.

In the last chapter you learned how to hold, support, and move your camcorder to get professional-quality shots. Now you will learn to better anticipate what to plan for on location so that you can capture the shots and scenes that you need for your next movie.

For example, the visual "feel" of your shot changes according to the lenses or lens settings you use, each with a different focal length. In this way you have a flexible range for interpreting a scene as you frame each shot. From a fixed position, the camera can pan, tilt and express interpretive angles to provide enriched continuity. In this chapter, we'll see how the zoom lenses on camcorders work with their automated systems for focus and exposure, and how zoom shots differ from static series.

A Look at Lenses

Camera lenses are the eyes of cinema. The variety of lenses that enable us to see up close and far away become the eyes of our minds. Whether you are using single "prime" lenses or choosing the settings on a zoom lens, your choice will affect the look and feel of the shots in your scene.

Before we cover the ins and outs of lenses, it's fitting to become familiar with a few of the terms used by cinematographers and videographers to define the kind of shots they take of their subjects:

- **EWA** extreme wide-angle, shows your subject from a far distance
- **WA** wide-angle shot, or wide

- **MS** medium shot, or normal shot
- **CU** close-up
- **BCU** big close-up
- **ECU** extreme close-up
- **LS** long shot
- **FS** full shot
- **ELS** extreme long shot

NOTE *Hang in there. We'll be showing you actual examples of what each kind of shot looks like, in practice, later on in this chapter.*

Wide-Angle Lens

The glass of the wide-angle lens bulges out at the center and can capture an image that pulls in much more of the peripheral area of the scene than a normal lens can. It achieves this through a form of optical distortion, but one where straight lines may appear curved and shapes can balloon beyond their normal proportions.

Where does a wide-angle lens work best? Well, an ECU (remember, that's extreme close-up) of an actor's face using a very wide lens setting runs the risk of unintended comedy. Wide-angle settings are the best for hand-held work because they are much more forgiving for bumps and unsteady movements.

In addition, in moving shots, a wide-angle causes areas of the scene at the sides to appear to go by more slowly than in scenes shot with a normal lens.

A wide-angle lens is ideal for a WA (wide-angle) shot.

Medium, or Normal, Lens

The medium lens is also called a normal lens because it most closely approaches the field of view and lack of distortion of unaided human vision. Objects don't appear much closer or further away than they do in real life. There are some photographers and filmmakers who try to do the majority of their shots with a normal lens setting to preserve a "more authentic" visual style.

In moving shots, a medium lens causes areas of the scene at the sides to appear to go by at a normal rate.

Use this lens for an MS, or medium shot.

Long, or Telephoto, Lens

The glass of the telephoto lens is narrower and longer than the glass in a normal lens. Like a telescope, it has a series of elements that, together, magnify objects at a distance to make them appear closer. In doing so, this lens also tends to flatten out the perspective of the scene and make everything seem to be sharing the same picture plane.

In moving shots, a long lens causes areas of the scene at the sides to appear to go by more rapidly than in scenes shot with a normal lens.

Use this lens for an LS, or long shot.

Zoom Lens

When a camera operator has to dismount one lens and mount another for the next shot, it takes up extra time and labor. To make this more efficient, motion picture cameras, especially the ones used for news, had three or more different focal length lenses mounted on a rotating turret.

The development of the zoom lens gave a great many more options for film and video camera work. A zoom lens is constructed with a complex series of concave and convex lens elements mounted in a tube that can expand and contract. Fully collapsed, the elements are closest together, and emulate the optics of a wide lens. Fully extended, the glass elements act as a telephoto lens. Sometimes referred to as a "glass trombone," a zoom lens has an almost infinite number of equivalent settings within its focal length range.

Zoom lenses are categorized by their power of magnification, and by their range. When Canon's professional-grade XL1 camcorder is described as equipped with a "16×" zoom lens, that means that the magnification of the full telephoto setting is 16 times more powerful than the least wide setting. That same lens is also defined as having a "5.5-85 mm focal length" range. That means that at its widest setting it is equivalent to a 5.5 mm lens, and at full telephoto it is equivalent to an 85 mm lens.

Looking at Electronic Zoom Lens Systems

There is hardly a consumer camcorder made today that doesn't come with a built-in electronic zoom lens system. Most models now have a system that is a combination of optical and digital zooming. Very few offer manual zooming now.

As an example, the Sony DCR-TRV 230 Digital 8 camcorder features a 25× optical, 700× digital zoom. The lens is described as 2.4-60 mm /f1.6. This means that from a wide setting of 2.4 mm to 25 times that, or 60 mm, it is zooming optically, and from 60 mm on to 700 times the wide setting, it is zooming digitally.

The widest aperture opening of the lens, which lets the maximum amount of light in, is an f-stop of f/1.6.

The digital zoom extends the camcorder's photographic range. At the maximum, the zoom lens on the Sony 230 is equivalent to 1,050 mm. That would be a big chunk of glass in optical. But the drawback is that the digital extended range is a magnification blowup, which makes small pixels larger. The image may reveal too much coarseness.

Camcorder manufacturing is so unevenly standardized that you need to test yours (or read a review in a computer or video magazine) to see what the results are along the zoom's full range. If you have a camcorder, you have a zoom lens. Learn to live well and prosper with it. Using an average camcorder, shooting the same urban location, here's a comparison of the differences between zooming and walking to describe the street scene from beginning to end.

Notice in Figures 6-1 to 6-3 how the magnification of the zoom maintains a good visual axis even as it flattens and magnifies the scene. In comparison, the shots that follow, Figures 6-4 to 6-6, show how moving the camera from point to point and maintaining a normal lens setting reveal areas and details unseen by the zoom.

FIGURE 6-1 Zoom wide.

FIGURE 6-2 Zoom medium shot.

FIGURE 6-3 Zoom telephoto.

FIGURE 6-4 Normal at the beginning of the street.

FIGURE 6-5 Normal midway down the street.

FIGURE 6-6 Normal at the end of the street.

Unlike professional interchangeable zoom lenses, your camcorder probably doesn't have any markings revealing lens settings. Most have a display in the viewfinder that appears when you activate the zoom motor buttons. They may look like a bar gauge with W for wide and T for telephoto [W-------×-------T] and lack an actual numeric setting. If the marker is at the center, you are probably at a medium, or normal setting.

Focus Issues

Focus is the adjustment of the lens elements so that the resolution of the subject is clear and sharp. Most camcorders have an auto-focus function, and the better ones have a manual focus option as well. The auto-focus judges the bounced-back light waves from the farthest reading it gets and focuses the lens on that plane. Auto-focus can be surprisingly good and reliable, but there are a few caveats.

Sometimes when there are several surfaces near each other the auto-focus "hunts" for the right one, and can ping-pong back and forth between them while you are filming. The end result is that the subject of your movie is suddenly in sharp focus and at other times blurry. If you see that happening, go to the manual focus option if it's available.

Here's how:

1. Set the manual focus option on your camcorder if it's available. If your camcorder has the feature, there will be a button or dial, or adjustable focus ring, which accesses this feature. Check your camcorder's documentation to see.
2. Manually zoom to the surface that you want to reference.
3. Adjust the focus so that your subject is as crisp as possible.
4. Zoom back to your original shot setting.
5. Record your shot.

Manual focus is the best way to ensure good focus in any scene. But you must always judge your shot and your scene. For instance, if your actor is near a wall that has a clock or a sign, you must make sure that a familiar readable element, like a clock, is in focus. Your audience will notice if it isn't. Let the face be a bit soft in a tradeoff for clarity.

Choosing Between Hard and Soft Focus

When you can adjust your focus manually, you have more opportunity for interpretive rendering of the scene. The brighter the lighting, the more you can use the manual exposure to stop down the iris of your lens, so the focus can be of higher resolution. The shot can provide the impact of razor-sharp detail and texture. This is hard focus.

There are other times when you may want a softer, more romantic or impressionist sense to the scene. By lowering the light level, and/or opening up the iris with the manual exposure, you can achieve that look. It may be better to employ the soft focus and let the light level remain to support the color. Beyond a certain point, soft focus begins to look grainy and pixilated.

Depth of Field

Most scenes have subjects and elements—near, close, and far—at different distances from the camera. Depth of field, or depth of focus, is the selective articulation for those relative distances. Video may not have the range of depth of field that film does, but depth of field still helps define a scene.

Depth of field techniques:

- Develop the scene so that all the elements are all well rendered and in sharp focus.
- A prime subject is highlighted by sharper focus than the others.

- Subjects can move in or out of a plane of focus for dramatic or instructional effect.
- The plane of focus can be moved to include and exclude subjects, by rack focusing.
- A shallow depth of field can selectively de-emphasize areas and backgrounds to make other areas stand out.

Depth of field is controlled by a combination of:

- **Aperture** The more you are able to close down the iris of the lens with the manual exposure (to make the aperture smaller), the sharper the focus will be.
- **Focal length** The wider you can shoot, the more spatial rendering you get (see Figure 6-7). The longer the lens setting, the closer together the subjects will appear, and the focus will be more consistent.

FIGURE 6-7 An ELS—extreme long shot, or establishing shot. Shows foreground-to-background depth of field.

Scene Composition

With every shot you make for every scene, you are engaging in the art of composition. You are enclosing an area of the natural or the man-made world within the frame of the camera, which, in turn, will be seen as the frame of the computer monitor, a TV set, or a projection on a screen when your movie is finished.

Every shot is making a statement, giving information, and contributing to the telling of a story. And each shot will end up in between two other shots in the editing, where they must all contribute to the flow of continuity. Your choices of what you include in the frame should be made to further all of these demands.

In an establishing shot, as shown back in Figure 6-2, the foreground element of the smokestack provides a natural framing device for the scale of the scene. The inclusion or the exclusion of scene elements can be decided on the basis of what best serves the action. As most shots follow the subject—the center of attention—it is often most appropriate to center the subject in the frame. But not always.

No, It's Not Nosy

Don't forget the nose room. No, that's not a facial enhancement department. It's a simple rule of composition that will ensure that your portraits and closeups will look well balanced. If you are shooting the subject when she is looking at the camera, you would normally take care not to chop off the top of her head. "Nose room" is not a problem when the person or object is facing directly towards or away from the camera. But when she is looking camera right or camera left, you need to leave enough room, or air space, between her face and the edge of the finished frame. If her nose is almost touching the frame, the results will be uncomfortably confining for the viewer. Even if it means that you must crop part of the back of her head, it will be better to let the sun shine through her profile.

The "nose room" concept also applies to objects. If you are shooting a car or radio or anything that has a definable front and back, make sure its "nose" is not pressing against the frame. Leaving space between the object and the frame is especially important when the subject is moving across the your field of view at a right angle. For example, if a person moves frame left to right, and you are doing a follow pan or tracking shot, it looks better to leave space in front of the movement, on the right side of the frame, to provide a visual destination.

The Rule of Thirds

Among the many classical lessons given to painters and designers for good composition, the rule of thirds, is the one that endures for film and video producers. It divides up the rectangular scene—like it does the painter's canvas—into nine sub-rectangles, like a tic-tac-toe game board, as shown in Figure 6-8. Here the lines of attraction converge not at the center, but in the left center subrectangle of the rule of thirds. Yet, the mast of the ship is in screen center, which contributes to the overall structure of the scene without dominating it.

The point of this exercise is not to suggest a rigid rule, but to free up your talent for more interesting compositions. Every shot need not be center-weighted. The human eye is, by nature, curious and exploratory, and takes pleasure in the exercise of discovery. The more viewers can feel they are collaborators and not passive receptors, the more they will enjoy your movie.

FIGURE 6-8 Take a look at this picture and see how it is framed to stimulate and move the eye.

Rack Focus

Focusing while filming is to rack focus. But you have to have established a measure of depth of field for this selective focusing to take place. You can rack focus from one subject to another to follow a key dramatic line. A step-by-step instructional sequence might illustrate a transition by racking focus from one control knob to a meter reading. You can rack from a hard to a soft focus, or vice versa, for a transition.

The best way to learn this technique is to practice, learning the fixed amount of movements of the focus knob so you know just how far to turn to home in on a particular subject. It may take a little trial and error to get it right, but it's a very effective skill to learn.

Framing Shots

Framing, or shot size, is the primary language of film and video production. The abbreviations, such as WA for wide-angle, and others described by their character such as zoom and profile, can be considered the "DNA" of moving picture production.

For the screenwriter and designer, these names provide a shorthand for developing a concept. For the producer, they speed along the organization of a project. For the director, they provide a command language for action. For the crew, they give everybody on the set a commonly understood jargon for working together.

The following shot names and descriptions are never meant to imply a cookie-cutter template system that is rigidly applied to all. The conventions of shot descriptions we're using here describe relative scales of visual composition of what is photographed in the frame. There is plenty of space within each description to allow for creativity on the part of videographer and director.

Static Shots

Static shots are not shots without motion—it's just the camera that is in a fixed position. The same area within a frame of a given shot does not determine the lens that is used. A MS could be shot with a wide-angle lens to render a softer, more rounded feel, or by a long lens to flatten out the details.

In this section we'll illustrate examples of each type of shot, so you can see how the impact and flavor of your movie can be influenced by the choices you make.

ELS (Extreme Long Shot, or Establishing Shot)

As shown back in Figure 6-1, a wide or medium-wide shot covers an area of environmental scale. As an establishing shot, it sets up the stage for closer action to follow. In a motion picture, you may first see an establishing shot of a city, and then zoom in on a building or street where the opening action occurs.

Master Shot

In a master shot scene the relationships between subjects are clear and the entire dramatic action for the scene could be played through without using other shots.

WA (Wide-Angle Shot, or Wide Shot)

As shown back in Figure 6-1, using the wide setting of the lens encompasses a broad area.

EWA (Extreme Wide-Angle)

The use of specialty or special effects lenses, where some distortion is unavoidable, is used for key scenes where an entire enclosed space, like a train terminal or a temple, is defined within one shot, and usually in deep focus. In exterior applications, an EWA could take in an entire landscape scene like a volcano or an avalanche.

LS / FS (Long Shot / Full Shot)

The long shot (see Figure 6-9) can reveal the whole figure and the immediate surroundings that define it.

MS (Medium Shot, or Normal Shot)

As we show in Figure 6-10, the medium shot frames the subject from the waist up, guiding the focus to the face and supporting the dialog.

CU (Close-Up)

The close-up is the frame for the face and intensifies the intimacy of the action and dialog. As we show in Figure 6-11, the neck and shoulders keep the face in bodily context. Also known as a tight shot.

ECU (Extreme Close-Up)

In Figure 6-12, the ECU focuses on expression of the face to the exclusion of all else. Also known as a big close-up.

FIGURE 6-9 A full shot of the figure.

FIGURE 6-10 Here's a typical medium shot of the subject of our movie.

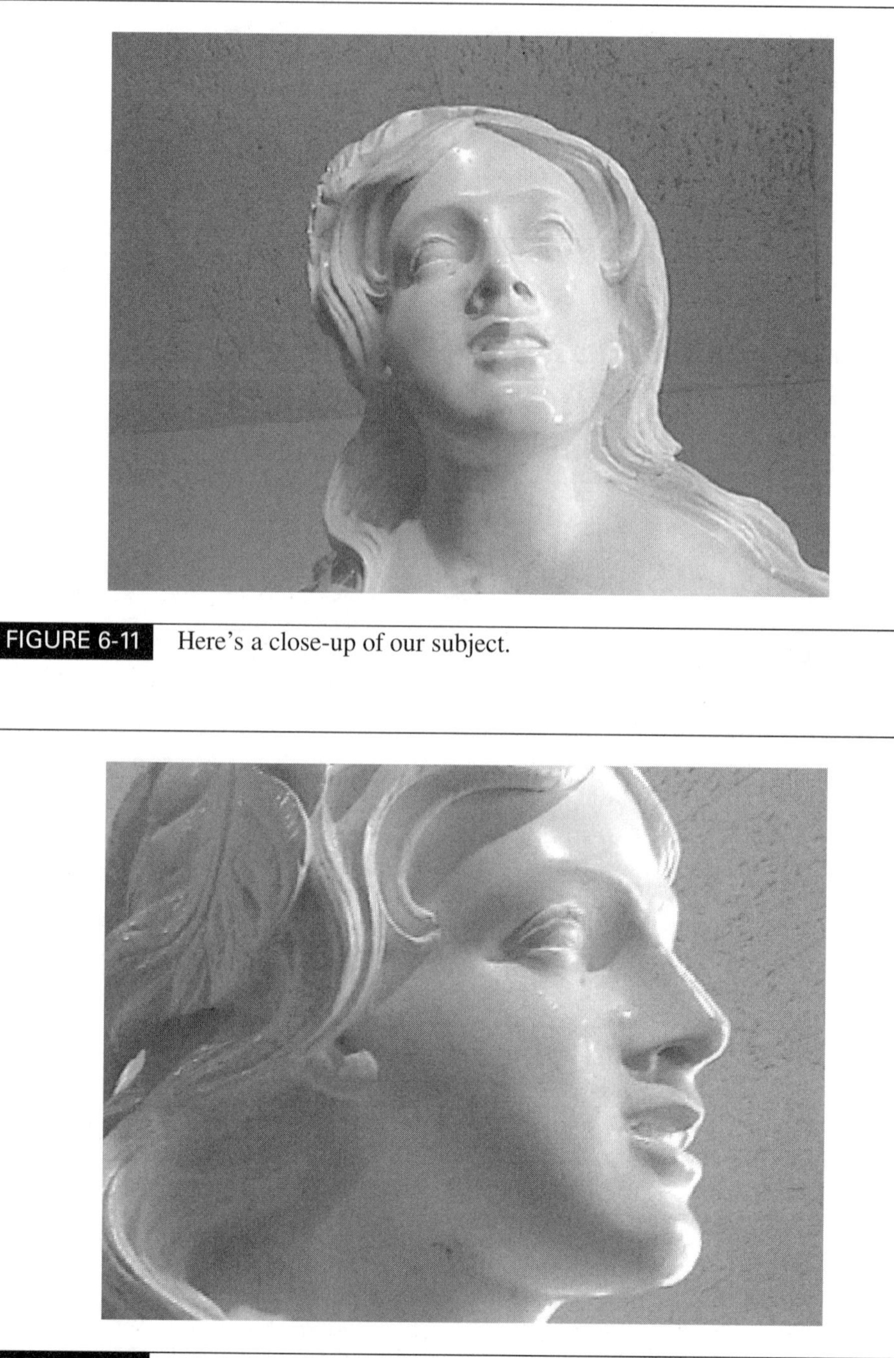

FIGURE 6-11 Here's a close-up of our subject.

FIGURE 6-12 Up close and personal, with our extreme close-up.

Profile, or Silhouette

A profile shot provides a sharp and well-defined line and form against a background. An actor's silhouette behind a screen reduces the figure to a strong, high-contrast form. Figure 6-13 illustrates an example.

Inserts, or Details

Virtually every production, from a commercial to *Cleopatra,* has brief shots of details, or insert shots, which can be the continuity glue of a complex range of actions. A sign that is seen by an actor, a telephone that suddenly rings, a door handle that means escape—these are usually CUs and ECUs that are shot out of continuity. The inserts in Figures 6-14, 6-15, 6-16, and 6-17 are elements found in the location shown in Figure 6-1—inserts to be edited into that movie. The camera operator picks them up in between scenes; many a camera roll sees its remaining few feet finished off with extra inserts.

FIGURE 6-13 Here's a profile shot of statuary against the sky.

FIGURE 6-14 An insert shot like this can help to link courses of events in your movies.

FIGURE 6-15 An insert shot of an unknown house number.

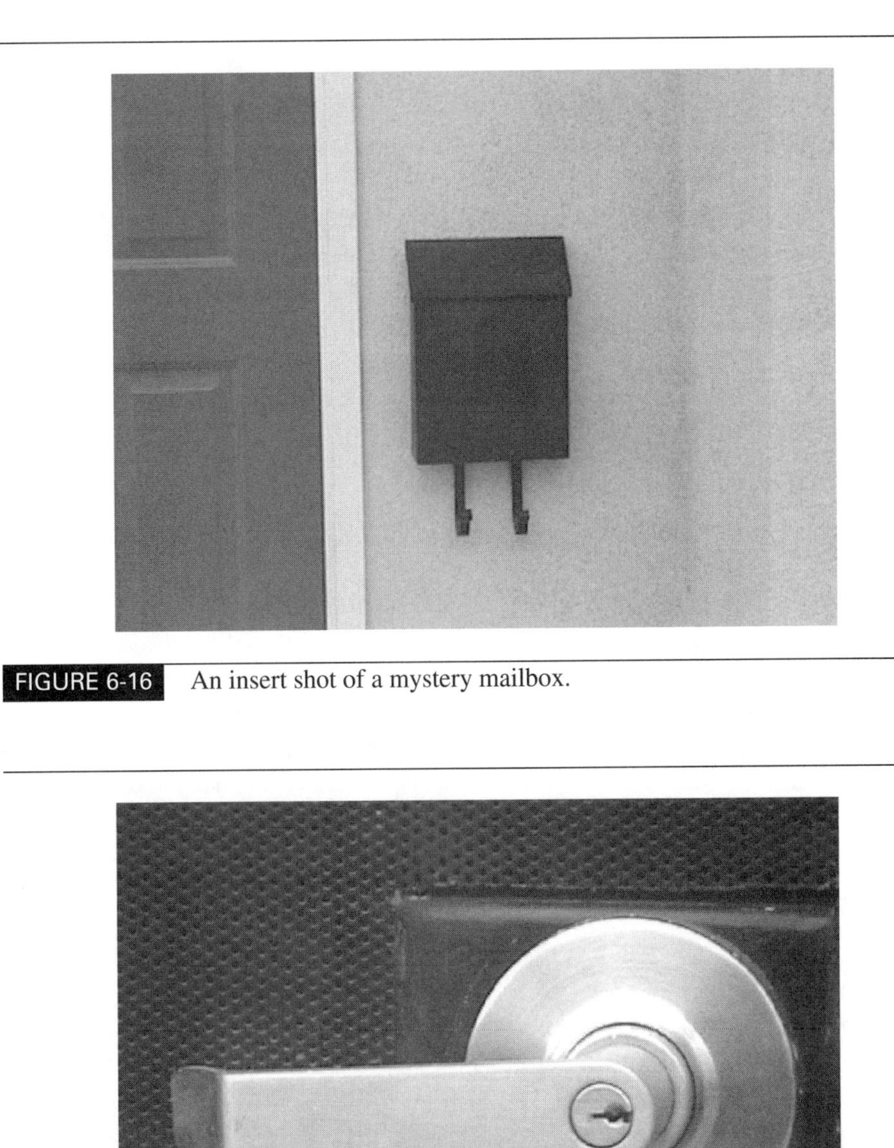

FIGURE 6-16 An insert shot of a mystery mailbox.

FIGURE 6-17 An insert shot of the door handle of fate.

People Shots

These shots, in different configurations, are oriented towards actors. But they are also freely used wherever these configurations appear in the shot, such as with cars in an industrial film or products in a commercial. They give your production a sense of a reality, something you can relate to.

Here are the common names used for people shots and their basic definitions:

- **One shot** One figure in the shot
- **Two shot** A pair of figures together
- **Three shot** Three figures in the shot
- **Group shot** Several figures in the shot
- **Crowd shot** A large number of figures in the shot.

TIP

If you don't have lots of extras around to fill a scene, you can create the impression of a large crowd simply by merging lots of small group shots, so it looks to the viewer that you are simply moving across the crowd.

Shot Movements

In a moving shot, like the tracking and dolly shots described in Chapter 5, the camera itself is in motion. But here it is the camera that is centered on a fixed position and the lens that is moving to capture larger areas, follow movement, or re-define angles of view.

Pan Shot, or Panning

The horizontal linear movement of the camera is one of the most familiar defining shots, as it maintains a comfortable equilibrium while describing the environment in a left-and-right direction similar to the way our eyes do. The pan left in Figure 6-18 describes an environment that would be difficult to encompass in one static shot.

A pan reveals information as it moves. Because it is a continuous shot, the pan is perceived as a connected and seamless visual experience. It is important to have well-defined start points and end points in a pan, so practicing the shot several times will ensure getting the best results.

FIGURE 6-18 The pan shot moves over a wide area.

TIP

One is never enough, or seldom at any rate. Unless it's a one-of-a -kind shot, it never hurts to do it a few times, and decide which to use in the "cutting room," which in this case is your copy of iMovie 2.

Pan Follow Shot, or Tracking Pan

The camera can define and reveal an area wider or longer than the focal length of the lens, but it can also follow or track a moving subject in a pan. Beginning in Figure 6-19, the camera at first tracks, or follows the ship as it moves to the right, and the background landscape moves behind it. At a key point, when the lens is normal to the subject—at a right angle—the camera stops panning and holds on point. The ship is then allowed to pass by on its own, in Figure 6-20, revealing its full length and scale, and without breaking the continuity of the shot (see Figure 6-21). Yes, almost like the opening of *Star Wars*. Almost.

FIGURE 6-19 Here's the first part of your tracking pan shot.

FIGURE 6-20 This is an intermediate angle of the action.

FIGURE 6-21 And this is near the final result, when the stern churns out of the frame.

Swish Pan or Flash Pan

You may not want to do it often, but a swish pan can often provide a direct and dynamic transition from one shot to another or one point in space to another. Move the rate of the pan fast enough so that it blurs the frame. You will have a comet-like streak of color and texture that will telegraph the transition.

The same technique can be applied to a tilt, in which the camera moves up or down. And that leads us to the next section.

Tilting: High Shots and Low Shots

A tilt applies to both a static and a moving shot where the camera is angled sharply down or up. In motion, a tilt is the vertical equivalent of a pan. In Figure 6-22, the camera is tilted down. Here, it can also be called a high-angle, or high shot. It provides a bird's-eye view of a scene, revealing action in plan.

Figure 6-23 shows a tilt up, or a low-angle, or low shot. It is a way of dramatically revealing a part of a scene and giving it a new perspective.

FIGURE 6-22 Here's our high shot, pointing downward.

FIGURE 6-23 From the bottom up, a low shot for your movie.

Did You Know?

The term Dutch angle came from 1940s Hollywood when many gifted directors, cameramen, and lighting technicians went there from Germany after World War II. Several were masters of the German Expressionist movement, producing creatively imaginative films styled with moody scenes in patterns of dark shadows and jagged forms. Their influence was felt in the dramatic and detective films of the times. But the friendly nickname "Dutch" that was given to all "good Germans" extended to their cinematic style as well, and endures today as in a Dutch tilt.

Dutch Tilt, or Dutch Angle

To "Dutch" an angle is to create a diagonal or oblique tilt. This angle is used to match the frame edge to a subject that is at an odd angle, or to create whimsy or tension. In Figure 6-24, the tug is Dutched to express its character and as a rhythmic shot element for the sequence yet to be edited.

NOTE *One of the famous (or infamous) uses of a Dutch tilt is the Batman TV show from the 1960s, the one that starred Adam West as the "Caped Crusader." The Dutch tilt was commonly used, along with those comic book captions, during the fight scenes.*

Reverse Angle

In a reverse angle shot, one shot follows another, each turned 180 degrees or so from the other. Using reverse angles is a way to refer to and reinforce the relationships between two subjects or areas. For example, Figures 6-22 and 6-23 are reverse angles of each other, and Figure 6-7 is, among other things, a reverse angle of Figure 6-22.

Zooming

The motorized automatic zoom lens on your camcorder provides an easy way to move from one lens setting to the next. It also encourages zoom shots, or zooming while filming.

Zoom Shot

The zoom shot is probably one of the most overused features in home movies. But the right zoom at the right time can be just as valid and valuable as the right pan or

FIGURE 6-24 A Dutch tilt provides a fascinating view of the subject of this scene.

tilt. We are so used to zoomed elements in film and TV that they may seem even natural. A good zoom doesn't draw attention to itself because it matches the way your own eye would naturally look more closely at something.

Any zoom is a magnification of a single image from far to near or near to far. Beginning in Figure 6-25 and ending in Figure 6-26, a zoom shot travels all the way down to the end of the street. This means that objects along the sides maintain their relative proportions to each other as defined in the start of the shot.

In comparison, the static equivalent of that zoom shot—a series of medium-wide shots, as seen in Figures 6-27 and 6-28, reveals the full dimensionality of the objects and spaces of the buildings. They change at each shot along the way, especially the environment you see at the end of the street that is opened up with the wider lens.

However, there isn't an inherent superior virtue in either approach—it all depends upon the movie you are trying to make. To capture a single swift signature of this street, the zoom shot might serve better in its decisive gesture. The series of wider shots would provide a better platform for the further development of personal profiles of the residents and the character of the housing. And in that movie, you might well be using zoom shots and inserts to tell their stories.

FIGURE 6-25 Your zoom shot begins here.

FIGURE 6-26 And ends here.

FIGURE 6-27 Showing the life of the street.

FIGURE 6-28 The medium wide shot shows the surrounding environment.

The Closing Scene

In this chapter, you took a crash course in cinematography. You discovered how different types of shots can evoke various moods and styles, and that by proper framing of your scene, you can give your movie a high level of professional spit and polish.

In our next chapter, you'll learn how lighting and exposure can combine to change the texture of your scene, or to help illuminate a subject or scene to its best advantage.

NOTE *The photos in this chapter are printed from single frame captures in iMovie 2, from footage shot by Tony with a Sony DCR-TRV230 Hi-8.*

Chapter 7

Working with Exposure and Lighting

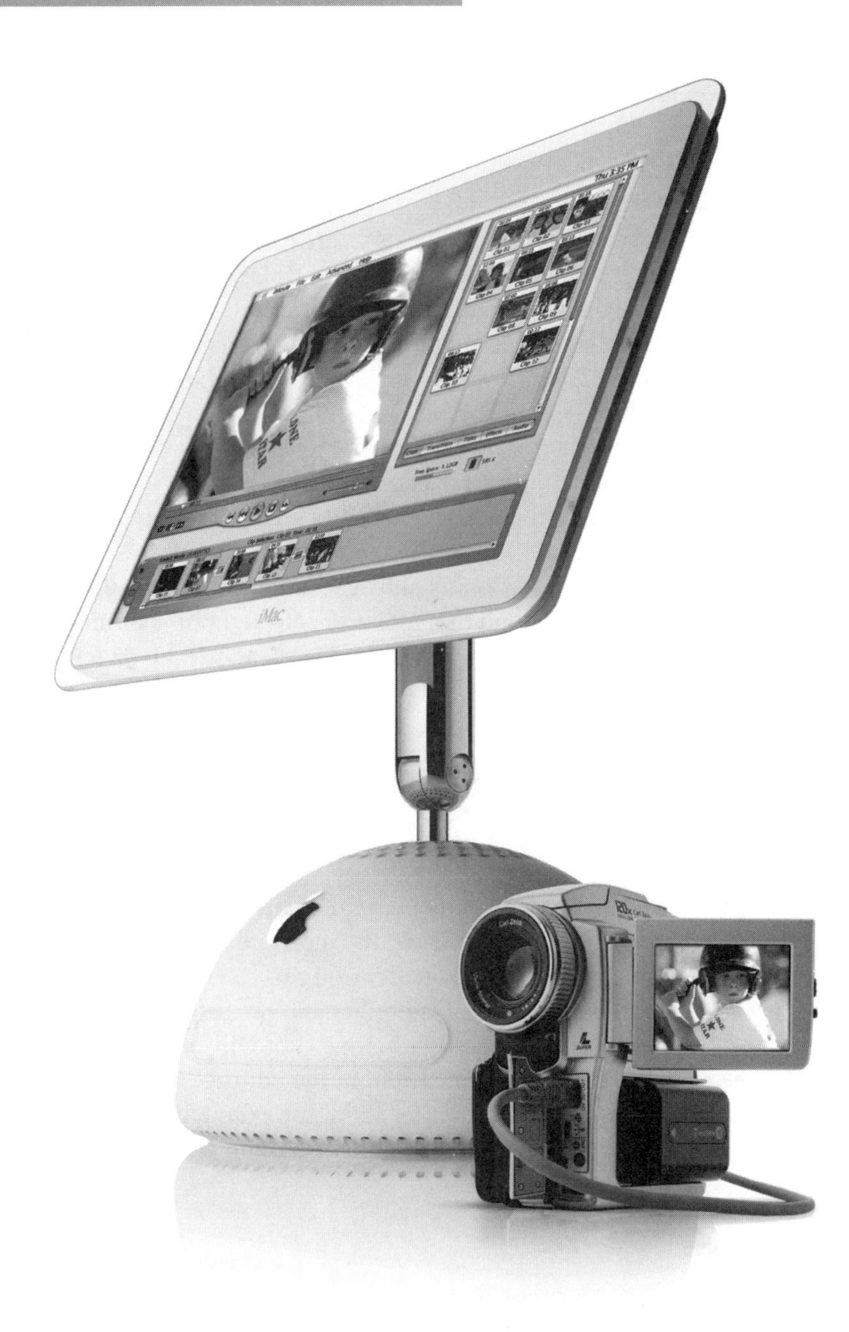

How to…

- Make the most of daylight shots
- Improvise with reflectors
- Use manual focus
- Learn about lighting media
- Make a basic lighting setup

It all begins with lighting. You may make dozens of great movies, all in daylight, without ever turning on the switch of an artificial light. But the sun, your primary point source lighting instrument, is a constantly changing and variable resource. In this chapter, you will learn about the simple strategies for making the most of your available lighting. You'll learn how to compensate for backlighting, reflection, and color correction with white balance.

In addition, we'll discuss manual exposure override, a feature on many camcorders that will give you more control over subject and area values in a scene.

Briefly, auto exposure programs can provide handy shortcuts for many exposure situations. Slow shutter settings can provide sharp capture for critical action at the expense of blurring fast moving subjects, and infrared sensitivity may be a useful resource for night-dark conditions. The various lighting instruments, lighting media and instrument placement for setting the scene will be reviewed in the pages that follow.

Understanding Daylight and Artificial Light

Daylight, our most constant standard of light, is actually a very dynamic, fluid and constantly changing resource. Throughout the day, the sun is always moving and changing the angle of its rays to any given point on the Earth; the nature of the atmospheric lens changes as the seasons do; and the moisture and temperature affecting the density of the air changes the quality of light.

During this ever-changing and usually unpredictable process, you, the videographer, need to make sure that the light in one shot will match all the others in the scene so that they will be consistent in the editing, and that flesh tones will look correct everywhere. The actors' skin, for example, will look unnatural when illuminated by more than one type of light.

Light for image exposure is measured by its color temperature. Outdoor light is usually bluish (about 5400 degrees K), except during sunrise and sunset. Artificial light is more constant, and lighting manufacturers are able to produce elements that will maintain a constant value throughout the lamp's life. Quartz halogen TV lights, for example, are reddish (3200 degrees K).

The problem with tungsten-based lamps like high-intensity floodlights is that their filaments age and get progressively less bright and more reddish. Common incandescent lighting is reddish (about 2000 degrees K color temperature). Fluorescent lights have a greenish cast.

White Balance

White balance is the camera's ability to correct color and tint when shooting under different lighting conditions including daylight, indoor and fluorescent lighting. Most auto-exposure systems in camcorders integrate white balance into their corrections. On some consumer cameras, manual white balance settings consist of exposure program choices such as "Indoor," "Sunny," and "Cloudy." If your camcorder has a manual white balance, you can obtain more color temperature reliability from scene to scene.

To manually white-balance follow these steps:

1. Hold up a white card.
2. Zoom into the white area to fill the frame.
3. Set the manual white-balance on the camera.
4. Zoom back to the shot setting.
5. Resume shooting until the light environment changes once again.

NOTE *Video has less range and latitude than film, so when exposure is too bright, white values may get bleached out. When it is too dark, you may get a grainy image without much color. The best image quality will be maintained by keeping your light level up at the optimum indicated by your camcorder's exposure setting .*

Adjusting Exposure With Your Camcorder

The automatic electronic exposure systems in full-featured camcorders today are so good they may sometimes appear to be guided by artificial intelligence. Nonetheless, they can't change the light—they can only adjust for it.

What they do better today than the earlier models did is to analyze the reflected light of the whole scene, and not just the brightest value and then the darkest value. They monitor it from second-to-second and yield an exposure setting that will be an average of the full spectrum of the light values it receives. That setting may be slightly darker than what your eyes perceive.

A Brief Look at Camcorder Exposure Tools

Camcorders admit light through the lens to expose each frame of video. They do this with the following:

- **Aperture** The lens opening is defined by the iris, which permits light to expose the CCD (Charge-Coupled Device) that digitizes the light information. The aperture size is calibrated in *F-Stop* numbers; such as 1/30; 1/15; 1/8; and 1/4. The larger the number, the smaller the lens opening.
- **The Iris** This is a variable leaf mechanism that expands and contracts to admit light into the lens. The smaller the aperture, the greater the depth of field.
- **Shutter** This mechanism controls the time of the exposure, or the length of time—expressed in fractions of a second—during which light is admitted. Standard shutter speed is 1/60 of a second. The faster the shutter speed, the better the lens can capture fast-moving action without blurring the image.

In today's camcorders, electronic design combines these classical camera features into integrated mechanisms, but the underlying principles remain the same.

Backlighting

If your camcorder has a backlight mode, you will be able to solve the most commonly-encountered exposure problem by simply pushing a button. Since auto exposure averages the light in a scene, if your subject is a figure against the sky, or beach or snow, the subject will look extremely dark as a result. In extreme cases, your subject will be so dark as to be almost unrecognizable against that bright background.

A backlight mode compensates for this by opening up the lens, giving the figure a better chance at a normal, and readable exposure. The tradeoff is that a beautiful cloud-filled sky may become brightly over-exposed and flat with a great loss of detail. On the other hand, if what you want is a profile or silhouette shot, then don't use the backlight mode.

Manual Exposure Override

The most reliable way to compensate for backlighting and for subjects that are a different brightness than near objects or backgrounds, is to use the manual exposure override. Even when the auto exposure is working perfectly, the dynamics of video making can conflict with its operation.

As you move your camera, and as the action moves past your lens, the overall scene light value may change. Just as auto-focus can sometimes be seen "hunting" between distance settings while you are taping, so too can auto exposure be caught hunting between f-stops in the same shot.

In an extended pan shot, the auto exposure may be seen to change two or three times between start point to end point. Rehearse your pan with an eye on exposure. If you see the auto exposure hunting, choose an exposure value that seems to serve the entire shot best, and lock down the manual exposure at that point. Now shoot the pan shot.

NOTE *If precise exposure is important to you, it never hurts to repeat a critical shot a few times, just to be sure you have at least one "take" that works.*

Exposure Control Methods

There are different exposure control methods used by different camcorder models. A common method is described as follows:

NOTE *We are assuming your camcorder does have a way to override automatic exposure. If it doesn't you'll have to bypass this material.*

1. Focus on the subject or area that you want to favor by your exposure, filling up the frame with the subject. It may be an area smaller than the scene.
2. Actuate the button or lever for manual exposure override.
3. An exposure indicator will appear in the viewfinder. It may be in the form of a bar indicator; [- --------×------- +] with the center representing average exposure. Others may express the range in numbered divisions.
4. Return to the shot position.
5. Record your shot.
6. To return to the auto exposure modes, activate the exposure control again.

Taking a Subject Reading

There are several other, more high-end systems that enable you to select the point in the frame area to measure, and then adjust and lock exposure. That way you don't have to leave and then return to your shot position. They include Sony's Push Focus and Canon's FlexiZone.

NOTE *If you're in doubt over the features your camcorder offers, check the specifications and manual, or contact the manufacturer if you still have questions.*

Using your camcorder as a light meter, you can prepare for a shooting sequence by going to each critical exposure area, take the subject reading, and then setting the exposure to each value for each respective shot. To adjust the exposure:

1. Actuate the button or lever for manual exposure override.
2. Use the dial or other control to move the setting to the point you have noted.
3. Record your shot.

You may also use this manual control to adjust to an exposure of brightness as seen through the viewfinder, or in the LCD viewer, that may seem optimum to you. This will give you more options for exposure control in your scenes.

For instance, instead of using the automatic backlight mode, you can determine the exposure setting for the subject's face and lock that down. This will ensure that the face, and not the body, will carry the optimum readable exposure.

TIP *Don't just depend on a visual display in the viewfinder or LCD of your camcorder. It doesn't hurt to do test shots with different exposure settings to be sure they will be satisfactory for your movie.*

Auto Exposure Programs

Many camcorders include a menu of auto exposure programs, or special settings that are represented by icons, and are named for location situations that could pose special problems. These programs custom configure exposure values for certain types of subjects, background or lighting, or some unsavory combination of all three.

For example, in Sony's TRV series they are listed as:

- **Spotlight** Prevents people's faces from appearing too white when subject is strongly front-lit. It is essentially the opposite of backlighting.
- **Soft Portrait** Brings out the subject while creating a soft background. It is a form of soft focus.
- **Sports Lesson** This mode minimizes shake on fast-moving subjects like tennis players.
- **Beach and Ski** Helps to prevent people's faces from appearing dark in strong light. It is a degree of backlighting.
- **Sunset & Moon** Enables you to maintain atmosphere when you are recording sunsets, general night views, fireworks, and neon. Exposure is leveled off at the low end.
- **Landscape** For recording distant subjects through a near surface such as a window or grill.
- **Low Lux** This mode makes subjects appear brighter in insufficient light.

How useful are these programs? They are not standardized between manufacturers, so a Canon program menu will look different than a Panasonic or JVC. You must test each of them for yourself to see what their results are. But they can be valuable shortcuts for fast-changing events in the field, and for certain environments or locations where you may find yourself shooting often. They can, if you're in a rush, save you lots of time for experimenting with various combinations of exposure and focus.

CAUTION *In addition to the differences in presets or automatic exposure settings from one manufacturer to another, don't depend on the description to lull you into a sense of security as to the results. It would be a good idea to test each preset in the situations in which they're configured against the standard setting to see how the changes affect your shots.*

Slow Shutter

If your camcorder has a slow shutter control setting, it will enable you to record dark images and dim scenes more clearly and sharply than with the iris completely open. The larger the shutter speed number, the slower the shutter speed. Your camcorder may have shutter speeds numbered at $\frac{1}{30}$, $\frac{1}{15}$, $\frac{1}{8}$, and $\frac{1}{4}$.

CAUTION *If you engage a slow shutter setting, the shot will be more vulnerable to bumps and shakes. If possible, try to mount the camcorder on a tripod or camera clamp and focus manually.*

Infrared

Infrared (IR) photography, developed for the military's night vision systems, enables you to record video in near total darkness. IR is one of those advanced technologies that has migrated down to appear in some moderately-priced camcorders.

With IR systems such as Sony's NightShot and Panasonic's IR Filter, a built-in infrared emittter lamp, located below the lens, illuminates the subject area. An internal IR filter interprets the light for recording. Daylight includes some infrared as part of its spectrum, but pure IR is a very narrow bandwidth of light, and is not visible to the human eye. You can see the IR emissions only through your camera. Your subject cannot.

For sharp resolution, the subject-to-camera distance illumination, about ten feet, is usually enough for a full or medium shot, but the IR can reveal a surprisingly large area for movement recognition. Sony's images are seen in an eerie green, and Panasonic gives you the option to record images in black and white, blue, or green. Unless you want to represent an alien's-eye-view, black and white might be the best editing choice. See Chapter 13 for information on changing color effects.

IR can be advantageous for uses such as:

- Nocturnal nature photography
- Security and surveillance monitoring, especially with a camcorder that has an intervalometer (a device setting the interval between shots), or programmable recording timer
- Inspection of difficult access areas, such as industrial voids, attics, and crawl spaces
- Experimental or dream sequences

Shooting in IR Mode

Here's some general advice to help guide you towards getting the best results from your IR shots:

NOTE *If the IR feature isn't present in your camcorder, it's not something you can add later on. You'll want to bypass this section, or use it for reference if you ever decide to upgrade to a more full-featured model.*

1. Turn on the IR function on your camcorder.
2. Switch to manual focus. This will probably be enacted automatically, as auto-focus can't "see" IR light waves.
3. Zoom to the subject and focus.
4. Zoom back to the shot setting and record.
5. Note that if you move the camera, the IR emitter pattern is revealed as if you were sweeping a flashlight beam over the scene area. If everything works as advertised, you'll end up with a shot that shows a lighting and exposure result similar to what you see in Figure 7-1.

Reflecting and Shading Light

Like in the military, one of the hard things about working in a movie crew is that you have to wake up and reach location before the light of dawn. The early morning and before sunset are "the golden hours" to directors of photography.

FIGURE 7-1 A night shot taken with infrared light by a Sony camcorder.

Many moviegoers may think that high noon, when you have the most sunlight, would be the ideal time to shoot a film. It is true that more light is flooding more areas, and there will be some locations where a full light beaming down from the sun will be the best for the angle. But it is the worst time to photograph actors; in fact it may make them look much worse than you expect, with harsher features (of course that may be appropriate for your particular setting). Early and late times of the day provide a softer natural light, but most important, the angle—almost horizontal—is the most flattering for human features.

TIP *Subjects with dark skin tone create a high contrast ratio that can be hard to handle. Keep the background on the neutral side—avoid white or bright colors. Put plenty of light on the subject and keep it even. On a light-skinned face, contrasty lighting often adds modeling and character. On a dark-skinned face the shadows don't seem as flattering*

Reflected Light

When shooting video in exterior locations, bright sunlight may cast dark shadows, and at the same time wash out the shadow detail and contribute to loss of definition. All that sun may overload the camera's CCDs as well.

Unfortunately, there are locations, such as when you're covering sports or events, where you must shoot in harsh sunlight. That's the time to use polarizing filters and a lens hood. Otherwise, look for locations that are illuminated by reflected light, or in which the sunlight is broken up by foliage, water, or other structures.

Reflectors are large flat white or silver surfaces, or even gold or black. The gold is good for warming up flesh tones. Umbrella reflectors, as you see in Figure 7-2, can "focus" the light from inside their bell-like shapes. Reflectors are anchored on stands with swivels for securing different angles, such as the one you see in Figure 7-3, where they can provide both key and fill lights for the subject. They may be further anchored with sandbags for stability. On locations where electrical power and supplemental lighting are not available, reflectors may make a great difference.

NOTE *Once you need to shoot many close-ups, the whole support structure changes. Even with all natural light shooting, the sun won't always be lighting the actor—or the subject of any kind—at the right angle. Shadows will be in the wrong places, or shouldn't be there at all. You may position the actor near a white stucco wall and enjoy a perfect exposure—until you need to do a reverse angle. And the color value cast by the reflecting surface may be wrong.*

FIGURE 7-2 Umbrella reflectors are a useful solution for getting proper reflected light.

FIGURE 7-3 Reflectors, which can be angled easily, can also clear up lighting irregularities.

Improvising Reflectors

All right, you are using a consumer grade camcorder, and we don't expect you to run to a professional dealer and rent tons of costly equipment to get good shots. There are always ways to do it on the cheap and still get great results.

For example, you can create your own reflectors using one of the following techniques:

- **An old movie screen** On a stand, it can serve for a normal angle reflection.
- **Card table** Tape white paper on the surface if it is too dark. Rest it on its side, using the folding legs to form angle bracing.
- **Umbrella** A rain umbrella with aluminum foil taped on the inside area may be a good substitute for the professional umbrella reflector.
- **Car window reflecting sun shade** Need we say more?
- **White foam core board** Available at art supply houses, this is a familiar tool for independent video. It can be a challenge to hold on to after the first big gust of wind hits the set, but if weather conditions aren't extreme, this may be a way to get the job done and not spend a bundle.

Shading

To control the lighting in a scene on an exterior location, sometimes you have to spend as much effort in shading, diffusing, and patterning the light as you do reflecting and amplifying it. Reflectors often do double-duty in shading areas of the scene from direct light. The camera position must often be shaded or the unit covered by an umbrella to keep the heat off equipment and crew and make it easier to see focus.

A wide variety of video gel and diffusion media are used not only in the studio, but on location, for controlling the light and color from both sunlight and artificial lights. Frames can hold gel sheets to correct the color of the light falling on the actors, or diffusers to soften it. When shooting an interior during daylight, the windows may be "gelled" with sheets of color correction gels to match the artificial light inside, yet expose the exterior outdoors to the camera. Lighting media are often combined and sandwiched, such as colors and patterns.

Here's an overview of the various filters and inserts that can be used to control light. They can fill in areas with textures for scenic character and link other illuminated areas together for continuity. Figure 7-4 shows some of the filter patterns available from professional supply shops.

FIGURE 7-4 Here are several of the many pattern designs available to control light areas and reflections.

- **Video color gels** Available as lamp inserts and in sheets in a wide variety of colors, for both additive effects and for color correction. There are patterns like mottled, marbled, abstract, and water.
- **Diffusion** Softens and evens the light. They range from hardly perceptible to total diffusion. Some are textured, such as scrim, silk, spun, and frost.
- **Patterns** Choose from a large variety of patterns, such as bare branches, bars, basket weave, beams, bricks, broken lines, grids, stars, and chain link fence.
- **Gobos** Lighting gobos are like spot patterns, to place a shape or pattern in a specific area. Custom gobos can be cut to fill, join, or mask areas in lighting design for a scene.

CAUTION *It's good to be resourceful in improvising your lighting setup, but lights, especially halogen or quartz-iodide bulbs, generate intense heat, and can ignite cloth sheet or paper diffusion media if they are positioned too close to the light source. It's safer to use flameproofed commercial video gel and diffusion media.*

TIP *A popular and cheap alternative to commercial diffusion is to hang a white bed sheet (or any other color, if you want color) over a window, or next to the subject in the outdoors if the light is coming from the side. If not used with artificial lighting, there is no risk of fire.*

Adding Lights to Fill Out the Scene

If you have ever seen a movie being shot on location, one of the first things you may have noticed was all the lighting equipment out there, even though it was being done in broad daylight. In order for the finished footage to look "natural" on the screen, reflected light must often be supplemented with electric lighting (see Figure 7-5). That may be the only way for you to control exposure values and conquer shadows.

NOTE *HMI, which is one of the most common lamp elements used in film and video, stands for Hydragyrum Mercury Medium arc-length Iodide.*

The crew positions for independent and amateur video—camera, sound, set, props, wardrobe—all are easier to do and are less physically challenging than is the lighting. The skill, knowledge, and, especially, experience needed for excellent location and studio lighting for a full production is daunting. This is why many, even low-scale productions may budget for a lighting technician.

They arrive in a truck equipped with just the right lighting instruments and power cords and accessories that are needed for your show. They set up, break and follow with the action, adjust on the fly, don't blow any fuses, know what to do in emergencies, and are out of there at the end of the day.

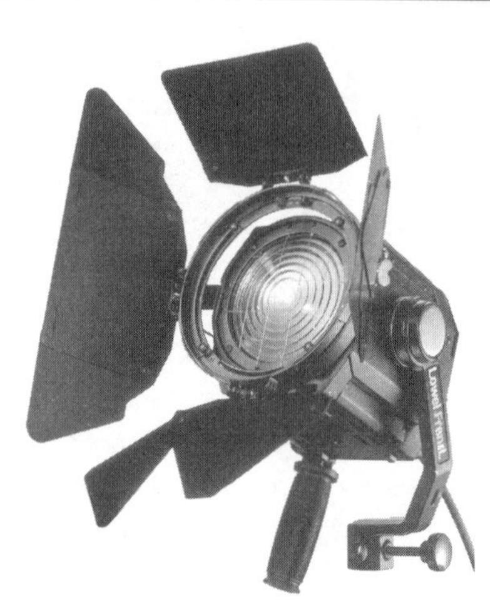

FIGURE 7-5 The Lowel Fren-L with barndoors has a focusing range from a wide even flood down to a tight spot.

Still, there is much you can do to light a scene on your own and to learn in the field. Try renting the lighting instruments you need. If you will be making videos on a regular basis, there are quartz lighting kits, such as the Lowel T/O GO Kit displayed in Figure 7-6, which are versatile and compact for travel. Most professional lighting kits also include tripods, AC power cords with on/off switches, carrying cases, and a supply of spare lamps (see Figure 7-7).

CAUTION *"Nickel Cadmium batteries have a 'memory effect' in which the voltage drops by two levels during discharge after shallow charge/discharge cycles. In application, when discharge and voltage is highly established, apparent decreases in capacity and operating voltage are shown." Sanyo Cadnica Engineering Handbook*

FIGURE 7-6 A Lowel T/O GO Kit can fly as carry-on baggage or fit in the trunk of your car.

FIGURE 7-7 A well-modeled portrait shot is lit with a Lowel Rifa-lite soft light from front fill, accented with a Pro key light from the back.

Supplemental Lighting

For occasional and improvised setups, you can use the following:

- **Camera-mounted light** These lights were developed for news cameras. Their fixed angle and limited beam separate the figure from the background, and so are ideal for shooting talking heads. Use sparingly, but be alert for the opportunity where they may be the best solution for the shot.
- **Sun Gun** A powerful battery-powered, hand-held quartz-halogen lamp that can be used for primary, fill, or backlighting in challenging field conditions and as a very flexible supplementary instrument.
- **Shop lights with stands** Available from hardware or home improvement stores, some construction-grade sets have halogen lamps.
- **Flood lamps with clamps** Again common in hardware stores and home improvement centers.

Preserving Your Home and Your Sanity for Home Video

Peter Utz has good advice for helping to preserve the home in home video:

"Don't overload power circuits. Electrical outlets for homes are generally equipped for 15 to 20 amps per circuit (and that circuit may be feeding several electrical outlets with other devices on it). Industrial electrical circuits may go up to 30 amps, but a single outlet may still be only capable of 20 amps. Just to be on the safe side, let's use 20 amps as our maximum as we do the following calculation:

A 500 watt bulb uses about 5 amps. A 1000 watt bulb uses about 10 amps. Add up all the lights you are using and see if you are exceeding the capacity of the circuit. Incidentally, if you switch all the lights on at the same time, the power surge will probably blow a fuse or circuit breaker, so activate the lights one at a time. If you are drawing a lot of power from one circuit, don't try to operate computers or VCRs from that same circuit—the lights may depress the voltage and may cause the computer or VCR to operate unreliably."

TIP *When setting up for an interior location, begin by working with the light that is already there. Identify all the "practicals"—the existing lighting fixtures. Increase the room's overall light level by replacing more powerful light bulbs in existing lamps.*

Three-Light Setup

The three-light setup is the fundamental lighting configuration and embodies the basics for most studio and location work. Lighting begins with the subject—an actor, seated or standing, who is lit frontally with the key light. As with all initial setups, the lights are mounted at a 45-degree angle looking down.

By itself, the key light will be somewhat harsh on the face. Follow with the fill light. Make it softer by reflecting the light off a wall, a reflector, and/or by putting a diffuser in front of the light. The scene is usually easier to light if the background is darker than the subject.

Mounting a light above and behind the subject will add a slight corona, or highlight, and will help to separate the subject from the background. This is called the back light. As you move and adjust these lights, you will begin to create a play of light and shadow on the subject, revealing depth, form, and mood. Figure 7-8 shows a typical three light setup as viewed from above.

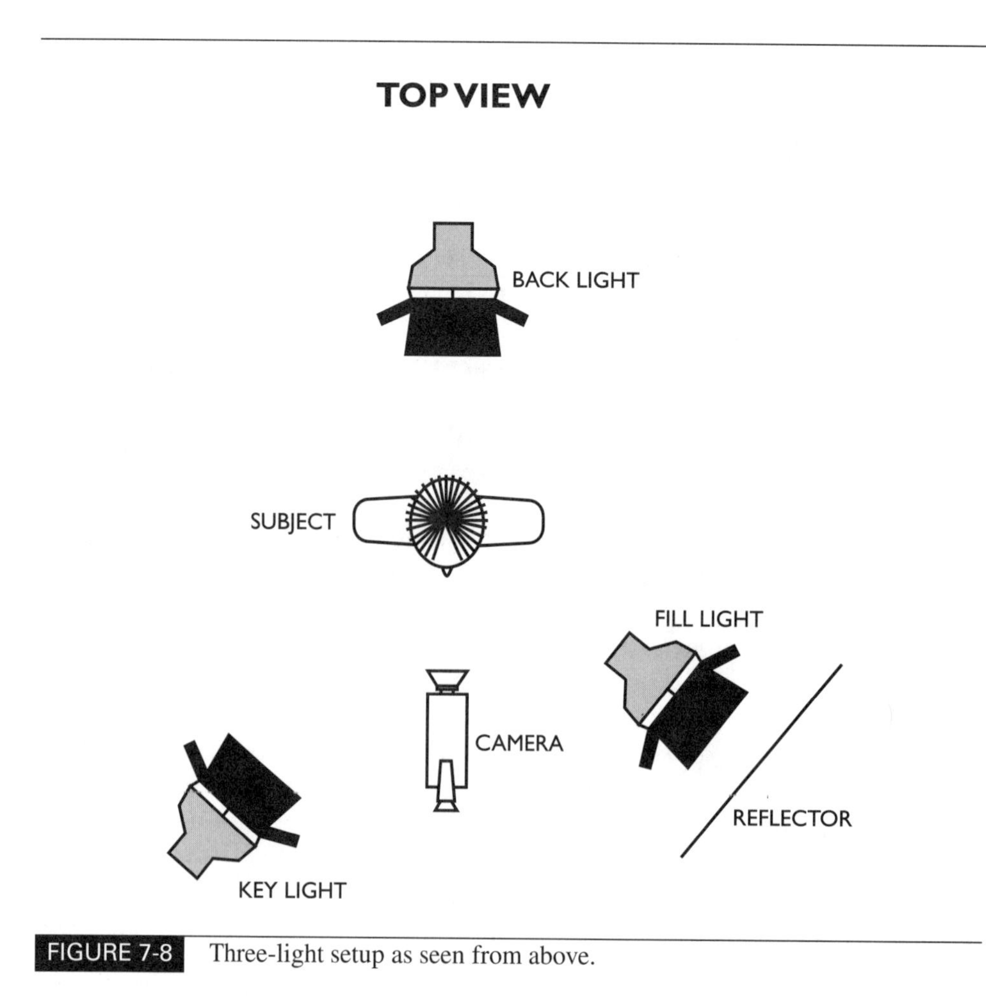

FIGURE 7-8 Three-light setup as seen from above.

The Closing Scene

As you see from this chapter, setting proper exposure values means going beyond the automatic settings of your camcorder. But it's not a complicated process. Lighting however, takes a little work, and even if you don't have the budget to hire a lighting truck, establishing the proper lighting, even for an exterior shot, can really help the final movie. Whether you are making an amateur movie, an industrial video, or you want to give a family event, such as a birthday or wedding, a polished look, a little work at proper lighting will truly pay off.

In the next chapter we'll cover the next phase of your movie, one that can be the most critical of all—the sound.

Chapter 8

Recording Sound

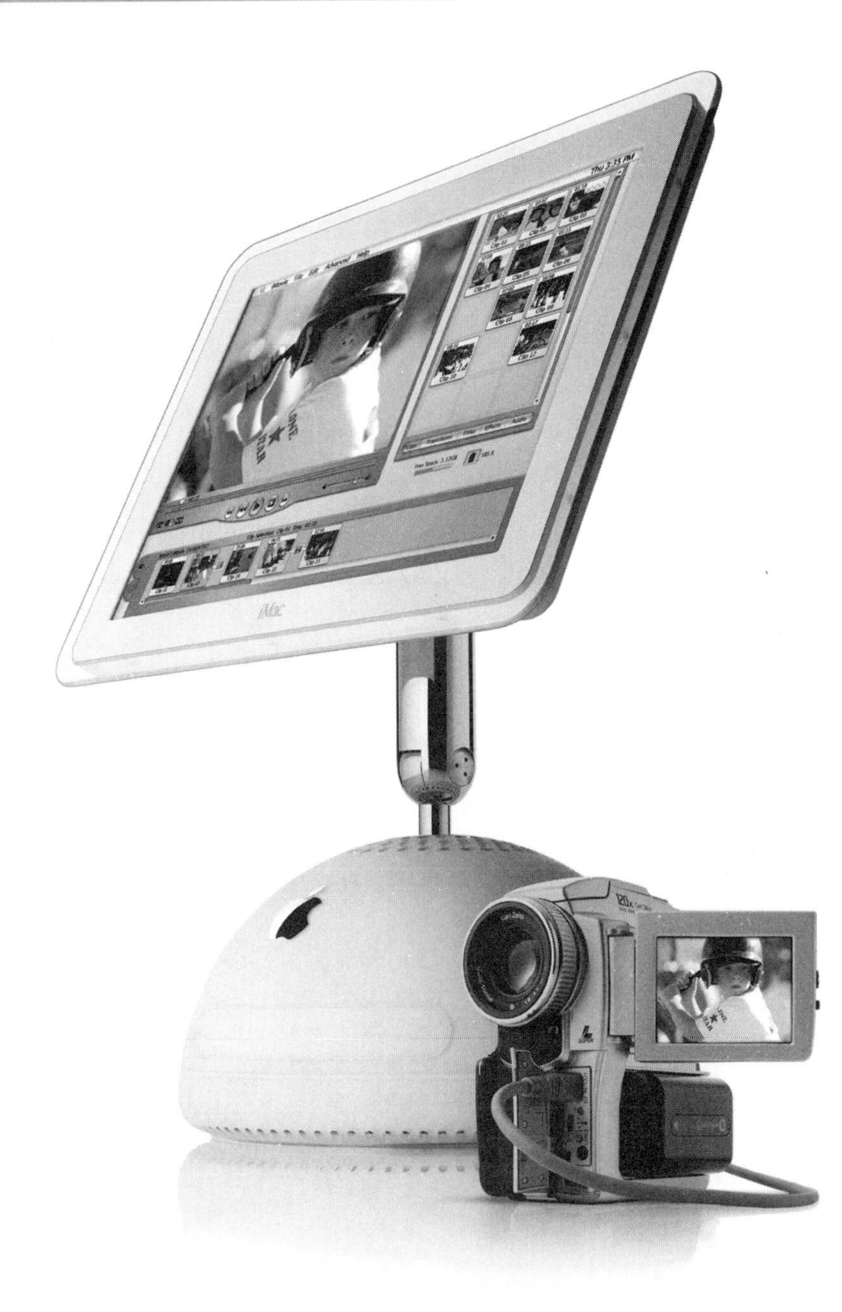

How to...

- Choose the right microphone
- Create depth of field in sound
- Learn about wireless microphone systems
- Monitor sound
- Use your camcorder as a sound recorder

They say sound makes the movie, and ever since the silent era ended, more and more emphasis has been placed on this significant factor.

Since most of your sound will be recorded at the same time as your visuals, this chapter covers the best ways to capture high-quality audio, especially on location. You'll learn about the limitations of the built-in microphone in your camcorder, and other options that are sure to improve sound quality.

There are similarities in the way different types of microphones and lenses hear and see things, and you'll learn how to recognize and choose the various types of external microphones best suited for particular needs, and how they may be supported and placed for the sonic picture you desire. For shooting from a location too far from your subject for a regular mic cable, you will learn about wireless microphone systems, including wireless lavaliers for actors (a mic worn on the actor's neck).

Another subject we'll cover is that of audio recorders, which can offer more kinds of expansion and flexibility in capturing sound. We'll also describe the importance of monitoring the sounds you're recording, and how you can make your camcorder do double duty as an audio recorder.

Understanding Sound and Microphones

Most microphones used in film and video production are condenser, or capacitor, microphones. Condensers interpret the sound pressure generated by sound waves that enter their apertures. The pressure moves and vibrates a lightweight membrane and a fixed plate that act as opposite sides of a capacitor. Together, they make sound waves into a changing electrical output that can be amplified and recorded. Comparable to the way that light that is reflected off a subject enters the camera lens and is interpreted by the CCD, the sound waves of a sound source are captured by a microphone and translated into an electrical pattern.

There is a further direct analogy between lenses and microphones. Here's the comparison between the common types of mics available (also see Figure 8-1):

- **Omni microphone** Like the wide-angle lens, an omni mic captures a wide and surrounding envelope of sound.
- **Cardioid microphone** A cardioid, or directional, microphone covers the area directly in front of the mic, like the field of a medium, or normal, lens.
- **Shotgun microphone** A shotgun, or line, microphone acts like the telephoto lens. It can capture distant sounds, or focus on the voice of just one actor.

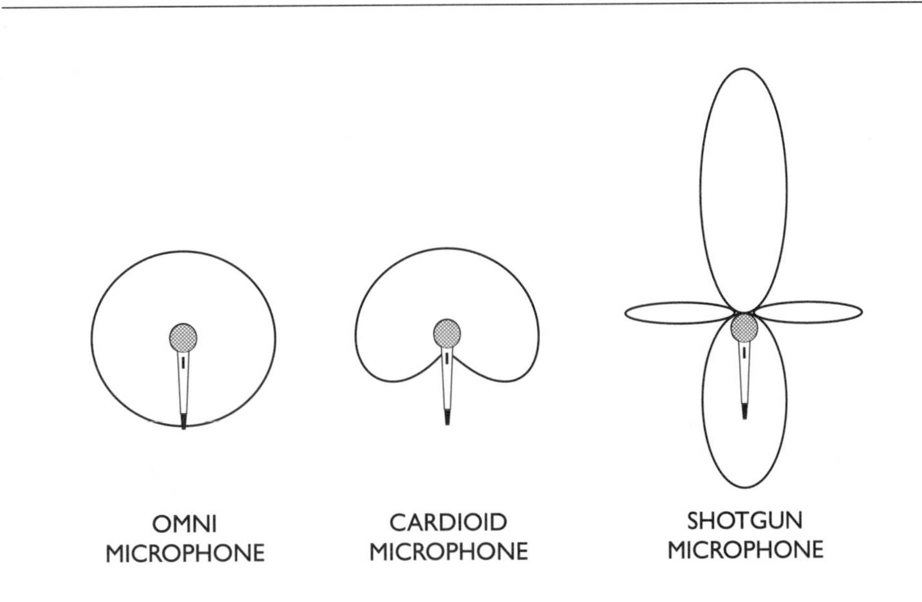

FIGURE 8-1 These drawings illustrate the sound recording directional patterns of different types of microphones.

Composition in Sound

Does that mean that you must match the microphone to the lens? Not necessarily. True, sound can be synchronous to action, which means that the viewer hears the sounds coming from the subjects in the frame. But you shouldn't be tied to that convention. For instance, it would be disruptive for the sound to jump around to follow a series of quick angle cuts that establishes an action or leads in a direction.

Voice-over and narration—as well as music—often "float" over a variety of angles and cuts, maintaining a constant axis of continuity. A first-person POV (point of view) sequence may combine the constant voice-over of the principal with the background sound of the scene environment, as well as a series of sounds from elements—close and far away—that the actor is looking at as the camera reveals them.

From the built-in microphone in your camcorder to the greater range and variety of external microphones, you can plan and design for a richer depth of field of sound in your movie. A scene may be set with a mix of a directional microphone for the main action, a shotgun for an actor speaking from a balcony, and an omni microphone for supporting environmental sound. Even the limitations of a built-in microphone can be greatly diversified when you edit your footage in iMovie 2, as you will see in Chapter 12. Adding and layering voice, ambient sound, and sound effects over the footage can endow a greater dimension to your movie.

Consider This...

Don't forget to record room tone when you're on location. When you edit your sound in iMovie 2, there may be many times when you'll need to insert spaces between dialog. A silent space will be heard as a flat drop-off, or even as a slight hiss. Here is where you need audio footage that has the the proper sound to fill those spaces. This is called room tone, room noise, or room sound. It is the general ambient noise in a space.

In an interior location, this noise could come from water pipes, air conditioning, or fans. At an exterior location, it could be from the wind, birds, or crowd noise. Even a sound studio at a broadcasting station has its own unique acoustic signature. Only an anechoic chamber, a specially insulated and isolated space used for audio engineering and testing, can be completely free from room noise.

Built-In Camera Microphones

Every camcorder comes with a built-in microphone. The least expensive models may be monophonic, but now most camcorder microphones are stereophonic. A mid-range Digital8 camera may have PCM (Pulse Code Modulation) stereo audio that records at a 96db dynamic range, which is a pretty decent level of digital sound. A camcorder acts as a kind of digital hub with the audio connectivity that it has on board.

Camera audio jacks are color coded on most models, so you can guess what they are without a score card:

- **Headphone jacks** These are green.
- **External microphone jacks** These are red, and a proper external microphone jack must offer plug-in power for those microphones that do not have their own built-in battery (check the product's specs).
- **Audio-Video jacks** These are yellow. Of the three plugs at the output end of the A/V connecting cable, the red and white plugs carry the left and right stereo audio channels. By connecting other units with these you can play back the audio through a TV or stereo system, or record the track on a tape recorder.

Camcorder microphones are designed to be directional. They record a field directly in front of the camera for about 20 to 30 feet. After that, the sound drops off.

Looking at the Advantages of Built-In Microphones

Although we are going to recommend other options in this chapter, built-in microphones actually have some important advantages:

- They are always there and never in the way.
- The camera is free from being tethered or encumbered by external microphone connections.
- They are fully compatible with your camcorder and automatically adjust volume and gain.

Looking at the Disadvantages of Built-in Microphones

On the other hand, not everything about the built-in mic is perfect. There are some serious limitations that can indeed hurt the quality of your videos:

- You can't place or position the built-in mic away from the camera to match or capture subject or action.
- They are configured within a design constraint—they must be very short in order to fit inside the camera case under the lens. This can limit sound quality.
- Even the high-end camcorders have microphones that do not have the accuracy of most mid-level external microphones, and will not capture the full CD-quality sound your videotape is capable of supporting.
- Built-in microphones may be vulnerable to wind noise.
- Some lower-end camcorders may have microphones that are not sufficiently isolated. The result is that your recordings will suffer from on-board machine noise, such as the sound of camera or zoom motors. Test for this by shooting a zoom sequence in a reasonably silent room. See if the playback returns equally as silent.

NOTE *You will also want to check published reviews of camcorders to see which ones have mics that are unusually sensitive to noises from the unit itself.*

External Microphones

An external microphone adds more cost and complexity to your setup, but it can also expand your range and professional control over the audio portions of your movie. You can design for richer and more dimensional sound that will support and reinforce the action.

NOTE *Here's an important option to consider. External microphones usually require the use of windscreens, which are foam cups or tubes that fit over the apertures and, for shotgun microphones, over the bodies as well. For exterior locations, there is wind, but even in the studio there are air currents from climate conditioning and floor action. In addition, when microphones are extremely close to the actor's mouths, they need to be protected from the pops and clicks that can occur from forceful dialog.*

For mobility, there are professional-quality camcorder microphones—both wired and wireless—in cardioid and shotgun configurations (see following). They mount on top of the camera case in the accessory shoe or an add-on mount. The variable microphone of Sony's ECM-HS1 Gun Zoom Microphone can be synchronized with the (Sony) camcorder's zoom feature to go from a cardioid to a shotgun focus in the same shot for audio-visual pickup of the zoomed subject.

Omnidirectional, or Omni, Microphones

The omni mic records a large bubble of sound from its source, as shown back in Figure 8-1. It picks up sound from just about every direction equally, and works about as well pointed away from the subject as it does pointed toward it—if the distances are equal, of course.

Omnis, like the one shown in Figure 8-2, are best suited for very "live" environmental, ambient and background sound, because they pick up all of the reverberation and echoes. In the field, they are better at resisting wind noise and mechanical or handling noise than directional microphones. Omnis are also less susceptible to "popping" caused by "plosives" in speech, such as *p*, *b* and *t*.

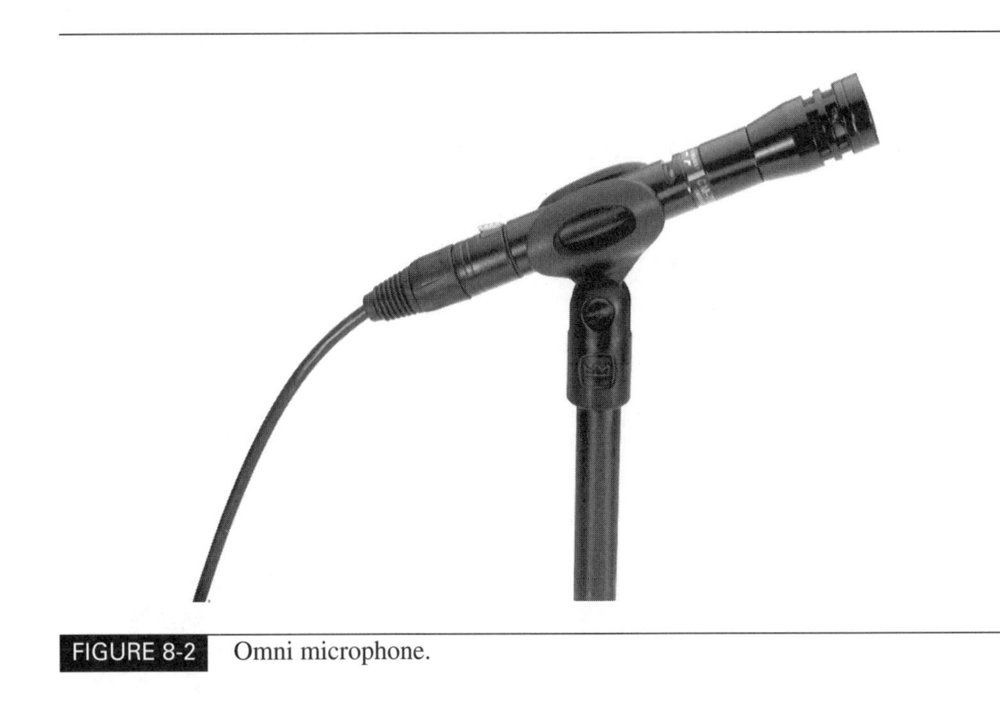

FIGURE 8-2 Omni microphone.

What Did They Say?

Have you ever used an external microphone with your camcorder and captured intermittent or no sound when recording? Here's good advice from audio visual provider United Visual:

"There is a good chance the problem is related to the external microphone jack. There is a lot of force put on the small external mic jack when a microphone is plugged into it. The weight of the mic cable alone can cause problems, but add to that someone tripping on the cord, or banging the protruding mic plug against something and you have a major problem. The jack itself is usually soldered to a circuit board inside, and this abuse will break the connections loose from the board. When this happens, your regular internal microphone will stop working or will work only intermittently when the jack happens to be making contact. This is because the jack has a built-in switch that disables the internal mic when an external one is used. To determine if this is your problem, try wiggling the jack with the tip of a pen while making a test recording. You will hear the sound cutting in and out if the jack is the culprit. The solution? Take the camcorder to a reputable service center and tell them where the problem is. The good news is, it is a relatively inexpensive repair."

Cardioid, or Directional, Microphones

Directional microphones, such as the one shown in Figure 8-3, are specially designed to respond best to sound from the front while tending to reject sound that arrives from other directions.

Shotgun Microphones

Also known as line, or unidirectional, microphones, shotguns can be focused over a long distance to accurately pick up a narrow sound, such as an actor's voice. Shotguns, an example of which is shown in Figure 8-4, receive that label because they are equipped with longer acoustic tubes than any other microphone.

CAUTION *It might be tempting to improvise a microphone windscreen. After all, they are just tubes of foam, aren't they? But not all foam is alike. Test it first. The same goes with improvising a windscreen for a built-in microphone. Taping a narrow strip of foam over the aperture might be just enough to break up the wind and make the difference, as long as you test it out first.*

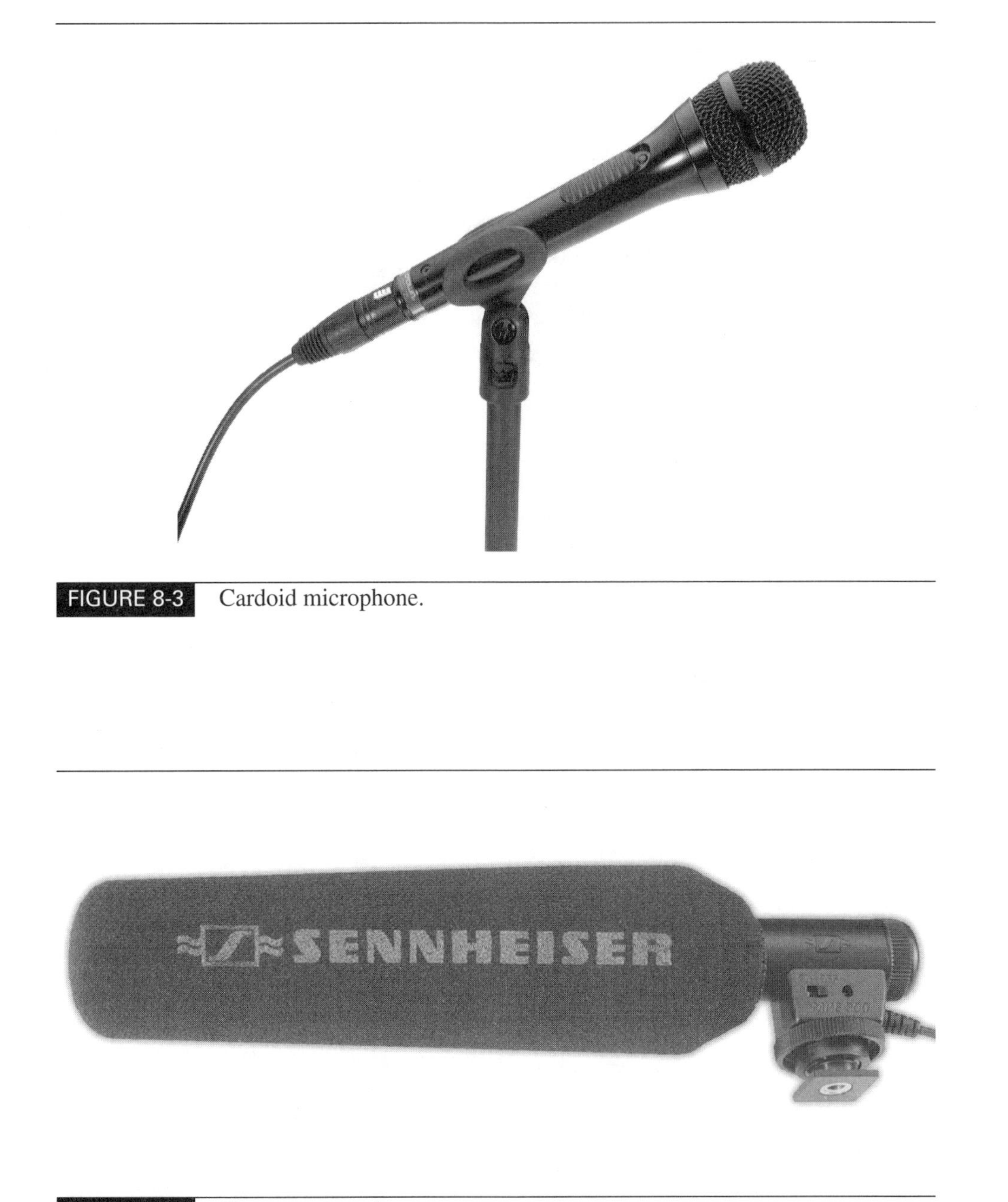

FIGURE 8-3 Cardoid microphone.

FIGURE 8-4 Shotgun microphone.

No Sound?

Check the audio input jack. Some camcorders have audio and video input jacks for making recordings from another VCR. In some cases, this jack has a built-in switch, just like the one described previously on the external mic jack, which disables the internal microphone. If you have a VCR and a dubbing cable with RCA/phono plugs on it you can make a test recording using these jacks. If you get sound on this recording, the problem may very well be the switch in the audio jack. Read the section above for more details on the cause and follow the "quick fix" instructions using a RCA/phono plug instead of a 3.5mm microphone plug to attempt to temporarily solve the problem.

Lavalier Microphones

Lavalier, or lapel microphones, or "lavs," are those clip-on miniature personal microphones that you may see worn by TV interviewees, panelists, and speakers (see Figure 8-5). They are very efficient semi-directional microphones that are designed to capture only the voice envelope of the person who is wearing one. They give a clean, condensed sound that can be better for processing for broadcast or Web.

What you don't see, but what the person wearing the mic feels, is the wire running down his or her torso or leg before it leads off to the microphone input or amplifier. What you really don't see are wireless lavs and, especially, ultraminiature lavs. These are connected to a body pack transmitter that contains batteries (see Figure 8-6). Such transmitters may need to be hidden in the actor's costume. Then you must then be alert to clothing noises.

NOTE *Wireless lavs have really liberated dramatic filming and all situations where there is a complexity of scenic elements, subject movement, and action with animals and vehicles.*

FIGURE 8-5 Lavalier microphone.

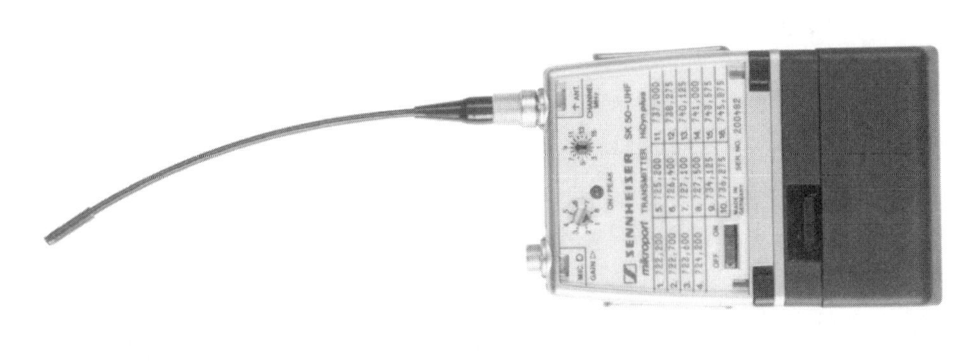

FIGURE 8-6 Wireless body pack.

Microphone Booms

Microphones mounted on a long pole, called a boom or a fishpole, are widely used in video and film to pick up sound when the microphone must be located outside the viewing angle of the camera. Any kind of microphone may be boom-mounted, but the most common are shotguns.

It takes a lot of patience and stamina to hold a position, sometimes hour after hour, and not let the pole, or its shadow, dip into the camera frame. Where possible, as in a studio, the microphone can be mounted on a boom arm stand, such as the one shown in Figure 8-7.

The crew member who handles the microphone boom, and often follows the action as it is moving, is called a boom operator.

NOTE *Which is better, a lav or a boom microphone? For drama, a mic on a boom captures a better mix of the actor's voice and the environmental tone, giving the shot a fuller dimension.*

Wireless Microphones

You may quickly pass the limits of how far you can stretch a microphone cord to reach a distant subject position, and you will need to go to wireless to record good quality sound. Wireless microphone systems can be rented. They can range from a single wireless lav and a small receiver that feeds into the camera's microphone input, to multiple microphone receiving, switching, and mixing stations (see Figure 8-8).

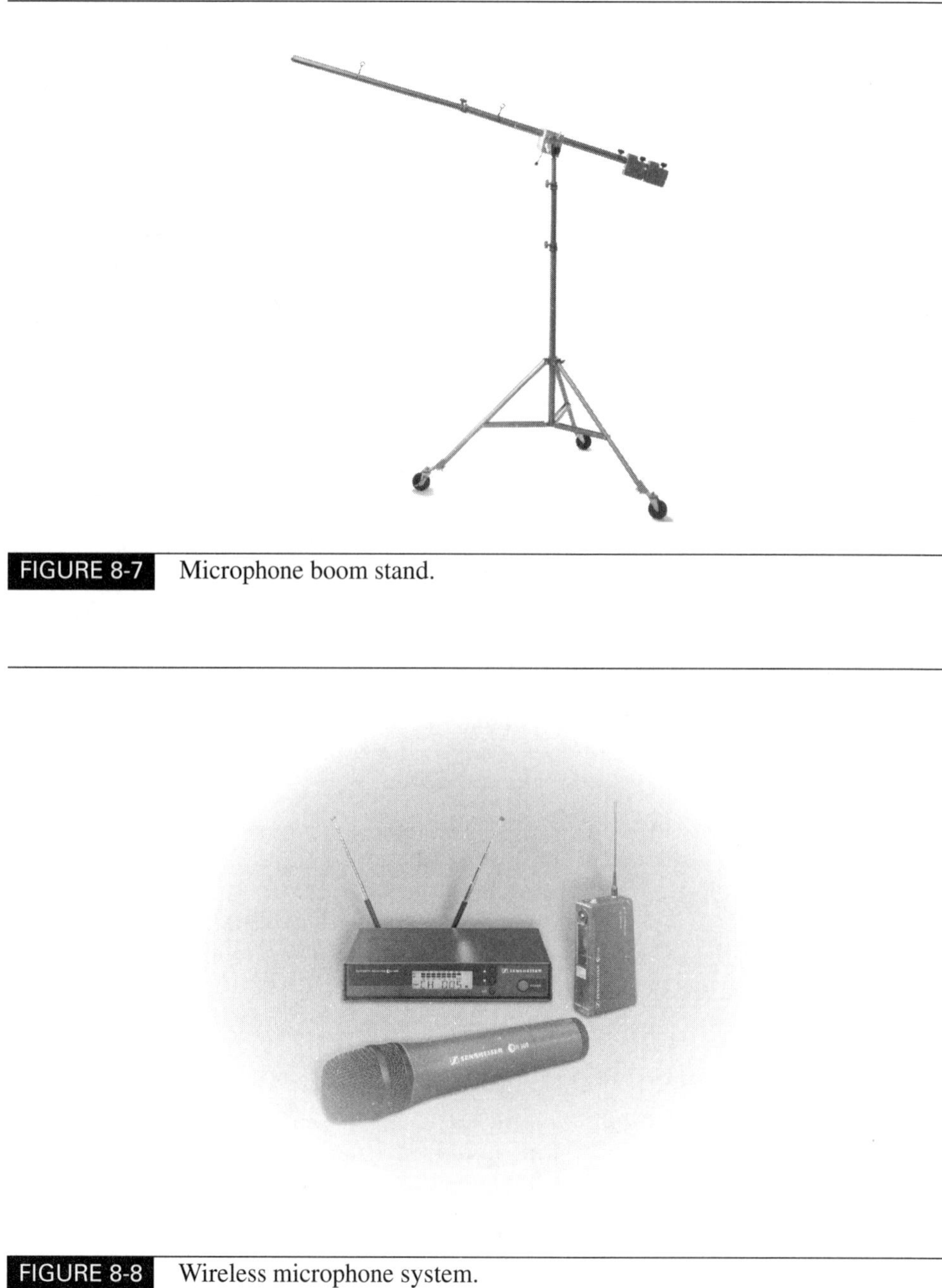

FIGURE 8-7 Microphone boom stand.

FIGURE 8-8 Wireless microphone system.

The practical maximum operating range of a wireless system varies from as little as 100 feet in heavily crowded indoor situations, to approximately 1,000 feet under open outdoor conditions.

Is there a downside to all this? Yes. Wireless systems are much more vulnerable to electric and electronic interference, which can sometimes come from unexpected sources such as ATMs, microwaves, and building security systems. Wireless frequencies are also shared with TV stations, communications equipment, and a large number of wireless microphone systems. Because of frequency sharing, there is always a chance that someone else in the area might be using the same frequency.

Audio Recorders

For both built-in and wired external microphones, the sound recording is integrated and synchronized with the video recording on the same tape, so you don't have to transfer the sound track for editing.

However, there may be production situations such as a sports event, a wedding, or other large event where you need to record sound from points very far away from the camera positions, and where wireless systems may not have the range needed by their antenna systems. Portable audio recorders can be used to pick up sound from those points, and the sound can be transferred later for editing.

This works as long as you don't need to have lipsynch (lip synchronization) communication with the camera, which is the most demanding of synchronization. Most sounds can be matched up to the picture in the editing or dubbing, but a close-up of a person speaking, if it is off by even one frame, will give the impression of a badly dubbed foreign film. A second similar camcorder may serve just as well—and give you yet another angle.

Using Double System Sound Recording

When the sound recording is captured by a separate, independent audio recorder, as is often the case in film and professional field video, the camera and the recorder must usually support a sync generator. This means that the wireless communication between camera and recorder is not sending the audio, as is the case in a wireless microphone system. It is sending a timing pulse signal that will remain consistent throughout the take. Portable professional DAT (Digital Audio Tape) recorders are most often used for double system sound, and can be rented in soundman kits.

When a theatrical movie is being shot, you may see a the second assistant cameraman thrust a slate, or clapper, in front of the lens, clap the frame down, and yell something like, "Scene three, take four!" That point will be the cue of the action and the place where the editor will match picture and sound.

But double system sync sound is one of those things that could be better left to larger budgets and bigger productions. For home movies and independent videos, try to limit your sound recording strategies to whatever can be fed, channeled, or mixed into the microphone input of your camcorder.

NOTE *The miniature blackboard with the chalked numbers in the hinged wooden frame that is the classical Hollywood slate has largely been replaced with electronic marker devices. Your own production could be well facilitated by the use of a simple notepad in front of the lens, as well as a verbal cue or clicker, to help mark your takes.*

Using MD Recorders for Field Work

One way to economically expand your field area of sound recording is with a miniature consumer MD (MiniDisc) recorder that has digital output, such the Sony MZR500PC MiniDisc player and recorder with USB PC link shown in Figure 8-9. These recorders can provide sound quality that is usually indistinguishable from sound produced by the much more expensive DATs. You should be able to match almost any cue in iMovie 2 that demands synchronization, short of lipsynch.

FIGURE 8-9 Sony's MZR500 MiniDisc player and recorder with USB PC link cable.

Monitoring Sound

One way to check on the sound recording in a shot is by playing it back and listening to the sound through the camcorder's internal speaker. By watching the picture on the LCD viewer, you can see how well the sound is relating to the action. But until you begin editing the footage in iMovie 2, you won't really be sure of the quality level of that sound recording.

The quality of a camcorder's speaker is not any better than the tiny internal speaker on a Mac. The best way to ensure that you are getting the sounds you want at the quality you demand, is to monitor your recording before and while filming. Wear a headset or pair of stereo headphones, like the one shown in Figure 8-10, which is plugged into the headphone jack on your camcorder. Just as what you see through the viewfinder is seeing what the camera will record, what you hear through the headphones is what the microphone hears and records.

NOTE *Even before recording, once your camera function is turned on, the microphone should be live. Then you can preview and test angles and positions to determine if you will get the right sounds for those shots. Just as important, you can preview for sound problems, such as interference or feedback from AC electrical sources, and intrusion noise such as traffic, vending machines, or a barking dog.*

FIGURE 8-10 Sennheiser stereo headphones.

Did You Know?

Sound designer Ben Burtt created the unique special effects sounds for the original *Star Wars.* Although the sequels had full budgets, we forget that George Lucas' original movie was shot on what today would be considered a shoestring budget, and the special effects people had to be especially creative to get the results they wanted.

Many effects were achieved by electronically modifying stock library sounds. Burtt transformed an elephant's bellow to become the screeching trajectory of a TIE Fighter, and blended segments of walruses and other animal sounds for the chesty roar of Chewbacca the Wookie.

But it was when he was out recording in the field, where his imagination could hear new wonders in ordinary sounds, that he did his signature work. The reverberations of his hammering on an antenna tower guy wire gave him laser blasts. Burtt spliced together the sounds of his TV set and an old 35 mm projector to create the *hummm* of a light saber, and he got the *whoosh* of Luke Skywalker's landspeeder by recording the roar of the Los Angeles Harbor Freeway heard through a vacuum-cleaner pipe.

Voice is the most important sound source to monitor because it can be the most deceptive. When you are actually filming, you may hear the actor or interviewee just fine. But that doesn't mean that the microphone can, or that there isn't some intrusive hum or rattle or wind noise that you will discover only upon playback. When you monitor the sound, you can focus your microphone for the best quality sound.

Using Your Camcorder as a Sound Recorder

Your camcorder, with its built-in stereo microphone, can double as a hand-held tape recorder for many sound-only applications. This can include sound recording for transfer to other media, as well as a more efficient way of capturing dialog, narration, room tone, ambient sound, and sound effects without needing to monitor the visual. But you should monitor the sound recording with headphones.

Here's some advice for using your camcorder to get good quality sound:

- **Shoot with the lens cap on** This will give you more freedom in the field, and cut down battery drain. Black footage is easy to recognize as sound-only shots in the editing stage.
- **Shoot insert cue shots** Shoot just a few frames of the person, object, or location whose sound you will be recording, then put the lens cap back on. This will help for reference in the editing.

- **Superimpose titles** If your camcorder has a superimpose titles function and a custom mode, you can identify shots on black footage with reference titles.
- **Card titles** Identify sound-only shots by shooting title cards. This is practical only in a studio and when using an external microphone. A card would probably get in the way of the built-in microphone.

Using Yourself as Sound: The Fine Art of Foley

You may feel sometimes that you are being asked to walk on fire to ever get your movie made, but it's more likely that you will walk on gravel, bubble wrap, or styrofoam egg cartons. You will be doing a Foley, named for Jack Foley, an old studio hand who made a fine art out of "recreating" sound effects. The Foley Artist can replace original sound completely or augment existing sounds to create a richer track. And virtually every movie and TV show you see—and hear—has a Foley track in the sound.

Unless you are recording your sequence with a low-mounted omnidirectional mic, its unlikely that your track will include all the secondary and tertiary noise of the action, such as footsteps, furniture movement, and the sounds of objects and props that the actors are using. The background noises of nature, traffic, or business activity must never be allowed to compete with voice. In fact, most sound for video recording is trying its best to capture dialog without the voice being compromised by any other interference.

Good micing focuses on and isolates the voice, even for whispers, sighs and gasps. Separate mics and tracks for ambient and background noise can be used, but it's not easy to include those decisive footsteps going down the corridor or that pivotal slap in the face.

Using digital technology in audio postproduction to clean up a dialogue track is time consuming and sometimes not possible. That's where ADR (Automated Dialogue Replacement) takes over and the dialogue editor conforms the ADR track with the sound effects, music, and all the rest, including the Foley track.

You may have already added some homemade sound effects to your movies with cheers, whistles, and applause. And by learning the basics of Foley, you can make a big difference in your sound track, making it more realistic where it counts—accentuating the action and defining the continuity.

Back in the early days of radio, before magnetic recording technology, all shows were live, including the colorful ranks of fifteen-minute adventure serials such as *The Lone Ranger*, *Bulldog Drummond*, and *Buck Rogers*. One corner of the broadcast studio would be set aside for the sound effects man and his Rube Goldberg jumble of odds and ends. A pair of coconut shells rattled on a wooden box would provide the sounds of galloping hoofbeats and a handful of cellophane crinkled close to the mic would emulate a campfire. Some things never change.

One of the first things you learn in Foleying, as in sound effects, is that not all sounds can be reliably re-generated from the object that made them. Inventive repurposing and improvisation is the rule. Said Foley artist Philip Rodrigues, seen in the studio in Figure 8-11, "Using many different kinds of shoes and lots of props—car fenders, plates, glasses, chairs, and just about anything I find at the side of the road—the Foley Artist can replace original sound completely or augment existing sounds to create a richer track."

Foley often creates sound effects as part of recreating action to match the continuity, but full sound effects go to the sound FX editor. Nowadays, that editor rarely creates a sound effects origin. Rather, he is more like a virtuoso theater organist, who plays from an enormous library of digital sound effects and various ways of modifying them. The Foley artist matches sounds to the action, which is looped on a rear projection screen in the studio. The scene loop is usually silent, but may have voice or cue tracks as well. The Foley artist here is as much of an actor as those who are visible in the final cut.

FIGURE 8-11 Foley artist Philip Rodrigues does the crunch.

Says Rodrigues; “Let’s say in a scene the actor grabs his gun, walks to his motorcycle, starts it up, and drives away...

- Foley would recreate these sounds: the leather jacket and jeans as the actor walks, footsteps (heavy cowboy boots!), the gun pickup and handling, handlebar grab and bike movement—and maybe the sound of some keys as one is slid into the lock.
- The sound FX editor would create the roar of the motorcycle engine starting and driving away, a tire squeal, and background ambiances (birds, wind etc.).
- In an ADR studio the actor would rerecord his line, ‘I’ll be back...,’ which was inaudible on location with the motorcycle engine running. The dialogue editor would conform the production and ADR into one. When played together, the tracks produce a seamless tapestry of sound.”

The Closing Scene

Getting good quality sound for your movie requires attention to detail and constant monitoring during the recording process. It also requires a touch of imagination. But as you discovered in this chapter, it doesn’t require expensive equipment to achieve clear, crisp dialog and atmospheric sound effects.

In our next chapter, you will begin to discover how you can bring your footage into iMovie 2 and get superlative results.

Part III

Editing Your iMovies

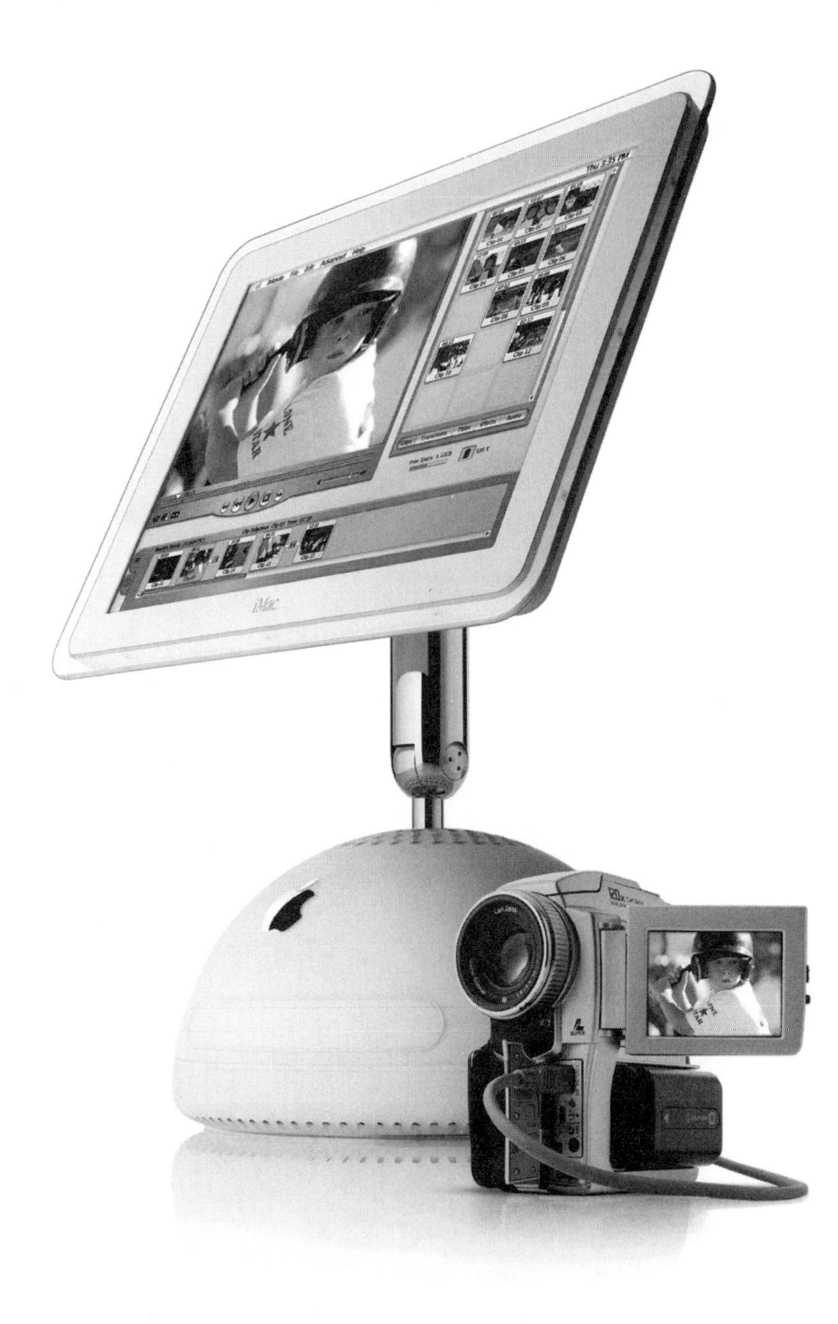

Chapter 9

Working With iMovie 2

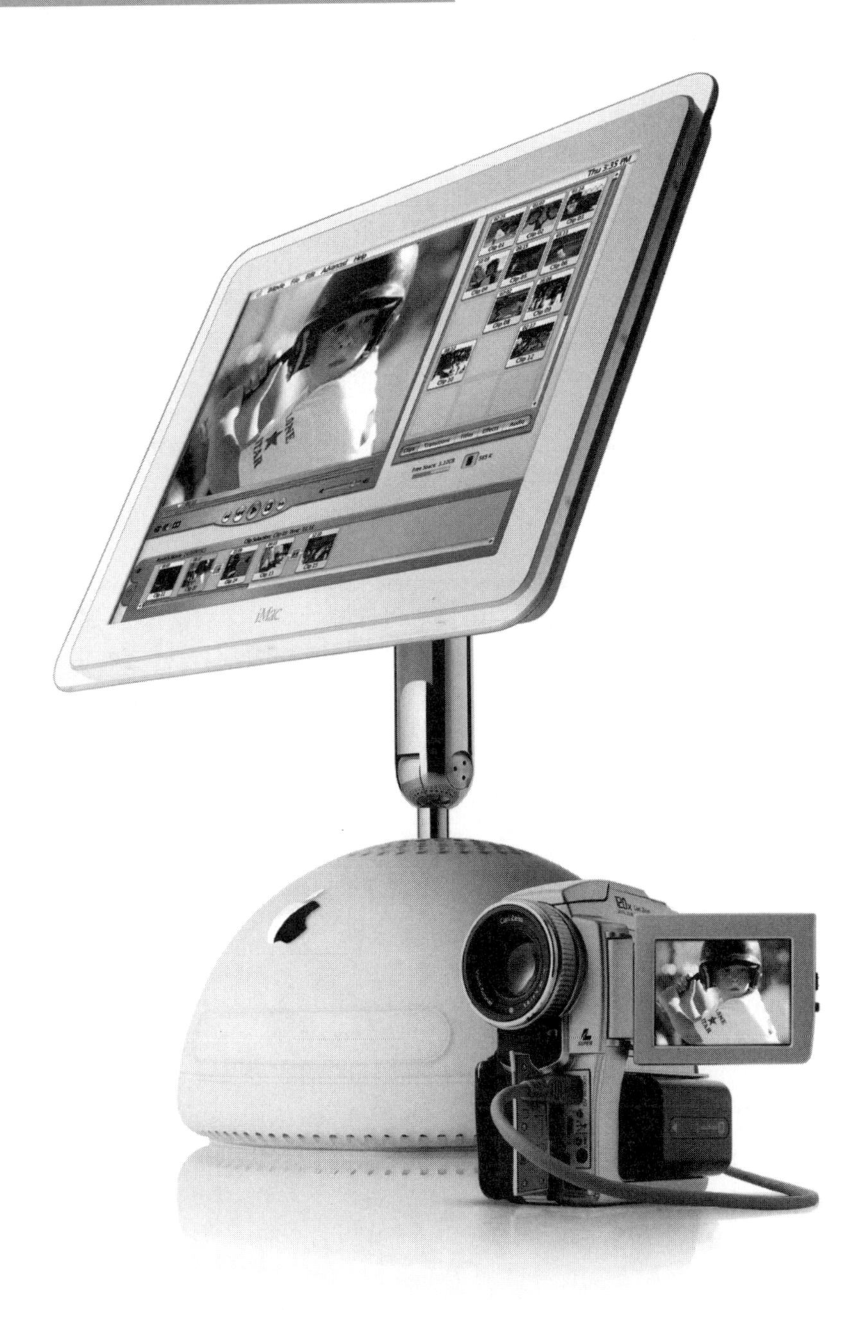

How to...

- Discover the Menus of iMovie 2
- Select preferences
- Capture a still frame
- Create a new project
- Install Plug-Ins

There are a wide variety of subjects and topics that you can make movies about using iMovie 2 for editing. Once complete, your own works become part of the great traditions of film, video and home movies.

In previous chapters, you've learned how to get your FireWire-equipped Macintosh ready for digital video. You discovered how to select the camcorder that best suits your needs and your budget. Armed with this basic tool of the trade, you then learned how to plan your productions with treatments, scripts and storyboards, and then scout locations and audition your talent to develop your concepts for the screen.

But assembling equipment and talent is only the beginning. You then learned how to support and move your camera to properly frame the action, and the best ways to expose the picture and record the sound.

Once you have that all-important footage to edit, you're ready to bring in iMovie 2.

In this chapter, we will begin to focus on iMovie 2 and how it gives you the organizational options to show the story that you want to tell using the footage you've shot. First, we'll review the menu commands, so you can see what choices are available as you begin to work with your project in iMovie 2's clip shelf. We will then take you through the process of adding audio and video effects and making titles, as your movie moves closer to completion.

A Look at the Parts of iMovie 2

For an application that is a complete audio-visual editing studio, iMovie 2 presents a very compact and orderly workspace, as you see in Figure 9-1. You are able to do all of the viewing, organizing and editing operations here without needing to leave the iMovie desktop and go to other menus and windows.

FIGURE 9-1 iMovie 2 puts your entire workspace in a single set of application windows.

NOTE

Because iMovie 2 takes over you entire desktop, it could make it harder if you are working with other applications as part of your movie project such as Microsoft Word for scripts, AppleWorks for storyboards and Adobe Photoshop for graphics. This is one instance where having a second monitor, as we discussed in Chapter 2, could make a big difference. Under Mac OS X, iMovie 2 even hides the Dock, which doesn't show up until you move the mouse down to where it's lodged.

You will be working with iMovie 2 often, so it should be easily and quickly available on your desktop. When you install Mac OS X 10.1 or later, the icon for iMovie 2 should be present and accounted for in the Dock. If it's not there, just drag the iMovie 2's icon from your Mac OS X Applications folder and drop it on the Dock.

To get started, just click the iMovie 2 icon in the Dock or double-click its icon in the Applications folder. The first time the application launches, the iMovie 2 Introduction will open with the iMovie 2 QuickTime splash movie and the introductory menu (see Figure 9-2).

The choice you'll want to make is the third, Open Tutorial, which brings us to the topic of the next section of this chapter.

FIGURE 9-2 Four choices from iMovie 2's introductory screen.

NOTE *No Tutorial button? Well, it only appears if you get iMovie 2 with your new Mac or order a copy of the CD version from Apple. Under Mac OS X, you may have to manually open your tutorial project from the copy of iMovie 2 installed in your Applications (Mac OS 9 folder), the place where older, Classic applications are usually stored. Even if you don't have the tutorial at hand, you can use the information offered here to help you get started using iMovie 2.*

Tutorial

Apple's Tutorial is a good example of a typical movie project and we'll be using it throughout this introduction to the iMovie 2 application. But the Tutorial isn't a movie—yet. As you can see in the Shelf shown back in Figure 9-1, it is a collection of six clips or shots, the raw footage so to speak. In Chapter 10, you will learn how to organize this raw footage into many different rhythms of small stories as you create your finished movie.

TIP *An iMovie document may contain an entire edited movie, or just a simple collection of unedited clips. If you double-click on it, it will open as a playable QuickTime movie window. You could place as many of these QuickTime movie windows as you want on any desktop, as a way of displaying and analyzing several motion clips, side-by-side, independent of the iMovie application, as long as QuickTime is installed on the computer.*

The Geography of iMovie 2

When you import your footage into iMovie 2 (and you'll more about that process beginning in Chapter 10), the clips from your chosen camera shots are first placed, stored, and organized in the Shelf. There are 15 panes that are visible within the Shelf frame, but you can store many more clips, scrolling up and down to reach them, the number of them limited only by memory.

NOTE *Any selected clip, such as the one with the picture of the dog in the Shelf shown in Figure 9-1, is highlighted with a yellow frame. You can click-and-drag the clips anywhere within the Shelf to sort and organize them. Delete by dragging a clip to the Project Trash or by selecting* COMMAND+DELETE.

TIP *Would you like to see a movie clip full screen? Selecting the Full-Screen button located to the right of the playback button, will start playing the clip, expanding to fill the screen of your monitor, and automatically returning you to iMovie 2's Monitor window on the desktop when the clip comes to its end.*

Let's tour the Monitor window first.

The Monitor window will display the first frame of the selected clip. Click the Play button to view clip in the Monitor, or click the Full Screen button to its right for a grander view, and at a size closer to a preview of what your audience will see.

The Volume slider to the right of the playback buttons will control the sound of playback, and of any sound effects you may want to try out. The Edit mode is selected here, the one you see when you are editing clips that you've imported into iMovie.

NOTE *If you click the little button at the lower left of the Monitor window and move it to the DV position, you'll be in Camera mode, where you can capture your clips from your camcorder. We'll tell you more about it in Chapter 10.*

The window at the right is Clip Viewer, where you store your shots, and the window at the bottom is the Timeline, where clips, titles, effects, transitions and other parts of your movie are assembled and previewed.

A Look at the Menus of iMovie 2

Most of iMovie 2's menus are clear and self-explanatory, and they efficiently take care of a lot of commands and functions in a few words. You would have many more menus and windows to deal with in a professional editing program like Apple's Final Cut Pro, an application that, by its nature, also requires a bit of a learning curve to master.

Instead of putting the menus in the back of the book, here is a listing that will give you a good initial familiarization with what's to come, and as a reference to come back to. We will go into more detail when we cover each of these menu topics.

iMovie Menu

Under Mac OS X, the iMovie 2 menu (see Figure 9-3) lists commands that address program-wide functions (similar commands may be found in the File and Edit menus of the Classic Mac OS version).

Preceded by the iMovie splash screen, the About iMovie window reveals what version of iMovie you have. The version being covered here is 2.1.1. The

FIGURE 9-3 The iMovie menu has basic program-wide functions.

other settings are standard for Mac OS X application, if needed to grab content for your project.

The final function is used to quit iMovie 2 (or just use COMMAND+Q if you prefer the keyboard method). If you're using Mac OS 9.*x*, the same command is found in the File menu.

NOTE *If you don't have the latest and greatest, check for updates at Apple's Web site. iMovie 2 2.1.1 is the version included when you install Mac OS X 10.1. We suggest you update, even if you're not using Mac OS X, because the newer version contains performance enhancements and bug fixes.*

The Preferences Dialogs

Unlike some programs, iMovie 2's Preferences dialog boxes are not complicated with lots of choices, but they provide enough sophistication to get the job done. Just click on any of the four (or three) available tabs to bring up a dialog box covering that category. Let's have a look:

- **Import Preferences** Your choices are shown in Figure 9-4. The first, *Automatically start new clip at scene break,* is an important feature that breaks up your camera footage into scenes as you import it, rather than coming in as one large piece of footage that you have to take apart manually. *Still Clips* lets you specify shots you took that are intended as stills and to delete scraps.

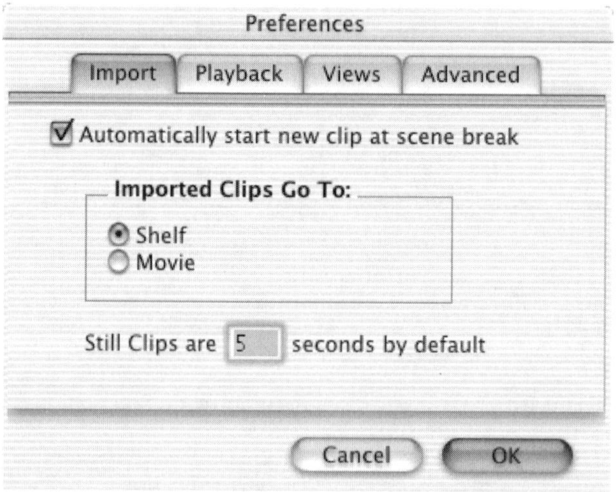

FIGURE 9-4 iMovie 2's Import Preferences offer only a few options.

- **Playback Preferences** The Video Settings dialog box (see Figure 9-5) gives you a Smoother Motion option for speedier playback at the expense of lower quality video on Macs without the fastest graphic cards, or Better Image, which emphasizes picture quality over playback speed.

NOTE *Is something missing? The Playback settings aren't available on faster Macs, since they have graphics chips (such as the NVIDIA GeForce2 MX or ATI Radeon) that are speedy enough to support good playback speeds at the maximum possible picture quality. So if you don't see this setting, don't be concerned; it just means you don't need it.*

- **Views Preferences** The Views preference box provides more options for seeing or not seeing information while editing. The Show More Details option, for example, will display both clip names and the duration of the clips in the Timeline window (see Figure 9-6).
- **Advanced Preferences** The final Preference tab (see Figure 9-7) has three important editing-related settings. You can separate audio from video in a clip, filter out extraneous sounds when importing, and play the video on your camcorder and in iMovie 2.

FIGURE 9-5 Weigh quality against speed when you select your video settings on a slower Mac.

FIGURE 9-6 iMovie 2's Views Preferences are limited to just four checkboxes.

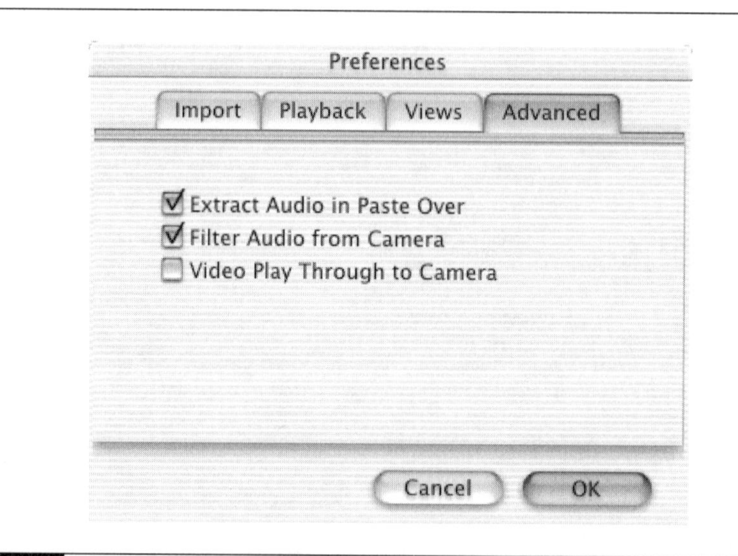

FIGURE 9-7 Choose your Advanced Preferences settings here.

iMovie 2's File Menu

The File menu (shown in Figure 9-8) offers a standard range of project editing choices:

- **New Project** (COMMAND+N) Create and name your new movie project.
- **Open Project** (COMMAND+O) Just what the command implies.
- **Save Project** (COMMAND+S) Save the work you've done in that project.
- **Export Movie** (COMMAND+E) You can record a movie from the desktop to a tape in your camera, to QuickTime (in various resolutions, depending on the quality level you want), or to VHS tape.
- **Save Frame As** (COMMAND+F) Affects just the selected frame.
- **Import File** (COMMAND+I) Use this command to import clips from your camcorder and many different types of media documents from other sources that you have on your Mac or on a networked drive.
- **Get Clip Info** (COMMAND+SHIFT+I) Discover more information about the clip you're working on.
- **Empty Trash** No, this isn't the system Trashcan. This command simply deletes the clips and other elements you've dragged to iMovie 2's own trash bin.

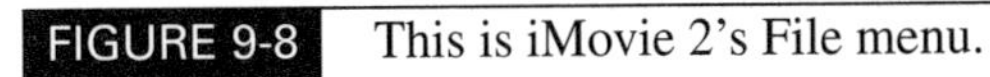

FIGURE 9-8 This is iMovie 2's File menu.

iMovie 2's Edit Menu

The Edit menu (shown in Figure 9-9) is also familiar territory and similar to what you'll see in other Mac applications.

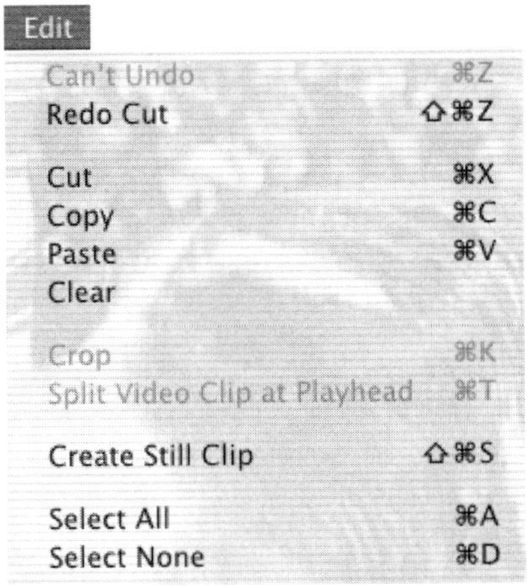

FIGURE 9-9 Here's iMovie 2's Edit menu.

The first group of commands are the ones you'll find in most any Mac application. In addition, iMovie 2 offers the following:

- **Crop** **COMMAND+K** This is used to grab just a portion of a frame.
- **Split Video at Playhead** **COMMAND+T** This command allows you to divide any clip into two or more clips. The Playhead is the marker that shows what frame you are on in a movie or a clip.
- **Create Still Clip** **SHIFT+COMMAND+S** Use this command to select any frame anywhere from among your clips, and it will appear as a still on the Shelf and also saved on your Mac's desktop as a PICT file. Still frames can be used as insert sequences in your movie, and even to create a slide show.

Advanced Menu

These commands (see Figure 9-10), apply a set of special purpose functions to help add special features to your project.

- **Extract Audio** **COMMAND+J** This command is used to separate the audio from your clip, so you can insert it into another place when editing your movie.
- **Paste Over at Playhead** **SHIFT+COMMAND+V** This command lets you paste a selected clip within another clip at the point at which you put the playhead.
- **Lock Audio Clip at Playhead** **COMMAND+L** You can use this command to precisely position an audio clip at a given point in your film.
- **Reverse Clip Direction** **COMMAND+R** As the title implies. This can be used to create some very interesting effects, as you can well imagine.
- **Restore Clip Media** If you want, this command puts things back the way it was originally.

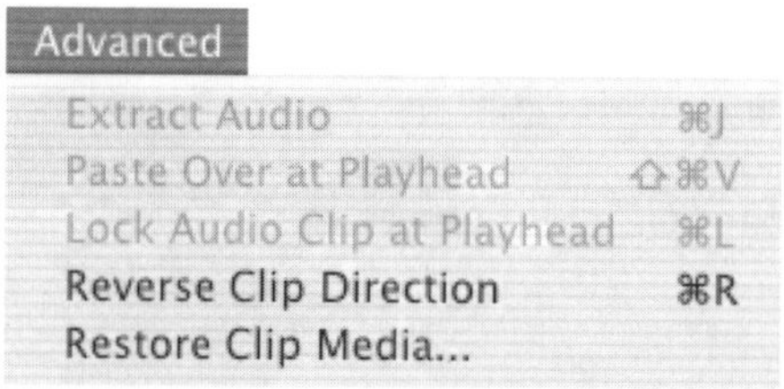

Advanced
Extract Audio ⌘J
Paste Over at Playhead ⇧⌘V
Lock Audio Clip at Playhead ⌘L
Reverse Clip Direction ⌘R
Restore Clip Media...

FIGURE 9-10 The Advanced menu.

Help

iMovie 2's Help feature, like many Mac programs, uses Apple's Help Viewer (see Figure 9-11) to provide quick definitions and explain functions for many parts of the application. Everything is just a single click away, by arrow or link. You can also get direct links to Apple's Web site for further information (this requires an Internet connection of course).

Installing Plug-in Packs

Plug-in Packs are software packages of extras and resources for iMovie 2. Such packages include animal sounds, additional backgrounds, effects, transitions, titles, music and sound effects. There are only a few so far, and most have come from Apple, although, in theory, third parties could provide their own enhancements.

FIGURE 9-11 This is iMovie 2's Help feature.

You can discover the latest and greatest add-ons for iMovie 2 by visiting Apple's iMovie Website at http://www.apple.com/imovie/.

To install plug-ins for iMovie under Mac OS X, just follow these instructions:

1. If iMovie 2 is running, quit the application.
2. Locate the Library folder inside your Home or Users folder.
3. Look for a folder labeled iMovie. If it's not there, go to the File menu and select New Folder, to make an "Untitled" folder and name it iMovie.
4. If you just created an iMovie folder or there is no Plug-ins folder present, make one, following the instructions in step 3.
5. Drag your iMovie Plug-in Pack and place it in the Plug-ins folder. The plug-ins will be available for the user who logs in under this directory next time iMovie 2 is launched.

CAUTION *The installation process we're describing only affects an individual User's or Home folder. If you want to have the plug-ins work system-wide, locate the Library folder at the top or root level of your Mac's hard drive, and then follow the instructions above to set up an iMovie folder. You'll need administrator's access to your Mac to create these folders and place files inside them.*

To install iMovie plug-ins under Mac OS 9.*x*, follow these directions:

1. If the application is running, quit iMovie 2.
2. On your hard disk, open your iMovie folder, and locate the folder labeled Resources and then the folder inside labeled Plugins.
3. Now drag the folder containing the iMovie add-ons into the Plugins folder.
4. Divide the contents of the add-ons folder into the appropriate category, such as the Effects Plug-Ins in the Effects folder, the Titles into the Titles folder, and so-on.

The next time you launch iMovie, the new plug-ins will be available along with the standard range of editing features as if they were built-in parts of the application.

NOTE

In addition to Apple's homegrown plug-in enhancements for iMovie 2, third parties are getting into the act. Virtix Inc. (http://www.virtix.com/) is marketing two packages of plug-ins. One, Bravo, incorporates 20 special effects including some pretty fancy laser, lighting, and smoke visualizations. The other, Echo, sports 18 transitions. Both products are available for sale from the company's Web site.

The Closing Scene

In this chapter, you discovered the various menu bar commands for iMovie 2, and the preferences available to enhance your work and simplify the editing process. You also learned how to add special plug-ins to add new dimensions to iMovie 2's feature-set.

In the next chapter, you will begin to work on your first editing project, first by importing video clips from your camcorder or from a movie file.

Chapter 10 Importing Video

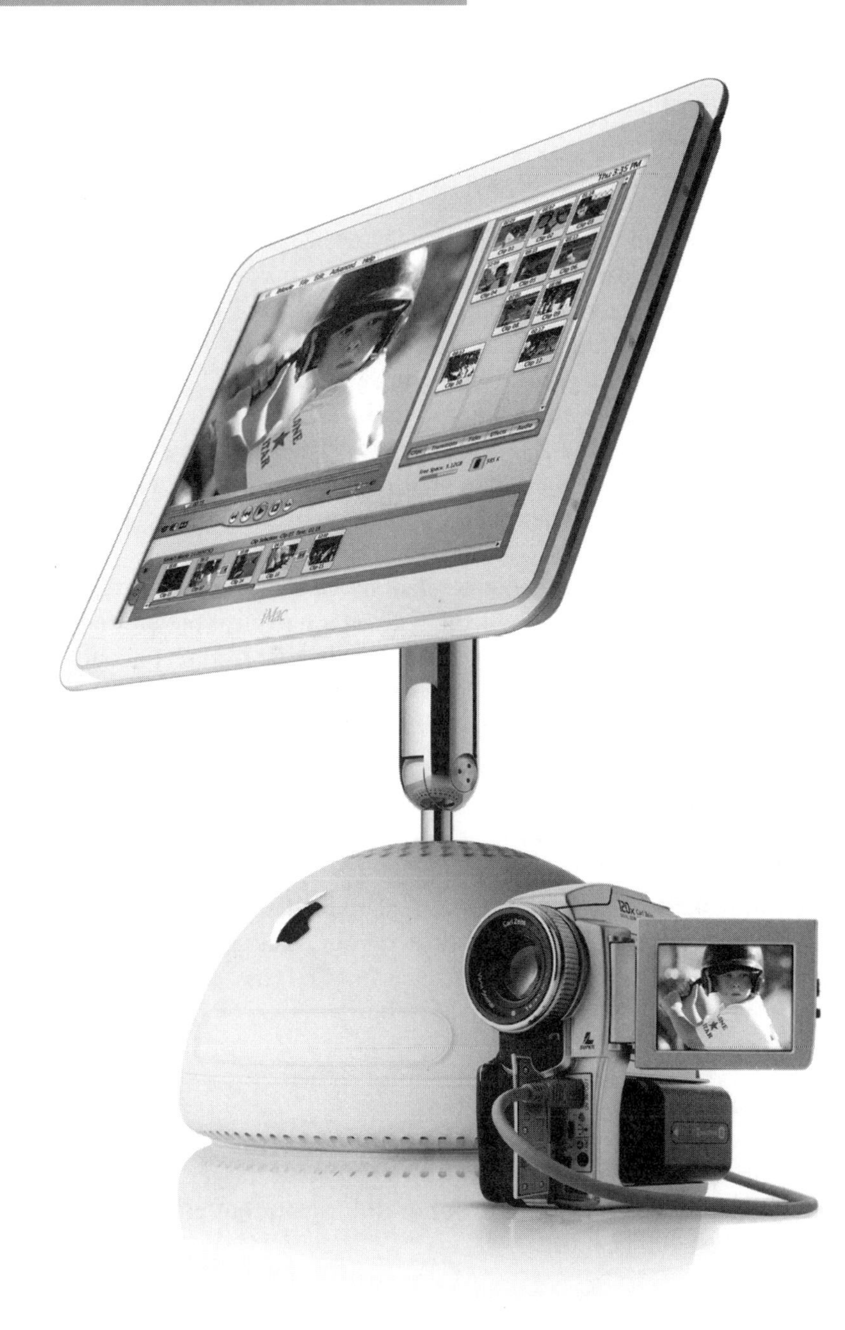

How to...

- Preview and crop footage
- Import video into iMovie 2
- Restore clip media
- Control Automatic Scene Detection
- Rename clips

It's here, where the FireWire meets the Mac, that iMovie 2 takes center stage. Because iMovie 2 gives you such a clear and easy path to editing, it makes all that production work you've done in capturing your footage worthwhile.

In this chapter, you'll setup and connect your camcorder with a FireWire cable to your Mac, and begin to edit by playing your camera footage to cue and review. A handy chart of shortcut commands will give you tips that will be helpful throughout iMovie 2. You'll also discover how importing the parts of the tape that you want can be done, thus creating the clips on the Shelf or lined up in the Clip Viewer. You'll understand how Automatic Scene Detection works in this process, and a way to turn it off when you want to.

Among the features you'll read about are the Free Space gauge, which keeps you up-to-date on file storage, and the Trash icon that you use to clear out unwanted footage for good (unless you use the Restore Clip Media first feature, of course).

As you learn the various ways to rename your clips, you will become more familiar with iMovie 2's files forms, which will be extremely helpful, because you will be creating many of them in your future movies.

Importing Video From Your Camcorder

Compared to filmmaking and professional video, taking the route the footage you just shot in your camcorder to individual clips on your desktop ready to edit, is like blinking through a Star Trek transporter. It's that fast and easy.

Setup and Connect

To capture those clips, you begin here:

1. Plug in the AC Power Adapter, or Battery Pack Charger, to your camcorder. Not only will you avoid draining your battery (and you

don't want to run out before you've captured all your frames), but you can charge it up at the same time.

CAUTION *We can't overemphasize the value of using that power adapter. Some camcorders have batteries with notoriously short life spans.*

2. Connect your camcorder to your computer with a FireWire cable.
3. Set your camcorder's power switch to its VCR, or VTR, mode.

Whatever kind of AC or charging system your camcorder may use, give it time to power up before you start importing your tape.

4. Insert the tape that you want to transfer, into your camcorder.
5. In iMovie 2, slide the little mode button below the iMovie 2 Monitor window from Edit mode to Camera mode. The Monitor window will change to blue, the Play head and Scrubber Bar will be replaced with the Import button.
6. When you see the Camera Connected message in the Monitor window (see Figure 10-1), you are ready to go.

Solving "Camera Disconnected" Problems

In the normal course of events, your camcorder should be immediately recognized, so you can check out your scenes and capture your footage.

But there may be situations where you just get a "Camera Disconnected" message instead, even though you are certain your camcorder is properly connected and switched on. If you encounter this sort of problem, you'll want to consider these solutions:

- **Is the Camcorder Compatible?** This is the big issue, and just because it may have a FireWire interface (usually labeled as IEEE 1394 or i.LINK), it's possible the unit may have compatibility problems with the Mac OS or iMovie 2. Apple keeps a current list of compatible camcorders (and a list of fixes for those partly compatible) at this Website: http://www.apple.com/imovie/shoot.html. If you've purchased a camcorder not on this list, you'll want to contact your dealer or the manufacturer about compatibility.

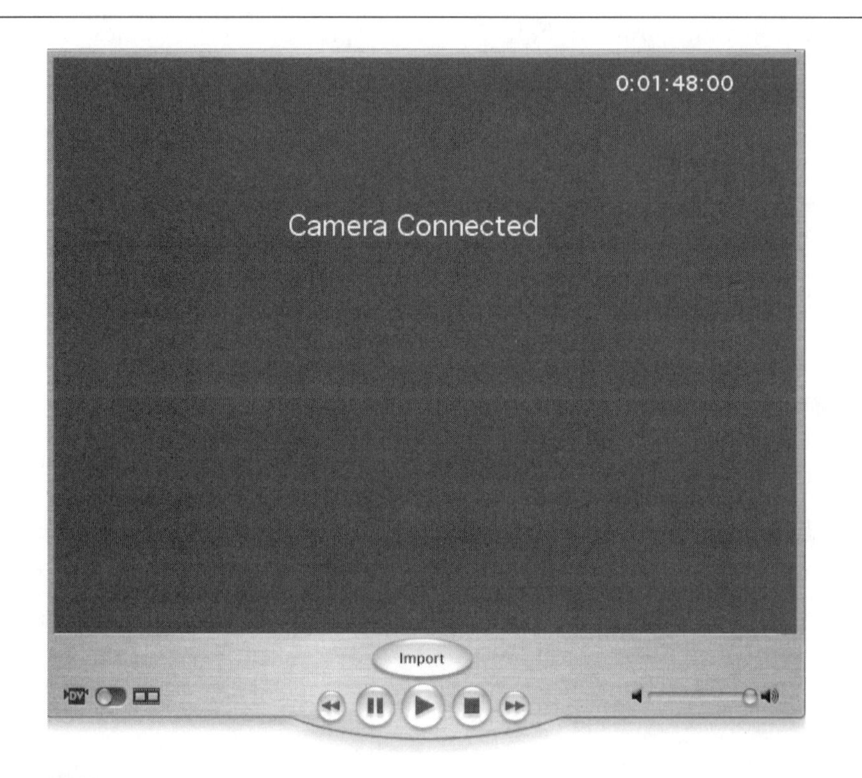

FIGURE 10-1 The Camera Connected message means that all systems are go for importing video.

- **Not Plugged In?** The standard syndrome. You plug it in the night before, but someone pulls out the FireWire plug behind your Mac while cleaning up the office. Double check all connections from camcorder to Mac. If you have another cable handy, give it a try. Also make sure that the AC adapter is properly connected. If it's hooked up to a power strip other than the one from which your Mac is running, make sure the power strip is on (it'll usually have a light to show it's powered on, but cheaper power strips have no visual indication at all).
- **Not Turned On?** Make sure the camcorder is on and in the VCR or VTR mode. Sometimes just turning the unit on or off again will establish a connection. You may also want to move iMovie 2's mode switch to Edit and then back to Camera.
- **FireWire Voodoo?** It's not just the SCSI standard that's subject to erratic behavior and inability to recognize attached devices. It sometimes happens

on busy FireWire ports as well. Rather than go through a long period of diagnostics, try just putting the camcorder on its own FireWire port (if you have a Mac with just one, such as the iBook, disconnect other devices). See if the camcorder is recognized that way. If you're using Mac OS 9.*x*, be sure that Apple's FireWire extensions have been enabled. You can check by launching Extensions Manager (available via the Apple menu, by choosing Control Panels) and seeing if the items labeled FireWire are checked. Either way a restart never hurts.

Previewing Your Scenes

Before you begin to import (capture) footage into iMovie 2, you'll want to double-check your clips to make sure that everything came out all right and to confirm the segments you want to bring into iMovie 2.

First click on the triangular Play button in the center (see Figure 10-2). It works like a remote control, and lets you play and preview your tape from your camcorder.

FIGURE 10-2 Before you import, you are free to play and preview the scenes on your tape.

iMovie 2 Playback Shortcuts

You don't have to point and click to shuttle through your video. iMovie 2 includes a healthy number of keyboard shortcuts that will simplify navigation through your footage. By using these shortcuts, you'll be able to pinpoint precisely a start and end point.

Here's the list:

iMovie Playback Shortcut Commands	
Play/Stop and Start/Stop Capture	Space bar
Playhead to beginning of movie	Home (not available on some keyboards)
Move Playhead to end of movie	End (not available on some keyboards)
Forward one frame	Right Arrow
Back one frame	Left Arrow
Forward ten frames	SHIFT+Right Arrow
Back ten frames	SHIFT+Left Arrow
Roll playhead forward	Hold down Right Arrow
Roll playhead backward	Hold down Left Arrow
Fast forward	COMMAND+]
Rewind	COMMAND+[
Sound volume up	Up Arrow
Sound volume down	Down Arrow
Delete clip	DELETE
Restore clip	COMMAND+Z

Use the iMovie controls to fast-forward, pause, and rewind to find the segments you want to use. Cue your tape to the start point where you want to import the scenes that you will be editing. If you have a lot of dead space footage on that tape, here is where you can plan on strategic cropping and selective importing.

Importing Video

Once you've established the start and stop points for a segment, you're ready to import it into iMovie 2, which means the actual clip will be copied to your Mac's hard drive.

Here's how to do it:

1. Click on the Import button, or press the spacebar on your keyboard, to start and stop importing. When you pause to stop capture, the Monitor will return to blue and the tape's time code will be displayed in the upper right-hand corner of the screen.

NOTE *As each clip is imported, a new clip will appear on the Shelf. The first clip will be numbered "Clip 01" and each one that follows will be consecutively numbered (see Figure 10-3). The first image of the clip will be displayed in the clip's frame. At the upper left corner, the length of the clip, in seconds, will be displayed. During the importing process, you will see the clip time increase until its end. Every clip reveals its duration with that time signature.*

2. Click Import again to stop the video capture process.

FIGURE 10-3 As you import your first scene, the first clip appears on the Shelf.

3. To end your importing session, switch from Camera mode to Edit mode.

NOTE *When you stop importing a scene before it is completed, it is the same thing as splitting a clip. That is, the clip that was created when you started importing that shot will end. If you resume importing, a new clip will appear on the Shelf starting at the point in the shot where you had stopped.*

Saving Clips to the Clip Viewer

If you'd rather save your clips directly to the Clip Viewer at the bottom of the iMovie 2 screen instead of the Shelf, follow these steps:

1. Go the iMovie 2 menu or the Edit menu with the Mac OS 9.*x* version.
2. Select Preferences to bring up the Preferences dialog box.
3. Click the Import tab.
4. Choose Imported Clips Go To: Movie.

Now the clips will be created one after another in a row in the Clip Viewer. If your shots were taken consecutively (the exact sequence you want for the finished video) you will be ready to edit your footage much quicker.

Automatic Scene Detection

iMovie 2 learned one of its best tricks from Final Cut Pro, where Apple developed Automatic Scene Detection. This is a very desirable capability for professional editing software. Instead of an entire tape streaming in as one long, huge document, where you would then have to slice and dice to separate one clip from another, Automatic Scene Detection does it, well, automatically.

Like those viewer-friendly VCR's that can skip commercials while taping, Automatic Scene Detection senses the change signal from the end of one scene to the beginning of the next. Here it is achieved by reading the time code that the camcorder's electronics write on each shot that you take, sensing when you switched from pause or standby to record mode and back again. But you may have a very good reason for wanting to defeat that measure, at least for a selected section of a tape, or even an entire tape, which would mean that all of the footage is captured on a single clip.

To switch off Automatic Scene Detection, follow these steps:

1. Go the iMovie menu or the Edit menu for the Mac OS 9.*x* version.
2. Choose Preferences, to open the Preferences dialog box.
3. Click the Import tab.
4. Uncheck Automatically start new clips at scene break. This will disable the feature and allow you to capture all that footage as a single clip.

NOTE *Be sure to activate Automatic Scene Detection if you want to turn on iMovie 2's ability to split clips at their proper break points. In addition, don't forget to set your camcorder's internal clock. This feature requires your camcorder's internal time code; flashing 12:00s won't do!*

About the Free Space Gauge

When you are importing footage, you are creating and storing iMovie 2 files on your hard drive. The free space gauge, located underneath the shelf, will give you up-to-date and running status on available storage space.

Here's how the gauge is set up:

- **Green** Space available.
- **Yellow** Nearing limit of available space.
- **Red** Disk is full.

When your free space gauge starts flashing yellow, it's time to think, and act, ahead. The first place to look for more disk space to accommodate your incoming clips is to the right of the gauge with the Trash icon. If you've trashed files but haven't emptied them, choose Empty Trash from iMovie 2's File menu to get rid of the footage.

CAUTION *Before you pull the plug (empty the Trash), take a moment to consider. Are there any edits you made in a clip that you may have second thoughts about? If so, take another look. Once you empty the Trash, they are gone with the wind.*

If there isn't enough storage space to be gained by deleting unwanted clips, then you will have to go back to your hard drive to see what you can delete to free up more space.

The readout to the right of the Trash icon reveals exactly how much storage space is taken up with discarded clips and stills. If there is any amount of storage space being taken up there, you'll want to empty the trash to free up that space.

Restoring Clip Media

Say you've deleted a bunch of clips and now you want to reuse the material you've discarded. Here's what to do:

1. Select the clip to be restored.

NOTE *There's no partial route here. You must restore all the edits that were shaved off of the clip to the state of a fully restored clip. Sort them out after the rescue.*

2. Go to the Advanced Menu.
3. Choose Restore Clip Media.
4. Confirm. The dialog will tell you exactly how much time is available at the beginning and at the end of the clip, as you see in Figure 10-4.

Confirm

This will restore the underlying media that was trimmed or split from this clip. 02:25 available at end of clip.

Okay to restore?

Cancel Restore

FIGURE 10-4 This will be your chance to restore that clip before it goes.

Renaming Your Clips

Now that you have your footage collected, all of your clips are named generically, such as Clip 01, etc. Being able to rename the clips beyond simple number identification will help greatly to prepare you for all the editing to come, as that, and the thumbnail preview in the clip, will ease the identification process.

Here's how to rename a clip in the Shelf or in the Clip Viewer:

1. Select the clip.
2. Select the label area in the bottom of the frame.
3. Enter the new name.
4. Deselect the clip.
5. Repeat the above four steps for each clip you want to rename. When you're finished (see Figure 10-5), your clips will be listed by the name you gave them.

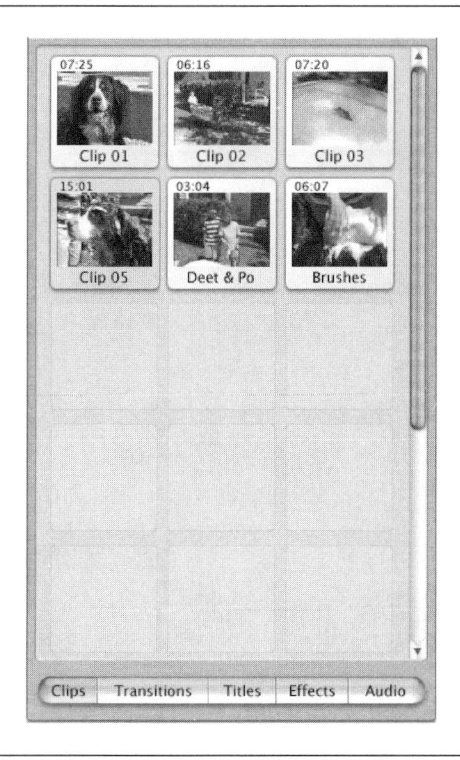

FIGURE 10-5 You can easily rename clips by selecting them on the Shelf.

You can also rename a clip via the Clip Info window. Here's how it's done:

1. Select the clip.
2. Double-click on the Clip frame.
3. The Clip Info window will open, as you see in Figure 10-6.

NOTE *The Clip info window also identifies the clip as a Media File, and its file size. The sound fade-in and fade out are displayed at their current settings, and you can change those levels here if you want. We will be learning more about sound files in Chapter 12.*

4. In the Name window, enter the new name of the clip.
5. Click OK. The Clip Info window will close, and the clip will be renamed as entered.

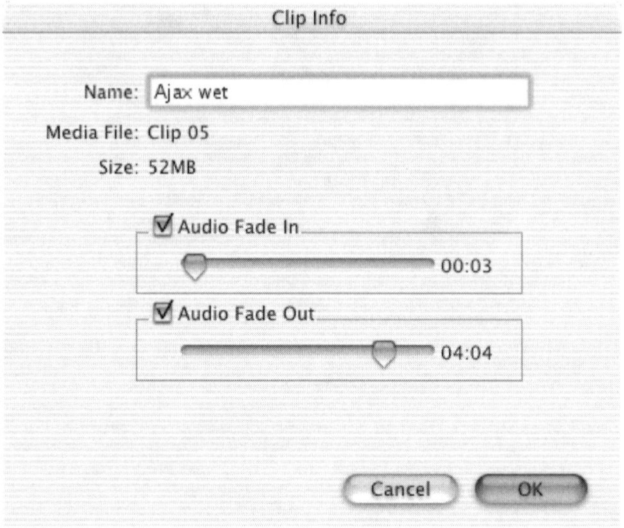

Clip Info

Name: Ajax wet

Media File: Clip 05

Size: 52MB

Audio Fade In 00:03

Audio Fade Out 04:04

Cancel OK

FIGURE 10-6 The Clip Info window has a space for you to rename a clip, if you haven't done so already on the Shelf.

NOTE

When you rename a clip imported from your camcorder in the Shelf, the name of the actual clip file isn't being changed, only the way it's identified in iMovie 2. No matter how many times you change the names of the clips, the original file will still be listed as Clip 01, etc. The reverse is true for QuickTime movies that you import into iMovie 2. The original files can be renamed in any way you want, same as any other Mac file, but they cannot be renamed within iMovie 2.

The Closing Scene

In this chapter you learned the first stages of editing your video in iMovie 2, how to import your clips, and rename them in the Shelf to make them easier to identity. You also discovered ways to deal with problems in getting iMovie 2 to recognize your camcorder.

In Chapter 11, you will continue on the road to an edited video, as you begin to edit your clips in the Timeline.

Chapter 11

Editing to the Timeline

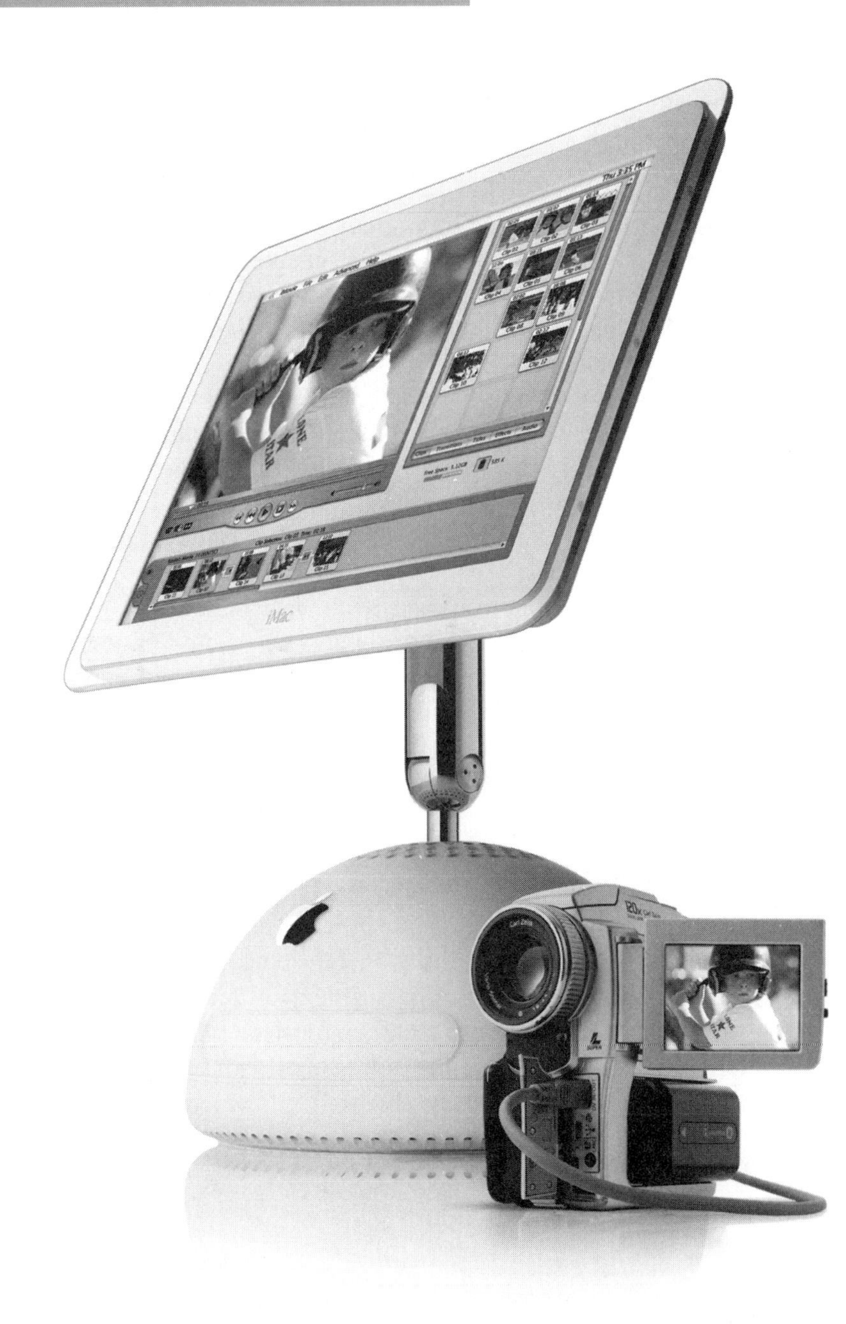

How to...

- Trim a video clip
- Split a video clip
- Restore footage to a video clip
- Edit video clips on the Clip Viewer
- Edit video clips on the Timeline

Now that you've got a foot in the editing room door, you can begin to organize your imagery to make up a complete iMovie. In this chapter, you'll learn how quickly and easily you can edit the footage you've just imported. You'll learn about trimming clips—how cropping and cutting can focus the action and direction and eliminate boredom.

iMovie 2 makes it all so easy. You can build continuity into your project by dragging and dropping the trimmed clips into the Clip Viewer, where you can run the sequences in playback. By splitting a video clip into smaller pieces, you can select and distribute them, creating even more editing options.

In the end, you'll discover that restoring all those clips is even easier than making them. As your sense of time in iMovie becomes even more precise and creative, you will start editing on the Timeline. There you can stretch the continuity for more detailed editing. iMovie 2's Motion Slider will really give you control of time, for fast and slow motion. With reverse clip direction, you can go back again, and even make time go backwards, just like in the movies!

Trimming a Video Clip

Even though you may have already deep-sixed large chunks of your raw footage as you imported it, and deleted more of the clips that landed on the Shelf, your editing has only just begun. As you organize the clips on the Shelf and arrange them on the Clip Viewer, a logical continuity will start to emerge from all this footage. By cropping and cutting, you can trim segments of many of your clips.

This is how you can shape the scenes so that they formulate the beginning, the middle, and the end—if not necessarily in that order at first—of what will become a finished iMovie. It's easy to do, and you are always free to change your mind and try something else. This is all part of the creative process.

Locating the Clip Segment to Trim

All right, let's begin. We'll assume here that you have already imported your videos into iMovie 2, just as we described in Chapter 10.

Now you're ready for the next step in post-production. Let's trim a clip.

1. Select a clip from the Shelf or from the Clip Viewer. It appears in the Monitor window.
2. Move the playhead along the scrubber bar to advance the clip. Find the point where you want to make the trim. The timecode readout displayed to the right of the playhead advances along with the continuity. You can note down those numbers for a list of alternative choices for trimming, and return to those points precisely (see Figure 11-1).

Here are a few pointers on moving the playhead to get the best possible performance and convenience:

- Press the space bar to start and stop playback.
- Click and drag with the mouse button to move the playhead.
- Use the arrow keys to make fine movements back and forth.
- If you don't want to be distracted by the sound track—or if you want to hear it better—adjust the volume control slider (see Figure 11-2).

FIGURE 11-1 The playhead marks the frame that is being displayed above.

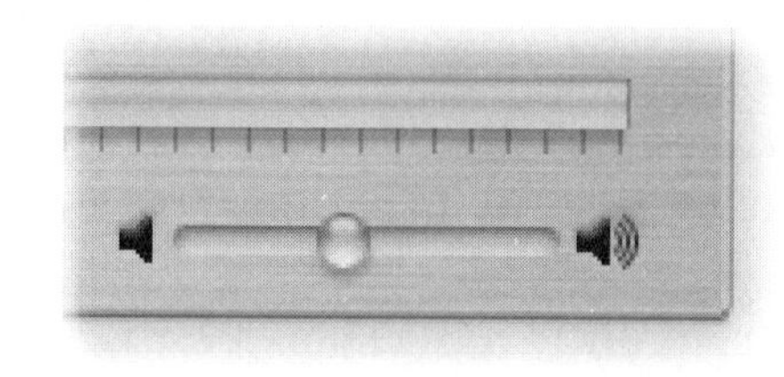

FIGURE 11-2 You can adjust the playback level with the volume control slider.

Cropping Your Clip

Cropping is the process of selecting the segment of a clip that you want to *keep.* Cutting is selecting a segment that you want to *lose.* Both are effective in shaping up your clips so they are as dramatically concise as they can be.

The advantage of cropping is that all you have to do is choose whatever segment of a clip you want to keep, and all the rest of the clip automatically goes away. You can select a segment at the beginning, at the end, or in the middle of a clip. If you choose a segment in the middle of a clip, as seen in Figure 11-3, the unneeded head and tail are gone in one stroke.

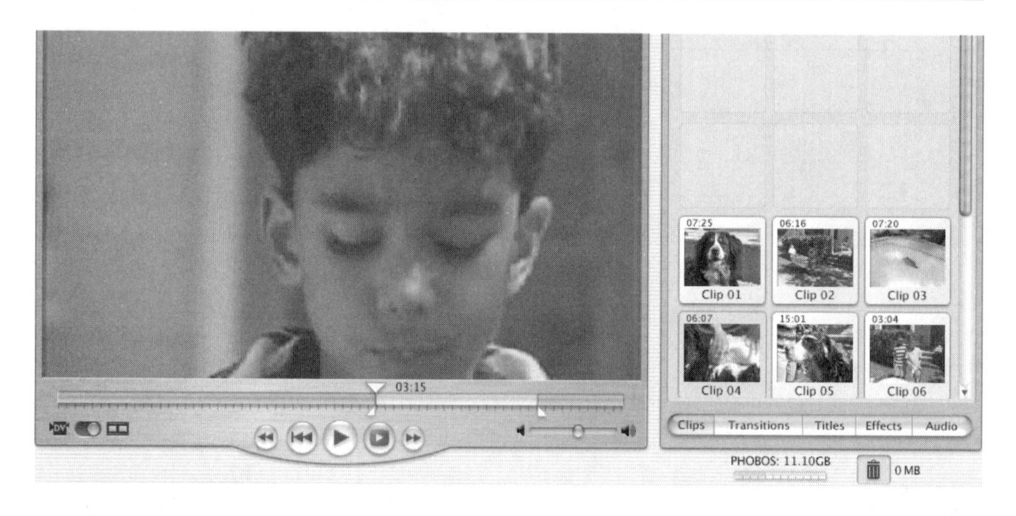

FIGURE 11-3 Cropping saves the central essence of your clip.

Here's how to crop a clip:

1. Select the clip you want to crop. It appears in the Monitor window.
2. Drag the playhead to the point in the clip where you want the segment to start. If you have a timecode marker as a reference, click on the scrubber bar and move the playhead to match the number.
3. Click and hold the mouse button underneath the scrubber bar. Two small triangular markers appear. They mark the in and out end points of a crop.

NOTE *You can click and drag either marker to the right or to the left. The scrubber bar turns yellow between the markers, indicating the length of the segment to be saved. You can adjust the trim further by moving the markers back and forth until you have just what you want. Once you have established a working crop, the arrow keys become active for even more precise frame-by-frame adjustments.*

4. Once you've established your start and end points, go to the Edit menu and select Crop. Or just press COMMAND+K.

NOTE *The clip now includes just the segment that you defined by the yellow bar, and all the rest is history.*

Restoring a Crop

If you change your mind and you want this history to repeat itself, you can undo the crop. But only if you do it right after you complete the crop, and if you haven't invoked a Save command.

To restore the crop, go to the Edit menu and select Undo Crop. Or press COMMAND+Z.

Cutting Your Clip

Cutting is a quick and easy way to shave down the length of a clip. Though used most often to cut off the head or the tail of a clip, such as in Figure 11-4, it can, like a crop, be used to edit in the middle of a clip. The difference is that whereas that middle selection in a crop *is* the final clip, in a cut you are discarding a piece *out* of the continuity. When you play back the edited clip, it will have joined together the segments to either side of the cut. If you made the cut in the

FIGURE 11-4 Cutting the part of the clip you don't want will leave the rest for the action.

middle of a movement, like a person turning, a pan, or a zoom, it will appear on the screen as a "jump cut," where the action is accelerated forward.

To make a cut, go through the same selection steps as for a crop, then go to the Edit menu and select Cut. Or press COMMAND+X.

Restoring a Cut

Whoops! Did you make a mistake, and cut the wrong segment? No problem. So long as you haven't saved your changes, you have one chance, and one chance only, to revert the clip to its former condition.

All you have to do is follow two simple steps:

1. Go to the Advanced menu and select Restore Clip Media.
2. Now go to the Edit menu and select Undo Cut. Or press COMMAND+Z.

But you can change your mind yet again if you decide that the cut really did work for you. Just go to the Edit menu and select Redo Cut.

Splitting a Video Clip

The split-clip is one of the fastest and most convenient of editing modes. Unlike the do-or-die trimming of crops and cuts, a split simply divides one clip into two clips, as in Figure 11-5 and, as you'll see shortly, Figure 11-7. Whatever parts that are left over "on the cutting room floor" from a split will still be sitting there on the Shelf in one piece if you ever want to go back for them.

Just as often you may want to move those new pieces around to different positions in the continuity of your video. Also use splits when you want to add an insert shot, or a transition, at that point within the original clip.

To split a clip:

1. Select the clip. It appears in the Monitor window.
2. Position the playback head on the scrubber bar where you want to make the split.
3. SHIFT+CLICK under the scrubber bar at the playback head. The markers appear together (see Figure 11-6).
4. Go to the Edit menu and select Split Video Clip at Playback Head, or type COMMAND+T.

FIGURE 11-5 Splitting a clip gives you two clips to use or lose.

FIGURE 11-6 Make your markers for the split.

Both halves of the split video clip appear on the Shelf as two separate clips. The leading original clip retains the name of the original clip; the second is labeled NAME/1, as shown in Figure 11-7. If you split that split—there's no limit—the clip that follows is labeled NAME/2, and so on.

Restoring a Split

All right, so maybe it didn't turn out the way you wanted. As with the process of cutting a clip, you can remove the split in a jiffy.

Just follow these steps:

1. Go to the Advanced menu and select Restore Clip Media (see Figure 11-8). Click Restore.
2. Now take a trip to the Edit menu and select Undo Split, or press COMMAND+Z.

FIGURE 11-7 Here's the original clip followed by the new clip, which begins where you made the split.

Edit | Advanced | Help

Extract Audio	⌘J
Paste Over at Playhead	⇧⌘V
Lock Audio Clip at Playhead	⌘L
Reverse Clip Direction	⌘R
Restore Clip Media...	

FIGURE 11-8 The Restore Clip Media option saves your tail.

NOTE *Of course, if you place both halves of the original into the Clip Viewer, they will be played through as an edit, as if the split never happened.*

CAUTION *Be careful with all of these undo's and restores. They will work only if you haven't emptied the Trash and haven't saved before undo or restore. You get only a single try at each—unless, of course, you haven't recorded over that original tape from your camera. You can always go back and import footage again. Play the tape back through the Monitor window until you reach the clips you want and import them for re-editing. This is another good reason to hold those camera original tapes "in the bank" until your project is truly finished.*

Editing in the Clip Viewer

You have already been placing clips in the Clip Viewer and you've seen how it collaborates with the Shelf in providing places to hold your clips while you crop, cut, and split your clips. From the Shelf, playback on the Monitor can only be one clip at a time, whichever one you have selected.

When you place clips in the Clip Viewer, it's like hooking together an electric train, with each clip as a car. If all the clips in the Clip Viewer are either all selected or all de-selected, all the clips are played back from left to right on the Monitor. If one or more contiguous clips are selected, only those are played back.

As the clips are played back, a vertical red progress bar cursor sweeps across the clips, keeping pace with the playback head above. When you have many clips in the Clip Viewer, like in Figure 11-9, this bar cursor helps you to keep track of which clip is visible in the Monitor and how far along in the clip you have gone.

The Clip Viewer is an editor's dream. No cranks and reels or splicing tape—just click and drag. You can move clips from the Shelf to the Clip Viewer and re-order

FIGURE 11-9 You're right on track in the Clip Viewer to see which frame in which clip is in the Monitor.

them there in any way you want to. Drop a clip in between two other clips. The two clips automatically move aside to make a space for the new one. Transitions, which we will investigate in Chapter 13, are dropped in here as well.

NOTE *As you add and subtract clips and re-order them, just tap on the space bar for the latest playback feedback on the continuity. Don't forget to use the full-screen playback mode often to get a sense of the sequence's real movement and impact. Along the way you can save different variations as Projects to use later to compare different editing strategies.*

Manipulating Time with iMovie

Film and video exercise the manipulation of space and time. Editing focuses on the time. In iMovie 2, time is as flexible as a rubber band. Every clip is the same size, and looks like a 35mm slide when in the Shelf and the Clip Viewer. Each displays its duration on the upper left-hand corner of its frame, such as "07.25," which is 7 seconds and 25 frames. 2:19:06 is a clip that is over two minutes long. iMovie 2 sees 30 frames in every video second.

When you drag or copy that clip into the Clip Viewer, that time duration is displayed on the upper frame of the Clip Viewer window. When more clips are added to the Clip Viewer, the window displays the identity and time of whichever clip is selected, as Clip Selection: Clip 05 Time: 08:18.

If all the clips are deselected, the Clip Viewer displays the total running time of all the clips—and transitions—together. This gives you an up-to-date reading of how long your finished iMovie is getting to be, as shown in Figure 11-10. NTSC stands for the National Television System Committee TV broadcasting format of 30 frames per second and 575 scan lines. That is the same format that your television set and VCR use if you are in the USA, and why iMovie is compatible with them.

Editing in the Timeline Viewer

To get an even more detailed look into iMovie time, go to the Timeline Viewer by clicking on the clock icon below the Clip Viewer's eye icon. All the clips that are nestled in the Clip Viewer will be there, but with a difference, as you can see in Figure 11-11.

The length of space each inhabits is proportional to the individual running time, and is identified with a thumbnail image. Below the top video track are the two tracks of the audio panel for the sound, which we will explore in Chapter 12.

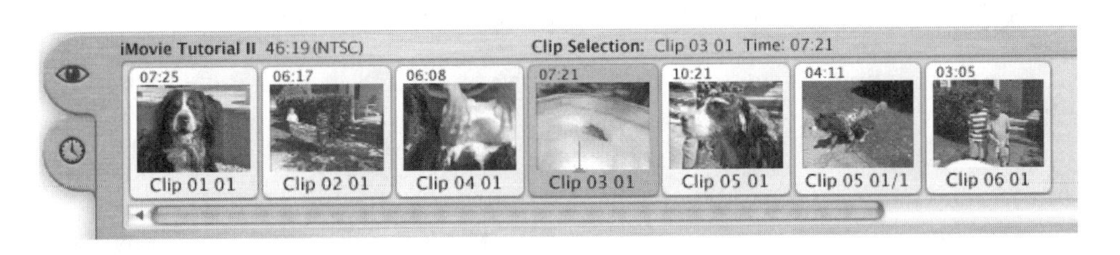

FIGURE 11-10 The Clip Viewer shows the selected clip information as well as the total running time of the rough edit continuity.

FIGURE 11-11 The Timeline Viewer mirrors what is in the Clip Viewer, but with a different continuity display and two audio tracks.

In the Timeline Viewer, you can't click and drag and drop as you can in the Clip Viewer. It is all cut, copy, and paste. Go back up to the Clip Viewer to do more structural re-ordering, and then come back down to the Timeline Viewer for detailed editing and sound.

The Timeline Viewer has its own playback head with a vertical line cursor that extends down through all video and sound tracks.

Fine Tuning with Clip Zoom Level

At the lower left level of the Timeline Viewer the Clip Zoom pop-up menu gives you ten levels of magnification of all three tracks. The greater the magnification, the easier it is to edit the video and sound tracks because each frame is extended and can be studied and controlled in more detail, as shown in Figure 11-12.

The continuity quickly extends off to the right and out of the frame, so you'll have to be prepared to do a lot of horizontal scrolling. Use the Auto 1X level for navigating the Timeline quickly, then raise the magnification for detailed editing.

Speeding Up and Slowing Down with the Motion Slider

At the bottom of the Timeline window, to the right of the Clip Zoom, you will find a real source of fun—the Motion Slider. With this tool you can make slow motion and accelerated motion run in any part of your video. If you've ever seen the Superman movies or TV series, you'll remember how the man of steel became "faster than a speeding bullet." Now you can do the very same thing with your child, for example, as he or she speeds through the grass or chases the family pet.

To change the speed of a clip:

1. Select one or more elements.
2. Adjust the motion slider to slow or fast.
3. Play the altered clip, and the continuity, to confirm.

You will see the clip on the Timeline expand or contract as you adjust the slider, as shown in Figure 11-13. If you select a transition, such as a fade-out, and change the speed, the portion of the clip that is hosting the transition will then play at that altered speed.

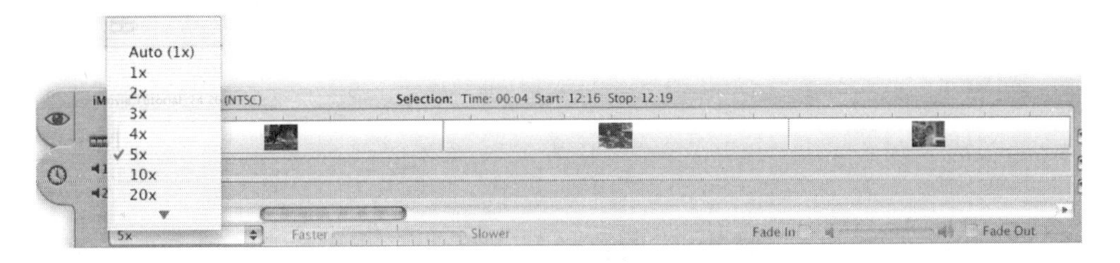

FIGURE 11-12 Adjusting the scale of the continuity in the Timeline with the Clip Zoom can help you fine-tune your edits.

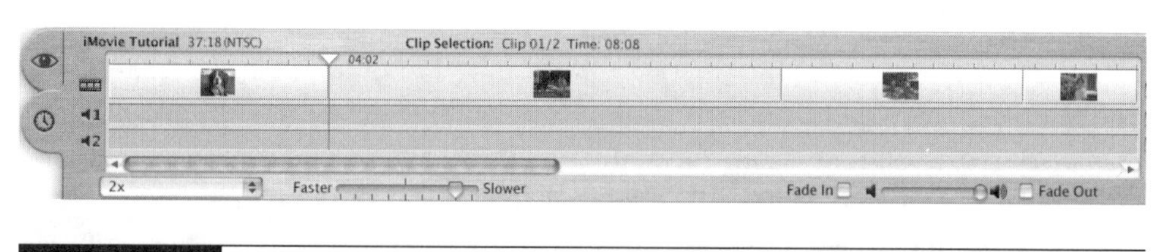

FIGURE 11-13 The Motion Slider will give your clip a slow or a fast ride.

NOTE *The sound track also changes speed. Dialogue is affected, and you will have to decide if voices like Chewbacca or the Chipmunks enhance the action or not. You may want to dub a separate audio track (we'll tell you how in Chapter 12).*

Changing the Direction of a Video Clip

Editing digital video in iMovie 2 is so flexible, it would seem that you can do everything but go backwards. Except that you *can* go backwards. Imagine showing a sequence of moves in reverse, as your spouse jumps backwards out of the family pool. You can rehearse this move right from the Monitor by moving the playback head back and forth. Of course, you have been doing that all the time now in your editing work.

To change the direction of a clip, just follow these two steps:

1. Select the clip you want to reverse.
2. In the Advanced menu choose Reverse Clip Direction or press COMMAND+R, as seen in Figure 11-14.

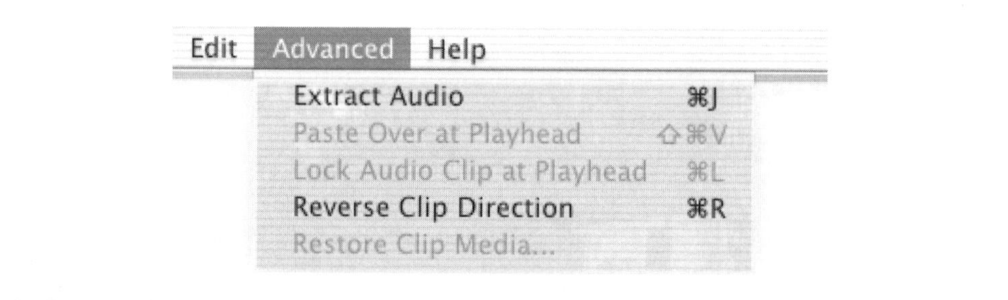

FIGURE 11-14 Forget something? They can run backwards to right where they started.

NOTE *When you engage that command, a left-pointing black triangle appears in the upper right-hand corner of the frame of the clip in the Clip Viewer. The last frame of the clip replaces what was the first frame. But now, the last is the first. The sound track also goes backwards. You may keep it for comedic or other-worldly effect, or paste over background or other sound to replace the reversed sound.*

Why Go Backwards?

When and why would you want to reverse the direction of a clip, unless you were producing a video version of *Alice in Wonderland*? There can be both practical and special effects applications for this editing mode.

Here are some practical reasons to go backwards in time:

- Change a direction for continuity. For example, in the Tutorial clip where the two children are carrying a tub from left to right, a reverse segment of it works with them going from right to left instead.
- Zoom or move from a distance and end the shot dead center on a tight target. To do this, begin the shot on the target, such as a face or a sign, and then zoom or move backwards, even erratically. When you reverse the clip, it will look like the camera was drawn by a magnet to the target image.

And just think of special effects possibilities. Here are some using, of course, the one we referred to earlier:

- The action of a child jumping into the pool can be reversed—see her rocket up into the air from underwater like a superhero!
- The crystal ball that shattered on the floor can reconstitute itself, and all is forgiven.
- You can demonstrate how easy it is to clean your messy tile floor by shooting the clean version, then pouring all sorts of stuff on it, from milk to syrup. When you reverse the shot, you see how rapidly that goop vanishes. Wouldn't it be nice if you could do the same in "real" life as opposed to "reel" life?

TIP *When you are including a reverse action shot in a scene for continuity, examine it very carefully for any "tell-tales." Watch out for even the slightest clue that anything unnatural is revealed, such as something falling "up," or a car going "backwards."*

The Closing Scene

In this chapter, you discovered how to work in iMovie 2's timeline, where real time becomes the clay that you can mold any way you want. Make time shorter or longer, speed it up, slow it down, or reverse its direction. The possibilities are almost endless.

In our next chapter, you'll extend your editing skills and discover more advanced video editing techniques, including one of the most important—the soundtrack.

Chapter 12
Editing Video and Sound

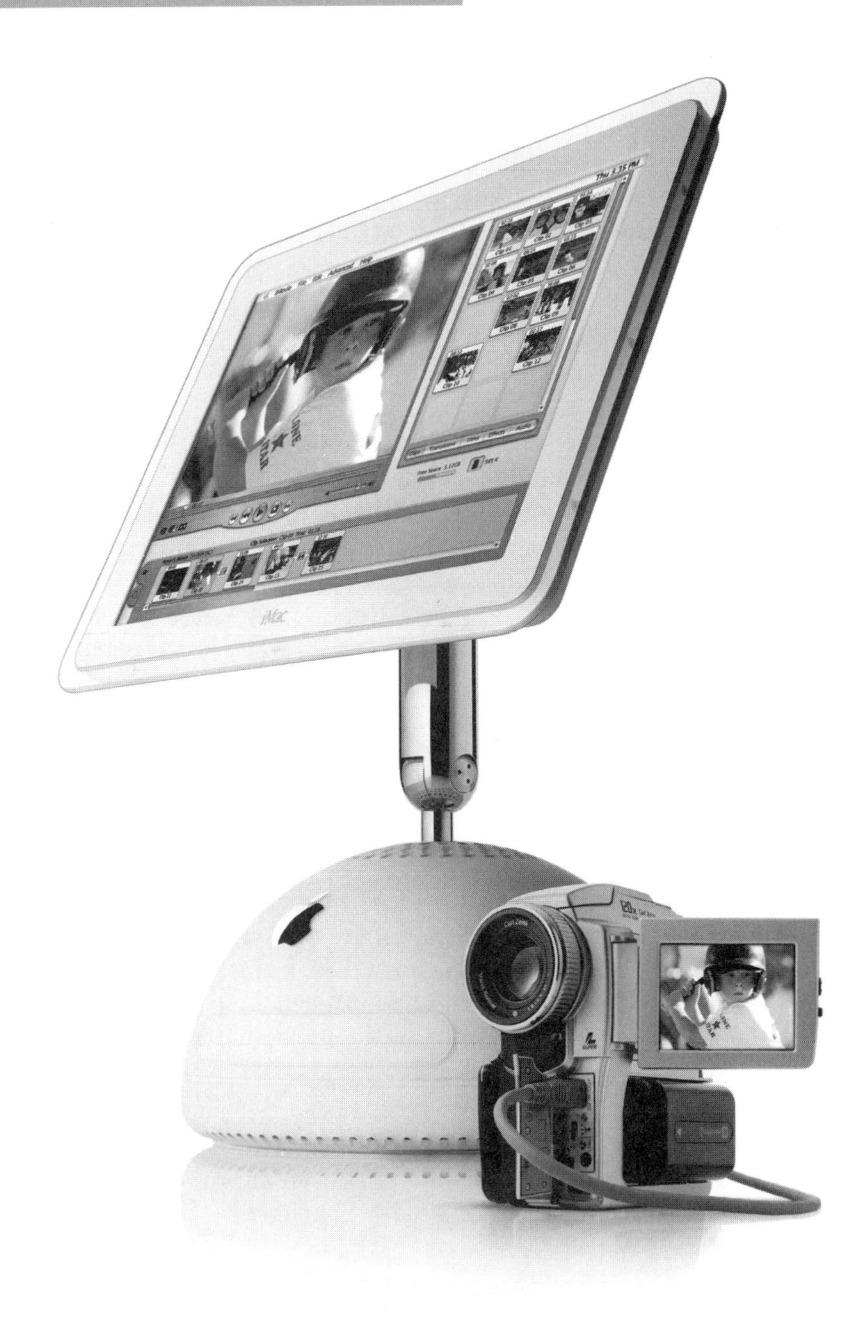

How to...

- Add sound effects
- Record your voice
- Add music from CDs
- Extract audio from the video
- Edit audio clips on the Timeline

Are you ready to make noise? Now that you've brought your videos into iMovie 2 and begun the editing process, here's where you can make noise—by recording and editing it to match and counterpoint your images. In this chapter, you'll become as familiar with the Timeline as you did with the Clip Viewer. You'll discover the joy of sound effects, and go on to using a microphone to record your voice, or an actor's voice, to add to the audio track.

But you aren't limited to the sounds you create yourself. The wide world of sound and music can be selectively brought into your iMovie by recording from an audio CD. The synchronized camera sound that was recorded on the same video clip can be extracted from the video for editing or re-assignment on the track. In this chapter, you'll also learn how to lock and unlock video and audio for tighter control.

In addition, editing the audio clips opens up an added dimension of creativity for your project as you trim, move, layer, and superimpose camera track, voice, music, and sound effects to give resonance and depth to the action in your video—all the way to the fade-out.

Trimming an Audio Clip

Only slide shows are silent. Professional slide shows, called multi-image presentations, have synchronized sound tracks. Sound is an integral part of the audio-visual experience. Even films of the silent era, from 1895 to 1927, were never a silent event. Movie palaces had pit orchestras, and most theaters had a great organ that could produce an amazing array of sound effects as well as soaring and surging musical accompaniment.

Your iMovie had sound the minute you pressed the start button on your camcorder. You are always shooting video with synchronized sound and, most often, it's in stereo. But your sound doesn't stop there. There are almost as many creative opportunities for your finished audio track as there are for the visual continuity.

Editing Sound on the Timeline

Look at the Timeline. Now select the Clip Viewer. The same clips are displayed in both. Any changes you make in one will be reflected in the other. You will be going back and forth between them to edit your iMovie.

As you learned in Chapter 11, the clips in the Timeline are identified by thumbnail images, and have a horizontal dimension based upon their time duration. You can cut, copy, and paste these clips here. The Clip Viewer reflects those changes. Because you can drag and drop in the Clip Viewer, that is where most of your structural editing will take place.

You can drag and drop transitions into the Timeline video track, and you can drag and drop audio into audio tracks 1 and 2. What's more, you can drag sound files from one track to the other, and drag sound effect files down from the audio panel.

There are several differences between iMovie 2 and the more professional editing environments like Final Cut Pro, but you can achieve similar results in both. One difference is that iMovie 2 has only two audio tracks besides the video audio. So, when you have recorded audio on two different tracks from two different microphones, such as from an omni and a lavalier, you can assign those sources to their own tracks in Final Cut Pro. With iMovie 2, you will need to do your mix-down to one track and import it into one track, or dedicate one mic to camera track, and import the other for audio track 1.

Another difference is that iMovie 2 does not have waveform sound clips, which show the audio sound signal as graphic peaks and valleys, rather than just as bars, enabling a more precise audio cut on a word or an effect.

You can achieve close audio cutting in iMovie 2, but it just takes a bit more trial and error. For instance, there is a scene in the Tutorial where the children cry, "Ohhh, Mattie!" when they encounter their muddy dog. That sound bite would be perfect to go under the dog wash title and over the intro music, as it does in Figure 12-1.

To extract the audio from that clip, unlock the audio and then drag the crop markers until the audio plays back with that sequence intact. Crop, and you have your bite to move wherever you want to in the Timeline. We'll go into locking later in the chapter.

Adding Sound Effects

One of the best ways to start with audio in iMovie 2 is by playing with sound effects (SFX), as shown in Figure 12-2. iMovie 2 comes with a built-in library of sound effects with the running time listed after each one. Open the audio panel and select each one to hear it play.

FIGURE 12-1 The intro gets off to a good start with the children's voices over the music and under the title.

Throughout your sound work, adjust the volume slider on the Monitor window to maintain a comfortable listening level. At the right end of the Timeline are three check boxes, one for each track. Remove the check mark and that track will be muted.

To manipulate the sound effects from the Tutorial, follow these steps:

1. Select Audio in the Design Panel.
2. Open the Tutorial project and select the Timeline.

FIGURE 12-2 Dropping a sound effect into the action gives it that added bite.

3. Move the playhead so that a closeup of the dog is shown in the Monitor.
4. Select Dog Bark from the sound effects window.
5. Click and drag it to the playhead in the Timeline.
6. Play back the scene.
7. Select the Dog Bark SFX on the Timeline.
8. Press COMMAND+X to delete the SFX.
9. Move the playhead so that a closeup of the dog is shown in the Monitor.
10. Select Cat Meow from the sound effects window.
11. Click and drag it to the playhead in the Timeline.
12. All set? Now just play back the scene to make sure everything works properly.

In the above steps, you have added a naturalistic sound effect, deleted it, and added another SFX in its place, which becomes out of context and humorous. This is how flexible and creative sound editing can be.

For a page full of free sounds for your iMovies, go to http://www.apple.com/imovie/freestuff/macosxaudio.html. The Sounds for your Scenes page offers downloads of music such as jazz, ambiance, and nature, plus sound effects sets like doors, people, space ships, and wind.

Adding Music from an Audio CD

Adding music, besides that of your own harmonica and kazoo, is made direct and simple in iMovie. CDs, CD-ROMs, and now DVDs are playable in most Macs, so the plumbing is there to pipe in the tunes. Select the audio panel and insert an audio CD. The CD's playlist appears in the music window as tracks, as shown in Figure 12-3. Though you may call them songs, neither they nor the

FIGURE 12-3 You can lay in music from Beethoven to the Beatles for your home video.

Playing Fair with Fair Use

Using copyrighted material of any kind always raises questions, even when you're making a home video. If you are using music, or any other material from commercial recordings, even just parts and not the whole, are you breaking a law and can you run into difficulty?

We aren't lawyers, and we don't play them on TV, so we can only give you general, common sense advice.

The answer is this: You can run into difficulty only if you use that media for personal gain. A home movie shown to friends and family is not being used for personal gain. A corporate communications video, even though it may not be seen outside the company, is considered a commercial product in itself. The home movie does not need to take into account permissions or fees. The corporate video and the independent video exhibited for admissions do. That's why most commercial videos of all kinds use stock royalty-free music, music for which they can get permission, music they can buy outright for a modest fee, or original music they commission from composers and performers.

At the core of all this is the principle of fair use. If you make an audiocassette of a CD that you have paid for so that you can play that same music in your car, or at a party, that is fair use. If you dub a few of these cassettes and give them to friends it may be frowned upon, but it probably won't be picked up by the radar. You also have the right to use a brief portion of copyrighted matter for review, commentary, and satire, although how much is somewhat of a gray area.

But if you dub large numbers of those cassettes and sell them at flea markets or over the Internet, then it is no longer fair use and you may run the risk of prosecution or, at the very least, legal action from the copyright holder.

disk's title will appear there. And, of course, there may be any kind of audio material on the CD, from nature sounds to the Gettysburg Address. To choose which track to record, if you haven't decided yet, click on the play button to listen to and review the selections.

To record music tracks for your iMovie 2 project, follow these steps:

1. Click and drag the playhead to where you want the music to start.
2. If you want to use the complete track, click and drag its name from the music window down to the playhead.
3. If you want to use an excerpt, click the Record Music button.

4. Click the Stop button when the playhead reaches the end-point of the excerpt.
5. Select the purple bar of the music file.
6. Type the name of the audio into the text box.
7. Play back your material to make sure the proper tracks were recorded.

When you boot up the music CD, iTunes will probably pop up, too (see Figure 12-4), providing another place to preview the tracks and to upload them to the Web or to your iPod.

Adding Voiceover

It's easy to add your voice, someone else's, or the entire barbershop quartet to the sound track. You can record voiceovers, dialogue, narration, or singing. You can do your own voice effects and homemade sound effects. The recorded sequence appears on Track 1 as an orange bar in iMovie 2, as seen in Figure 12-5. You can move that sequence under any of your footage. If you want to pursue more serious media sound for your iMovies, there is a wealth of third-party, Macintosh-compatible sound

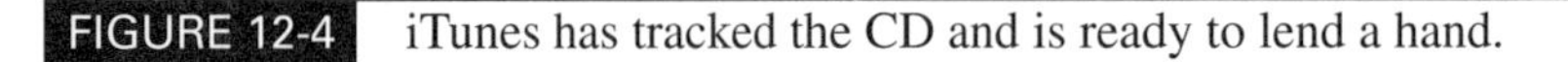

FIGURE 12-4 iTunes has tracked the CD and is ready to lend a hand.

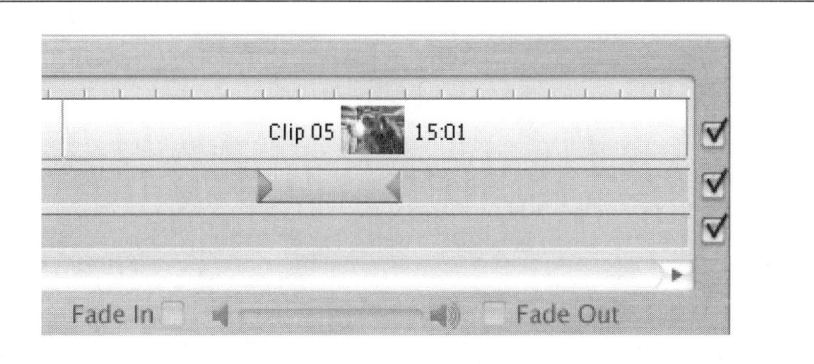

FIGURE 12-5 Your voice tracks are recorded on audio Track 1 as orange bars.

mixing, editing, and effects hardware and software solutions available. Alan Glenn's SndSampler, for example, allows for waveform display and transforms.

Just remember that if the voice track is placed under a close-up of a person who is not speaking, it will read as a voiceover of what that person is hearing or perhaps thinking. Also, if the person in the close-up is speaking, the recorded voice will conflict with that person's speaking action.

If you have an iMac or a PowerBook, you can use the built-in microphone. The older G3 and G4 towers come with a separate PlainTalk microphone that you plug into a microphone jack in the back. The PlainTalk mics come with an 8-foot cord, so you may want to use it with the other computers for more studio flexibility.

NOTE *Many USB microphones work, and standard microphones need an adapter to fit into a Mac jack.*

CAUTION *Because of the degradation of audio quality with analog inputs, Apple no longer has mic jacks on its computers, which means you'll have to consider the USB option for audio input, or use an analog>USB mic jack converter like the one from Griffin Technology.*

To record a voiceover, do the following:

1. Connect the external microphone if necessary.
2. Select Audio in the Design Panel. The Record Voice button becomes active.
3. Position the playhead to the point on the Timeline where you want the voice track to begin.

4. Test the sound level by rehearsing into the microphone. The VU bar above the button scans from green, which is acceptable (see Figure 12-6), to amber, which is marginal, and to red, which is distortion.

CAUTION *One of the shortcomings of digital audio is the lack of room for mistakes. If your signal goes into the red area, even slightly, the audible distortion can be downright irritating. On the other hand, if you record onto an analog source, such as a plain old cassette deck, you'll be able to jump into the red area to a fair degree before the distortion comes objectionable. So be careful about setting levels.*

5. Click on Record Voice and begin your action.
6. Click on Stop when you have finished.

Renaming an Audio Clip

There are two ways to name and re-name an audio clip. Final Cut Pro displays the name on the audio clip bar, but you have to look elsewhere in iMovie 2. When you change the name in one of these modes, it is repeated in the other.

To display the audio clip name:

1. Select the clip.
2. The name of the clip appears on the top frame of the Timeline as Audio Selection. A clip like a sound effect shows its name, but is not renamable there. Other clips, like voice, CD, and extracted audio, offer a text box.
3. Type a name or a new name in the text box.

By opening the clip's Clip Info window, you can also see the file size and select Audio Fade In and Audio Fade Out, as seen in Figure 12-7.

FIGURE 12-6 With the voice recording level at around mid-point of the VU bar, the sound quality should sound good in the movie.

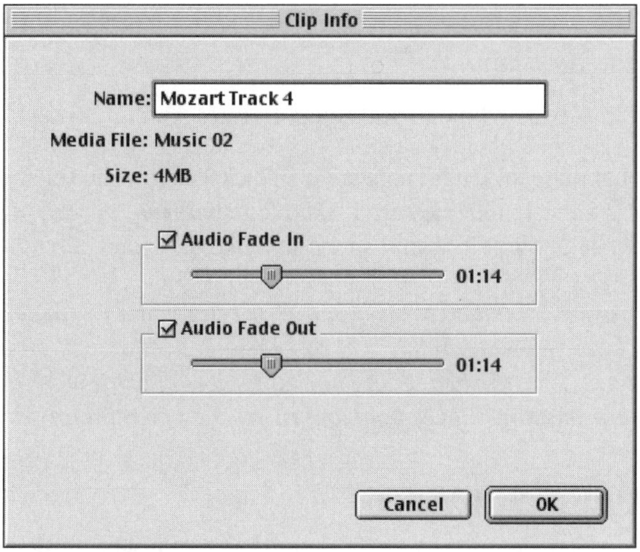

FIGURE 12-7 Name that clip and do the fade.

To open the Clip Info window:

1. Double-click on the audio clip. The Clip Info window opens.
2. Type in the name in the text box.
3. Select and adjust the fades if you want that effect.
4. Click OK.

Extracting Audio from a Video Clip

You can hear it, but you can't see it. That's the camera audio in the video clip on the Timeline. But there is a way to remove it and separate it for other audio editing. But remember—when you have extracted the audio, that video clip will be forever mute. Once you unlock and move that audio elsewhere, that video clip will play silent.

That may be just what you want if you plan to substitute music for that scene. Otherwise, make a copy of that video clip and store it off to the right in the Timeline in case you want to go back to that original.

To extract audio just follow these easy steps:

1. Select the video clip.
2. Go to the Advanced menu and select Extract Audio, or press COMMAND+J.

An orange bar of equal length appears on Track 1 below the selected video clip. Orange pushpins indicate that they are locked together now, as seen in Figure 12- 8. When you play back, it will look and sound just like the video clip did before.

NOTE *It's always a good idea to test your work after you do it, in case the results aren't what you want. While you can easily repeat an edit process, so long as material isn't trashed, going back after lots of extra work has been done on your project only takes time and raises the potential for frustration.*

Locking Audio and Video

Locking, which occurred when you extracted the audio, keeps the two clips synchronized together. You can move any audio clip anywhere and lock it to any other video clip. You can select two audio tracks underneath a video clip and lock all three. And you can unlock clips and delete and move them around some more. Move the playhead to mark the position of the lock.

To lock audio and video:

1. Select the audio clip.
2. Go to the Advanced menu and select Lock Audio Clip at Playhead, or press COMMAND+L.

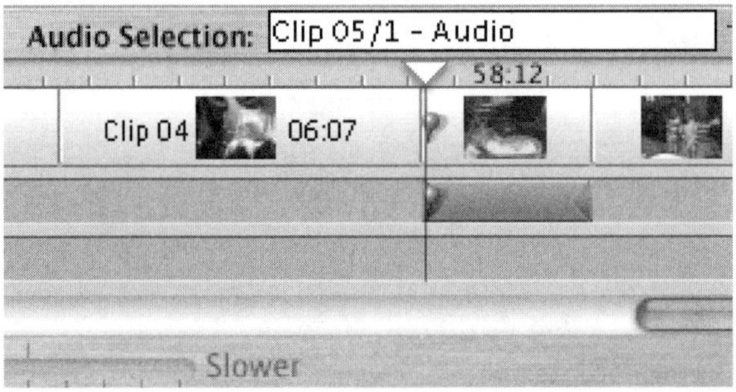

Audio Selection: Clip 05/1 - Audio
58:12
Clip 04 06:07
Slower

FIGURE 12-8 The pushpins ensure that the extracted audio remains in synch with the video clip, until you decide to move it or modify it.

To unlock audio and video:

1. Select the audio clip.
2. Go to the Advanced menu and select Unlock Audio Clip, or press COMMAND+L.

Editing Audio Clips

The gray triangles at the ends of the audio, voice, and music clip bars are the crop markers. Click and drag them to the points on the clip where you want to crop. Use the arrow keys for more precise positioning. If you try to cut that section, the whole clip will disappear. You need to cut by cropping, which defines the section that you keep, as seen in Figure 12-9. Since you can't see the audio track, use the position of the playhead in the picture to judge the position of your editing marks. As you drag the playhead, often you will leave behind a faint line on the Timeline, which is a "ghost playhead," a temporary marker that you can use as an editing target. Play over the marked clip until the playback confirms what you want to hear in the final edit.

To edit an audio clip:

1. Move the crop markers to the desired locations on the clip.
2. Go to the Edit menu and select Crop, or press COMMAND+K.

Editing is also designing and moving the layers of video, SFX, voice, and music in the three tracks in relation to each other so that you will have depth of action and ambiance in the movie. You can also superimpose one clip over another, and they will play simultaneously at the juxtaposition. You can drop a SFX right on top of a clip without any cropping. It's like having three audio tracks without having to have a multitrack recording device.

FIGURE 12-9 Locking audio and video and cropping the audio clips builds a strong and dynamic continuity.

Adjusting the Volume of Audio Clips

An important part of designing the audio, with several elements combining in different ways, is in controlling the relative volumes of the camera, music, and voice. This is especially important during the playback process, where you don't want to constantly hunt for the level control to lower the volume of a noisy passage or bring up the level of quiet conversation.

To adjust the audio level of a clip:

1. Select the clip or multiple clips to share the same level.
2. Click and drag the Fade volume slider (see Figure 12-10) to the level you want.
3. Deselect the clip and play it back.

When you select an audio clip, the Fade volume slider moves to indicate the level at which the clip has been set.

NOTE *Some volume variation is important for the impact of your movie. A dramatic scene, for example, may be enhanced by raised voices, louder sound effects, and music. But too much of a good thing can only be irritating. You aren't remaking Star Wars here, or are you?*

Fading in and Fading out

There are two ways to fade in and out for an audio clip. One is within the Clip Info window, as discussed in previous sections of this chapter. There you can adjust the rate of fade separately for in and out.

The Fade volume slider at the bottom of the Timeline window (again take a look at Figure 12-10) has check boxes for in and out fades which are preset to

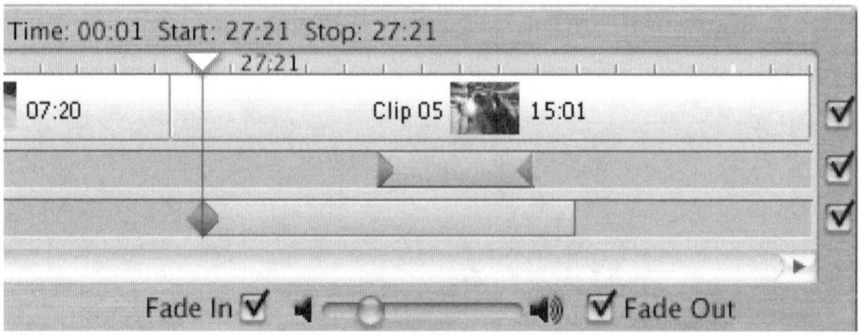

FIGURE 12-10 The Fade volume slider provides an easy and visible way of coming and going gracefully.

be short average-length fades. Select the clip and check or uncheck the boxes to set the fades.

The Closing Scene

As you discovered in this chapter, the audio element of your movie is as important as the visual. When you combine a carefully edited soundtrack with well-edited video, the impact of your production is enhanced substantially. Don't consider audio just as a necessary add-on to your movie, but as an important part of the picture to convey your story.

In our next chapter, we'll return to the video, and show you how to add transitions and special effects to give your movie a more professional spit and polish and greater impact, regardless of your intended audience.

Part IV

Advanced Editing Techniques

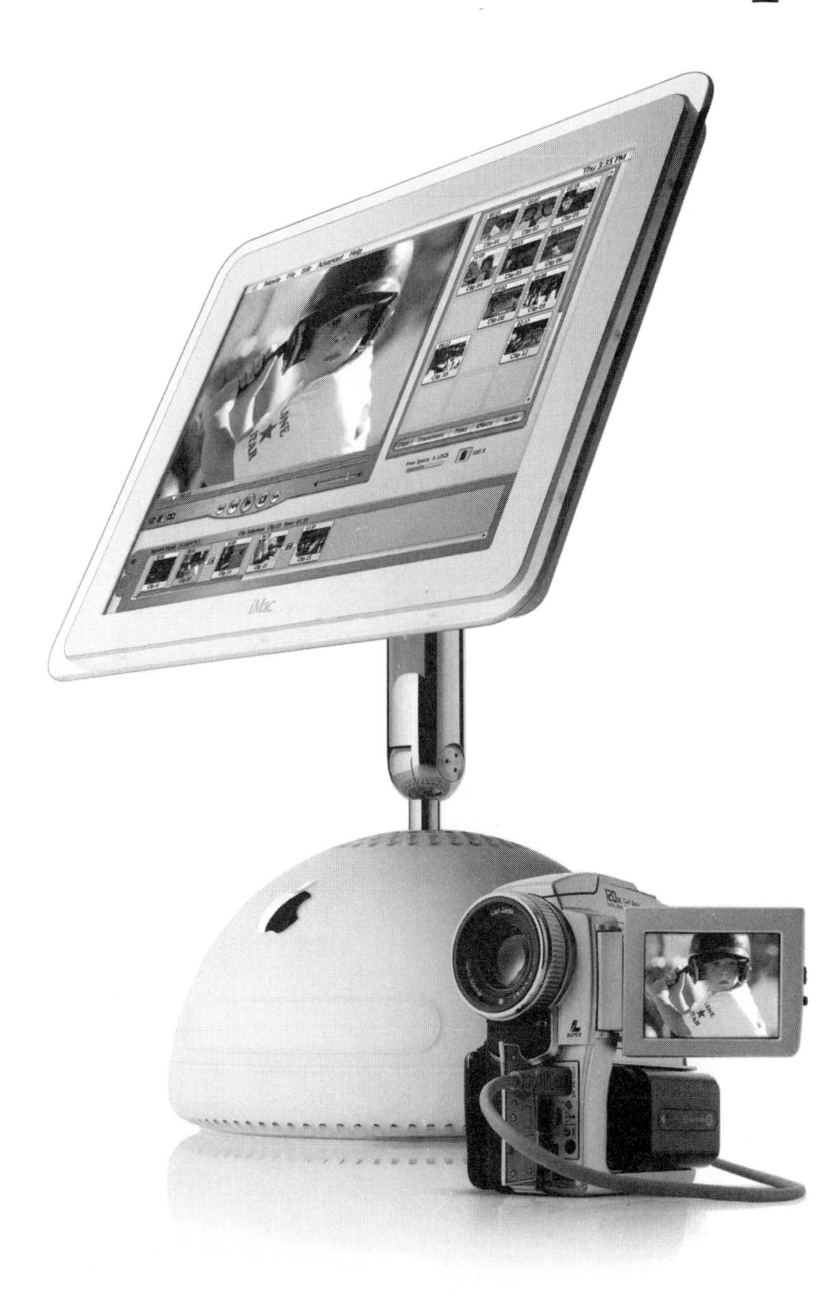

Chapter 13 Adding Effects and Transitions

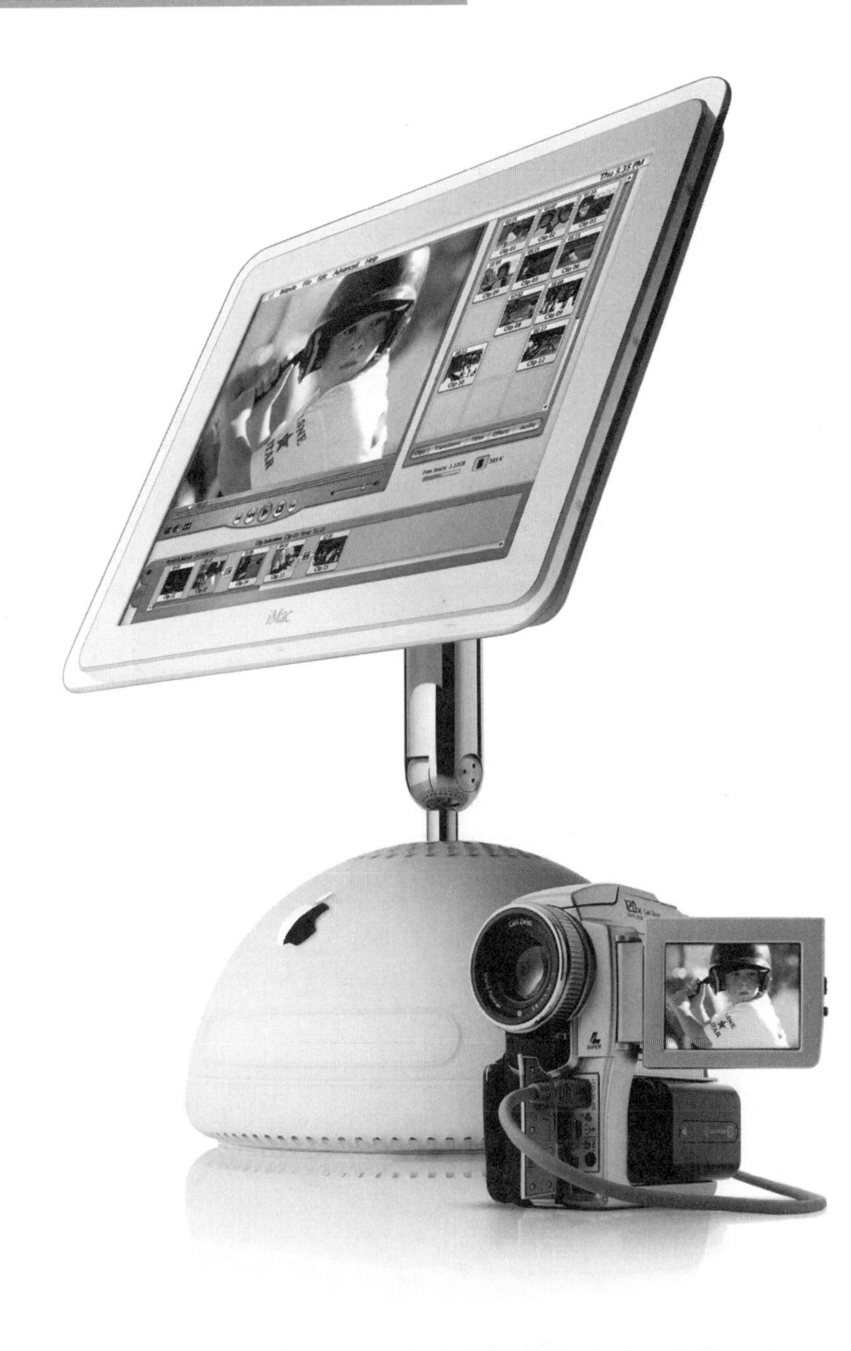

How to...

- Correct the color in a scene
- Turn a color clip into black and white
- Create strong and elegant mirror patterns
- Link scenes with fades and dissolves
- Make graphic transitions that form circles or squares

Effects and transitions are powerful digital tools that will give you the means to improve, modify, and shape your scenes and the way that they are connected together. In this chapter, you'll learn how to apply the effects from the iMovie special effects library by sampling, previewing, and testing them on a clip. You'll see how corrective effects will enable you to adjust colors, including hue and lightness, and go on to manipulate sharpness, brightness, and contrast. In addition, you'll learn how classic effects of black and white and sepia can frame those vintage inserts. You'll be pleased to know that iMovie's special effects are a magician's treasure chest of ripples, flashes, mirrors, and ghost trails—and, they're simple to master. The sophisticated transitions like fades, circles, dissolves, pushes, warps, and radials can bring a bit of Hollywood into your monitor.

Effects

Effects are so much a part of our commercial movies, videos, and broadcast, they have become integrated with our visual imaginations. Special effects have been with movies from the very beginning, as Georges Melies demonstrated in 1902 with his *Trip to the Moon*. He combined his stage magician's box of tricks and rewinding the camera exposures to create a short story of joyful wonder that still works for audiences today.

iMovie 2 comes with a bountiful library of transitions, effects, and titles, all which are complex and powerful digital tools, yet easy to use. Special effects or titles houses in Hollywood would have charged thousands of dollars to create these same elements before the days of digital.

NOTE *Make sure you have updated your copy of iMovie 2 with the Plug-in Pack 2, as we have done here, available free from the Apple Web site. This package gives you these additional special effects and other goodies to further enhance your movie editing creativity.*

Is There Too Much of a Good Thing?

Having all that power at your disposal is a double-edged sword, and it's so very easy to get carried away. Here are some points to consider in the actions of effects and transitions, and the titles that we will work with in Chapter 14.

- Is the action appropriate and meaningful for the clip and the continuity?
- If the clip is too short, there may not be enough frames to support the action of the effect.
- These actions will add to the file size of your iMovie.
- These actions are also processor-intensive, so you shouldn't count on doing much multi-tasking until their rendering is completed.

Some Common Sense Advice on Adding Special Effects

You can apply effects and transitions on either the Clip Viewer or the Timeline, but things tend to stay clearer on the Clip Viewer. Select a portion of a clip and apply the effect there. You can even combine effects on the same clip, such as coming in on a Soft Focus and going out on a Sharpen.

Though there are ways to stop an effect and restore the clip, it's not a bad idea to make a working copy of a clip when you are trying out many variations on your video.

Effects have more variables than transitions do, and some effects have further unique values, as many as three. Your touch on any one of the controls will initiate a preview in the panel window.

TIP *To test your work, just click on the Preview button and the preview will appear in the Monitor window.*

In preview mode the effect hasn't been fully rendered yet, and the pace may appear slow and jerky in the Monitor. Until the effect is committed and rendered, it can't be displayed in the full screen mode. When a clip has been fully rendered, it will be awarded an "fx" at the upper right-hand corner of the clip frame. If you want to go back and edit the effect some more, click on Update after you are finished and the clip will be re-rendered.

Adding Special Effects

All ready? Let's add some special effects to your video.

1. Select Effects from iMovie's Design Panel (see Figure 13-1).
2. Select the clip or combined clips to be treated.
3. Adjust the Effect In and Effect Out sliders. Frame readouts appear in the lower left and right corners of the preview window.
4. Adjust the other variables until previews, both in the panel window and in the Monitor, and confirm your final settings.
5. Click Apply.

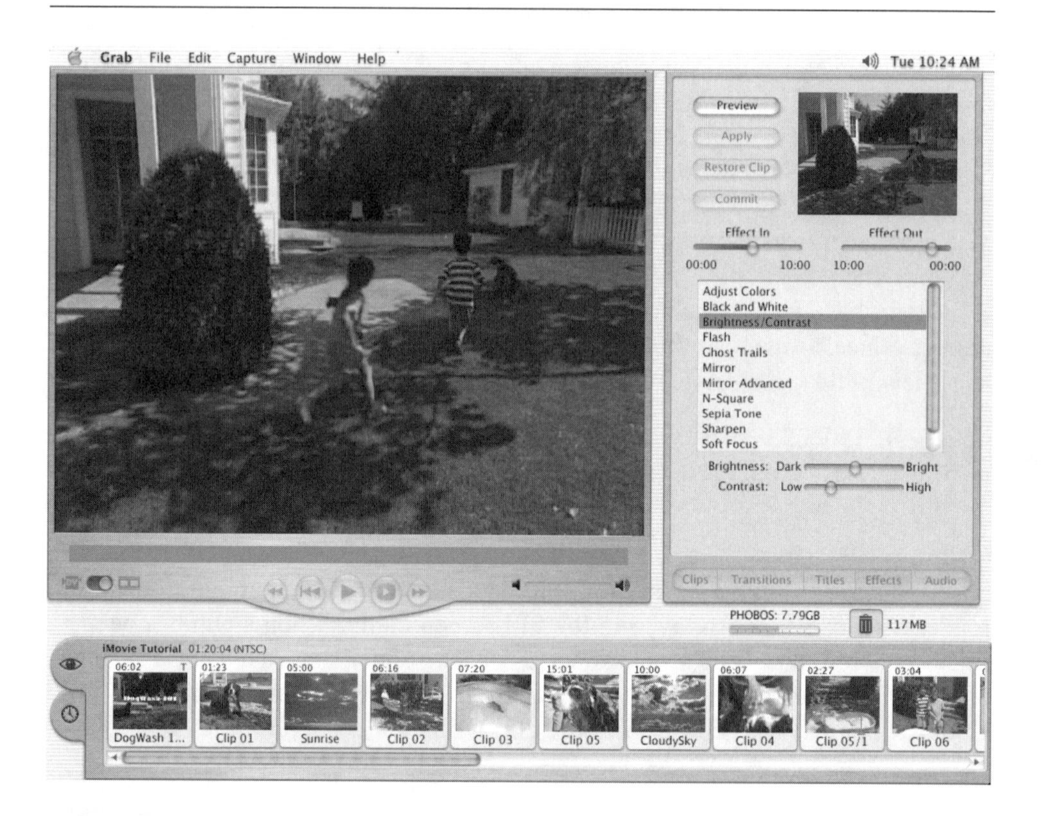

FIGURE 13-1 Pick your special effects from this wide selection.

6. A red line cursor progresses on the clip in the Clip Viewer with a running readout of frames rendered.
7. If you change your mind and want to skip the effect, click Restore Clip, or press COMMAND+Z.
8. Click Commit if you are sure of the effect and want to move on.
9. To stop an effect in progress, press COMMAND+Z.

Applying Corrective Effect

Adding special effects is just one way to enhance your movie. Another is to apply a corrective effect. What if, for example, you have great footage—one-of-a-kind shots—but the colors are dark, or way off. Do you just throw it all away and start again? Or tolerate the imperfections for the greater good?

Fortunately, iMovie 2 gives you a different option. The corrective actions we're about to describe are similar to what is done, not so much in a special effects department of a studio, but in the timing and color correction areas of a film lab.

It is here that you may be able to rescue a clip that was underexposed or overexposed, as in Figure 13-2, or adjust the hue for a face that was getting too much red from the reflection off of a fire engine. These effects are equally useful for inspired touches where part of a scene needs to brighten or gray down just at the right moment.

NOTE *Unfortunately, the arrow keys aren't active here, so be prepared for a certain amount of trial and error to get these sights just right.*

Adjust Colors

The following tools are available to adjust the colors in your clips:

- **Hue Shift** You can shift the entire scene's spectrum by sliding from red/yellow on the left to green/blue on the right.
- **Color** This adjusts a range from black and white, to gray, to full color, to vivid color.
- **Lightness** From dark to bright, you can adjust the reading of the whole scene to soften or darken it.

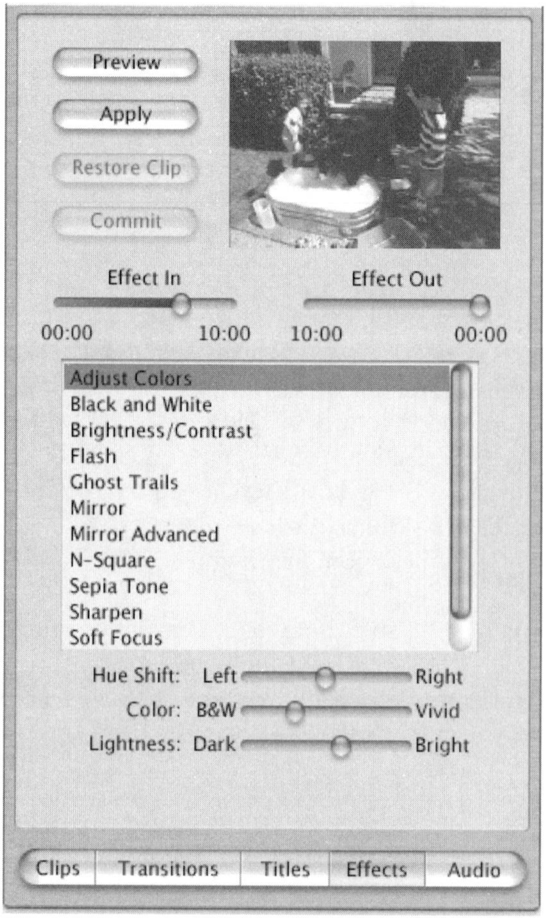

FIGURE 13-2 Adjusting colors and restoring values.

About Brightness/Contrast

Brightness is similar to Lightness, but instead of making the image softer and fainter, an increase in the brightness adjustment makes the pixels glow with illumination. The image displays a more absolute spectrum, from solid black to pure white.

Contrast is a tool you may use the most often, as even a little bit can help to invest a scene with more definition and readability.

Sharpen

Sharpen is another useful tool which can enhance the tone and texture of the subjects of a shot. It can make hair look more alive, a field of grass more deep and dimensional, and type more readable.

Classic Effects

In addition to touching up the colors in your footage, you can also make some basic changes that'll give your movies a unique point of view.

Black and White and Sepia

Black and white and sepia (brownish tint) can both be used as special effects, but their primary usefulness is in emulating or integrating with classic modes of cinema and photography. If you are intercutting transfers of old black and white home movies or industrial footage, you can render the contemporary scenes in the same way if it is meaningful for showing comparisons. You can change a clip to black and white in the Adjust Colors effect at the B&W color slider.

Some films of the silent era were released in sepia tone, but it is more likely that you will want to use this mode (see Figure 13-3) when you are including shots of antique photographs printed in sepia. Because both of these modes allow for bringing the effect in and out in the shot, you can program a graceful transition from the black and white or sepia material into or out of the contemporary color footage.

Special Effects

Special effects can enhance and re-emphasize reality, direct and redirect action, interpret an internal point of view, or provide an expressive and dynamic reminder of reality. For example, Water Ripple could add texture to the surface of a pool, add movement to a wind-blown banner, or portray a distorted world as seen through the eyes of a drunkard. It's all up to you to sample, experiment, test, and run.

Soft Focus

Soft Focus is a tool that can be used as a corrective effect. As a special effect (see Figure 13-4), it is strongest when seen in process, and works better in a close-up than it does in a long shot. It can, however, lend an atmospheric transformation to a landscape or background in a long shot.

FIGURE 13-3 Sepia gives an image a soft monotone effect as well as the shift in color.

Water Ripple

The ripples (shown in Figure 13-5) are parallel and run in a diagonal direction. From a medium shot to a long shot it can work as a texture. The closer the shot is, the more extreme and surreal the distortion will be.

Flash

Flash can be used as a single-point effect like a spotlight that briefly highlights a subject at an action in the shot. With the In and Out at 00.00 and the Count at Max, it can provide a constant disco-like flashing effect throughout the clip.

Ghost Trails

Ghost Trails (see Figure 13-6) could be used in an industrial or training video to emphasize and highlight motion study, but as an effect its applications are usually for the poetic. It has been seen applied in sports videos, where the actions of basketball players create a strong and dynamic composition in space.

FIGURE 13-4 Soft focus can suggest the nostalgia of time remembered.

Mirror and Mirror Advanced

The Mirror effects can be incisive and elegant in their symmetries, but also overwhelming in their domination of the frame. They may bring people together or apart, or symbolize a collective effort building to a climax. Or they may just be decorative and interesting, especially when the pattern they create is held at the end of the clip, as in Figure 13-7.

N-Square

At the minimum setting, with four panes, the n-square is like a mirror effect, but as you slide towards the maximum, it generates so many panes that it produces a pictorial field like wallpaper. It may be just what you want, perhaps like Figure 13-8. More than any other, this effect says "computer graphics."

FIGURE 13-5 The rippling effect spreading over this sunset scene makes an awesome exit.

Transitions

Movies and videos are constantly in motion, even when a single frame is on the screen. As your editing process has been evolving, you have been weaving together frames, clips, scenes, and sequences. By and large, your transitions have been made cut by cut. Most transitions can be used as the intro or the exit of a sequence, or even of the movie, where it comes from black or goes to black. Some effects can be used as transitions, applied at the tail of one clip and at the head of the next. You will find many ways that transitions may be used as effects.

Adding a Transition Follow these steps to add a transition to your iMovie:

1. With your project open, select Transitions from the Design Panel.
2. Select two clips and choose a Transition.

FIGURE 13-6 Girl, boy, and dog meet the need for speed, and make ghost tracks doing it.

3. Adjust the speed slider.
4. Preview the Transition.
5. Click and drag the Transition to the Clip Viewer and drop it in between the two clips you want to join. The Transition link appears and a red progress line below it paces the rendering.

Changing a Transition Follow these steps to edit your transition:

1. Select the Transition in the Clip Viewer.
2. Make the changes in speed, or direction, for Push.
3. Click Update.
4. A red progress line below the Transition pace the rendering.

FIGURE 13-7 A meeting in the mirror.

Removing a Transition Follow these steps to delete a transition:

1. Go the Edit menu and select Undo Add Transition or press COMMAND+Z.
2. Drag the Transition to the trashcan.

Linking Transitions

Linking transitions are those that connect two clips together and build the continuity of the movie by bringing you, the viewer, along with them. They are described in detail in this section.

Fade In and Fade Out

The most familiar transition is the fade, coming to or from black, or sometimes leading to a hard cut with the next scene. A fade-out-fade-in can provide a mental transition for

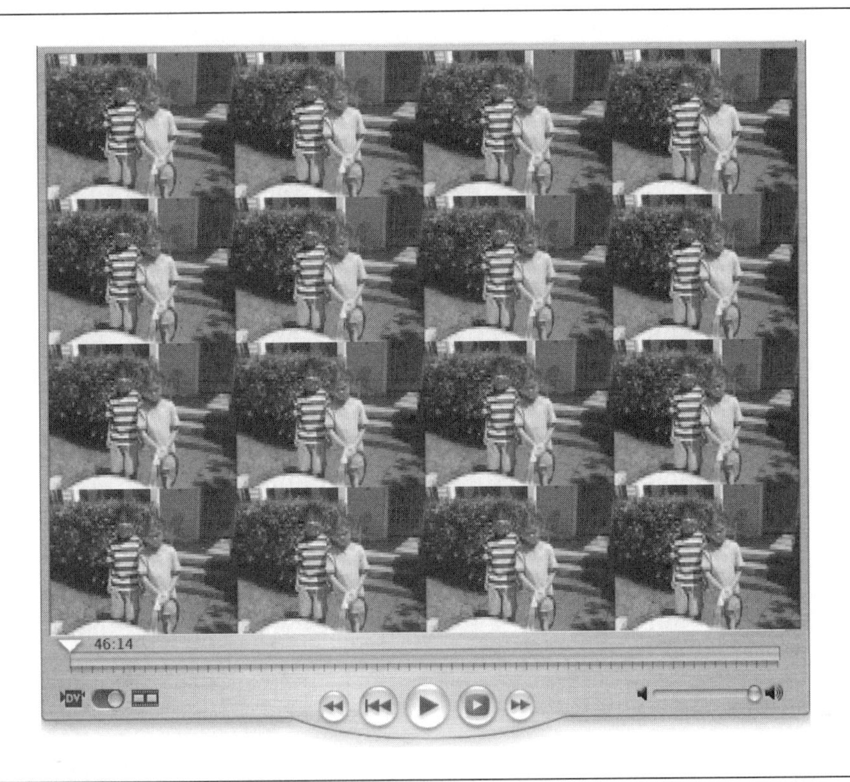

FIGURE 13-8 N-Square generates compound interests.

a change of location or the passage of time. You can adjust the speed of the fade from a quick bump to a duration that stretches up to four seconds, which provides plenty of latitude for fine-tuning.

Cross Dissolve

The cross dissolve (see Figure 13-9) is one of the most familiar transitions, as it merges and mixes what you are seeing in the outgoing scene with what you are seeing in the incoming scene. Of course, you can do a cross dissolve from a fade out to the head of the next scene for an even smoother way to introduce the incoming scene. As with most of the transitions that follow, once you create a moment where one image is superimposed over the other, you must take into consideration the design that they make together on the screen. You may go back to trimming the head and tail of the linked clips so that the forms match or complement each other, no matter how briefly.

FIGURE 13-9 The cross dissolve is a gateway between two moving scenes and their subjects.

Overlap

If you have struck upon a very meaningful juxtaposition of the outgoing and incoming images, you may want to go to an Overlap (see Figure 13-10) where the last frame of the outgoing is held as the new clip begins, bringing more emphasis on that transitory mid-point.

Push

A versatile tool, the push can be considered as much as an effect and a graphic transition as a linking transition. As shown in Figure 13-11, a four-way compass direction button enables your push to go horizontally, a perfect linking transition, or to go up or down like an elevator. With a four-second maximum, it can give you plenty of time for the audience to read the incoming and outgoing scenes.

FIGURE 13-10 These two hot tubbers had their heads in the clouds.

A meaningful push up might be used for the scene of a house under construction being replaced by the finished house.

Graphic Transitions

These are transitions, but their movements are so emblematically defined by their forms that the circle, or square, takes on a life of its own. Use them; they are fun to try out. Graphic transitions had their heyday in the movie serials of the 1940s such as *Flash Gordon Conquers the Universe*, which George Lucas paid homage to in his *Star Wars.*

Circle Closing and Circle Opening

The moving circle, contracting or expanding, was one of the first transition effects in cinema. Called an iris in or iris out (see Figure 13-12), it was a

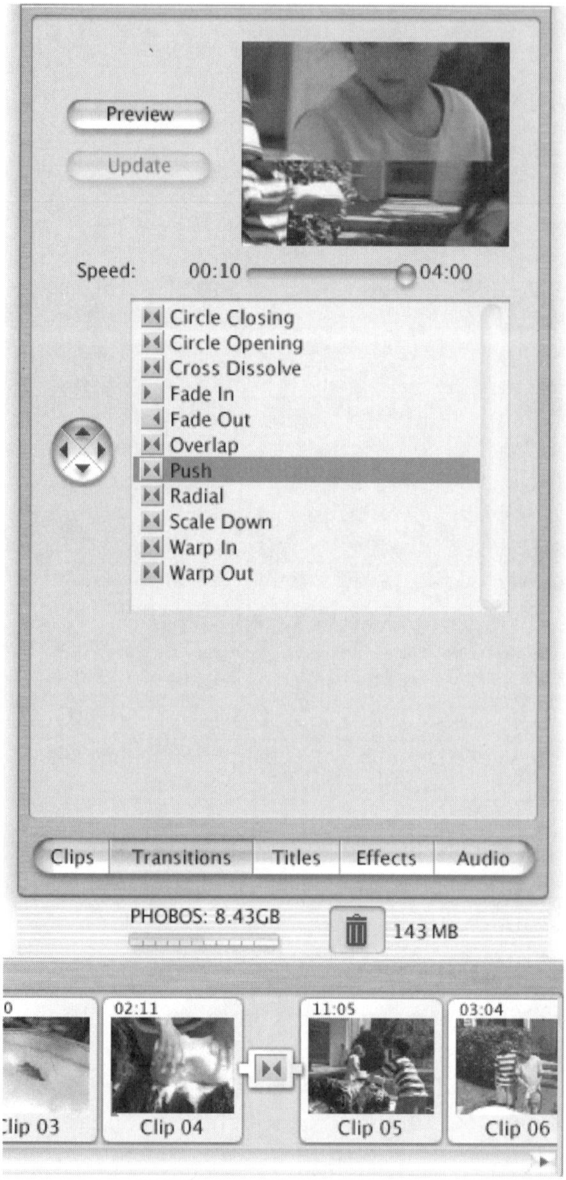

FIGURE 13-11 This sequence is elevated with a Push.

FIGURE 13-12 The sky will open up for a smiling face when you use the circle opening.

reflection of the theatrical spotlight used in those days to highlight the live stage acts that entertained the audiences before the feature film. The circle opening makes a good revelation, and the circle closing helps to focus in on the clue. Don't you wish you had a circular object in the frame?

Warp In and Warp Out

The warps are like the circles in their actions, but are more contemporary in their forms. The warp in focuses down a bow tie/butterfly shaped window, but the warp out irises out with a twist of the weird with a ripple-like ocular distortion of its frame, as seen in Figure 13-13. This could be seen either as a strong open, or an odd comment, depending on how you use it.

FIGURE 13-13 A warped frame of reference reveals the hidden dog.

Radial

The radial is a dynamic graphic movement, though iMovie gives you just a clockwise rotation. This is the picture that could be worth a thousand words—or minutes—as it can imply the progress of time as well as a progression from one scene to the next, as in Figure 13-14.

Wash In

The wash in is like a negative fade. Whereas a fade in comes in from black and a fade out returns to black, a wash in comes in from a bright white screen to normal exposure. It can be a good transition from a bright outdoor scene into a dark interior.

FIGURE 13-14 The radial transition sweeps away one face for the next.

Scale Down

Like circle closing, scale down (shown in Figure 13-15) also windows the outgoing shot down to a miniature and then makes it disappear into the incoming shot. It has just one screen end-point, unlike professional effects where you may be able to define the target area on the screen. Yet scale down may be just the window of opportunity for that special transition in your iMovie.

The Closing Scene

Special effects and transitions are the icing on cake in a movie. Apply your imagination to the task and you will take your iMovie into a totally new direction, and entertain and delight your audience in the bargain.

In Chapter 14, you'll be ready for the finishing touches, when you add text, titles, and captions to your iMovie.

FIGURE 13-15 And there goes Wonder Dog, scaling up, up into the sunset!

Chapter 14

Adding Text and Titles

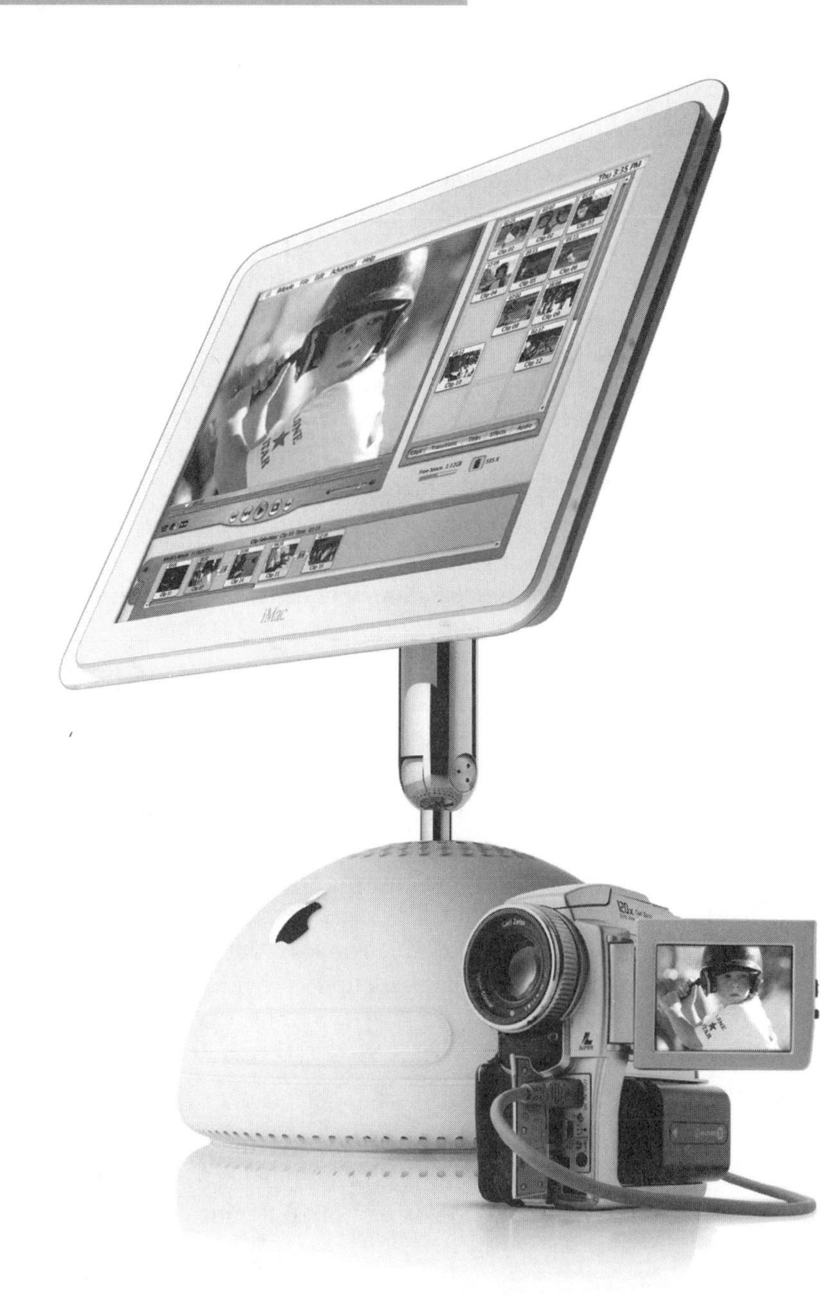

How to...

- Add a title to a clip using different fonts and colors
- Bring in titles from different directions on the screen
- Use subtitles for informational applications
- Give credits where credits are due
- Make a slide show

Now that you've forged your footage into a good story, it deserves professional-looking titles. iMovie has an impressive text and titles tool shop that will enable you to design and install a wide array of styles and configurations. A good background for your titles can come from scenic and detail footage you have shot, or from other graphic sources—or the background can be black.

In this chapter, you'll learn how to add a title to a clip after choosing fonts, sizes, colors, and actions, and you'll learn how to edit and change that title. By sampling, manipulating, and previewing, you will tailor the title to complement and enhance the scene it covers. There are standard titles that come up front and center, lines that bounce, others that drift—and rolling credits that tell us who's on first. There are flying words and letters, titles that scroll and zoom, and subtitles that can imitate a typewriter, CNN, or MTV. You'll never have to worry about settling for homemade titles that look like ransom notes. The hardest thing will be telling yours apart from the ones on TV.

Text and Titles

Even with all of the visual breadth and expression of your images, your audience will still need a title to give them perspective and credits to give you credit. iMovie's action-packed titles library provides everything you need. Titles are text. If you are making a documentary, training, or educational movie, you may employ some of these title modes as text to mark and explain things at different points along the way.

You can drop a title in any clip, or make a black background for that professional look. You can use effects in the title clip to provide a dynamic and interesting background for the text.

Shoot a Background Check

Titles can also be where you find them. When you are making a travel video, you may catch a shot of a road sign, kiosk, or festival banner that can contribute key words to your title. If the name of the school is part of your educational title, get a shot of the building's entry sign. Think ahead and plan to find location shots that can serve as backgrounds and frames for your titles that will support the subject and character of your movie. They could be a city skyline, a beachfront, or an ancient wall.

Integrate titles into background and action. Plan shots that will frame the title, and carry on into the continuity. You could start off the travel video with that scenic pan, but begin with a long hold on the stone wall—long enough for the title sequence—then make the pan, all in the same unbroken shot.

You can build your own library of backgrounds and backdrops with your camera when you see interesting and useful surfaces and textures. For a ready-made library of free backgrounds, go to http://www.apple.com/imovie, click on Enhance, and navigate to Apple's Background Sets link. Download the sets that appeal to you. They include Abstract, Artwork, Gradation, and Nature, as seen in Figures 14-1 and 14-2. Import them into iMovie and they will appear on the Shelf.

FIGURE 14-1 A dramatic cloudscape can open your titles wide.

FIGURE 14-2 A background like this promises a well-seasoned story.

Designing Titles

It's easy to add a title or subtitle to your movie and tweak it till it's just right.

Creating a Title Follow these steps to create your title:

1. Select Titles in the Design Panel.
2. Select the clip in the Clip Viewer or the Timeline.
3. Type in the title in the text box.
4. Choose a font from the Font Menu.
5. Select the size of the font with the slider.
6. Choose a Title mode from the list.

7. Select the Speed of your title's display from the slider.
8. Select the Pause point from the slider.
9. Click Preview.
10. Click and drag the title name from the menu and drop it on the clip that will host the title. A red line cursor progresses on the clip with a running readout of frames rendered.

Editing a Title Once your title has been created, it's not set in stone. It can be easily edited to meet your changing requirements:

1. Select the clip that contains the title you want to edit.
2. Make the needed changes.
3. Click Update. A red line cursor progresses on the clip with a running readout of frames rendered.

Deleting a Title Did you change your mind? Maybe you don't want to use a title at all on some of your footage. Here's how to delete it:

1. Select the clip to be restored.
2. Press Delete. The clip will be restored to its state before the title was added.

Entering a Title

Most of the title modes offer two lines in the text box. If you want more, create and add successive titles. For those modes that offer a Multiple option, as seen in Figure 14-3, you can go on and extend the title text much further. All that text won't be displayed in one frame, however, each two-line phrase will follow the last. This is why the multiple option is so good for credits.

When you add a title to a clip, it will appear as soon as the clip displays. If you want the title to begin later on in the clip, it's easy enough to do:

1. Drag the playback head to the frame where you want the title to begin.
2. Split the clip, using the COMMAND+T shortcut.
3. Add the title to the new clip. When you play it back, the continuity will remain intact with the title coming in at the later point.

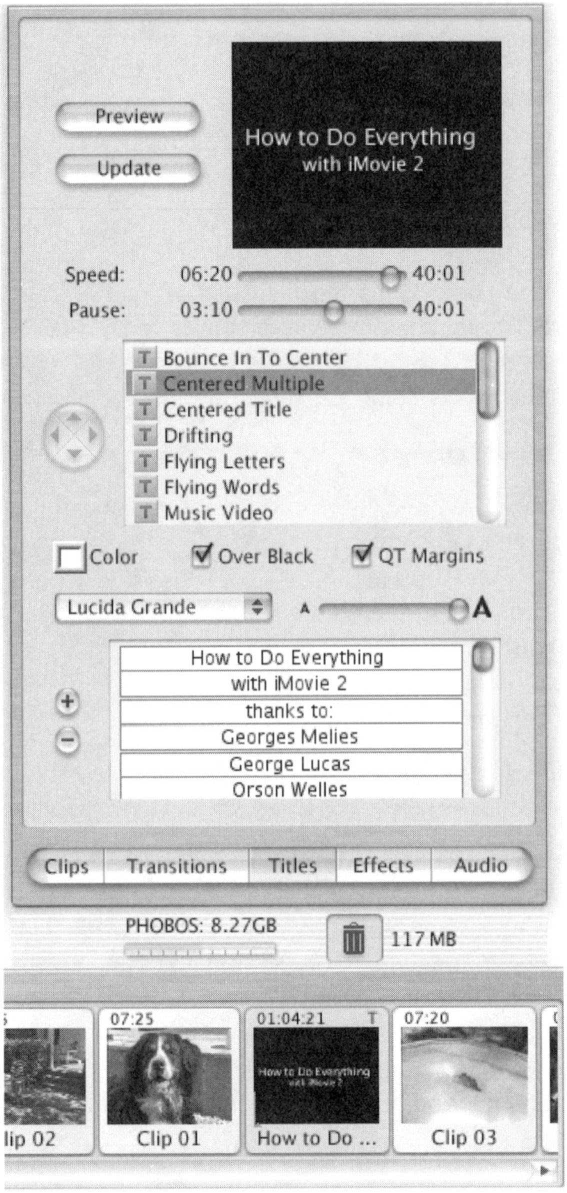

FIGURE 14-3 The Titles panel offers options to choose and preview your completed title.

Choosing Fonts

The best way to decide which font you want to use is by checking the Over Black option and choosing white from the color palette. You will be able to see the character and design of the font the most clearly here. There will be opportunities to exploit specialty fonts, but the simpler, cleaner, and bolder the font style is, the better it will read in all the ways that your iMovies will be seen. You can choose font colors after you have previewed the clips to see what works best over each scene.

And if you like a test just the way it is, you can instantly create an all-black title. Just click and drag the title mode name from the menu and drop it between the right clips and it will read the same as it did in the preview. A new black-background clip has been created! The QT Margins checkbox is to enable the title text to extend closer to the borders of the frame. The Normal mode respects the TV safe area, but, if you are distributing this movie on QuickTime, that won't be necessary.

CAUTION *If you have a large font library on your Mac, you'll be tempted to use some of your favorite fonts to create a special effect, even if it's not very readable when played on a TV. A title isn't very useful if it can't be read, so you'll want to test the fonts carefully before picking the ones you want to use.*

Adding Title Modes

Sample and preview the different title modes that are described below. You need to be able to see how their animations move and contrast against the moving footage they will go over.

When a title on a clip has been fully rendered, the clip will be awarded a "T" at the upper right-hand corner of its frame. At the bottom of the clip frame you will see the first words of the title, or, if you have chosen the Music Video title, it will say "Music Video." Select that text. You will see that it becomes an active text box, and you can type over the existing text. This will not affect or change the resident title. This feature can be used to create a handy identifier for action in that clip.

Title Styles

In addition to changing text, font, and color, there are other ways you can set up a title for maximum impact. We'll list them in this section.

Centered Title

This is the most familiar of standard titles, with a clear and strong imprint as it fades in, pauses, and then fades out, as seen in Figure 14-4.

FIGURE 14-4 The centered title says it all, up front and center.

Centered Multiple

This title expands upon the centered title by adding more sets of lines that fade in and out, following the lead title set. This makes room for more information, such as opening credits and backstory warmup.

Action Titles

These are titles with some measure of motion design and animation. Some have directional controls that provide even more variety in the way they can come in and out of the screen.

Your choices are listed below:

- **Bounce In to Center** The top line floats down from above, and the bottom line comes up from below, and they meet in the middle with a slight bounce like two hands clapping. It's a snappy way to start (check out Figure 14-5), especially if you have a sound cue or accent that will exclaim the contact.

- **Drifting** Drifting is a graceful counterpoint between the upper and the lower lines as they float past each other in opposite directions (as shown in Figure 14-6). It is an effect that works best with shorter rather than longer titles.
- **Rolling Centered Credits and Rolling Credits** "Roll credits!" is the refrain of TV directors. The rolling credits feature (see Figure 14-7) provides a way to roll up, from bottom to top, a fair amount of information, such as credits or lists of any kind. You can add following sets in this mode to make up for the time limitations, and they will read as if they were all part of the same feed.

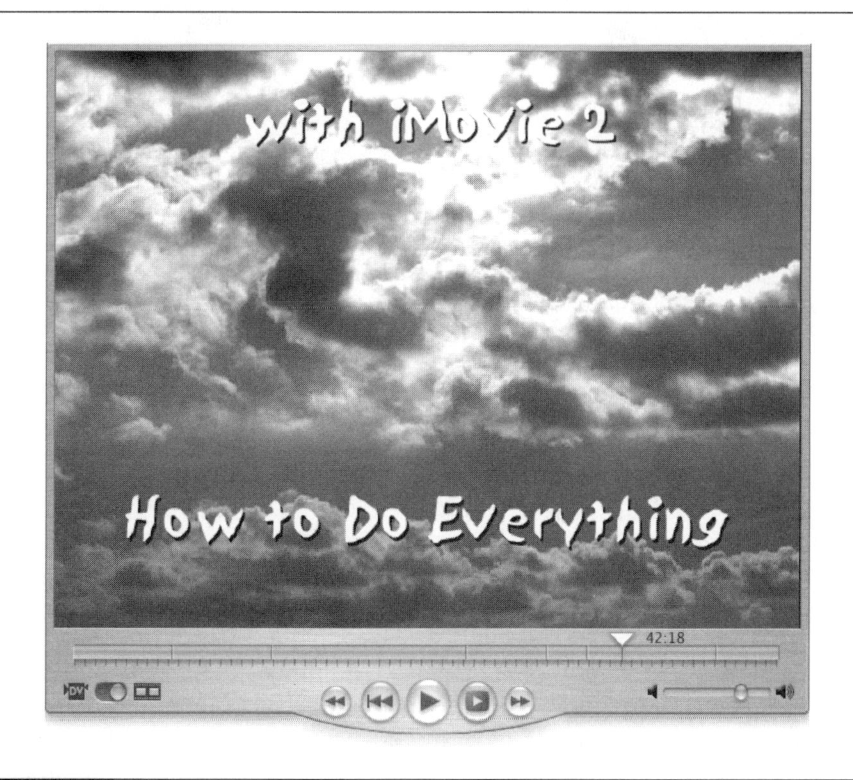

FIGURE 14-5 Top and bottom float down and up and past each other to center.

FIGURE 14-6 This just drifted in.

- **Scroll with Pause** The scroll with pause is similar to the centered title, but it comes in to the center, then holds, and goes off. It will do this from four directions. The result is a rhythmic emphasis that can be effective for a series of statements, like starring role credits.
- **Scrolling Block** The scrolling block offers the largest text window and the greatest text area, which can roll up or down. This can display more information than rolling credits.
- **Flying Letters and Flying Words** Watching letters and words fly in from above or below is dramatic and graphically interesting. When the letters fly in they are additive, spelling out the words one at a time. If this action is done too fast, though, the words can be hard to read and

FIGURE 14-7 And no humans were abused during the making of this picture.

follow. Flying words like the ones seen in Figure 14-8 are stately and authoritative.

- **Zoom and Zoom Multiple** The zooms have a central and dynamic impact as they expand up out of the center, fill, hold, and fade. The zoom multiple (see Figure 14-9) can telegraph sock-it-to-you credits and exclamations.

Subtitles

Whether designed as a special effect, as help for the hearing impaired, or as multilingual or educational enhancement, subtitles may be an important weapon in your arsenal.

FIGURE 14-8 The words fly in from above to tell the story.

Here's a list of iMovie's subtitle formats:

- **Subtitle and Subtitle Multiple** Subtitles are not only good for serving multiple language videos, they're useful in many other informational applications where you don't want the main action to be intruded upon. The subtitle multiple (shown in Figure 14-10) fades up each line one at a time. You can combine titles and subtitles in the same clip for more extensive screen notation.
- **Stripe Subtitle** Following the network style of CNN and Fox News, as seen in Figure 14-11, you can take advantage of the universally effective stripe subtitle. Superimposed over the gradient stripe, the title is clear and visible no matter the color or brightness of the changing scene.

FIGURE 14-9 Text zooms from the center to fill the screen. The effect is enhanced here by the spray.

Text

Using text is one way to give your titles an understated look, conveying authenticity. Here are two possibilities:

14

- **Typewriter** Do you remember typewriters? As a title that builds along one letter at a time, the Typewriter mode delivers the stamp of authenticity. Composed more like a subtitle than a title, this text makes its statement without getting in the way. The sample shown in Figure 14-12 is in the American Typewriter font.
- **Music Video** Styled like the text blocks composed to label the performances on MTV, this mode has a large text box and is very flexible. As seen in Figure 14-13, it comes in from left or right, and can be tabbed towards the center.

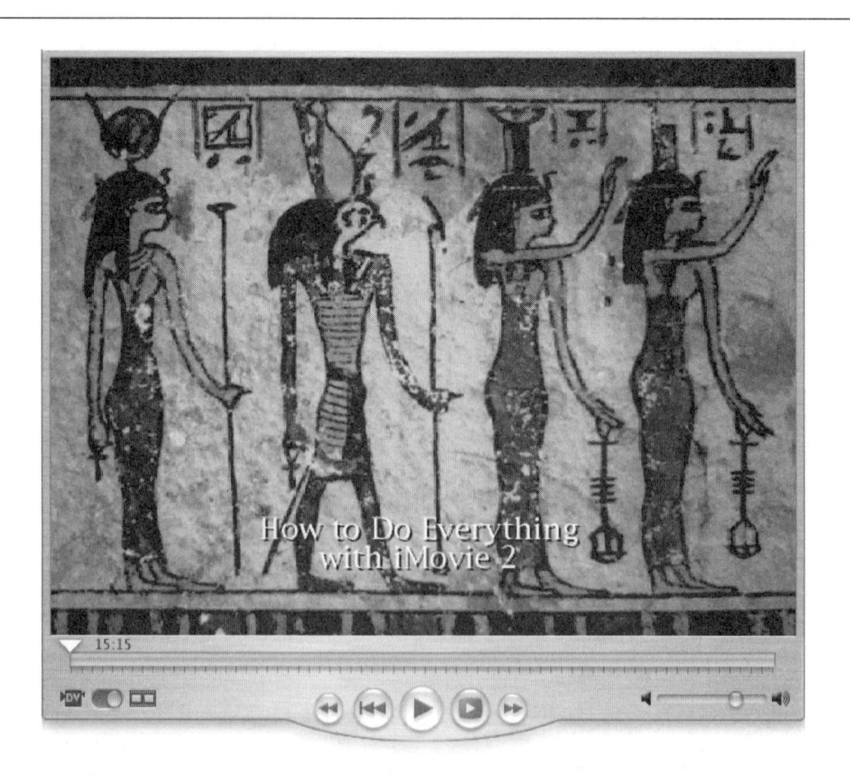

FIGURE 14-10 And so the ancients have sub-scribed.

Make a Slide Show

You may have made the transition from still photography to slide shows, and then graduated from slides to movies, but now slide shows can be easier than ever with iMovie. And they can go a lot further than the living room wall.

An iMovie slide show can be saved and played back as an iMovie. It can be exported and saved as a QuickTime movie and copied to tape, CD-ROM, or DVD, and sent over the Web, as you will see in later chapters. Slide shows can also be created within QuickTime Player Pro, AppleWorks, and iPhoto. But why do a slide show when you can make a movie?

Your iMovie slide show can serve many purposes:

- There are some movies whose stories are longer than their best shots.
- Slide shows can be a great way of showing a group of stills from your digital camera.

FIGURE 14-11 The stripe subtitle reads clear as a banner, no matter what the scene.

- There are many applications where the stop-and-go selectivity of a slide show format is more practical and advantageous than a continuous movie. Examples are presentations for education, training, real estate offerings, corporate communications, and public displays.
- The wealth of iMovies' transitions, effects, titles, and sound can enrich the slide show well beyond the means of most other slide show authoring environments.

Slide Home

The first thing to do is create a new project for your slide show. If you want to distinguish your movies from your slide shows in the collections of your Pictures

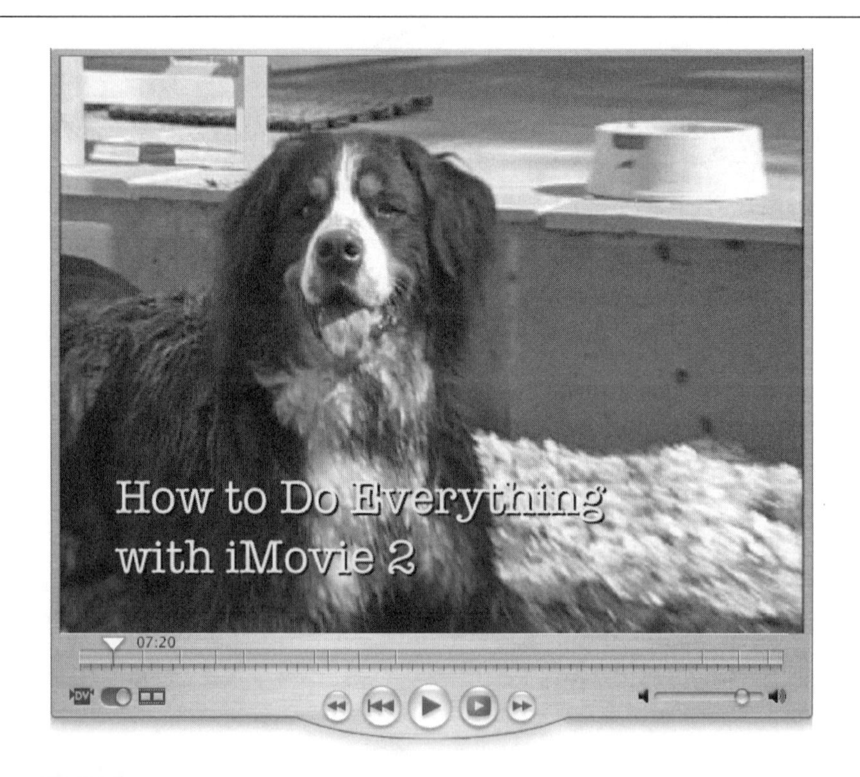

FIGURE 14-12 The typewriter text tells it like it is.

or Media folder, you might title them beginning with "slide," as we do here for *DogWash 101*, a qualifying instructional tutorial for advanced canine cleanliness.

1. From the File menu, select New Project, and create a new folder called Slide Shows in the same folder where your Movies and Picture folders are.
2. Name your slide show *Slides; DogWash 101*. Click Save and you're ready to go. The title now appears on the top frame of the Clip Viewer. The Shelf and Monitor are blank.

Slide Sources

As with any movie you make with iMovie 2, you can import a variety of different kinds of images to incorporate into your project. You can directly import still image files in these formats: PICT, GIF, BMP, and Photoshop. You can use iPhoto to import the images you took with your digital camera. For motion files, use the DV Stream

FIGURE 14-13 The music video text puts the credit where it won't intrude on the action.

setting, which enables you to import images from movies through QuickTime Player Pro and from other iMovies.

1. For this slide show, go to the File menu and select Import.
2. Open the iMovie Tutorial, and then its Media folder. You will see the six Tutorial Clips, but they will be grayed out and unavailable.
3. To activate the set of six clips, select the DV Stream file from the Show pop-up menu. Select the clips and import them; they appear on the Shelf as the grist for your mill.

NOTE *If you don't have the iMovie Tutorial at hand, don't despair. You can follow these steps with your own photo collection to get an idea of how easy it is to make a slide show in iMovie 2.*

Snapping Stills from Clips

Designing a good, logical slideshow that hits the high points of the story while filling the spaces with warmth and color, starts when you choose the frames from the footage that you have available. Sketch a rough outline of what the continuity requires in order to support the theme and the action, which here is a celebration of the simple joys of family life with children and pets. As you go through the clips, don't be afraid to choose some frames simply because they look good. They can contribute to the flow when you are further along in development.

To extract a frame from a clip:

1. Choose the clip that you want to start with. The first frame appears in the Monitor window.
2. Play the clip and position the frame you want to extract underneath the playhead.
3. From the File menu select Save Frame As, or press COMMAND+F. The Save Frame dialog box opens, as seen in Figure 14-14.
4. Create a new folder for the frames you will be saving.
5. Type a name for the frame in the Name text box.
6. Click Save.

NOTE *The default file format, as displayed in the Format menu, is Macintosh PICT File. This is the format you want to use in iMovie 2. The second choice in the menu, JPEG, is what you would choose if you wanted to e-mail this frame image.*

As you save the frames, they will accumulate in the frame folder. To bring the frames into iMovie 2, import them into the project. They appear on the Shelf. Each frame is labeled as a .pict file, and timed with a default duration of five seconds—long enough to be recognized, but brief enough to be seen as a still.

TIP *It's usually helpful to import each frame you extract from a clip as soon as you have finished with it. This way you will see the material you are working with as you progress. And we might as well refer to those frames as slides from now on.*

FIGURE 14-14 Saving that frame for a slide.

Sliding Along

Editing your slide show is not much different from editing a movie, so you are already more than one step along. We can start by arranging the slides in the clip viewer, as you see in Figure 14-15. Play the sequence to review the material. At five seconds per slide, there is plenty of time to get a sense of each slide image. Now re-arrange and delete slides to work towards the continuity you want to see.

Changing the Duration of a Slide's Display

The default duration of five seconds may seem too long, too short, or even just right. Follow these steps to change that default setting if you would like it to be different, as shown in Figure 14-16.

FIGURE 14-15 With a slide show, what you see here is what you will get.

1. From the iMovie menu, select Preferences.
2. Choose the Import tab.
3. In the Still Clips default text box, type in number of seconds for the new setting.
4. Click OK.

As you edit the slide show, you will want to set different durations for different slides. It's easy to change how long each slide stays on the screen.

1. Select the slide you want to change.
2. In the Image Selection Time text box on the Clip Viewer (see Figure 14-17), type in the new duration.
3. Deselect the slide. The slide will now play for that new length of time.

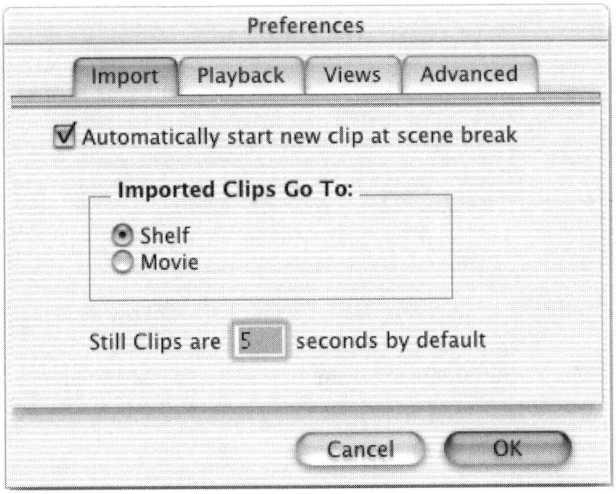

Preferences
Import
Playback
Views
Advanced
Automatically start new clip at scene break
Imported Clips Go To:
Shelf
Movie
Still Clips are 5 seconds by default
Cancel
OK

FIGURE 14-16 Change the default duration here.

Cinematic Strokes

Because you are sculpting an audiovisual slide show out of the raw material of video clips, the rules are different than if you were composing a series of still photos. You may find opportunities in strategically chosen groups of frames that can provide an effect or an expression in the slides.

For instance, the three frames shown in Figure 14-18, that were part of a zoom shot, can give us a "slide zoom" that you can bring in and hold under a title. The two frames from the clip shown in Figure 14-19 give the slides the means to telegraph the subject's personality.

Image Selection: Dog11.pict Time: 00:07:00
05:00
Dog8.pict
02:00
Dog9.pict
07:00
Dog11.pict
03:00
Dog10.pict

FIGURE 14-17 Change the slide duration here.

14

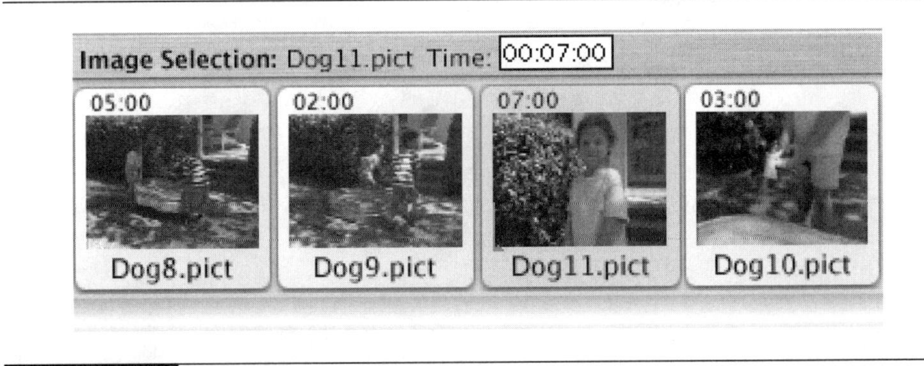

FIGURE 14-18 The "zoomescence" of the clip was captured to give a rise to the slides.

Transitions in Slides

All the transitions in the iMovie repertory are available for your slide show. Because the durations you set for slides may often be shorter than that of the average clip, you need to allow for the overlap time within the slide time for the transition to work. For instance, in the fades that bracket the seven-slide sequence show in Figure 14-20, the duration of the first slide was set higher to absorb the incoming fade. As far as iMovie is concerned, a 5-second slide is just a 5-second clip with identical frames.

Even when you have allowed enough time for both slides on either side of a transition, some graphic transitions, like radial, scale down, and warp in may be too overwhelming in a slide show. Cross dissolve, push, and overlap can work very well between still images.

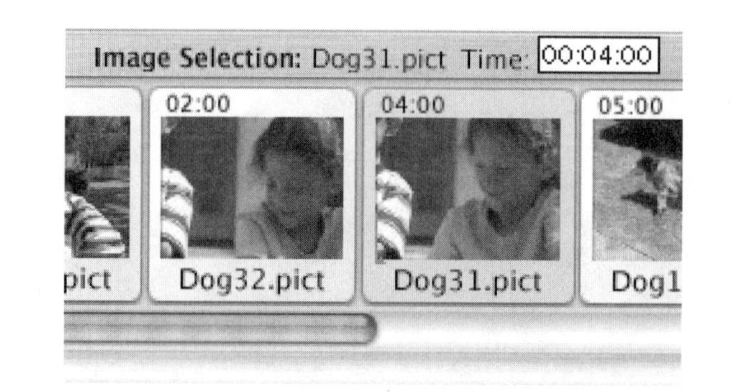

FIGURE 14-19 The moment of a smile is opened wider between two slides.

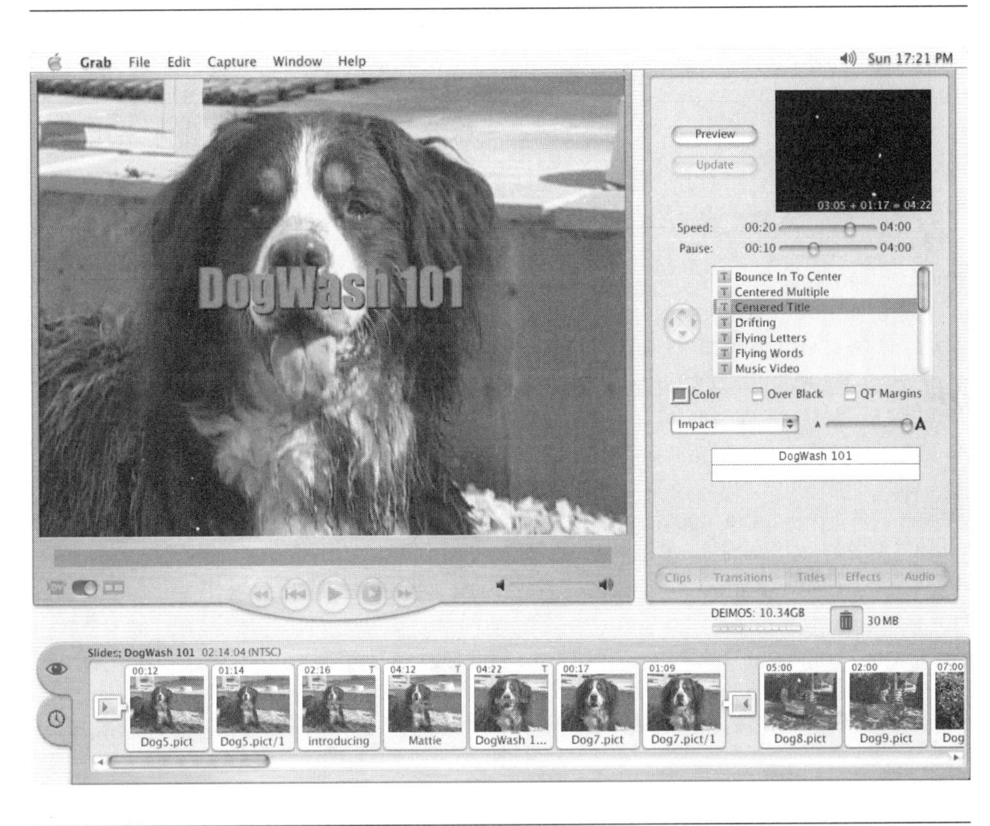

FIGURE 14-20 Mattie the Wonder Dog makes her silver slide debut.

Effects in Slides

Corrective and classic effects can provide a great deal of creative latitude for slide images. The same caution of allowing enough time for transitions goes for dynamic special effects like mirrors and n-square.

Titles in Slides

In movies, titles are often laid over still images and backgrounds, so most titles available in iMovie work well for slides. Some of the more vivid action titles, however, might make the slides that follow look limp by comparison.

For beginning or inserting a title, the action of splitting a clip works the same on a slide as it does with a movie clip, because slides are really "mini-clips" anyway. Even a one-second clip can be split into fractions of a second—not that it would leave you much to work with. As shown back in Figure 14-20, by using splits and adjusting slide durations, you can have full use of titles and transitions in a solid slide show.

Audio in Slides

How you design the audio portion of your slide show depends mostly upon how you will be presenting it. If it is to be displayed as a show, from beginning to end without interruption, then music, sound effects, and narration can be laid in much as you would in a movie. You might record your narration first, if the slides are meant to illustrate and supplement your personal story about *Mattie the Wonder Dog*. Then you would tailor the continuity to match your topic points. For a friends-and-family kind of slide show, laying in a soft background music track would be the best choice to support your live, in-person narration.

It is when you need to be able to stop and start within the show, like during a PowerPoint presentation, that your audio may be absent, or discontinuous and supplementary, for certain sequences of the show. In corporate communications applications, there may be several sequences where different personnel would be quoted, and those voice-overs would be specific to certain slides. You, as the presenter, would let each play through, and then advance to the next point, where you, would continue the narration "live." iMovie 2 is so flexible that you can choose to have video clips interspersed with slides within your presentation.

The Closing Scene

With a little effort and imagination, you can finish off your movie or slide show (or combination movie/slide show!) with the judicious use of titles, subtitles, and captions—all of which combine to convey a message, or just to credit the hard-working folks responsible for your production.

All finished? Not quite. You may want to spruce up your video with some stock footage, or add special artwork to convey an emotional message. In Chapter 15, we look to outside sources for this additional material.

Chapter 15 Expanding Your Sources

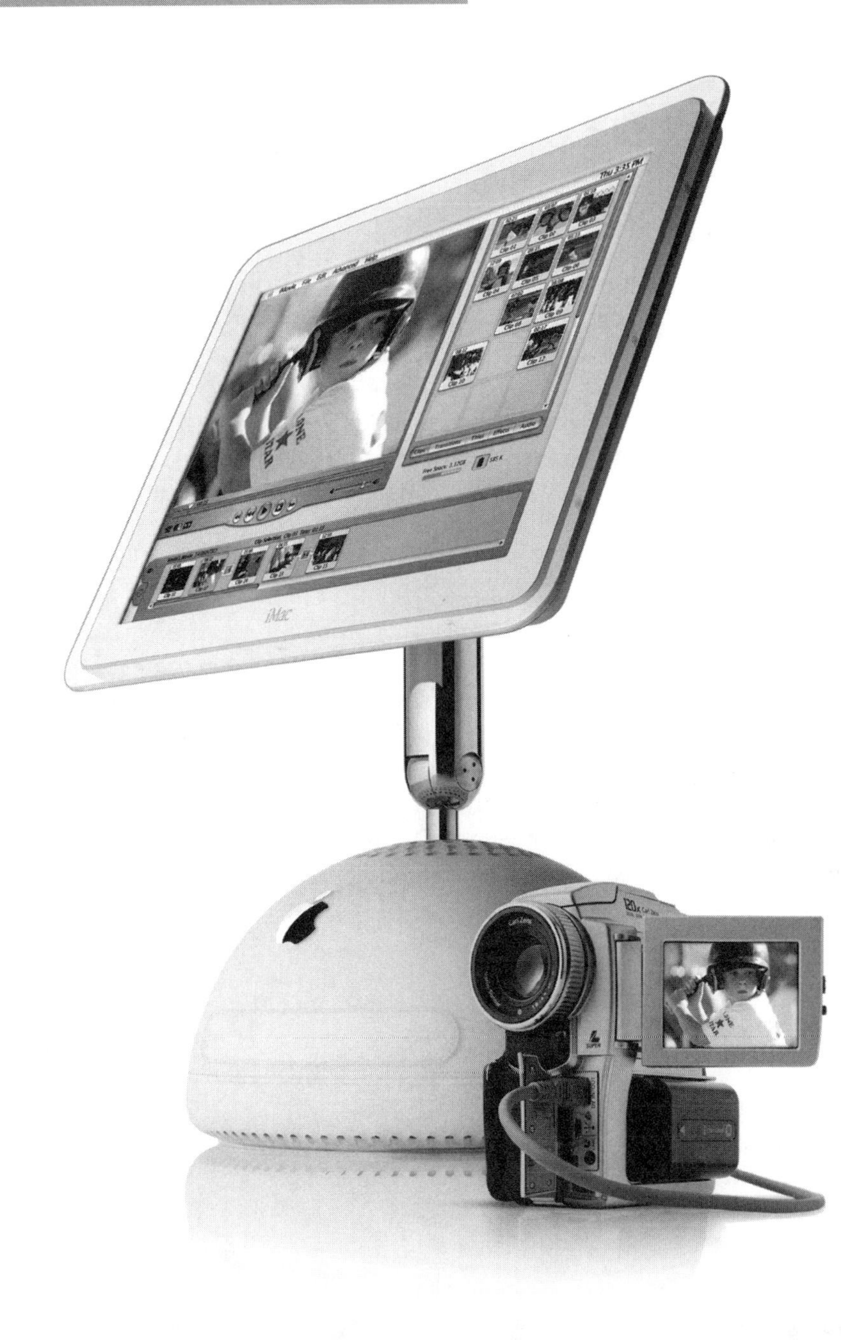

How to…

- Add artwork and photos
- Locate and use stock footage
- Incorporate broadcast footage
- Use your vintage films
- Use your vintage analog videos
- Use webcams
- Create animation and visual effects

So far in this book, you've discovered the ins and outs of editing your videos in iMovie 2. From importing your video to reshaping it according to your needs and your imagination, you've seen how easy it is to design and expand your story in a huge variety of ways.

Up till now, though, you have been working primarily with the footage you've shot with your DV camcorder. This is, by far, the easiest way to work with iMovie 2, because all you need is the camcorder, the FireWire cable, and the time it takes to import your video onto your Mac (which can be measured by the duration of your original video).

But footage from your camcorder isn't the only source of material for your iMovie. It may be just a part of it, enhanced by still pictures and movies from other sources. Or you may simply use other sources for the raw footage.

In this chapter, we'll focus on the alternatives. You'll discover how to take still pictures and artwork and use them to full advantage in making your video. In addition, you'll learn how to harness other sources for video material, such as your own older films and videos, as well as broadcast footage. You'll even learn how to harness the awesome power of stock footage to give your video an incredibly professional look and feel.

Using Flat Art and Photos

A video of your teenager's sixteenth birthday begins with a montage of black and white photos, first showing her in her mother's arms hours after birth, then showing her as a toddler, and, finally, showing her going off to grade school. The last image then fades into her smiling face as she sits amid a huge pile of presents.

Add an appropriate musical background, and this could be an effective and even emotional alternative to the standard birthday video. Another variation is to intersperse the black and white photos with brief video clips of family members reminiscing about the birthday girl.

Instead of superimposing titles and captions onto one of your video clips or a black screen, you can use photos and artwork as backgrounds to deliver brief, tantalizing hints about the movie you're about to present.

Whether a photo from your family album, a picture of a special vacation spot, or an image of a famous oil painting, artwork and photos provide another way to give life to your story. Since your Mac is billed as the hub of your digital lifestyle, you'll find many ways to bring in those pictures for use in iMovie2. They include:

- **Digital Photos** Some camcorders can take stills but, for best quality, a dedicated digital camera can deliver superb picture quality—in some cases rivaling traditional film photography. Most digital cameras these days come with Macintosh software and, if you're using Mac OS X, you'll find you probably can use the built-in Image Capture software to download the pictures from your camera's memory card. Better, consider Apple's iPhoto (see Figure 15-1), a clever application that can manage your digital photo library, from the import process, to editing and cropping, and even to posting your images in an online photo album.
- **Scanner** Don't have a digital camcorder? Or perhaps your photo albums consist of regular prints made from film negatives. Here's where you can harness the power of one of those low-cost personal scanners to capture the images from photos, original artwork, even books, and convert them to digital format so you can view and edit them on your Mac. Scanners are sometimes given free as premiums with a new computer purchase, and many are available for less than $100 (see Figure 15-2). Others can cost upwards of a grand. Is there a difference? If you are preparing digital artwork for the publishing industry, you need the absolute best quality, but for online use or for images you're going to insert into an iMovie 2 production, a minor difference in picture sharpness won't be noticeable.

Using Stock Footage

When you see a wartime scene in a movie or TV show where soldiers are massing at a beachfront, or tanks are firing at each other in battle, do you really think all that footage is done by a movie company's special effects team? Not every movie has the budget to create such difficult and expensive shots from scratch. Many productions, particularly those on TV, are done in a far more inventive fashion, using existing shots that capture those specialized moments. It's called stock footage.

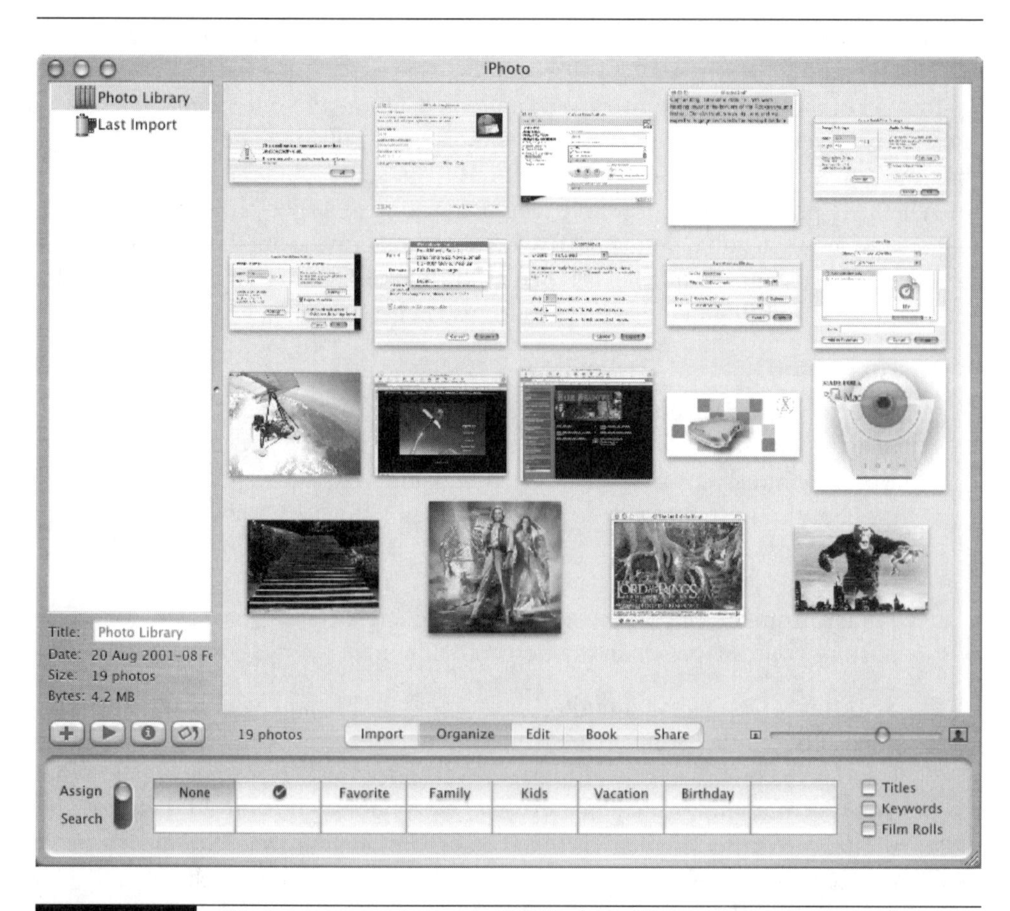

FIGURE 15-1 iPhoto can organize your digital photo library, a great source of material for iMovie.

NOTE *Some low budget TV shows actually make original footage of special effects sequences, but just reuse those shots over and over again throughout the series to save work and keep budgets really low. Back in the 1950s, for example, the highly popular Superman TV series, starring the late George Reeves, used the same primitive flying scenes over and over again, often several times in the very same episode. And how many times do you recall Clark Kent running into that same storeroom, pulling off his glasses, and opening his suit, ready to change into the man of steel? Consider the Flash Gordon movie serials of the 1930s, where the same shots of spaceships taking off and landing were regularly reused.*

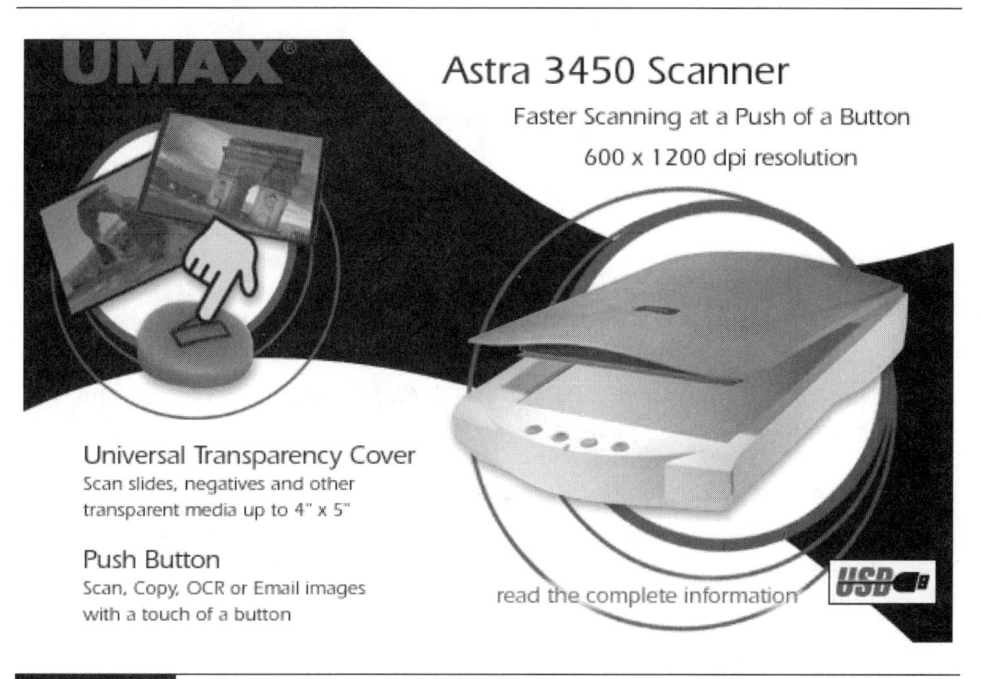

FIGURE 15-2 Umax is one company that builds low-cost scanners of extremely high quality.

But you don't have to be a professional movie producer to benefit from stock footage, and there's a wealth of it to be found if you do a little judicious searching on the Internet.

A Word About File Formats

iMovie 2 reads still photos in Adobe Photoshop, BMP (a Windows bitmap picture format), GIF, JPEG, and PICT formats, and can import QuickTime clips. But what about the ubiquitous Windows AVI format? How do you handle that? One way is Apple's QuickTime video player, which can import clips in the Windows-based AVI format and export them as QuickTime. However, to unlock this and other capabilities in QuickTime, you have to first upgrade to the Pro version, at $29.95, to access the extra import and export features.

And what about those other popular media formats, such as the one used by Microsoft's Windows Media Player or RealVideo? Sorry, but they're not going to work. Fortunately, you have so many choices in QuickTime format, you should be able to fill most any need without having to worry about converting some other format.

A Survey of Stock Footage Resources

Here's a listing of some popular sources of stock footage, along with a brief description of what they offer:

NOTE *We are mentioning these sites for information purposes only, not to recommend any particular site as best for your purposes. As with any online resource, we recommend you check them out thoroughly or solicit recommendations from other users before you order footage. If you surf the Internet regularly, no doubt you'll find additional resources that will suit your needs.*

- **Adventure Productions (www.aerial-stockfootage.com)** This stock footage source concentrates on custom solutions rather than prepackaged collections. Its specialty is extreme sports action, depicting such high-pressure activities as hang gliding in various locations around the world (see Figure 15-3). You'll want to contact the company directly to check for footage and pricing.

FIGURE 15-3 Maybe you wouldn't want to do this yourself, but a picture of this sort of activity may do wonders for your video footage.

- **Artbeats (www.artbeats.com)** The stock in trade of Artbeats is royalty-free digital stock footage. The material is available for unlimited use, and is available in CD-ROM collections that are grouped by topic and title. Clips can be sampled in single frame, thumbnail clips, or storyboard form before you place your order.
- **Easymotion (www.easymotion.com)** This source specializes in "royalty-free animation motion graphics" (see Figure 15-4). Footage is available on CD-ROM in QuickTime format, and is designed for use in presentations and broadcasting. Products are listed by topic, and sample clips are available for download.
- **Environmental Media Corporation (www.envmedia.com/stock.htm)** This is a special-purpose resource, which is designed to provide footage of plants and animals for classroom instruction on environmental issues. Footage

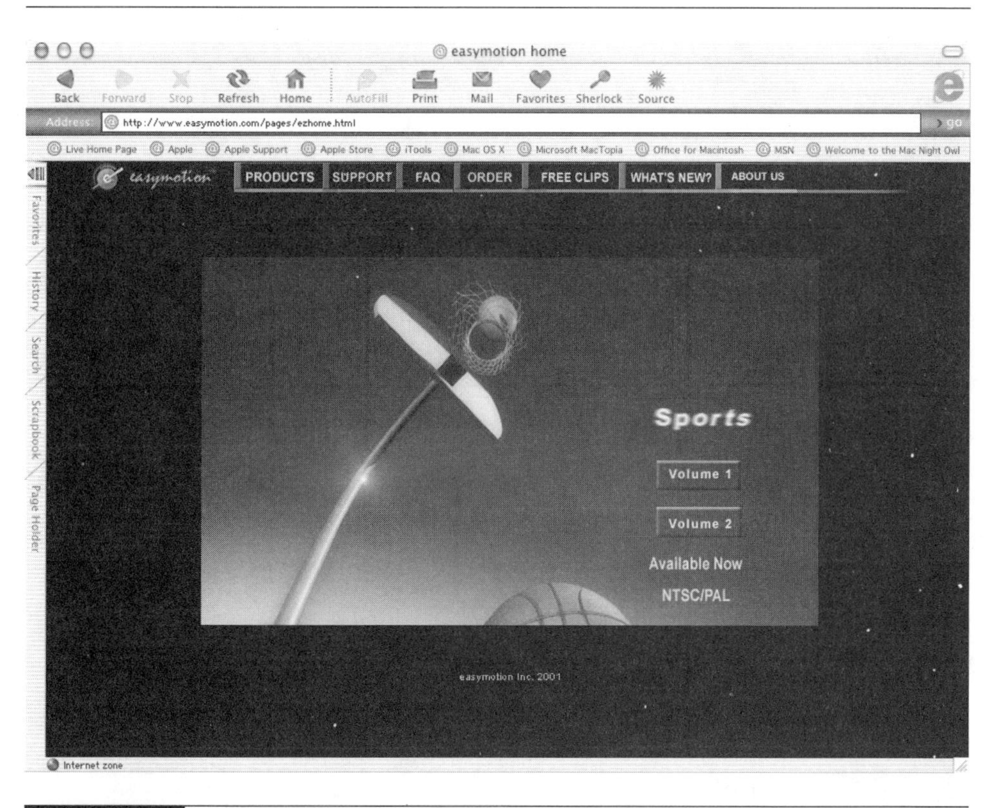

FIGURE 15-4. This site offers an extensive lineup of quality footage.

is available on video, CD-ROM, or DVD. They also offer special licenses for broadcast use of the footage.

- **Getty Images Creative (http://creative.gettyimages.com/source/motion/)** This is a single resource (see Figure 15-5) that culls its offerings from a variety of resources. Footage is available in two forms—one is royalty free, and the other is rights protected, where the footage is licensed for specific use, and pricing depends on how or where the movie will be distributed. Footage is available on video or CD-ROM.

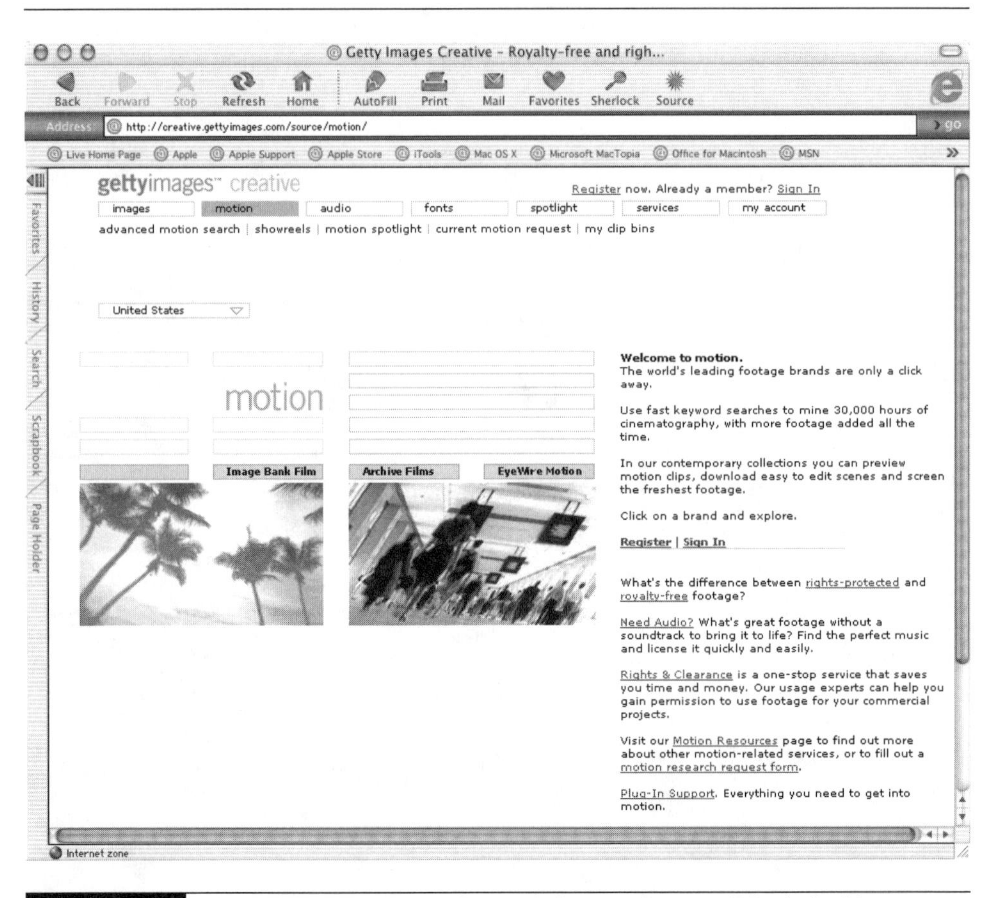

FIGURE 15-5 One of many resources for stock footage for your iMovie 2 videos.

- **Historic Films (www.historicfilms.com)** As the title implies, Historic Films specializes in stock footage covering a wide ranger of subjects, dating from 1985 through 1990. You'll find such diverse material as outtakes from newsreels to some of the most exciting moments from television, including segments from *The Ed Sullivan Show* and *The Steve Allen Show.* Material is licensed on a per-use basis, and sample clips can be downloaded from the company's Web site.
- **Show Poppers (www.showpoppers.com)** Show Poppers offers a single collection of royalty-free clips on DVD, consisting of scenic- and wildlife-based footage. The package also includes music tracks, all in QuickTime format. While a full description of all the offerings was lacking at the company's Web site, there seems to be enough variety to cover lots of background footage needs.

NOTE *At the time we checked the company's site, sample clips weren't yet available, but they should be by the time you read this book.*

- **WPA Film Library (www.mpihomevideo.com/stockfootage.html)** This company offers some 60,000 hours of film and video covering a host of subjects from popular culture to geography. Film and video materials (see Figure 15-6) are licensed on a per-use basis. You can choose from DVD or video versions, and sample footage is available for download.

A Warning About Copyrights

When you film your own material, your only concern is a release for non-family members. But when you start incorporating outside footage to flesh out your movies, you run up against the copyright laws, which are particularly stringent as to how such footage can be used. And the same holds true for images from published books or images of artwork.

In a most general sense, the best type of outside footage is what is called "royalty free." Mass-market clip art is offered in this same way to graphic artists. What this means is that you pay just one up-front cost for the footage and you are free to use it thereafter within the limits of the license agreement. If royalties are charged, you'd have to come up with a payment on a per-copy or per-use basis.

Another licensing agreement offered by some sources, "rights protected," means you pay for rights to use the footage depending on your needs and how it is to be distributed. If you expand your distribution plans, you have to go back to the source and purchase an additional license.

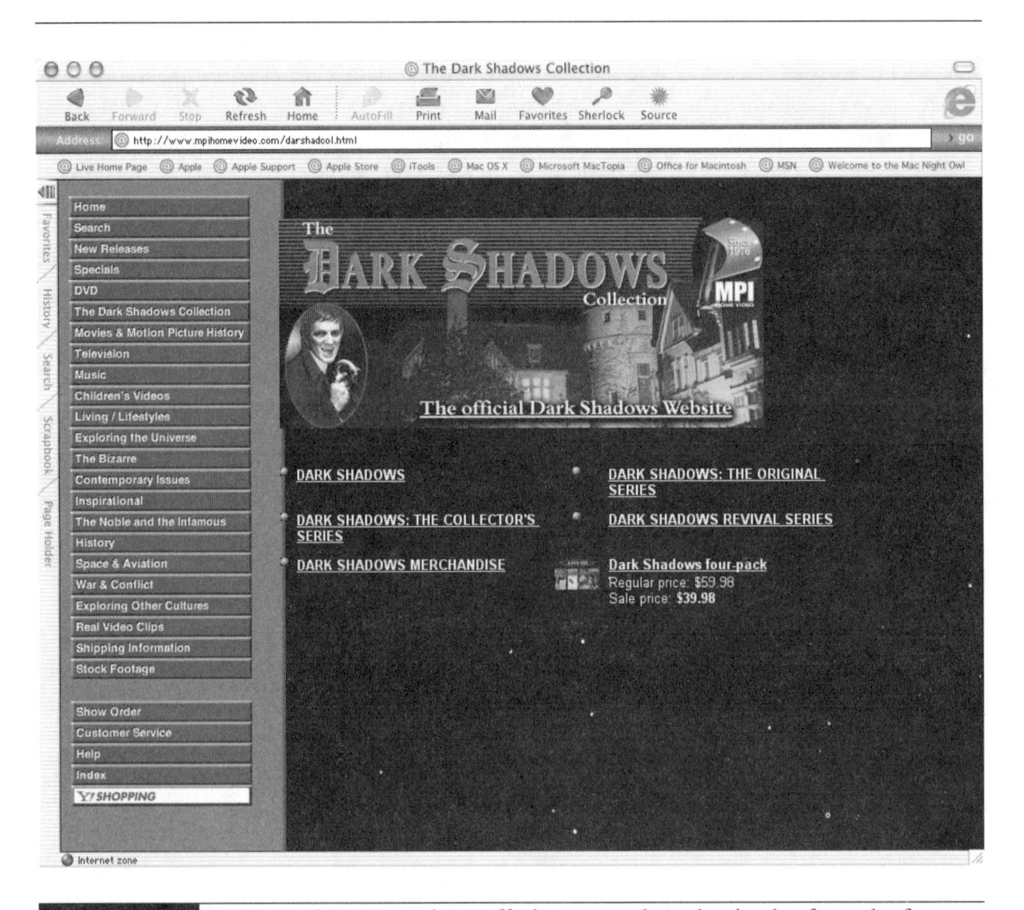

FIGURE 15-6 Among the more unique offerings are selected episodes from the famous TV gothic serial, *Dark Shadows*.

When it comes to commercial films, the answer is that studio lawyers won't go after you if you just copy footage for your personal use, such as showing a beaming up sequence from *Star Trek*, but if you attempt to distribute a movie containing that footage, you'll run afoul of copyright and piracy laws.

TIP

You may be able to use a limited amount of commercial footage using the "fair use" provisions of the copyright laws. These allow you to run excerpts of copyrighted material for commentary, news, educational use, and satire. However, since the exact amount of copyrighted material you might be able to use in this fashion is essentially a gray area, it is still best to seek permission from the network or studio that owns the footage before you use it.

Using Broadcast Footage for Home Videos

You are watching TV and find some simply awesome scenes that you'd love to use in your home video, or perhaps you see that important presidential address that would be nice to show in your child's classroom.

In iMovie 2 you can edit footage from a variety of sources, so this may indeed be a perfect opportunity to obtain footage that you could never shoot yourself. If that's on your mind, with a few cautions, here's a brief listing of the ways you can acquire that footage on your Mac.

CAUTION *Before you attempt to use commercial broadcast footage in your video, you'll want to read the section entitled "A Warning About Copyrights," in this chapter. For personal use, it should be no problem, but as soon as you plan to take the movie that contains this footage beyond your family unit, you risk running afoul of copyright laws.*

- **VCR** The regular household VCR is a great tool for recording that cool car chase or spectacular explosion or outer space epic from commercial or cable TV. Once you've acquired your footage, you can easily hook up your DV camcorder to your VCR and transfer it; some camcorders even come with cables for a simple one-step hookup. Some camcorders will even let you do pass-through, where you can direct the signal straight to your Mac's FireWire port without having to record it first.

NOTE *Don't expect great quality on a regular VHS VCR because its resolution is less than half that of even the cheapest DV camcorder. A better resource is S-VHS, a higher resolution version that'll offer pretty sharp pictures (although these models tend to suffer from a bit of extra video noise).*

TIP *A better way to get good quality video from broadcast sources is to use a system that records digital video onto a hard drive. If you opt for the higher quality setting for such a device, you can get some pretty good looking footage, but you'll need to use your camcorder or a separate adapter module, such as Formac Studio (see Figure 15-7), to grab the video signal and bring it to your Mac.*

- **Direct from TV** You can hook your DV camcorder up to a TV and record the broadcasts directly. The advantage of this technique is quality. Your camcorder is probably capable of producing a higher quality image

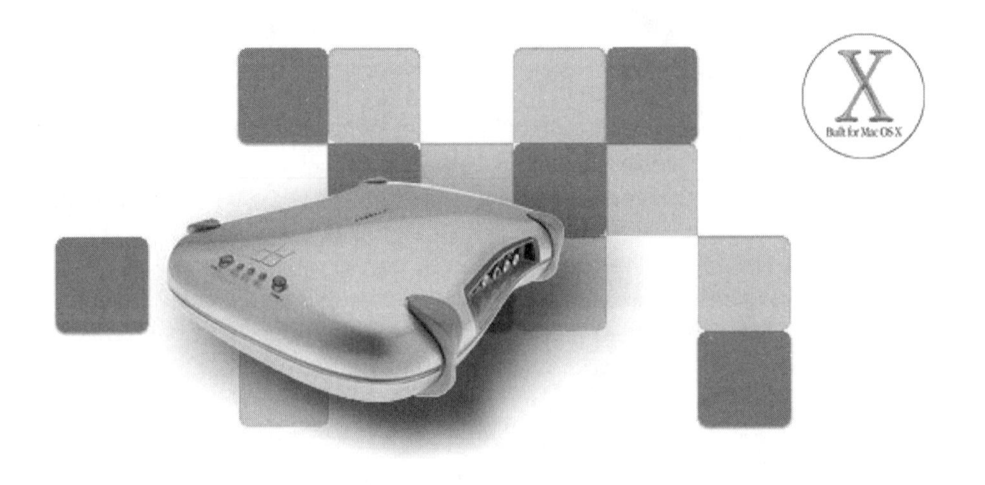

FIGURE 15-7 This breakout box lets you convert video formats, and brings them to your Mac's FireWire port.

than is available from your broadcast resource—it will be limited by the reception quality. Digital cable and satellite are the best sources.

- **TV Card** A video card capable of receiving broadcasts, such as the ATI XCLAIM TV USB Edition, can capture incoming broadcast sequences as QuickTime movies. For the most part, however, some products may not be of use, for they may play broadcast TV but not capture it directly. Worse, the slow speed of the USB peripheral bus will conspire to limit picture quality rather severely. You'll want to consult the documentation to be sure.

NOTE *How do you hook up your DV camcorder to your VCR or TV? It's usually just a matter of plugging in the cables and setting the camcorder to VCR record mode to receive the signal. Consult your user guide for the specifics for your particular make and model.*

Using Your Own Vintage Film Footage

All right, you've lived through all the home video generations. When it was vogue, you made 8mm videos, Super8, even videos with sound. Perhaps you even ventured into film documentary territory and went to 16mm. But now that we're in the digital hub generation, just how do you handle all those old reels of film?

We suppose you could do it fast and dirty and just shoot directly off the projection screen, but don't expect good quality any more than you might expect good quality from shooting footage from a TV screen or computer monitor.

But there are alternatives, the best one of which is to transfer all that footage onto video for easy capture to your Mac and editing in iMovie 2.

So how do you accomplish that task? Here are two ways:

- **Supermarket or superstore** This is the fast and dirty way. These stores contract with a service to do their photo finishing and simple conversions from 8mm and Super8 to VHS. You pay on a per reel basis. Don't expect great picture quality, but for a casual home video, it maybe sufficient.
- **Video production house** This is a better alternative. Some of the firms that shoot videos for special family events or corporate use also have dubbing facilities to transfer your reels to a finished video. You'll want to check out pricing, and perhaps see a sample tape to be sure it's what you want. Try to get DV tape or DVD, if you can, for the best possible quality.

NOTE *Before sending off the old reels for dubbing, you might want to play them first, in case you can discard a few reels that you may not want to see again or use as material for your iMovie 2 projects.*

Using Your Own Vintage Video Tapes

Do you have an older camcorder, perhaps in VHS or 8mm format, or just some tapes someone shot of a child's birthday or a wedding? Likely they're just sitting around catching dust in a closet. Maybe you don't really intend to ever view them again, because separating the wheat from the chaff isn't worth the bother.

What you'd really like to do is to copy those videos onto your Mac and cull the really good stuff and make up a video showing the highlights—all the classic shots you've taken over the years, and none of the boring footage that makes seeing the videos a chore even for relatives who are devoted to capturing family history.

There are two ways to transfer these videos:

- **Copy to your DV camcorder** The same connection you use to connect your camcorder to a TV set or VCR can be used to record videos from another camcorder or tape deck. Here you can be a little selective, copying only the footage you truly want to edit. Once it's copied, you can import the footage into iMovie 2 in the same fashion as any other footage, just as we described in Chapter 10.

- **Transfer it directly** Use an outboard conversion device, such as the Formac Studio, or a camcorder that can pass through the signal and import directly into iMovie 2. This is the route to the best possible quality, since you aren't transferring to another tape. Either way, chapter 10 will tell you how to bring in the footage for editing.

Using Webcams

Art imitating life again. Peter Weir's biting take on a person's life caught by hidden cameras in *The Truman Show* and Ron Howard's lighthearted variation, *EdTV*, once seemed interesting if unlikely curiosities. But more and more people are actually hooking up miniature cameras—webcams—to their PCs and using them not just for two-way communication, but to present interactive diaries of their lives to the public.

Some even charge a special access fee for the privilege, and provide content that is definitely to the far side of PG rated.

While a webcam's actual picture capturing capabilities are usually limited to single frame, this may serve as a suitable resource for material. You may, for example, have an online conference with a friend or family member on the other side of the world, then capture his or her image for use in a family movie.

Here's a brief list of some popular webcams worth a second look:

- **ADS Technologies PYRO WebCam and Card** This entrant in the desktop camera arena uses your Mac's FireWire port, rather than USB, and is thus capable of delivering better video. The company even provides a FireWire card for older G3 Mac desktops. The specifications include a maximum resolution of 640×480 pixels, with a frame rate of 30fps. This product handles videoconferencing chores courtesy of SmithMicro's VideoLink software.
- **ZoomCam—USB for Macintosh Computers** Well known as a manufacturer of telecommunications products such as modems, Zoom makes a USB camera (see Figure 15-8) that promises to capture stills at up to 704×576 pixels, plus full-color, live-motion video. The unit is

FIGURE 15-8 Bearing a stylish look that blends nicely with Macs, the ZoomCam is a low-cost way to bring in video images to your Mac.

powered by the USB bus, and teleconferencing chores are handled by CU-SeeMe. Special features include variable focus from 1.5 inches to infinity and automatic exposure capability.

Adding Animation and Visual Effects

Animation Software

Thousands upon thousands of ugly insects surrounded an unwary victim in Universal's special-effects ridden remake of *The Mummy* (see Figure 15-9), but no actual insects were used in the shooting of those horrific scenes. Instead, the moviemakers, for this and many other scenes, used computer animation programs to create masses of insects, swirling deserts, half-formed creatures, and ancient Egyptian cities torn asunder by mysterious forces.

From simple backgrounds to incredibly complex battle scenes, computer animators can deliver realistic visual effects without props or models. From TV's *Ally McBeal* to *Star Wars Episode II: Attack of the Clones*, banks of artists are kept busy rendering scores of images to enhance films and TV.

FIGURE 15-9 This is the underground chamber in which the mummy was first located.

Like any artistic skill, it takes a lot of time and effort to learn computer animation, but if you have already cut your teeth on such graphics programs as Adobe Photoshop and Illustrator, you may find it possible to adapt to the next level of computer-based artistry.

Several programs are available to develop animation, and some of these are the very same programs used in the entertainment industry. But the best of the breed doesn't come cheap:

- **LightWave 3D** From Newtek, this $2,495 animation program has been used to create visual effects in such recent films as *Black Hawk Down* and *The Time Machine* (see Figure 15-10). And on television, both *Enterprise* and *The X-Files* are among the shows that get full treatment with visuals courtesy of LightWave 3D. More information is available from http://www.newtek.com.

- **Maya** From the Alias|Wavefront™ division of SGI, this $7,500 application is a standby for such famous special effects houses as Digital Domain and Industrial Light and Magic. You've seen the results in such movies as *Lord of the Rings* (see Figure 15-11) and, of course, *Star Wars Episode I and II*. Even

FIGURE 15-10

FIGURE 15-11 Maya, a program you can run on your Mac, was used for many of the stunning visual effects in this film.

15

better, if you want to develop your skills at computer animation, you can download a copy of the free Maya Personal Learning Edition of the program, designed strictly for practice and non-commercial use, from the publisher's Web site at www.aliaswavefront.com/freemaya.

- **Toon Boom Studio** If your animation interests are closer to Mickey Mouse than to Jar-Jar Binks, you might want to take a look at Toon Boom Studio, a $374 2D animation application that has garnered high praise from Mac magazines. Although oriented more towards Web use, the animation quality is quite good for your movies. One of the program's clever features is an automatic lip sync analyzer that enables you to easily match your voiceovers to the characters in your cartoon. You can learn more about the software from the publisher's Web site at http://www.toonboomstudio.com/main/.

Stop Motion Animation

Although they're not household names, Willis O'Brien and Ray Harryhausen have produced works that have thrilled millions and millions of moviegoers for decades. O'Brien's brilliant execution of the famous 50-foot ape, King Kong (see Figure 15-12), stands as a monument to this incredibly labor-intensive technique. Who can forget the

FIGURE 15-12 An incredible feat of stop-motion animation, *King Kong* is brought to life.

beautiful lifelike, lumbering creature that conveyed such heart-felt emotion. Few movie characters have had such an impact.

NOTE *For the sake of this discussion, we won't get into the low-cost Asian-made King Kong films, which simply used a man in a monkey suit to create the big ape!*

Harryhausen got his feet wet in the business in the 1940s, and worked with O'Brien on such films as *Mighty Joe Young*, another story about an oversized gorilla. Later on Harryhausen gained fame on his own as the visual effects mastermind for such films as *Earth Versus the Flying Saucers, The Seventh Voyage of Sinbad*, and *Clash of the Titans.*

Although the artwork and results were different, highly impressive and, in many respects, as realistic as anything that is being done these days with computer animation, all of these effects were created using the techniques of drawn, or cell, animation—the same type of animation used in the creation of cartoons.

Incredibly detailed models of the creatures or objects are created, which are capable of very flexible, fluid movement. They are filmed one frame at a time. Between each frame, the model is moved ever so slightly. Remember that, at 24 frames per second, hundreds and hundreds of shots are necessary to convey even a few seconds of action in the completed movie.

Footage for even a brief sequence may take months to complete. It takes unimaginable patience and loving attention to detail to produce a realistic result. One false movement and the effect is lost. It's also probably a dying profession, since most animation these days is done on a computer, but if you have a feeling for arts and crafts and you can build dolls and puppets, this may be a technique you'll want to experiment with or master for one of your movies. Even if you aren't skilled at crafting models, you could, with careful attention to detail, buy off-the-shelf models of dinosaurs and planes and even toy puppets and use them to advantage in adding some extremely imaginative scenes to your videos.

The Closing Scene

The footage you shot with your DV camcorder isn't the only source for video material. By judiciously gathering videos, both old and new, plus other footage and images from other sources, you will have a vast resource of material that will give your completed video an unusual level of originality. If you are willing to develop some new skills, you may even want to explore the fabulous world of computer animation or the old art of stop-motion animation to create your visual enhancements. You'll stand out from the crowd in many ways.

Our next chapter focuses on the ways you can copy your movie, ranging from videotape to a QuickTime movie that you can email or post on the Internet.

Part V

Sharing iMovies

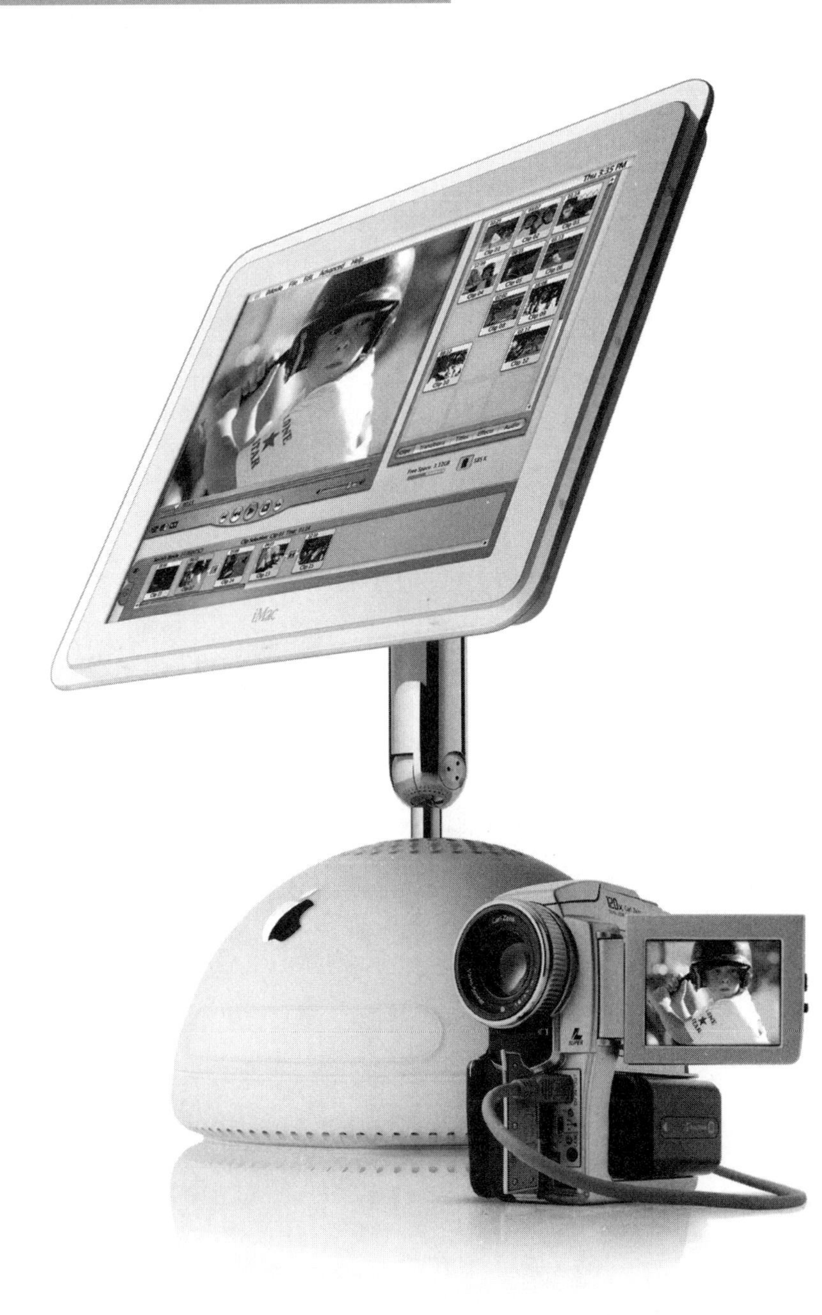

Chapter 16 Making Copies of Your iMovies

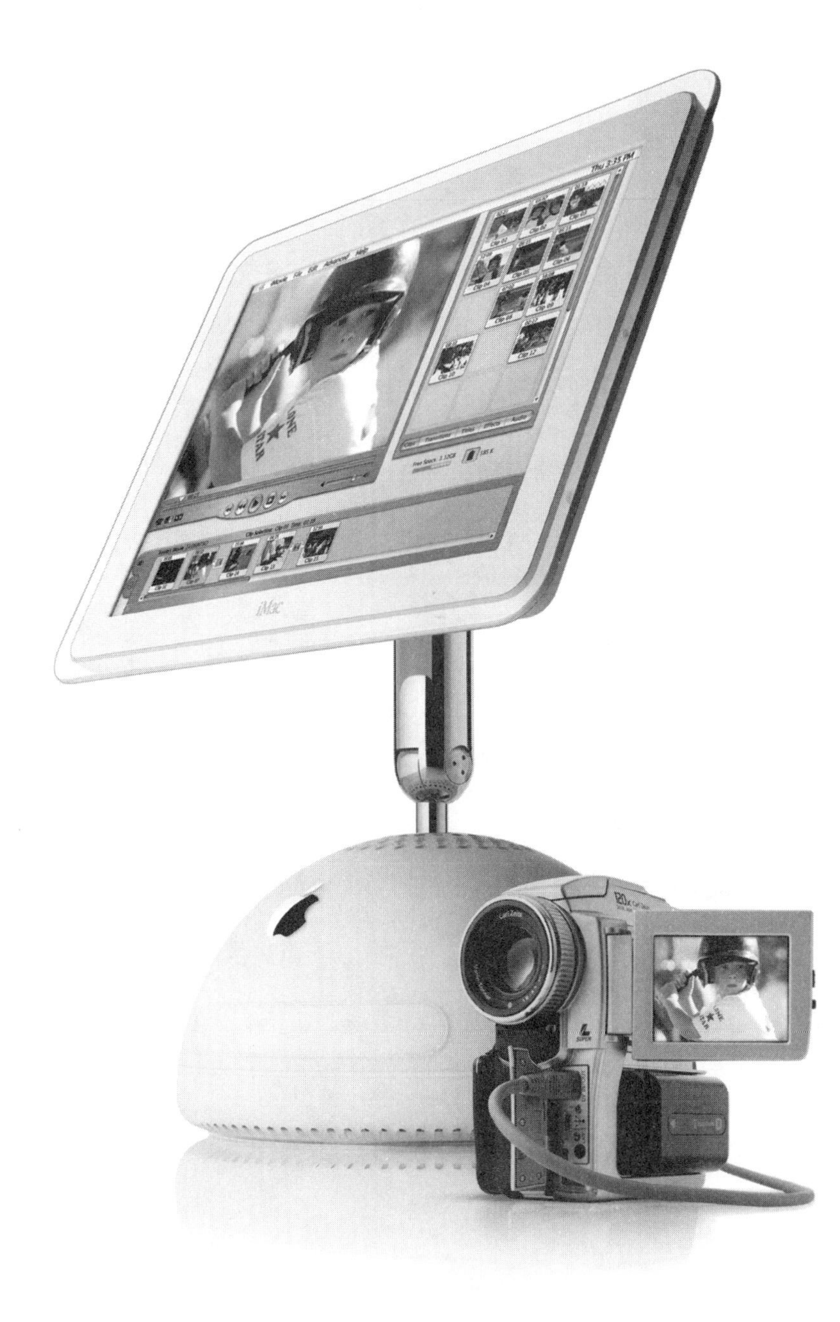

How to...

- Export your video to DV Tape
- Export your video to VHS
- Export your video to CD-ROM
- Export your video to QuickTime
- Exhibit your video on a TV or projector

All right, you've put all the elements together. You have assembled your clips, added stock footage or still pictures, then you've added sound and visual effects, fancy titles, and transitions. Your movie is ready, and you're pleased with the results.

But what comes next? What do you do with your movie? Do you just open iMovie 2 and play it back on your Mac? Not exactly. The next step of the process is to convert the movie to a format for viewing by others. Your options are extensive, depending on your needs. You can, for example, copy the movie back to your DV camcorder or a regular VHS tape, or make a QuickTime movie, or simply play it back on a regular TV or through a projector.

We'll cover the options in this chapter, along with some suggestions as to which techniques are best for your needs.

Exporting to DV Tape

Since much of your footage no doubt came from a DV camcorder, the easiest thing to do is to export the completed movie onto a blank tape. In fact, this is the standard operating mode for iMovie 2, and it gives you a high level of flexibility as far as viewing your finished production. What's more, since you are working in the digital domain, the quality level will be superb—essentially as good as the original.

Before you are ready to proceed, you'll want to recheck your footage. This is not a casual task, as it's very easy to overlook a mistake during the rush to finish your work. You don't want a misplaced cut, missing audio track, or an error in your title to be part of your final version.

One way to make sure you don't miss anything is to play your movie back several times, focusing on a different aspect of production each time. The first playback may be simply to get the overall look and feel of your movie. On successive playbacks, you'll want to concentrate one at a time on the editing, the sound track, the special effects and transitions, and the titles.

One often-overlooked item is continuity. If your movie has a number of scenes designed to show a continuous sequence of events that may have been shot out of order, you'll want to check to make sure that your actors suddenly don't lose a jacket or a shirt, or suffer from a sudden change in the color of their garments. Night shouldn't suddenly change to day without explanation, and a coffee cup shouldn't disappear or appear for no reason.

NOTE *Even commercial movies suffer from silly mistakes. Look at the scene in As Good As It Gets where Helen Hunt wants to drive a Saab convertible off the highway to listen to Greg Kinnear talk of his sad childhood. On the highway the top is down, but when it pulls to the stop, the top is suddenly up.*

If you made a mistake, now's the time to correct it.

TIP *If you're the organized type, you might even want to create a short checklist, with a separate entry for each element of your production, so you can easily check off the items as you preview your footage. In traditional Hollywood, that search-for-oversight task would go to the "script girl," or "continuity girl." Today, that title has been corrected to "continuity supervisor."*

NOTE *Checking out titles can be a bit tricky. It's very easy for your mind to compensate for a common typo, such as "hte" for "the." Even professional proofreaders may overlook a common mistake if they so much as blink.*

Here's what to do once your editing is complete:

1. Connect your DV camcorder to your Mac's FireWire port.
2. Turn it on and place it in VTR mode, and make sure a tape with enough room to record the movie is installed.
3. Choose Export from the File menu.
4. Select Camera from the Export popup menu in the Export Movie dialog box (see Figure 16-1).

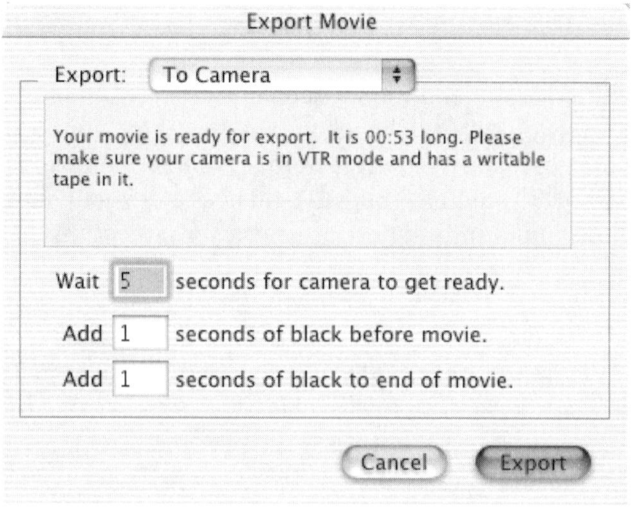

FIGURE 16-1 Prepare to export your iMovie from here.

5. If you want to give yourself a little extra time to get the camcorder running, select a specific Wait time (it's 5 seconds by default). You can also add a blank or black interval at the beginning and end of the movie. One second is normal, but you might want to add a longer interval at the end of the movie if you plan to export several projects to the same time, to provide a reasonable degree of separation.
6. Click Export to send the movie to your camcorder. Your movie will be played back in real time and copied to tape, so just sit back and relax till it's done.

NOTE *Exporting to tape requires lots of processor power, so you may see your movie playback stutter a little on your Mac's screen, especially if you have a G3 rather than G4 processor. Don't despair. All the data will be copied to your tape in good order.*

CAUTION *Under Mac OS 9, do not attempt to work in other programs while iMovie 2 is doing its stuff. Even if it works, you risk dropped frames as the Classic Mac OS tries to juggle tasks. Even though Mac OS X's preemptive multitasking is more resilient to such problems, you'll want to restrict your work to some non-processor intensive tasks, perhaps entering text into a word processing document or reading something on the screen, while your movie is being exported.*

About Multiple Generations

Once you have a VHS copy, you may be tempted to make duplicates right from that tape, especially if you have a second tape deck around or are willing to spring an extra $75 or so for an extra low-cost VCR. While this may be convenient, it won't do anything for the quality of your finished production. For one thing, you are already losing a substantial amount of quality dubbing to VHS. A copy of that tape will have more video noise and inferior sharpness—how much depends on the quality of your deck.

An alternative may be to use a S-VHS deck for masters. S-VHS offers up to 400 lines of resolution, compared to approximately 240 lines on regular VHS, which means less quality loss from the original DV version. The JVC S3900U, for example, lists for $249.95, but usually sells for less than $200 at a consumer electronics store.

NOTE *Although S-VHS usually requires a special tape to record in the high quality picture mode, at a cost at least twice that of regular tape, some decks, such as the ones from JVC, offer an ET option. This enables you to use regular videotape and gain most of the quality enhancement the S-VHS format provides without having to buy special tape.*

Another advantage of S-VHS and some of the higher cost VHS decks is Hi-Fi sound. This sound format uses the video heads to provide near-CD quality reproduction. Even if you do not opt for S-VHS, consider hi-fi an imperative. The normal audio quality of VHS is hardly better than an FM table radio, which means music and sound effects will not be heard to their best advantage. Hi-fi decks cost only slightly more than regular models.

Exporting Your iMovie to VHS Tape

What's the ultimate destination for your iMovie? Do you intend to just keep it on a DV tape, or do you want to make copies in other video formats, such as VHS, so they can be distributed to folks who don't have DV camcorders?

Depending on the end result you want, there are two ways to perform this task. The first is simple enough. Just make a DV copy as described above, then connect your VCR to your camcorder and make a dub.

Follow these steps:

1. Connect your VCR to the camcorder, following the instructions in your user guide.
2. Place a blank tape in your VCR.
3. Cue the DV tape that contains your iMovie to the start of the black portion.
4. Put the VCR in the record mode, but press the Pause button to halt tape motion.

CAUTION *Be sure your VCR is set to the high or LP speed. The lower speed setting will put three times as much material on a tape, but at a substantial loss of picture quality.*

5. Start the VCR, pressing the Pause button to begin recording.
6. Press the playback button on your camcorder.
7. When you've finished, press the Stop button on your VCR and then the stop button on your camcorder.

Showing Your Video on a TV or Video Projector

You don't have to export a video or make a tape copy if you just want to see your video on a TV or video projector. There are a number of options available to you for direct full screen playback.

How is it done? Some video projectors can be hooked up directly to the VGA output on your Mac. Apple PowerBooks feature composite video and S-video connections for direct hookup to different video sources, such as a TV or VCR. The iBook has a composite video jack and the newest models have a special VGA slot for external displays.

NOTE *Any iMac with FireWire has a VGA port that can be used to mirror the picture of your internal display. On the slot-load iMacs, the jack is located at the lower rear, and Apple supplies a special cover plate to protect the jack. You'll find a custom video output jack at the rear of the flat-panel iMac, the same as the one on the current generation iBook, but this one requires a custom adapter plug from Apple.*

To play back your video on a TV projector, follow these steps:

1. Shut down your Mac or put it into Sleep mode.
2. Connect your Mac to the external video source with the appropriate connection cable. On some models you'll have to buy a cable from a dealer.
3. Turn on your Mac.
4. Open your iMovie 2 project.
5. Press the Full Screen button to playback your video in full-screen mode.
6. To end playback, press the spacebar.

TIP *If you want to make a simultaneous tape copy of the movie while you're playing it back, just hook up a VCR to your TV or video project and start recording as soon as full-screen playback commences.*

A Look at Video Projectors

It may seem as if we've come full circle. In the old days, you used a projector to view movies. Depending on your needs and budget, there is a wide variety of video projection devices available from such companies as Epson, 3M, and ViewSonic (shown here).

You can expect to pay upwards of two grand for the projector, plus the cost of a screen. Most of the popular models hook up in essentially the same fashion, to the VGA port of your Mac. Most support the standard range of display resolutions, such as 800×600 and 1024×768, so setups should be easy.

NOTE *When hooked up to an Apple laptop, the projector mirrors the picture you see on your screen, assuming the feature is supported on your particular model. If you have a single video port on your desktop Power Mac, you might want to consider getting a second display adapter, so you can use a regular monitor and the projector at the same time. Beginning with the new products introduced in January 2002, all Power Mac G4s ship with video cards that can support two displays.*

In addition to acquiring a good projection system, you will also want to consider getting a good quality audio system to go with it. Most Macs have pretty basic sound systems, and your movie will have far greater impact if you can include superior sound along with the superior picture.

Most of the major speaker makers have computer sound systems. The Cambridge SoundWorks division of Creative Labs, for example, has a huge line of high quality systems, at prices that start at $40 for the PC Works system. A particularly decorative and high quality system emerges from the labs of Harman/Kardon. The $199 SoundSticks, shown here, consist of two upright "sticks" containing four speakers each, plus a transparent woofer module.

NOTE *Speakers with standard mini-jacks will work on any personal computer without special software, although a sound card is required on a Windows PC. However, USB speakers, such as the SoundSticks, depend on the operating system having the proper USB drivers (officially it requires Mac OS 9.0.4 or later). Apple's Pro Speakers work only on a Mac with a special connector and built-in amplifiers, such as recent model Power Mac G4s, and the flat-panel iMac.*

NOTE *If you opt for a computer speaker system, it's not a bad idea to give a listen to the offerings at a local retailer. Evaluating speaker quality is a very individual process, and even if a reviewer or your best friend says a product sounds great, you may feel otherwise when you set it up in your own installation.*

Putting Your Movie on CD-ROM

One of the most popular transport mediums is CD-ROM. Since Apple began to include internal CD burners on new Macs, which include a simple Finder-level CD burning feature, the process of making a CD of anything has become butter smooth. And even before Apple got into the act, there were dozens of external CD burners around and easy-to-use software such as Roxio's Toast and CharisMac's Discribe, either of which could make short work of CD creation chores.

A CD may be a useful way to store a collection of short clips, up to the format's maximum of 650MB or 700MB, depending on the type of CD. To export your movie to a form that's suitable for CD-ROM, with sufficient resolution for playback on most drives, just follow the instructions for exporting QuickTime movies later in this chapter.

Using QuickTime

Apple's QuickTime technology is one of a few products that have stood the test of time. Since it appeared in 1991, QuickTime has become an essential element of the Mac operating system, an extensible file format that has expanded and flourished in the ensuing years.

At its core, QuickTime software enables you to play back multimedia files, sound, and video. Tens of millions of Mac and Windows users depend on QuickTime technology for playing back everything from movie trailers to home movies.

Why Upgrade to QuickTime Pro

Although QuickTime is available free of charge on the Mac or windows platform, you don't get all the features that way. No doubt, you've seen and grown tired of those little banners asking you to upgrade to QuickTime Pro. You might wonder if the $29.95 asking price is worth the bother. Doesn't QuickTime Player already enable you to play movies?

The answer depends on your needs. There are ten new features to be found in QuickTime Pro simply by entering your registration information into the QuickTime Player application. Here's the short list:

- **Play full screen movies** This may be one of the best features. If you've spent hours downloading those huge movie trailers from the Internet, wouldn't it be nice to be able to have the pictures fill your Mac's entire screen? The result is especially striking if you have one of Apple's gorgeous 22-inch Cinema Display LCD monitors.
- **Build a personal movie library** All right, you have finally retrieved the latest *Spider-Man* trailer, but after viewing it, you find that, when you click on the down arrow at the right end of the playback controls, there's no option to save the movie. What gives? In order to save those cool trailers, you have to upgrade to QuickTime Pro.

NOTE *Copyright restrictions may prevent you from saving some movie trailers, or exporting them to DV. So if you run into a problem when you try to save, even with QuickTime Pro present and accounted for, don't assume something is wrong with your setup.*

- **High-bandwidth trailers and other exclusive content** Unfortunately, not all the QuickTime files are available, unless you have the Pro version. You have to ante-up to join this exclusive club.
- **Limited video editing tools** Well, this is a book about iMovie 2, so we won't dwell on this option, but QuickTime Pro unlocks a small subset of simple video editing options. You'll still prefer iMovie 2 for most of your work, except, maybe, "splicing" a couple of clips together, but we're mentioning this capability strictly for your information.
- **Create simple slide shows** Again you can do it with iMovie 2. But QuickTime Pro enables you do simple slide shows, complete with a simple soundtrack for narration or background music.
- **Make a custom media skin** Don't like the look of the standard QuickTime Player? We know the brushed metal look can be a little controversial. Well, Apple has provided detailed instructions at its Web site (http://www.apple.com/quicktime/products/tutorials/mediaskins/) that show you how to exercise your artistic skills to build a new skin for the program, using such graphics programs as Adobe Photoshop.

- **Import and export movie and sound clips** This is one feature that can really help you in assembling clips for your iMovie 2 projects. With QuickTime Pro activated, you can take advantage of the ability to convert dozens of multimedia files, including the Windows AVI format, which will greatly extend the kinds of files you can handle in your iMovie.
- **Simple audio and video editing** Don't want to use iMovie 2 just for a quick touch-up job? QuickTime Pro enables you to handle simple editing chores, such as color, brightness, and sound balance, after which you can save in the format of your choice.
- **Prepare your movie for streaming on the Web** QuickTime Pro helps you get your movies ready to roll if you want to embed them at your Web site or deliver them in a streaming presentation from a Web sever.
- **Use AppleScript** One of the unsung heroes of the Mac operating system is AppleScript. It's a system-wide automation feature that enables you to perform repetitive tasks by launching a simple application or activating a function from an application. You can learn more about using this handy feature from the AppleScript Web site at http://www.apple.com/applescript.

NOTE *To help you develop your scripting abilities, Apple includes a number of sample scripts with Mac OS 9 and Mac OS X. Additional offerings, including an online tutorial, are available at the Web site.*

A Short Primer on Using QuickTime

Installed on your new Mac is the application that will provide your most direct exposure to QuickTime—QuickTime Player (see Figure 16-2). Whether you use the Classic Mac OS or Mac OS X, the look and feel of the player will be very much the same.

Like any player program on the Mac, the controls are fashioned after those of a VCR or a CD/DVD player. Click the Play button to start a movie, click it again to stop. There are also controls to jump to the beginning or end of a clip, rewind or fast forward. Volume is set via a slider control.

A Look at QuickTime Player

Here's a brief look at the basic operation of QuickTime Player, with the "Pro" upgrade. After your experience with iMovie 2, no doubt you'll find many

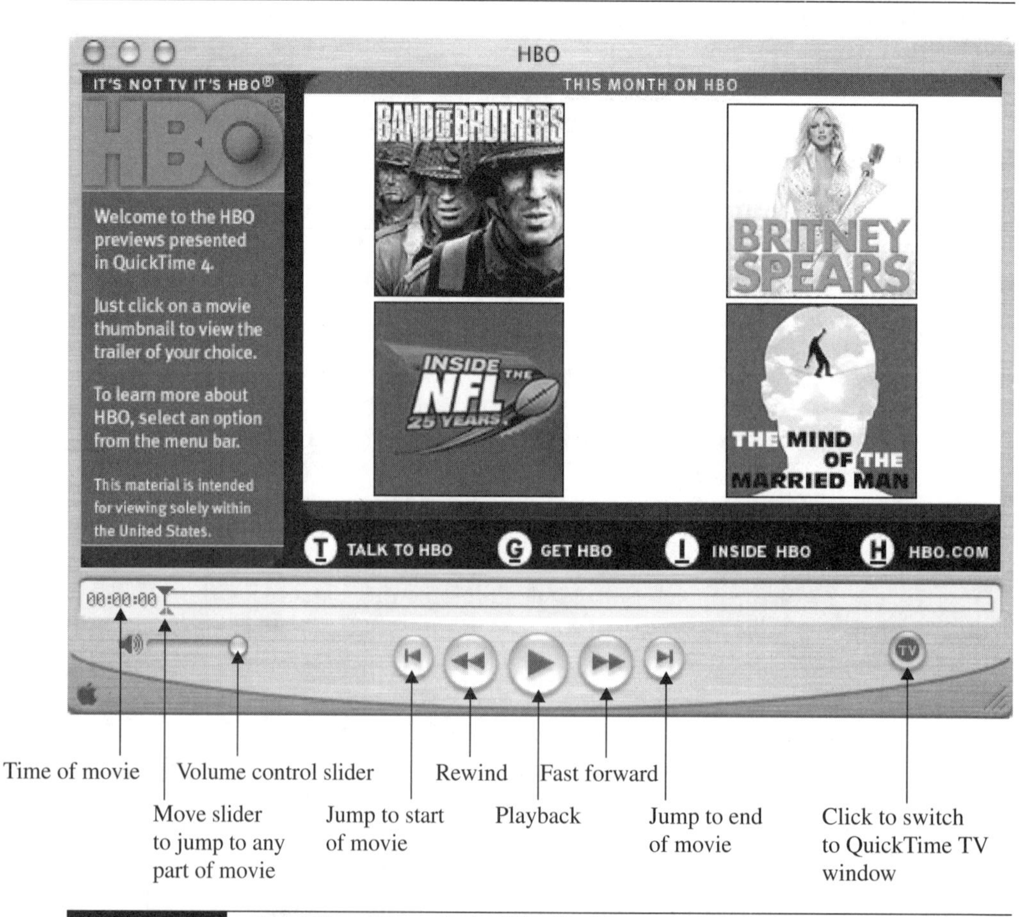

FIGURE 16-2 QuickTime Player is the "face" of the typical QuickTime user experience.

similarities. But there are a few distinct differences, largely because QuickTime Player is, despite the extensive import and export capabilities, a playback tool rather than an editing tool.

To open a QuickTime movie, all it usually takes is a double-click on the file, and QuickTime player will launch. If, for some reason, the application doesn't launch, you can always open QuickTime Player first, then choose Open from the File menu to select your file, and it'll open in a convenient playback window appropriately sized for the specific movie file.

Introducing QuickTime TV

Apple has entered into partnerships with a number of production cable and broadcast TV networks to deliver streaming broadcasts. For fast access, just click the TV button at the lower right of any QuickTime Player window (see Figure 16-3).

Once you select a specific network, you'll see a list of available broadcasts that will open in still another player window.

QuickTime Player Preferences

Program options are simple. Just choose Player Preferences from the Preferences submenu in the QuickTime Player application window under Mac OS X (it's in the Edit menu under Mac OS 9), and you'll see a small number of movie and sound handling options (see Figure 16-4).

FIGURE 16-3 Click on a network icon to see the program listing.

General Preferences

Movies:

Open movies in new players

Automatically play movies when opened

Sound:

Play sound in frontmost player only

Play sound when application is in background

Favorites:

Ask before replacing favorite items

Hot Picks:

Show Hot Picks movie automatically

Cancel OK

FIGURE 16-4 Click on an option to activate that preference.

- **Movies** The first option, checked by default, opens a movie in a brand new player window, rather than in the existing one. You might want to uncheck it to lessen desktop clutter. The second option, when checked, automatically plays your movies as soon as they're opened.
- **Sound** To avoid confusion, keep the first option checked, and only the movie in the frontmost player window will produce sound. Then again, if you want a really strange effect, I suppose you could uncheck this option. The second one, also checked by default, will produce audible sound even if you move to another application while your QuickTime movie is being played back.
- **Favorites** One of the convenient options in the QTV menu is that you can add a movie to your Favorites. When this option is checked, you'll be warned if you are attempting to replace an existing item among your Favorites.
- **Hot Picks** When you launch QuickTime Player, you will see a list of movie Hot Picks. This feature requires access to your ISP, and if you don't want to be connected automatically, feel free to turn it off. This feature works best if you have a full time Internet connection, such as DSL or cable.

QuickTime Player's File Menu

Basic player options are handled via the File menu. In addition to opening a new player window, you can open movies or pictures in a player window, save your movie files (an option activated by QuickTime Pro, as you recall) and import and export movies in a host of file formats.

Table 16-1 shows the full list of file formats processed by QuickTime 5.

File

New Player	⌘N
Open Movie in New Player...	⌘O
Open Image Sequence...	
Open URL in New Player...	⌘U
Close	⌘W
Save	⌘S
Save As...	
Import...	
Export...	⌘E
Page Setup...	
Print...	⌘P

NOTE *This list was complete as this book went to press; remember that things change quickly in the world of digital imaging!*

QuickTime Player's Edit Menu

The unlocked, QuickTime Pro version adds some simple video editing tools that are available from the Edit menu. We'll cover basic QuickTime movie editing a little later in this chapter.

Edit

Undo	⌘Z
Cut	⌘X
Copy	⌘C
Paste	⌘V
Clear	
Select All	⌘A
Select None	⌘B
Add	⌥⌘V
Add Scaled	⌥⇧⌘V
Replace	⇧⌘V
Trim	
Enable Tracks...	
Extract Tracks...	
Delete Tracks...	
Find...	⌘F
Find Again	⌘G

QuickTime Player's Movie Menu

Do you want to show a movie full screen, filling all the available area on your Mac's display? Do you want to loop a movie, or just make incremental size charges? Other commands enable you to handle some simple sound and video touch-ups. The Movie menu will provide the tools you need.

Movie

Loop	⌘L
Loop Back and Forth	
Half Size	⌘0
Normal Size	⌘1
Double Size	⌘2
Fill Screen	⌘3
Present Movie...	⌘M
Show Sound Controls	
Show Video Controls	⌘K
Get Movie Properties	⌘J
Play Selection Only	⌘T
Play All Frames	
Play All Movies	
Go To Poster Frame	
Set Poster Frame	
Choose Language...	

Import File Formats	Export File Formats
3DMF	AIFF
AIFF	AU
AU	AVI
Audio CD Data (Macintosh)	BMP
AVI	DV Stream
BMP	FLC
Cubic VR	Image Sequence movie exporters
DLS	JPEG/JFIF
DV	MacPaint
FlashPix	MIDI
FLC	PhotoShop
GIF	PICT
JPEG/JFIF	PNG
Karaoke	QuickTime Image
MacPaint	QuickTime Movie
Macromedia Flash 4	SGI
MIDI	System 7 Sound
MPEG-1(Playback / Streaming)	Targa
MP3(MPEG-1, Layer 3)	Text
M3U(MP3 Playlist files)	TIFF
Photoshop	WAV
PICS	
PICT	
PLS	
PNG	
QuickTime Image File	
QuickTime Movie	
SF2 (SoundFont 2)	
SGI	
Sound	
Targa	
Text	
TIFF	
TIFF Fax	
Virtual Reality (VR)	
Wave	

TABLE 16-1 Import and Export File Formats Processed by QuickTime 5

Getting Basic Information About a Movie

QuickTime Player can display some basic information about a movie in a Properties window. To access this feature, follow these steps:

1. Open the movie you want to check. For this example, we're using one of the trailers for the Columbia Pictures production, *Spider-Man*, based on the famous Marvel comic book.
2. Go to the Movie menu and choose Get Movie Properties, which will bring up the information screen shown in Figure 16-5.
3. To discover more about a particular movie file, click the pop-up menu at the left, which will give you Sound Track and Video Track options.
4. To learn more about a particular component, click on the right menu. This brings you nine options (shown in Figure 16-6) that you can use to learn more about the movie or adjust the playback settings. Auto Play, for example, enables you to modify the movie file so it begins to play

FIGURE 16-5 Click on an entry in the Properties category to learn more.

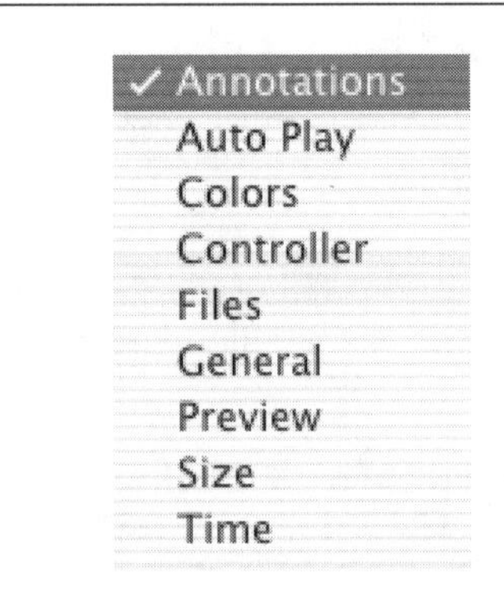

FIGURE 16-6 Click on a menu to learn more about a movie clip or adjust a setting.

back as soon as it's owned. The Controller option enables you to choose which style playback controls will appear (or none, if you decide).

Basic QuickTime Movie Editing

This book is designed to show you how easy and convenient it is to edit your videos in iMovie 2. However, QuickTime Player upgraded to the Pro version may be a useful companion to give a video a quick shave and haircut, and a fast ticket to streaming and the Web.

Here's how you'd perform some basic editing chores with the program:

1. Open your movie file in QuickTime Player.
2. If you want to add an audio track to a movie, choose Import from the file menu and select the sound you want to bring in. When the sound is brought into QuickTime Player, it'll open in a new player window.
3. Go to the Edit menu and choose Select All to select the audio track.
4. Choose Copy from the Edit menu to put the sound clip in the clipboard.
5. Position the playback head at the location in your movie where you want the sound to begin.
6. Go to the Edit menu, and choose Add. The sound will be put in the movie, right at the point you selected.

NOTE *The same basic process can be followed to copy and insert movie tracks from another clip into the player window for the movie to which you want to insert that material.*

7. To adjust the sound balance of you clip, choose Show Sound Controls from the Movie menu and you'll see three controls for balance, bass and treble, in your player window (see Figure 16-7).
8. Click on the plus and minus buttons to adjust sound balance.
9. You can also adjust the brightness of your clip to match the rest by choosing Show Video Controls from the Movie menu and clicking on the brightness level you want.
10. All done? Choose Save from the File menu to store your edits.

FIGURE 16-7 Adjust the sound quality of your movie with these three extra controls.

Importing QuickTime Movies

As you've discovered, there are many sources for material for your iMovie, in addition to the footage you've shot with your video camera. One of those sources is another QuickTime movie, if it's in the proper format. This gives you a host of options, particularly if you're just using a movie for personal use, for viewing by family or friends.

Here's how to import a QuickTime movie:

1. Open the movie in QuickTime Player.

To follow these steps, you need QuickTime Pro, a $29.95 upgrade for QuickTime users that is available from Apple's Web site.

2. Use Export from the File menu and select Movie to DV Stream from the Export menu in the Save exported file as dialog box (see Figure 16-8).
3. Name your movie clip and click the Save button.
4. Once the file has been converted, return to iMovie 2, and choose Import from the File menu.
5. Locate and select the movie in the Import From dialog box (see Figure 16-9).

Save exported file as...
Save As: QuickTime.dv
Where: Documents
Export: Movie to DV Stream
Options...
Use: Default Settings
Cancel
Save

FIGURE 16-8 Convert your QuickTime movie here so it can be imported into iMovie 2.

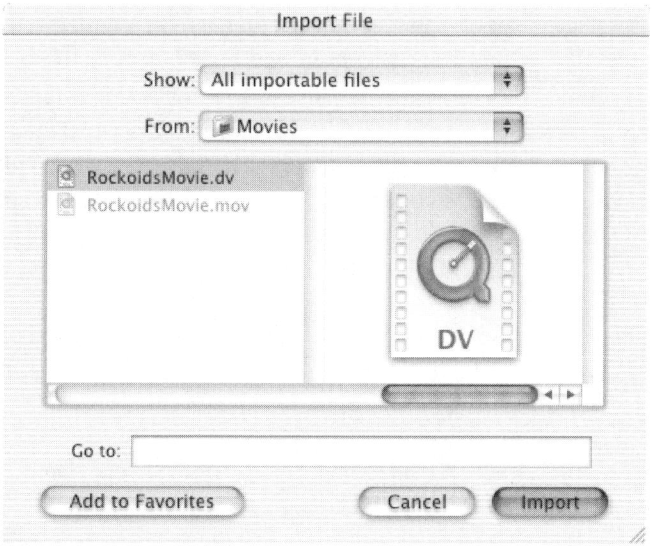

FIGURE 16-9 Select your converted QuickTime movie here.

6. Click the Import button. The movie will appear in the Clip Shelf along with your other clips, ready for placement in the Timeline for further editing.

Exporting QuickTime Movies

Apple's QuickTime movie format is world-famous and used by professionals around the globe. You'll also find a wealth of QuickTime movie export options in iMovie 2, so you can conveniently tailor the output quality to your needs. You don't even have to be an expert at making a specific choice, because the default options that you see when you choose to Export your video in this format are plentiful.

Let's have a look at your choices:

NOTE *When you select a particular option for export, you'll see a display in the dialog box showing the size of the video frame, the frame rate, and details about the sound and video compression used.*

- **Email Movie** There are limits to how big you can make your movie for email. For one thing, most people still surf the Web with dial-up modems, usually getting far worse than those advertised 56K speeds. Secondly, ISPs generally place limits at the size of files that can be emailed—usually from 2MB to 5MB—which means you will not be able to send a high-quality video of more than a few seconds duration without running into a roadblock one way or the other. The Email Movie setting in iMovie 2 skirts this juggling act as much as possible, keeping the file size small with decent view quality with a 160×120 image window, 10 frames per second speed, and mono sound.

NOTE *This format requires that the viewer have QuickTime 4 or later. If your intended recipient has a vintage Mac or PC with an older version of QuickTime installed, tell him he can get the latest version, free, from Apple's Web site.*

TIP *If you've signed up with Apple's iTools, you get 20MB of free storage space at Apple's Web site (with more available at extra cost). This is a neat way to store a larger video for download by friends and family, at the risk of making it available to anyone else who may want to access your "Public" files.*

- **Web Movie** Streaming video. Imagine having someone click on a link at your Web site, and up comes your movie. It can be a full movie with sound, or just a few recycling clips, as Apple used on its Web site when it introduced the flat-panel version of the iMac. To show how easy it was to move the screen, Apple showed it moving up and down and sideways in big steps on their home page. Again, sizes are kept pretty small—240×180—and the frame rate is slow—12 frames per second—but this setting should be sufficient to deliver a neat enhancement to your site.
- **Streaming Web Movie** Ever see a live broadcast of a special event online, such as a Macworld keynote address? This is accomplished by streaming video, where the content is spoon fed to recipients based on the ability of their computers to process the material. This format has the same quality level as a Web movie, and is designed to be used in conjunction with Apple's QuickTime Streaming Web Server software, which works with Apple's Mac OS X 10.1 Server to deliver the video across the Internet.
- **CD-ROM Movie** Used for playback from CD drives, this format delivers stereo sound, a window size of 360×240, and 15 frames per second. That's quite good, and enough to produce some pretty compelling performance in a variety of environments.

- **Full Quality** Where only the best will suit, this setting produces a QuickTime movie that matches the original DV source as closely as possible. The maximum window size is 720×480, with 29.97 frames per second, and thus is suitable for professional use. The output can be brought into other programs, such as Final Cut Pro, for further editing.
- **Expert** The pre-built settings are sufficient to deliver the highest quality level for the various purposes listed above. But you do not have to stick with those settings. You can choose Expert (see Figure 16-10) and select custom Image and Audio compression options, depending on your needs. One of the recommended Image options, the Sorenson Video codec, takes longer to process and creates larger sized files, but it ensures the maximum possible quality, virtually indistinguishable from the original.

NOTE *The nuts and bolts of a particular compression codec are arcane and beyond the scope of this book. If you want to learn about the Sorenson codec, for example, you can visit the company's Web site at http://www.sorenson.com. This video compression technique, by the way, is commonly used for movie trailers, such as the ones for Star Wars I and Star Wars II, which is evidence of its high quality.*

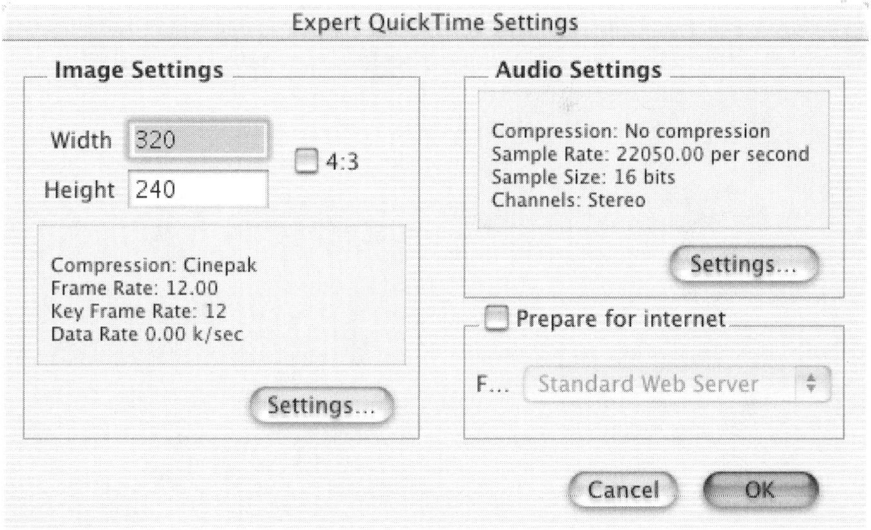

FIGURE 16-10 If you want to further customize your export options, feel free to experiment with some of the offerings in the Expert dialog box.

Ready to begin. Just follow these steps:

1. With your completed iMovie project opened, choose Export from the File menu.
2. Select the appropriate format from the Exports pop-up menu (see Figure 16-11).
3. Click the Export button. Be patient, depending on the speed of your Mac, its hard drive, and the QuickTime format you selected, a number of minutes may transpire until the process is done. But you'll see a progress bar to indicate how it's all progressing and when the process is finished.

TIP *Mac OS X's preemptive multitasking feature gives you the freedom to do other work on your Mac while your iMovie is being exported. But there are no miracles, and the process will go quicker if you stay away from processor-intensive tasks while the Mac's processor is crunching the data from your iMovie.*

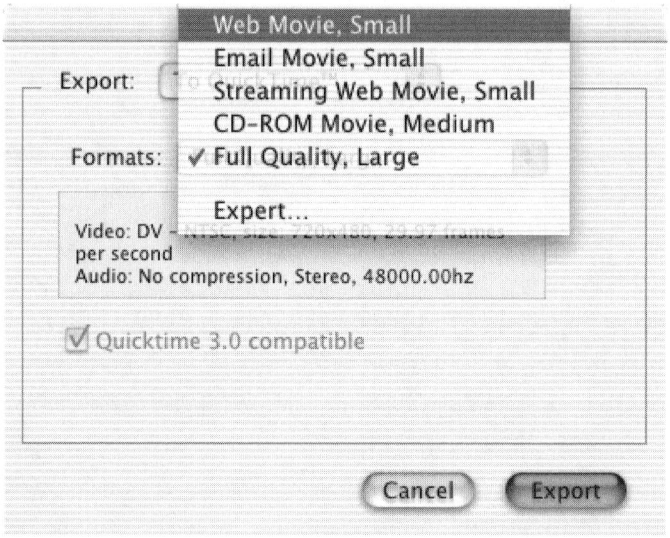

FIGURE 16-11 Select from five pre-built formats, or customize the one you want.

What About DVD?

Good question. DVD is the hottest video format out there—a great way to deliver videos with superb quality, even on inexpensive equipment. Apple has a terrific way to prepare your movies for DVD, an application called iDVD 2. But it takes more than a few pages to tell you how the program works and how you can harness its power to make professional caliber menus with motion and fancy backgrounds. So we've devoted a full chapter to the subject. You'll want to read Chapter 18 for all the details.

The Closing Scene

This chapter covered all the ways you can save your iMovie project for the end user, whether it's your family, your friends, or your business. As you can see, the choices are extensive, and you have many options for saving your video as a file or a completed tape.

In our next chapter, we'll focus more tightly on Web-based movies. Whether for your own personal Web site or your business Web site, you'll find that plenty of options are available for showing your movie in a high-quality format, even for folks who don't have the fastest Internet connection.

Chapter 17

Making iMovies for the Web

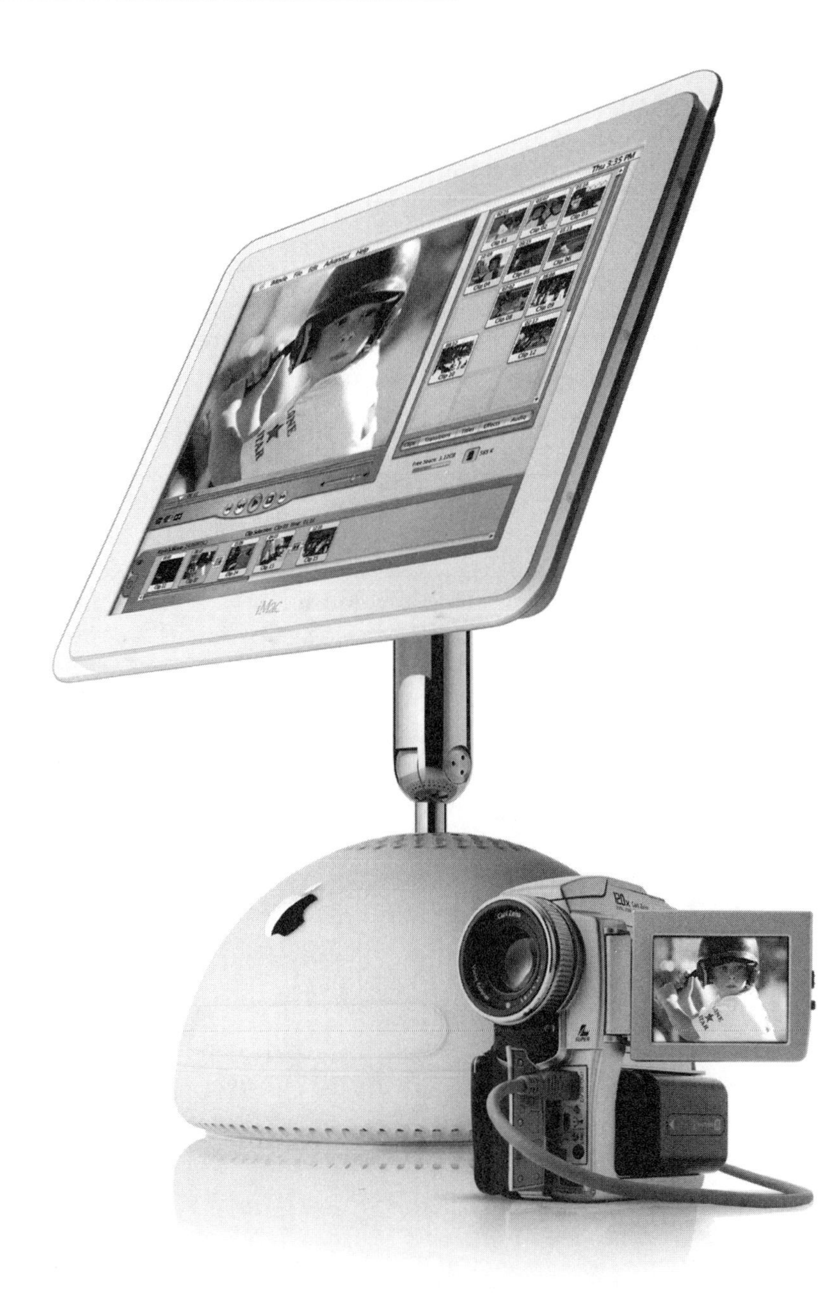

How to...

- Compress your iMovie
- Email your iMovie
- Post your iMovie on the Web
- Stream an iMovie on the Web

How many times have you checked out a movie trailer on the Web before going down to your local multiplex to see it? Tens of millions have downloaded trailers for a wide range of movies from *Star Wars* to *Spider-Man*, and movie companies use the Internet as a major venue for promotion of their multimillion-dollar epics.

It stands to reason, then, that the Internet might be a great way for you to show off your iMovie to family, friends, or, perhaps, potential business contacts. So we've devoted this chapter to explaining how you can use email or a Web site to make your iMovies available to others.

We will also briefly cover another option available, and that is streaming your video from the Web. Maybe we'll be seeing your movie trailer in the near future!

Emailing Your iMovie

Perhaps the simplest way to have people view your iMovie is to email it to them. But what sounds simple can often be something else again. Part of the problem is that just about every ISP we know puts up a cold, hard limit on the size of files you can send.

Those limits range from as little as 2MB for sending files from an AOL member to someone outside the service, to as much as 5MB or 10MB. Regardless, there are significant limits to the quality and length of the movie you can send.

For example, a 53-second clip, based on the iMovie tutorial and some fancy titles, and exported using iMovie's default email setup (see Figure 17-1), consumes approximately 1.4MB of storage space. If your ISP allows you up to 5MB file transfers, you may safely get away with a three-minute movie, but that's about it.

NOTE *All right, we admit it. 1.4 times three doesn't add up to 5MB. What gives? When you send a file attachment, it has to be encoded by your email software, and that process adds some overhead. In fact, a three-minute clip may end up being too long once it's encoded. You'll want to keep total file size to somewhere between 3.5 and 4MB.*

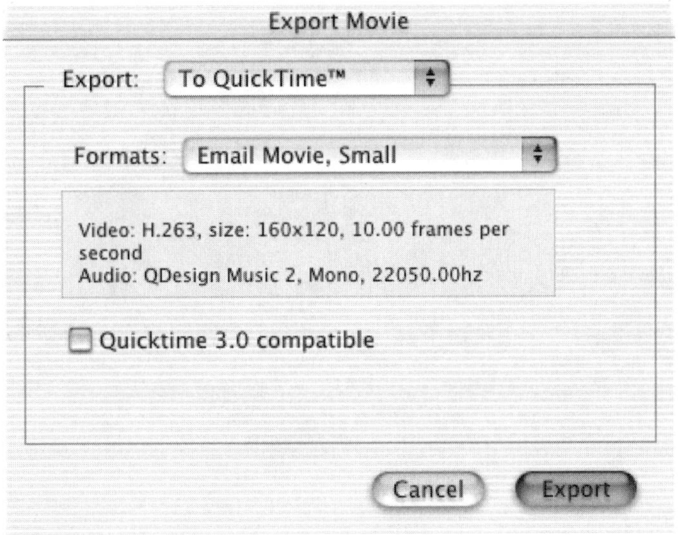

FIGURE 17-1 Exporting this movie to email format gives you viewable quality and small file size, but not small enough.

If you want to send a larger movie, you'll want to consider some of the other options described in this chapter, such as posting a copy on your iDisk.

NOTE *What about using Aladdin's StuffIt to compress your movie file? Will that help? A little, but since a QuickTime movie is already compressed to a large degree, the difference isn't all that great. That 1.4MB movie file, for example, will shrink to about 1.2MB when you use DropStuff or StuffIt Deluxe to compress it. If you're file is earmarked to a Windows user, you'll want to consider DropZip, an Aladdin utility that compresses files in the most popular PC format. Regardless, compression will help a little, but it's not a solution.*

Playing Your iMovie

Once the recipients receive your iMovie, they can use Apple's QuickTime Player, or any movie player application compatible with QuickTime, to see your movie in all its glory (see Figure 17-2).

FIGURE 17-2 One of the *Star Wars Episode II* trailers as shown in QuickTime Player.

All Macs produced in recent years come with QuickTime software already installed. QuickTime is also available for Windows users, so you don't have to convert your PC-using friends to a new computing platform. Just tell them they can get a free copy of the latest version from Apple at http://www.apple.com/quicktime.

NOTE *A special version of QuickTime, QuickTime Pro, includes enhanced file import and export options and is a useful adjunct to iMovie 2 for bringing in clips that would otherwise not be compatible. We told you more about QuickTime in Chapter 16.*

Posting Your Movie for Downloading

If you don't want to limit quality or length, another option is to post your movie for downloading on a Web site or, using Apple's iTools, your own iDisk.

Apple's iTools (see Figure 17-3) is a suite of free services that gives you four useful features. These include a mac.com email address, the ability to send iCards with personal and business announcements, the ability to create a personal Web

FIGURE 17-3 iTools offers a useful set of free enhancements to the Mac user's experience.

site, and up to 20MB of free storage space (more is available on a sliding fee schedule from Apple).

TIP *In addition to its prestige, having an email address that doesn't depend on a specific ISP is a useful way to keep a single email address, especially if you must move from home to office accounts or travel to cities where your ISP doesn't have access. Unfortunately, the email feature doesn't work for AOL and CompuServe users.*

NOTE *In addition to the standard set of features, Apple routinely deposits software updates and a collection of interesting Mac OS X software on your iDisk. Just check out the Software folder for the latest offerings—they change regularly.*

Joining iTools

If you're a Mac OS X user, you probably set up an iTools account when you set up your new operating system, but if you haven't, here's what to do:

1. Open the System Preferences application and click the Internet icon.
2. With the iTools tab selected, click the Sign up button.

NOTE *Still a Mac OS 9 user? Just log into Apple's iTools Web site at http://www.apple.com/itools and follow the instructions for setting up your account.*

3. Your Web browser will be launched, and you'll be asked to create a unique user name and a password and provide a short set of personal information, including your name and address.

NOTE *Since there are millions of iTools users, creating a unique name may require a bit of work. So be prepared to try different names until one takes. Also, when you create a password, for maximum security, it's best to use a random set of lower and upper case letters and numbers. So you may remember, mY23mAc39, but it would be difficult for password surfers to get that exact combo.*

4. Once you set up your iTools account, you can call up your iDisk Public folder and put your iMovie file there. Under Mac OS X, you access your iDisk via the Go menu, or just press COMMAND+OPTION+I. Depending on the speed of your ISP, your iDisk should show up as a drive icon on your Mac's desktop in just a few seconds.

NOTE *For Mac OS 9, you can call up your iDisk at Apple's iTools Web site. Once you've brought up the iDisk icon, you can make an alias of it for a quick return.*

Uploading and Retrieving Your iMovie

All set up with an iTools account? Here's how to set up your iMovie file for downloading by others:

1. Open your iDisk, using the instructions provided above.
2. Drag and drop (upload), the iMovie file into your iDisk's Public folder (see Figure 17-4).

NOTE *The time it takes to send the file, of course, depends on how fast you can transfer files over your ISP, and the same is true for the time it takes for others to get that file. In general, expect those file transfers to take longer if you simply put the files on your iDisk. Your mileage may vary, even with a broadband connection, but if you find the slowdown is significant, you may want to embed the movie in your iTools Home Page (see below) and see if performance is any better.*

3. To access the files in your Public folder, your contacts need to use the following URL: http://idisk.mac.com/member_name/Public. The member name is, of course, the user name you have established as an iTools member.

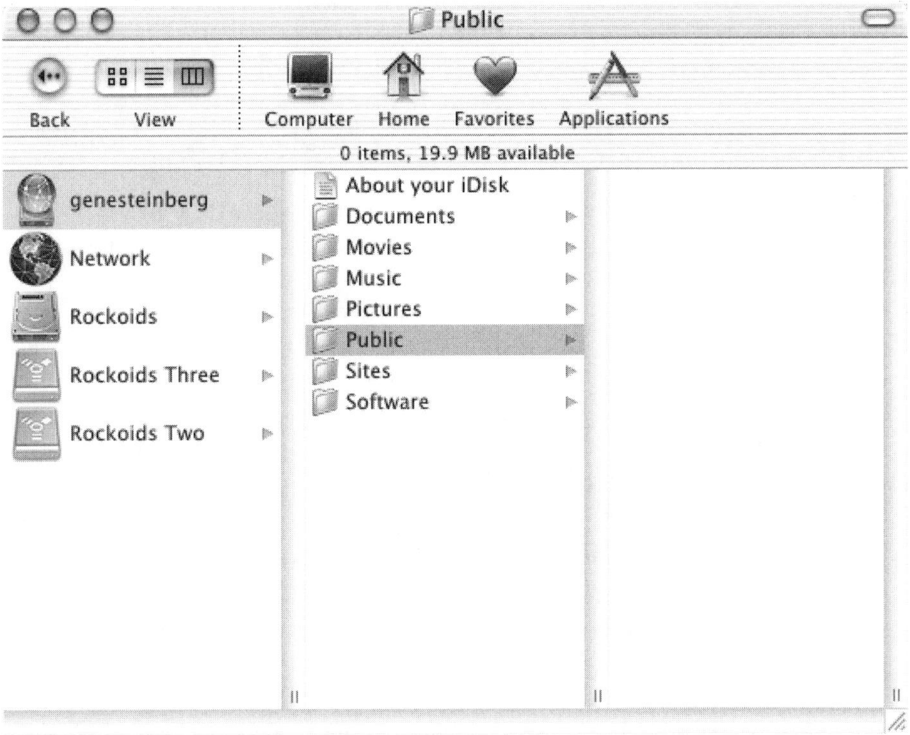

FIGURE 17-4 Place your completed iMovie in this folder for upload to your personal iDisk.

TIP

You can also embed your iMovie in your iTools Home Page. Just follow the simple point and click instructions when you create or edit your personal Web site and visitors to your site will be able to access your movie with just one click. You can, of course, use your own Web authoring software and simply upload your files to your iDisk (the files go into your Sites folder).

NOTE

You aren't limited to iTools to post your movies and photos. Most ISPs, including AOL, give you free storage space to set up a personal Web site where you can post your files. You'll want to check the support information your ISP provides on how to access your personal storage space.

CAUTION

What about security? All right, here's the downside. When you set up a Web site or put your iMovie in your iDisk's Public folder, it's available to anyone who has Internet access. If you want to limit your audience, you may want to put the files in a private FTP area, available only to those who use the proper username and password. Check with your ISP about how this might be set up.

A Brief Guide to Adding a Video on a Web Page

If you're not using one of these free Web site building tools, you'll find it's still quite easy to add a link to your iMovie, or even to embed it on a Web page, so it begins to play back as soon as it's downloaded.

We'll cover the basics of how it's done here. If you're using a graphical Web authoring tool, such as Adobe GoLive or Macromedia Dreamweaver, you'll want to consult your user guides and help menus on how to insert multimedia content into your Web page.

Creating an External Link

The simplest way to set up this kind of link is to upload your movie to your Web site, and then put a simple Web link on your page that points to the movie. When a site visitor click the link, the file is downloaded to his Mac or PC, and the appropriate QuickTime player application launches to run the movie.

Here's how it's done, using regular HTML coding.

1. Confirm that your movie file has the proper file name. You can get away without a file extension on your Mac, but on the Internet, it won't work, so you'll want to make sure that the .mov extension is appended to your QuickTime movie file name.

2. For maximum efficiency, make sure your movie was exported in Web Movie configuration, as described in Chapter 16. This provides a reasonable tradeoff between picture quality and file size.
3. Enter the following command in your Web document to access and identify the movie file:

```
<A HREF="[filelocation]/filename.mov">
```

NOTE *In addition to the file name, you must name the location, or directory path, of the file on your Web site's server, so it can be found.*

CAUTION *Be sure you include the proper HTML prefix, http://, in your tag. If it's not there, the tag won't work. It's also a good idea to test your page to make sure the movie is being selected and is downloading properly.*

4. Type a label that will tell your site visitors what they're receiving, such as "My Favorite Movie", and then add the following command to complete the link.

```
</A>
```

When you publish your Web page, your iMovie is just a click way.

TIP *Would you like to put up one of those "tool tip" blurbs to announce your movie when someone moves a mouse above your link? This command works in Internet Explorer, which has the largest market penetration (even on the Mac platform). When you create your "A HREF" link include this tag within the brackets:*

```
title="[insert blurb here]"
```

Creating an Embedded Link

Ever see a QuickTime movie window right in the middle of a Web page, complete with playback controls? As soon as the page is displayed, the movie begins to play. This is a really neat effect you can do yourself through some very simple codes.

NOTE *In order for site visitors to see the embedded movie, they will need to have a Web browser with QuickTime plug-in installed. This is standard on a Mac, and available as an option for Windows users who download the add-on from Apple's web site.*

Here's the simple command structure to make it happen:

1. As in the previous section, first make sure your movie file is properly named with a .mov extension.
2. Locate the portion of your HTML document where you want to embed the movie, and enter this command:

```
<EMBED SRC="[filelocation]/filename.mov"
```

3. For playback controls to appear in their proper location, you need to manually enter the width and height of the movie window. We'll use 240×180, which is the standard Web Movie export format for iMovie. Thus:

```
WIDTH=240 HEIGHT=180
```

4. Do you want your site visitors to start the playback manually, or have it begin automatically as soon as the movie is downloaded? To have playback begin automatically, use this command:

```
AUTOSTART=true
```

CAUTION *Don't forget the controller if you want to give your visitors the ability to control playback. Apple's official recommendation is that you add 16 pixels to a movie's height to accommodate the controller. That means, if your movie has a height of 180 pixels, like the one cited in the example above, you should make the height 196. Almost there. Here's still another command, one you can use to have the video play over and over again, the same as the Loop mode in QuickTime Player:*

```
LOOP=true
```

5. When you're done, close the command with a > symbol, and you're ready to publish your page complete with embedded video.

CAUTION *Remember that you must keep your iMovie in the precise spot pointed to on your Web page for the movie to download and play. You move it, and the link will simply be invalid.*

Where Do You Put that Plug-in? When you install Mac OS X, your QuickTime plug-in is present and accounted for, in the Library > Internet Plug-ins folder at the root or top level of your hard drive. Most of your native Web browsers, and even the Mac OS X versions of AOL and CompuServe, will be able to recognize that folder, so you won't have to do anything to make QuickTime work on your Mac.

Under Mac OS 9, each browser keeps its own counsel and has its own plug-ins folder for its own copy of a plug-in. What's more confusing is that many Macs end up with several copies of a browser. One of your long-suffering authors once checked out a first generation iMac to solve an Internet connection problem and found a grand total of half a dozen copies of Netscape strewn across the computer's hard drive. Each copy had a unique collection of Internet plug-ins, and QuickTime might work on one, but not the other.

Now it's perfectly true that the QuickTime installer for the Classic Mac OS should be putting the proper plug-ins in their proper locations upon initial installation. But, if you add a new browser later on, the latest version might not be there—just the one that might be bundled with the browser. Fortunately, you'll find copies of the browser plug-ins in the QuickTime folder in your Classic Mac OS's Applications folder. You can install these directly yourself. The files bear the labels "QuickTime Plugin" and "QuickTimePlugin.class."

Under Windows, there is also a Plug-ins directory, which is in your browser's application folder. Because of the greater complexity of Windows, however, it's usually best to let the QuickTime installer sort all this out during the installation. What you are concerned about is the end result—that your movies will play normally when they're accessed from a Web site by a Windows user.

Worse, Microsoft removed support for plug-ins beginning with Internet Explorer 5.5 SP2, which means that Windows users need to install QuickTime 5.0.5 or later, which includes an ActiveX control that enables your QuickTime movies to play (see Figure 17-5). Nothing comes easy.

TIP

If you want to ensure maximum flexibility for Windows visitors to your site, you'll want to code your Web pages as follows, so that embedded QuickTime movies will play properly regardless of whether a traditional plug-in or ActiveX control is needed. This code is just a sample, and assumes a standard-sized movie, with sufficient space for the controller buttons, and automatic play enabled. It will also provide the automatic link your site visitors need to quickly retrieve the right plug-in:

```
<OBJECTCLASSID="clsid:02BF25D5-8C17-4B23-BC80-D3488ABDDC6B" WIDTH="160"
HEIGHT="144" CODEBASE="http://www.apple.com/qtactivex/qtplugin.cab">
        <PARAM name="SRC" VALUE="[name of movie file]">
        <PARAM name="AUTOPLAY" VALUE="true">
        <PARAM name="CONTROLLER" VALUE="false">
        <EMBED SRC="[name of movie file] "WIDTH="160" HEIGHT="144"
        AUTOPLAY="true" CONTROLLER="false"
        PLUGINSPAGE="http://www.apple.com/quicktime/download/">
        </EMBED>
</OBJECT>
```

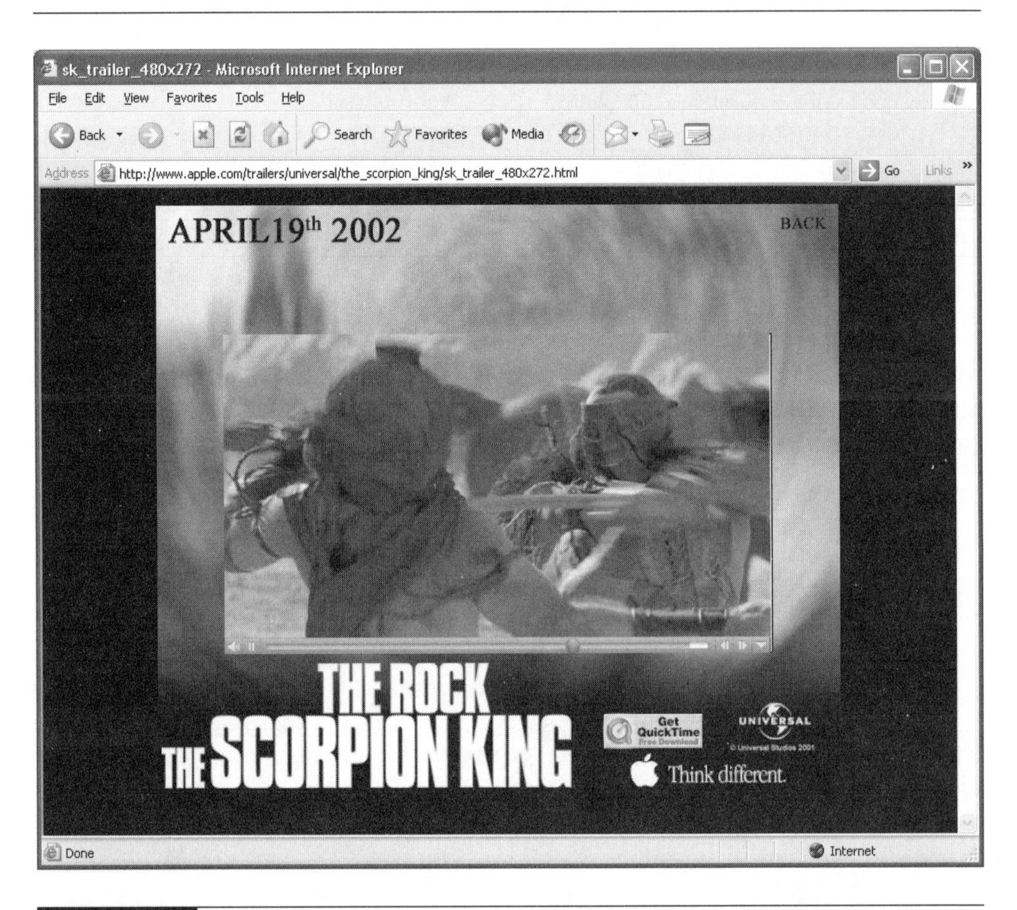

FIGURE 17-5 Under Windows XP, Internet Explorer 6 requires an ActiveX control to play a QuickTime movie such as the trailer for Universal's *The Scorpion King*.

Streaming Your Movie

Did you ever witness one of Steve Jobs' world-famous Macworld keynote addresses via QuickTime, live on the Web? As new Macs are rolled out, there's Mr. Jobs in his famous turtleneck shirt telling us about the company's latest insanely great product.

Of course, with tens or hundreds of thousands of simultaneous viewers, it takes an awful lot of server horsepower to accomplish that task and, even then, viewers are often turned away disappointed because they can't get a good connection or any connection at all.

It's also possible for you to stream your video using Apple's free QuickTime Streaming Server software, which works with Mac OS X Server to deliver streams for up to 3,000 simultaneous users.

While setting up and managing a Web server is beyond the scope of this book, we suggest you point your Web browser to http://www.apple.com/quicktime/products/qtss/ for more information on how to set up both server and movies.

Your first step to streaming video is a simple one, since your iMovie can be exported as a streaming web movie.

Here are some other considerations:

- **You need a business-level broadband ISP or T1 line** Dial-up ISPs are far too slow to stream video. Also, upload speeds are often throttled by cable or DSL services to a fraction of the upload speed, and they usually prohibit use of their consumer-level services for Web servers. You will need to contact your local phone company or ISP for information on what to do.

CAUTION *Take the limits about using your Mac as a Web server seriously. If your ISP catches you in the act, as it were, they can cut off your service and you will have no right of appeal. You might get a warning the first time—or maybe not, depending on how often the facilities are abused.*

- **Devote your Mac to this task alone** Even with Mac OS X's industrial-strength multitasking, if you want to stream video on a regular basis, you should dedicate a single computer to performing this task alone. Apple's official recommendation for its QuickTime Streaming Server software calls for a G3 or better with a minimum of 128MB of RAM and 4GB of hard disk storage space. But to use Mac OS X Server, a G4, whether a Macintosh Server or Power Mac, and a minimum of 512MB of RAM are essential for good performance.

TIP *The best approach is usually to look for a third-party Web hosting service to handle your needs. Depending on the service, they can even dedicate a single computer to managing your video streams if the bandwidth requires it. However you add up the cost, from ISP hookup to the hardware itself, this is often the best way unless you have a large business with the proper hardware and connections already in place.*

The Closing Scene

The Web is not the final frontier for your iMovie. It is just another handy way to circulate your movie to others, whether family, friends, business contacts, or the public at large.

In our next and final chapter, we'll show you how easy it is to transfer your iMovie to DVD, using Apple's clever DVD authoring tool, iDVD 2.

Chapter 18

Transferring Your Videos to DVD with iDVD 2

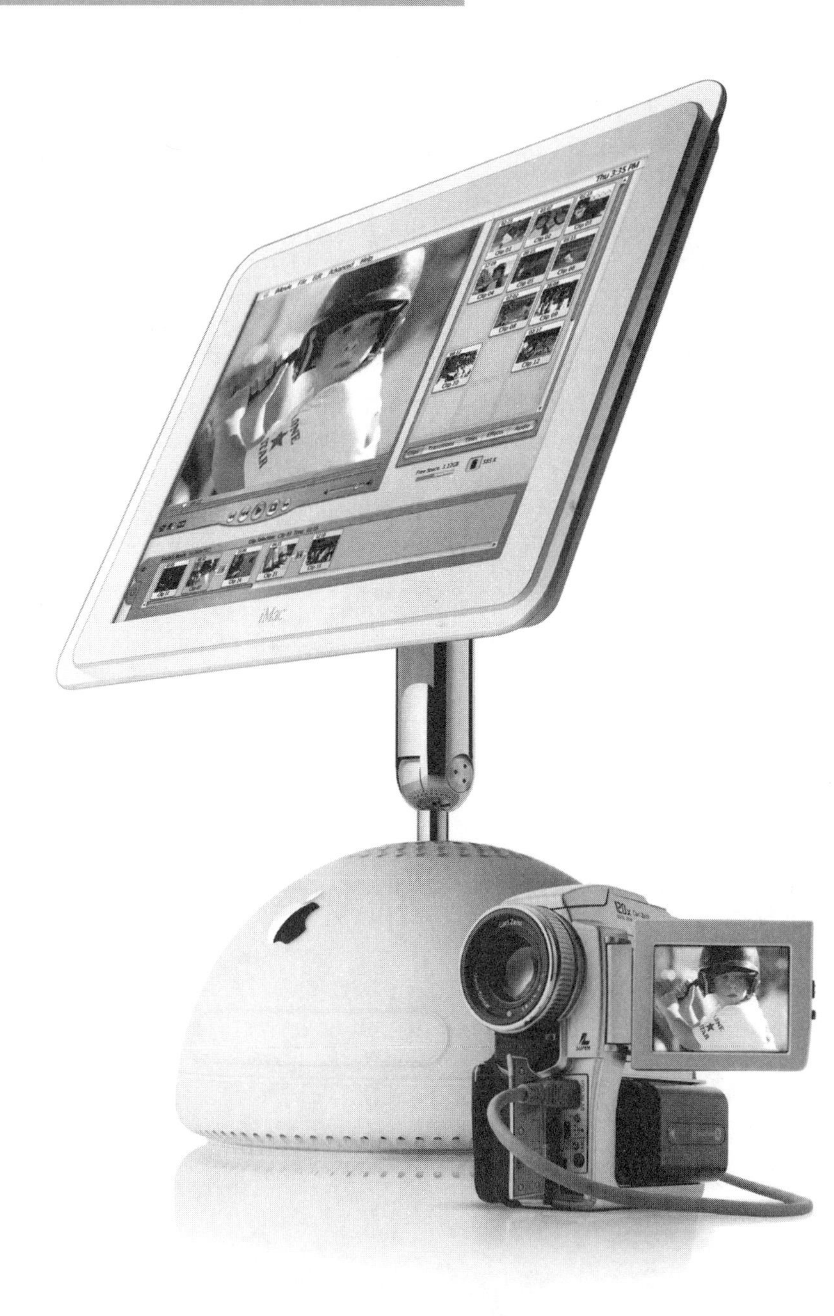

How to…

- Prepare your videos for a DVD
- Import video into iDVD 2
- Customize menus
- Add a slideshow and motion menus
- Make a DVD copy of your video

The era of the VCR is coming to a close. As with LP records and cassette tapes, a product from the digital world is destined to supplant the VCR in the next few years. That product, an outgrowth of CD technology, is the DVD—short for Digital Versatile Disc. DVD players and movies are the hot-ticket items at consumer electronic stores and even your local supermarket.

A single 5-1/4 inch DVD, for example, can come in a variety of forms. Movies may be pressed on a single side, on both sides, or even on two layers to increase capacity. In the end, though, you get something that delivers a full-length motion picture with an image that's at least twice as sharp as an image delivered by a VHS tape, with genuine Dolby Digital and, sometimes, DTS surround sound—all at a cost of just a few bucks more than a music CD.

It was only a matter of time before the cost of making your own DVDs became affordable. One of the DVD recorders to hit the personal computer world was the famous Pioneer DVR-103, a drive that can burn not only DVDs, but CDs as well. Apple put the drive in a Power Mac G4, dubbed it "SuperDrive," and introduced a clever application, iDVD, that enables you to create professional-looking DVD menus in minutes, and then burn a DVD that will work on most recent DVD players.

NOTE *You don't need to spend big bucks on a high-end professional Mac to make your DVDs. The ultra-slick, flat-panel version of the ever-popular iMac comes in a version that includes a SuperDrive. Talk about making DVDs on the cheap!*

In this chapter, we'll tell you how to take the movie you've just edited in iMovie 2 and, courtesy of Apple's iDVD 2, press your own DVD. Whether you're a video pro who needs to make a demo disk or a professional-grade picture of a wedding or graduation, an editor, or just a home video hobbyist, it doesn't get more exciting than this.

Introducing iDVD 2

Before we tell you about all the good things you can do with iDVD 2, we do want to mention some limitations, the first of which deals with capacity. iDVD 2 is a consumer application, and the DVDs you make with it are limited to 90 minutes in length with up to 99 images in a slide show and six items in a single menu. None of the exotic options, such as multiple-layer or two-sided DVDs, are possible.

The second limitation is that you are making General, or consumer-level DVDs, which means they cannot be used for Authoring, or mastering, a professional DVD and you certainly cannot use it to make copies of commercial recordings. All of these can be accomplished, though, in Apple's $999.00 professional package, DVD Studio Pro 1.1.

There is one more limitation, and is that not all DVD players read discs made with iDVD 2. The reason is that the DVD format is steadily evolving, and the standards have been expanded over time. If you have a very old DVD player, you may run into trouble.

Fortunately, Apple runs regular tests on supported devices. Check the Apple Web site at http://www.apple.com/dvd/compatibility/ for the latest compatibility list. You'll see that a great number of players, including DVD drives on computers, are supported by manufacturers all the way from Aiwa to Zenith.

NOTE *If your player isn't listed, don't assume it won't work, especially if it's a newer model. Apple can't test everything out there. However, since DVD player prices have come down so much, you may be able to replace your old unit with a new one that offers more features and better picture quality for a fraction of the price you paid originally.*

iDVD 2 Hardware Requirements

The version of iDVD we're writing about in this chapter is a major upgrade to the program. As with the original version, you need one of the new flat-screen iMacs with a G4 processor, or a Power Mac G4. Either should be equipped with Apple's SuperDrive.

The application also requires Mac OS 10.1 or later, and a minimum of 256MB of RAM installed, with 384MB recommended by Apple. All supported models have the minimum amount of RAM, and upgrades are cheap and easy to install.

NOTE *If you have a Power Mac G4 with the original version of iDVD, you can still use it under Mac OS 9.x, but you will not find many of the features listed here. In addition, iDVD doesn't support third party DVD-R drives, even if they use the very same Pioneer mechanism (DVR-103 on the Power Mac G4 and DVD-104 on the iMac) that Apple uses. Don't ask us why—we only work here.*

iDVD 2 Features

When DVDs first came out, they were very much like a videotape or a disc. You just inserted the disc and it began to play. However, movie studios soon realized that they could take advantage of the vast storage capacity of the DVD and include value-added content, such as out-takes, alternate endings, director's commentaries, games, and so on and so forth. Some DVDs include more extras than movies.

The movie studios also put in fancy navigation menus, so you can click your way through the vast amount of extra content.

Now wouldn't it be nice if you could do the very same thing yourself, creating professional looking navigation menus for accessing the various videos and even still pictures? That's just one of the delights of iDVD 2, as you'll soon discover.

Here's a brief look at some of the features of this marvelous little application:

- **Simple to add clips** You can drag and drop QuickTime movie files directly into iDVD 2, or just use the Import feature to grab your iMovie 2 files and other multimedia material.
- **Make a slide show** In addition to putting movies on your DVD, you can assemble digital pictures and create a slide show, complete with a sound track. This is tailor-made for company presentations.
- **Built-in menu themes** Pick from a small selection of still menus, or take your own digital pictures and make your own.
- **Motion menus** Just like Hollywood, take a video clip and use it for a background menu or button. Or do both. You can use one of the menu themes that come with iDVD 2 or exercise your creativity and create your own.
- **Easy previewing** Just click the Preview button to check out your work, so there are no nasty surprises after you burn a DVD.
- **One-button DVD burning** It works the same way as iTunes, Apple's popular jukebox application. Click the Burn button and follow the prompts.
- **Ninety-minute recording capacity** You can record projects that last up to 90 minutes, with a few caveats. First off, video quality suffers when you go over 60 minutes because of the added compression needed to fit the video on a single DVD. Also, Apple recommends that individual movies be kept to 60

minutes or less, which still means you can add two or more movies, slides and so forth.

iDVD 2 Preferences

iDVD 2 is designed to be smooth and easy to use, so, as with iMovie 2, you won't find extensive and confusing menus and preferences. But we'll cover the basics here, to help you get used to the choices available.

For example, the preferences dialog box, available from the application menu (see Figure 18-1), has just a handful of options.

- **Video Standard** Choose the default NTSC for North America or PAL for other countries where that standard is in effect.
- **Delete rendered files after closing a project** Assuming you never intend to make another copy of that DVD, this may be all right, but it's better to leave it checked, in case something happens during the burning process. You don't want to redo the work again, especially if you spent a lot of time customizing menus.
- **Show Watermark** Do you want the Apple logo or not? Decide here.

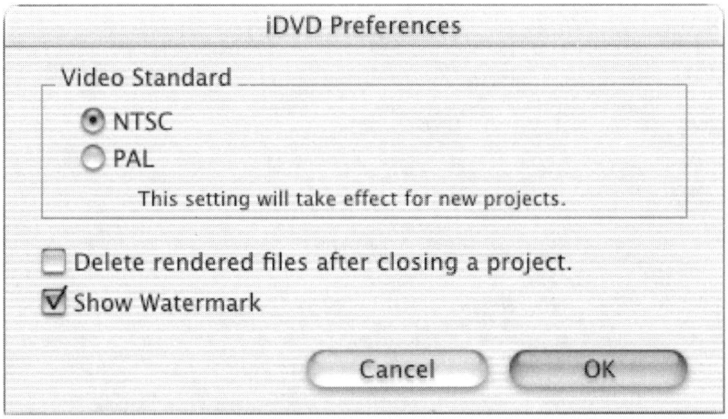

FIGURE 18-1 Set a few preferences for iDVD 2 here.

Reviewing iDVD 2 Menu Bar Commands

The labels are straightforward, simple, with no complexities, so we'll cover the choices ever so briefly, and then we'll get to the meat of this chapter:

- **iDVD application menu** This is, essentially, your standard application menu, with an About iDVD command and access to the Preferences dialog box.
- **File menu** Shown in Figure 18-2. You can open and save your DVD projects here, and access a menu of recent projects. The lone commercial tie-in for this application is the Buy DVD Media command, which opens your Web browser and takes you to an online ordering page where you can buy more blank DVDs from Apple Computer. The final command burns your DVD.
- **Project menu** You'll find a limited number of choices here (see Figure 18-3). Project Info delivers the cold, hard facts about the material you're putting on your DVD, and Show Theme Panel delivers a set of convenient dialog boxes where you can customize your DVD menu. We'll get to these shortly. The other key options are the ability to add a folder and a slideshow on your DVD menu.
- **Advanced menu** Some key choices are available to you here. One, Show TV Safe Area, enables you to see only that part of the picture that will appear within the standard TV screen aspect ratio (4:3). No doubt only a small number

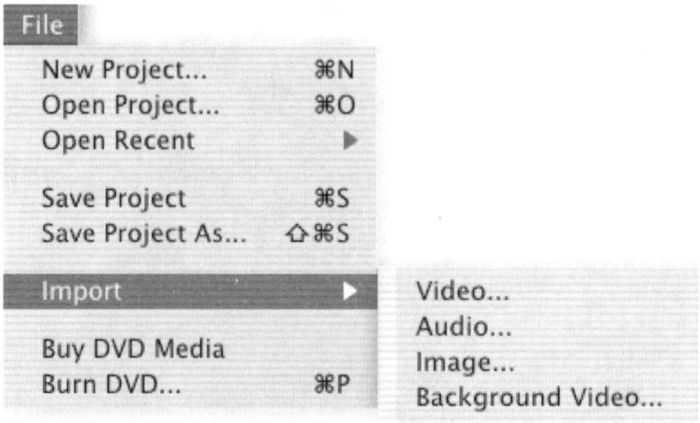

FIGURE 18-2 Open projects, save projects, and burn your DVD from this menu.

Project
Project Info... ⌘I
Show Theme Panel ⇧⌘B
Add Folder ⌘K
Add Slideshow ⌘L
Go Back ⌘B

FIGURE 18-3 Access the Theme Panel and other features from this menu.

of you have those nifty widescreen TVs yet. The Motion command brings up the choice of producing a Motion menu. The other two commands are used to apply themes to a project or to a folder.

iDVD 2 Editing Shortcuts

As with iMovie 2, using a handful of useful iDVD 2 keyboard shortcuts will help speed up your work, particularly if you'd rather avoid the mouse.

Here's the list, shown in the order in which these commands appear in iDVD 2's menu bar:

IDVD 2 Keyboard Shortcuts	
New Project	COMMAND+N
Open Project	COMMAND+O
Save Project	COMMAND+S
Save Project As	COMMAND+SHIFT+S
Burn DVD	COMMAND+P
Project Info	COMMAND+I
Show Theme Panel	COMMAND+SHIFT+B
Go Back	COMMAND+B
Show TV Safe Area	COMMAND+T
Motion Menus	COMMAND+J

Using the Theme Panel

In keeping with iDVD 2's convenient drag and drop interface, iDVD 2 includes some simple yet powerful ways to select from a pre-built set of menu themes and to customize them in a reasonably wide fashion.

To bring up the Themes Panel, just choose Show Theme Panel from the Project menu or type COMMAND+SHIFT+B. Here's a look at the selections you'll see when you click the tabs:

- **Themes** Choose from the standard selection (see Figure 18-4), shown in thumbnails, so you can get a sense of how they'll look. If you click on the All pop-up menu, you can restrict the list to Motion themes, Picture only themes, or Picture with audio. Using a theme is simply a matter of dragging it to your project window.
- **Customize** Once you've picked a theme you like, you aren't locked into its default setup. In fact you don't even have to use a standard background theme. The Customize dialog box (shown in Figure 18-5) gives you a fair number of options to create your own themes, or customize the one that's set up for you, simply by dragging a new picture into the Image/Movie well. As you'll see later in this chapter, you can also change title fonts and layout and the shape and positioning of the buttons you use.
- **Status** As you learned earlier in this chapter, you can create a DVD of up to 90 minutes, but you must limit a single video to 60 minutes duration. The Status dialog box displays the duration of each element or asset of your project, so you can keep tabs on how things are going.

TIP

If your videos are running too long, there's nothing wrong with creating two DVDs. Even commercial videos sometimes come on two discs, with the second one containing special content to enhance the entertainment value. You'll want to divide your DVD at logical break points should you decide to go this route, however. Perhaps place the beginning of your documentary on the first DVD and maybe the background information and conclusion on the second DVD.

Exporting Your iMovie 2 Video to iDVD 2

If you have followed the steps in the first 17 chapters to shoot a video and edit an iMovie 2 project, you are just about ready to bring all that work into iDVD 2, and make a DVD.

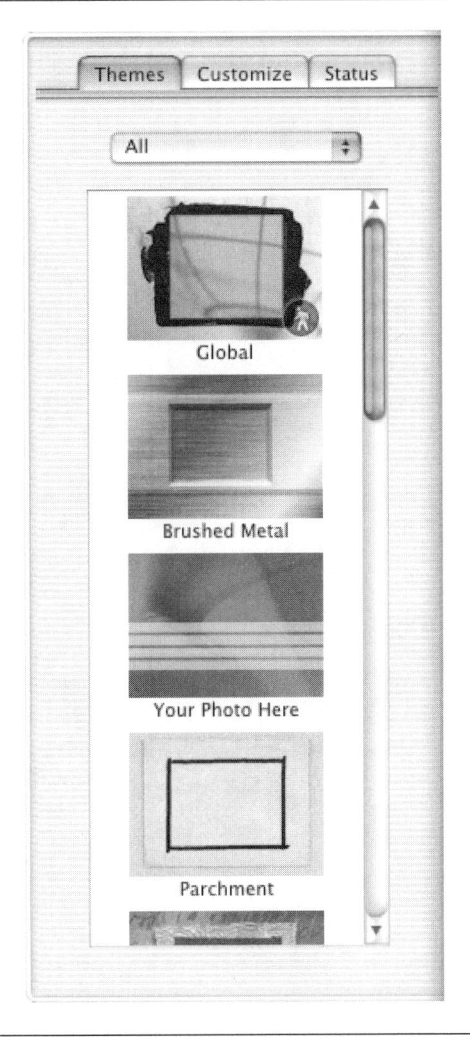

FIGURE 18-4 Drag and drop the theme you like to get started.

You just have to follow a few more steps to make it happen:

1. With your edited project on the screen in iMovie 2, choose Export Movie from the File menu. You'll see an Export Movie dialog box.
2. Select For iDVD from the Export to pop-up menu (see Figure 18-6).

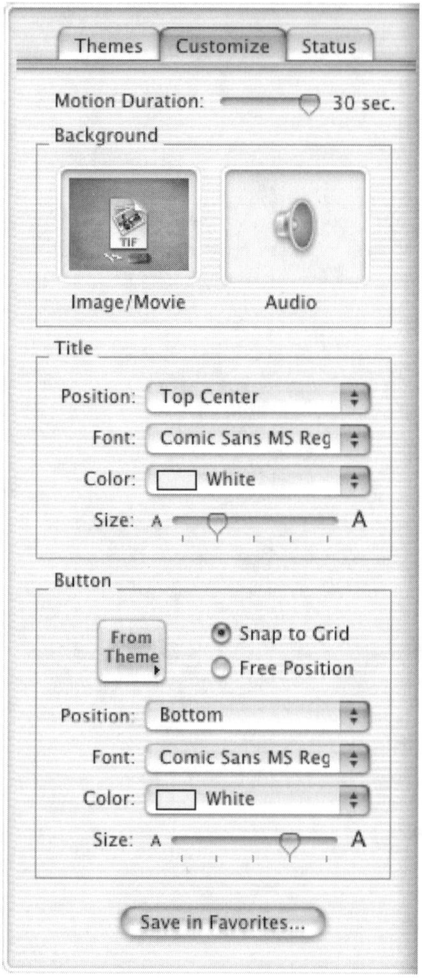

FIGURE 18-5 Modify an existing theme or create one of your own here.

NOTE *The preceding instructions require that you have iMovie 2.0.3 or later. If you haven't upgraded, you will need to export your movie in QuickTime format, choosing Full Quality from among the listed formats to get a good quality DVD.*

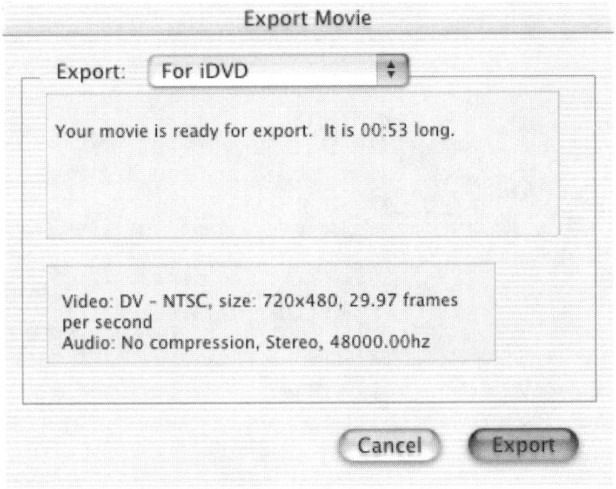

FIGURE 18-6 Save your project in iDVD 2 form to simplify the task of making a DVD.

CAUTION *The files used in your project must be on your Mac's hard drive. You cannot add items from a CD or DVD, because those files will not be available to iDVD when you remove the discs to burn your DVD—the files are read during the burning process.*

3. In the Save As dialog box, give your project a name for easy identification later on. Depending on the size of the project and the speed of your Mac, it will probably take several minutes for the export file to be created.

Other Supported Formats

You aren't limited to an iMovie 2 project in iDVD 2. You can use any QuickTime movie with a linear video track, and JPEG and PICT formatted pictures for your slideshows. Sorry folks, you can't use movies in QuickTime VR, MPEG, Flash or other streaming video formats.

Setting Up a New Project in iDVD 2

All ready? Let's make a DVD. To begin your new project, just follow these steps:

1. Launch iDVD and click New Project on the startup screen, which is shown in Figure 18-7.

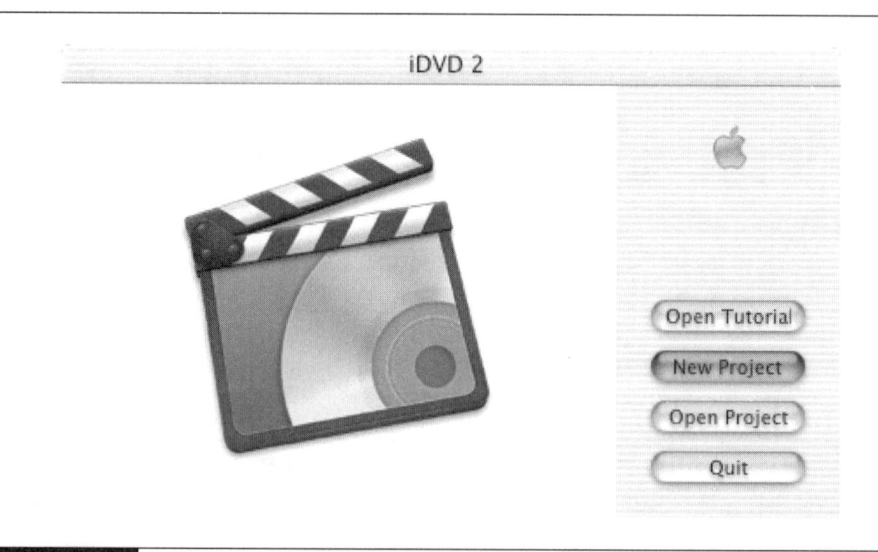

FIGURE 18-7 If you don't have an existing project, or you've opened iDVD for the first time, this screen appears.

2. Name your project in the Save as dialog box that appears next (see Figure 18-8). Now you're ready to bring in your videos and create themes and menus.

CAUTION *As desktop publishing software usually does, iDVD 2 keeps tabs on the files that are used in your project while the application is open, but cannot update itself to reflect the files you may have moved or deleted. So you should not move or rename any of those files, because the disc you burn will be missing those items. If you remove a QuickTime file, however, you will be asked to locate it via an open dialog box. If you cancel that dialog box the application will freeze.*

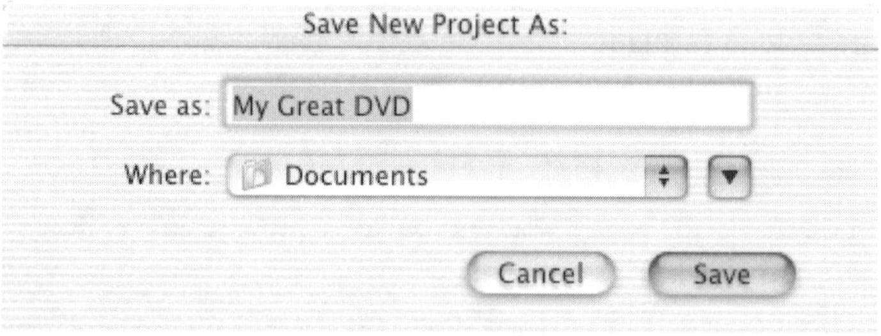

FIGURE 18-8 Name your DVD project in this dialog box.

Importing a Video

All set? Now you're ready to bring your movie into iDVD. This is an ultra-simple process that takes just seconds to do.

Here's how to accomplish the task:

1. Locate the movie file and drag it into the background of your DVD project window (or menu).
2. If the file isn't easily found via drag and drop, choose Import Video from the File menu and locate the movie file.

NOTE *When you bring a movie into iDVD, it'll appear in a button that contains the name of the movie file (minus the .mov extension). Your DVD menu can have up to six buttons; if you need more buttons, you have to create more menus. We explain the process later in this chapter.*

Choosing a Theme

The look of your DVD is decided by your choice of theme, the background images, movies and buttons that set your project apart from all the others. Fortunately, you have a number of choices in iDVD 2 that will give your movie a special touch of individuality.

Here's how to pick a theme:

1. With your iDVD 2 project opened, open the Theme Panel, if it's not already present and accounted for. You can locate the Show Theme Panel command in the Project Menu, the Theme button in the project window, or press COMMAND+SHIFT+B. The command, by the way, toggles to Hide Theme Panel if it's on display.
2. Click on a theme that suits your fancy and drag and drop it into the project window.
3. If you want to add a Motion theme, click on Motion in the pop-up menu at the top of the Themes drawer to see what's available before you drag it into the project window.
4. If you select a Motion theme, you can preview it by clicking on the Motion button (a second click will stop play of the Motion theme).

NOTE *If you decide to use another theme, no problem. Just drag and drop the new one into your project window. And, oh yes, be sure to save your work periodically so you don't lose it in the event your Mac crashes or iDVD quits. While this happens only rarely under Mac OS X, it's better to be safe rather than sorry.*

Customizing Your Theme

Do you find the array of background themes in iDVD 2 a little too limiting? No problem. Feel free to create one of your own. The ability to customize an existing theme or use a different one is one of the compelling features of iDVD 2 that will help give your disc a unique flair and impact.

Here's how to customize your theme:

1. With the Themes drawer open, click on the Customize tab (take a look again at Figure 18-5).
2. If you want to use a different background image, locate the image and drag it into the Image/Movie well. You can use a PICT or JPEG picture or just drag a movie file if you want to use a motion background. Audio tracks for a motion menu go in the Audio well.

NOTE *You can, of course, incorporate an image by dragging it right to your project window or any individual button or menu, but we assume you might want to customize position, font, and button style too.*

CAUTION *Images used for the background should be sized at 640×480 pixels to fit within the normal aspect ratio of a TV image. If the picture has a wider aspect ratio, you'll see black borders at the top and bottom.*

3. If you want to change the position, font, and style of title text, make the changes you want in the Title category in the Customize drawer.
4. Change the size, shape, and title text formatting in the Button category.
5. Once you've made your changes, you can drag the completed background image to your project window or an individual button.

TIP *Want to reuse your custom theme? No problem. Just click the Save in Favorites button at the bottom of the Customize drawer, give it a name and it'll be available in the Favorites category of the Themes pop-up menu.*

Adding Extra Menus

We assume that, for most purposes, having six buttons is sufficient to incorporate a normal number of videos on your DVD. But if you want to use a number of shorter clips, you may find six buttons just too limiting.

Fortunately, the clever designers of iDVD 2 found a way to get around this limitation.

1. To add another menu, click the Folder icon in your project window, which creates an empty folder in your project window.
2. Give the folder a name, such as "Special Features," "More Goodies," or whatever suits.
3. Drag the movie files into the new folder. When your project is done, clicking on this extra menu button will bring up a new menu in the finished project.

NOTE *By default, a Back button is placed within the second menu, which viewers must click to return to the main menu.*

Changing Title Text

As you've seen so far in your discovery of the great tools available in iDVD 2, whatever you put there gets a default title, based on the name of your file. But you don't have to stick with defaults. To change a title, click on the text window to select it, just like any old text box, and change it to what you want.

Use the Customize drawer to change positioning and type style to fit your needs.

NOTE *You can use any font available on your Mac for your title text. Since the title displays in the exact font and style, feel free to experiment and pick what works best.*

Creating a Slideshow

You aren't limited to movies in iDVD 2. Still pictures presented as slideshows can have their own brand of motion and pacing simply through the time you set for each picture and the addition of an audio track to give the presentation forward focus.

Here's how to make a slideshow:

1. With your iDVD 2 project open, click the Slideshow button to make a new button.
2. Give the button a name, such as "My Photos," and double click that button to bring up a window where you can place your photos.
3. Drag the pictures that make up your slideshow from the Media folder and place them in the slideshow window.
4. Should you want to add narration and music to your slideshow, just drag the file containing the material to the audio well.

NOTE *You can add audio files to the Audio well by dragging and dropping into it a QuickTime file with an audio track. iDVD 2 will use the first soundtrack in that file (and that includes MP3 and AIFF). When you use a narration, you'll want to select Fit To Audio from the Slide Duration menu (also see the tip below).*

5. We're getting close to the finish line here. To display right and left navigation arrows on the menu, click the checkbox labeled "Display <> on image." That way, the viewer can easily move from slide to slide.

TIP *If you'd rather have the slides advance automatically, click the Slide Duration button in your DVD project menu to bring up a menu where you can select the time for each slide—from 1 second up to 10 seconds. The final option, Fit To Audio, enables the audio track to trigger the next slide.*

6. All done? Click the Return button (the one with the curved arrow) to complete the slideshow setup process.

Adding a Custom Preview Image

Normally, when you set up a picture menu, it'll display the first frame in a movie or a slide. But you don't have to use that standard image.

In order to change it, simply drag the slider above the button to pick another image from your movie or slideshow. If you prefer to use a different picture, you can drag a different image file from your Mac's hard drive to any iDVD button and use that one instead. Nifty.

Ready to Check Your Project?

All right, blank DVDs are getting cheaper all the time, but there's no sense wasting them on a project that isn't quite ready, so iDVD 2 has a Preview option to enable you to check everything out before you burn your DVD.

Here's how it works:

1. If your project has motion background and buttons, click the Motion button to activate them.
2. Now simply click the Preview button to turn on the preview mode. When you click Preview, a remote control window appears (see Figure 18-9), which enables you to test out each function. It's similar to the remote on many regular DVD players, and it's easy to navigate in a similar way. Here's what to do:
   - **Playback controls** Click a button to play back your videos, pause, or move forward and backward among the videos. Typical of Mac multimedia software, the slider at the bottom of the remote is used for volume level.
   - **Arrow buttons** Use the appropriate arrow button and the Enter button to choose and activate buttons in your DVD's menu.

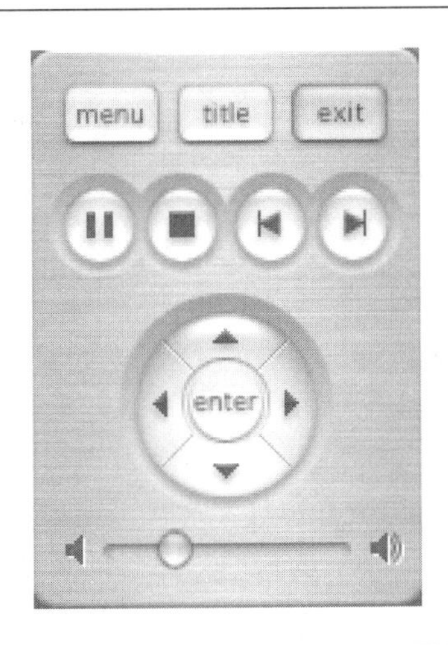

FIGURE 18-9 Use this onscreen remote control to navigate through your movies, menus, and buttons.

- **Next button** Use this control to travel through the slides in your slideshow.
- **Menu button** One click of this button takes you to the menu you've made for your movie.
- **Title button** A click of this button moves you directly to the main title or first DVD menu, the one you will see when you first put in a DVD and the menu appears on your screen.

TIP *Watching a movie or slideshow? When you click Menu or Title to see either item, another click of the Menu button will return you to what you were watching, exactly where it left off.*

3. All finished? Take another look to be sure everything works as advertised (see Figure 18-10), then just click Preview again or Exit on the remote control to leave Preview mode.

Ready to Burn?

Once you've set up your project the way you want, there's just one step remaining before you can enjoy that DVD in all its glory, and that's to burn the DVD. After all the work you've done so far, you'll find this process is the easiest of all, though you have to wait a bit for it to happen.

How's how it's done:

1. With your DVD project ready to roll, click the Burn button in iDVD's application window twice.

CAUTION *Be careful about naming your DVD. You cannot use such keyboard characters as $ or & in the name, or a word space. If your title does contain a word space, such as Rockoids Movie, the DV will be named Rockoids_Movie.*

2. When you see the prompt, place a blank DVD-R disc in your Mac or iMac's SuperDrive and close the drive tray. Over the next few minutes, your project will be encoded and written onto a DVD. You'll see an onscreen prompt when it's done.

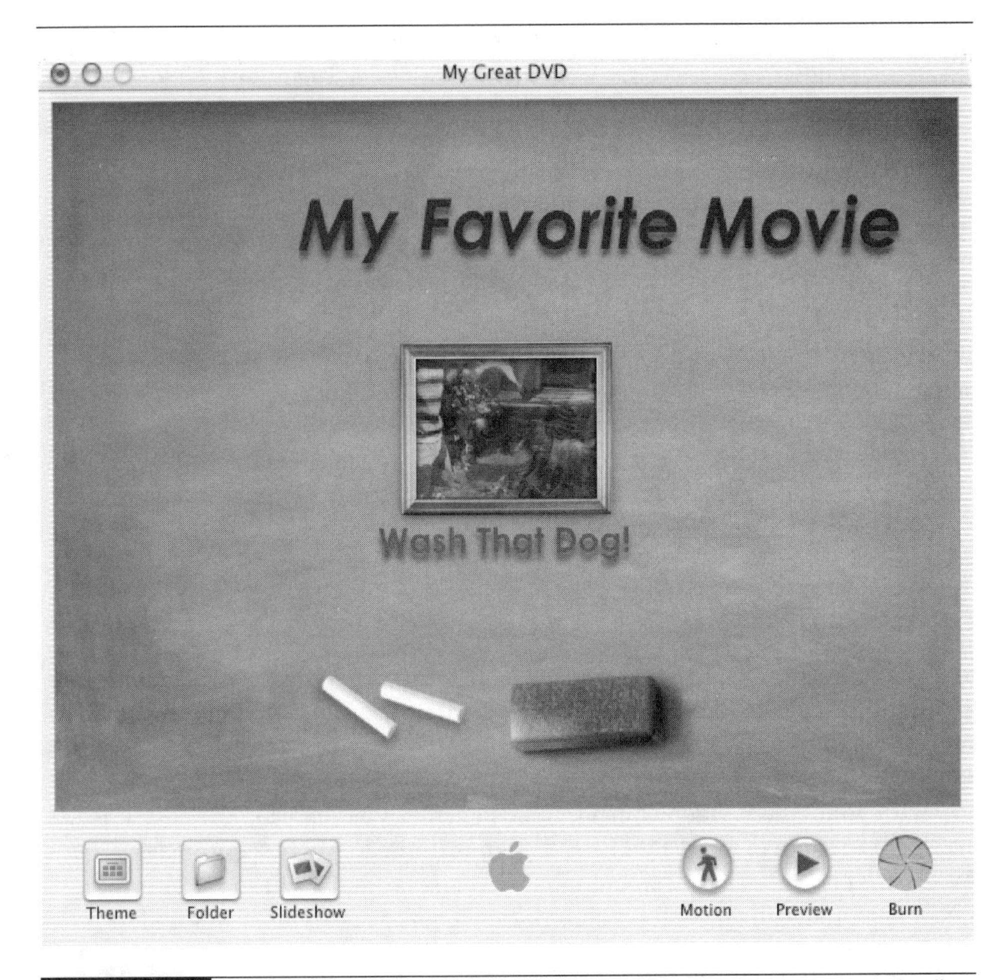

FIGURE 18-10 Give your completed DVD menu a final check before you burn the disc.

NOTE *There are many variables in determining how long it'll take to burn a DVD. It depends on the content of the project and how much encoding is necessary, as well as the speed of your Mac's processor, but figure on two to three minutes for each minute of video. If you have a Mac with dual processors, burning goes much faster, but not twice as fast.*

CAUTION *While your Power Mac and flat-panel iMac are supremely powerful computers, you need to observe some cautions when burning a DVD. First and foremost, don't run other applications while burning is in progress, as it may slow down the process or cause a data error. Make sure you don't press the Eject key on your keyboard, because it will abort the project and eject the DVD before the job is completed.*

DVD Playback Problems

As soon as you finish burning a DVD, it's a good idea to try it out on your Mac. Just reinsert the completed DVD into the drive, launch the DVD Player application (located in the Applications folder), and test your DVD to make sure the videos, slideshows, and menus that you added all work as they did when you previewed them.

So long as the DVD works properly on your Mac, it will run properly on any consumer DVD player that supports the DVD-R format.

The Closing Scene

As we come to the end of this book, we hope the experience has been both informative and fun. Through 18 chapters, you have learned about the wonders and simplicity of iMovie 2, how to choose the right camcorder and accessories, and how to make and edit videos with professional spit and polish.

With your edited video at hand, in this chapter you learned how easy it is to transfer your movie to DVD. The next step is limited only by your imagination. Whether you just want to capture family events, or you have aspirations to become a professional videographer or moviemaker, iMovie 2 is a wonderful environment to show off your creativity.

Welcome to the wonderful world of movies.

Appendix A Troubleshooting

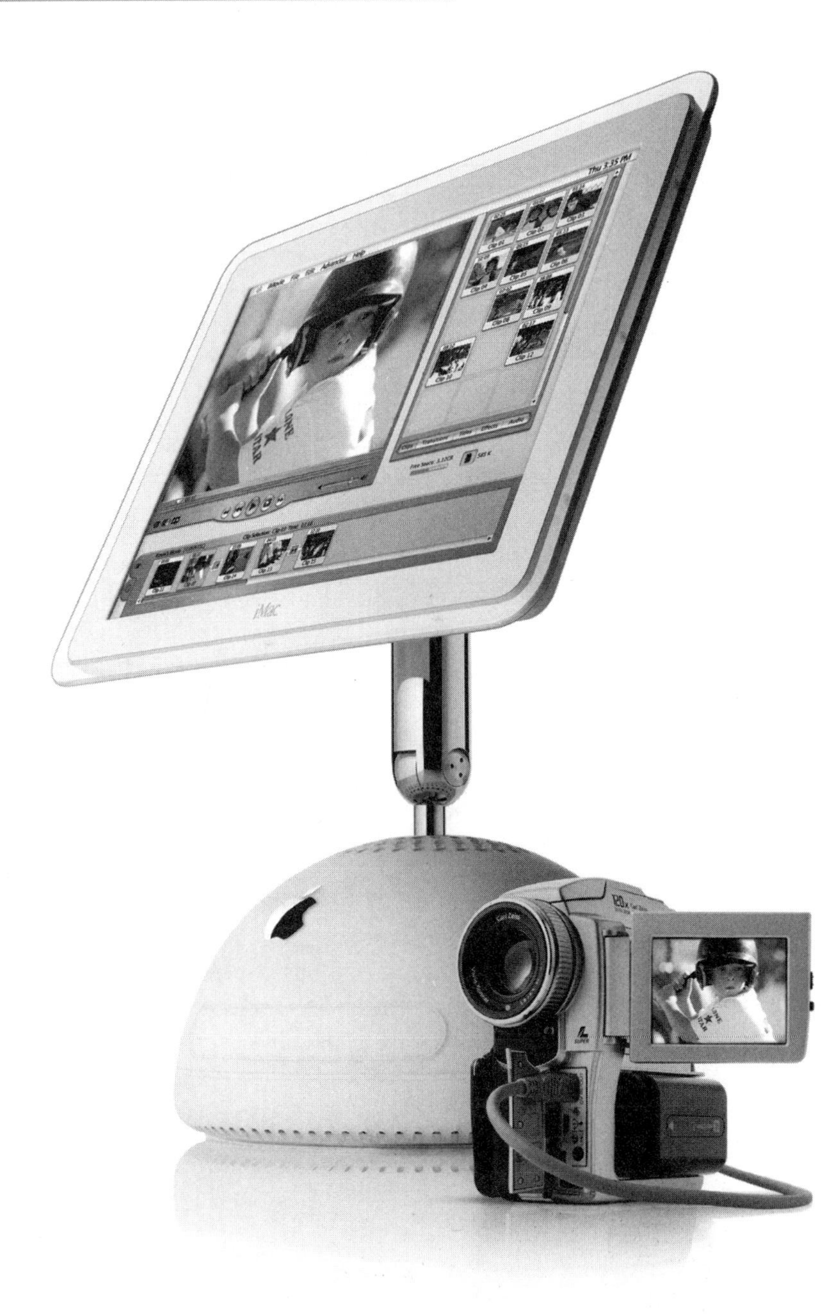

How to…

- Check your manual focus
- Use your remote control
- Make a smoother pan
- Find online technical support

Question I am trying to use manual focus to zoom into a distant target to get the best sharpness, but it just gets blurry when I go that far. What am I doing wrong?

Answer If your camcorder, like many, has a combination manual and digital zoom, try turning off the digital zoom function as well as the autofocus function, and just go on manual. You may be shooting beyond the distance covered by the manual zoom. If you must capture that distant frame, let digital zoom and autofocus do their jobs. Otherwise, you may lead a sharper life by just abandoning digital zoom altogether.

Question I try to use my remote control from behind a tripod setup, and nothing happens. Is it broken?

Answer Most infrared receivers are mounted on the front of the camcorder, usually below the lens and microphones. This is to accommodate the popular "get me in the shot" shot where you are positioned way in front of the camera. You'll just have to hold the remote near enough to, and pointing at, the bottom front of the camcorder for the IR signal to register.

Question I am using a good photography tripod with a pan head, but even though I sight through the viewfinder, I am getting rough movement. How do I perform this function smoothly, as they do in the movies?

Answer With careful trial-and-error adjustment of the knobs, you can often get quite acceptable pans with one of these tripods. They will have to be slow or medium speed pans. Further, use your viewfinder to set up the shot with its start point and end points, but don't try to view and pan at the same time. Use the LCD screen, but if you have your points set up well, just concentrate on making a smooth movement.

Question My camcorder has a neat option where you can shoot in the 16:9 aspect ratio, so that the screen will have the same proportions as I see in the movie theater. But when I import that footage into iMovie, the frames are in the normal 4:3 ratio. How can I fix this?

Answer iMovie 2 is a consumer editing tool, and not intended for professional use, although some use it that way. At this time, it does not recognize or support the 16:9 options offered by some of the camcorder manufacturers.

But we may have a solution for you: Are you comfortable creating graphics with a program like AppleWorks or Adobe Photoshop that you import to integrate into your editing? If you are, you could make a black and white PICT mask overlay that would configure the finished frame to look just as widescreen as what you saw through your viewfinder. Of course, this wouldn't help for footage shot with those few camcorders that have an anamorphic lens setting to capture true 16:9. Everything will still look elongated and distorted.

Question I am all set up to import footage from my camcorder, but it is not coming through. Is something wrong with my camcorder, or my Mac?

Answer Assuming you have connected your camcorder to its AC adapter that is plugged into an outlet, make sure that your setup's FireWire is not in conflict or competition with any other FireWire device. In other words, try plugging it directly into the Mac's FireWire port, rather than have it daisy-chained from another device (although in theory that should work too).

In addition, iMovie will sense how much footage is incoming, and if it doesn't find enough potential storage capacity in your available disk space, it will not be able to capture the footage. So make sure you have plenty of free storage space to store that video.

Question All right, I was short on hard disk space, so I added some external storage, and it still won't come through. I'm getting desperate here.

Answer The external storage system you added may not be fast enough for iMovie, or may not be compatible. iMovie won't work with floppy drives, SuperDisks or Zip drives, and iMovie may not yet be able to recognize some other removable storage devices such as Orbs or other emerging formats. In addition, don't even think about trying to store iMovie footage on a drive connected to your Mac's USB port, which is far too slow for efficient video capture.

Question When I play back a movie to be viewed on a television set, some of the image is cut off around the edges. How do I fix it?

Answer Your picture is overscanning. Turn off the QT Margins check box in the Titles panel. Now it will be restored with the TV Safe Area safe again.

Question My footage is being imported as one long reel instead of being broken down into shot-by-shot clips. I suppose I can work this way, but it'll take a lot longer to split up the footage so I can edit out the bad parts.

Answer Don't give up the ship. Check to see if your Automatic Scene Detection is turned off. Go to the iMovie menu, open Preferences, and select Import. There you can select Automatically start new clips at scene break. If this was already selected, then check to see if your camera's time and date was set. If it wasn't, this will be enough to throw off the Automatic Scene Detection.

Question I seemed to have lost one of my sound tracks while I was editing the audio. Can I bring it back?

Answer Take a look at the right side of the timeline and see if one or more of those three check boxes for the video and the two audio tracks got unchecked somehow. If they did, that track will be muted.

Question I've got the tracks back, but now the sound isn't loud enough. Can I make it louder?

Answer First check the Volume slider on the Monitor window. If that doesn't raise the level enough, then it may be your computer sound level. Go to the Sound preferences window and choose the Output tab. Adjust the Main volume slider. While you are at it, you might check the Show volume in menu bar box below as well.

Question I have an iMac running Mac OS 9.1, with 128MB of RAM. It was enough to make iMovie work, but now when I play things back, playback stutters; it's not fluid. I can't use it this way. Is there a fix?

Answer The Classic Mac OS version of virtual memory, which is turned on by default, works fine to extend usable memory, but sometimes it hurts playback of multimedia files. A good way to see if this is the cause of your problem is to open the Memory Control Panel, turn Virtual Memory off and restart. See if playback is better.

Question My iMac works fine under Mac OS X, but I can't get full screen playback of QuickTime movies to work right. It looks like a bunch of still pictures, rather than a movie. Is there a fix?

Answer Older iMacs and other Macs using older generation ATI graphics chips, such as the RAGE PRO, are short-changed under Mac OS X. Multimedia performance isn't going to be quite up to the level of Mac OS 9. Apple's solution is to switch to thousands of colors in the Displays preference panel of the System Preferences application.

NOTE *As this book went to press, we understand that ATI was looking into the possibility of updating drivers for its older graphics chips to work better under Mac OS X, but had made no final decisions about it. This has been a constant bugaboo for many Mac users who have complained about the lack of support, but it's a matter way beyond the scope of this book.*

Question I tried to import some GIF and JPEG pictures into iMovie 2 under Mac OS X, but some of these pictures were dimmed out; I couldn't get them. When I tried under Mac OS 9, it worked fine. What's wrong?

Answer Try using Mac OS X's image viewer application, Preview. If Preview can open these files, you should be able to export the files so iMovie 2 can see them. Once the pictures are opened in Preview, use the Export command from Preview's File menu to convert to JPEG or PICT formats; it doesn't matter if the picture was already a JPEG. Once the pictures are saved in the new or updated format, you should be able to easily import them into iMovie 2 for Mac OS X.

Question Whenever I import a clip into iMovie 2 under Mac OS 9, the clip goes into iMovie's trash can rather than on the shelf. What am I doing wrong?

Answer By any chance, are you using an Aurora Igniter video capture board from Aurora Video Systems on your Mac? If so, there is an apparent extension conflict with the Aurora Igniter INIT extension. The solution is to open Extensions Manager via the Control Panels submenu in the Apple menu, disable this extension and restart. If you need to use your Aurora Igniter, you can reenable this extension after you've finished importing your clips into iMovie 2.

Question I followed the instructions in Chapter 18 to the letter to create a DVD with iDVD 2, but when I checked my completed DVD there were blank spots; segments were missing. Why?

Answer iDVD 2, like iMovie (and most of your favorite graphic applications), simply creates a link to a file that you bring into it for your DVD. If you move or delete the original file, iDVD2 won't have the data it needs to encode the movie onto your DVD. So leave the originals alone until your project is complete.

Question I wanted to try iDVD 2, but it's only available for Mac OS X, and I'm using Mac OS 9. How do I make a DVD?

Answer While the original version of iDVD lacks some of the neat features of the upgraded version, such as motion menus, you can get a perfectly satisfactory DVD from its simple interface. Many of the instructions we gave you in Chapter 18 apply in almost the same fashion to the original release.

Appendix B Web References

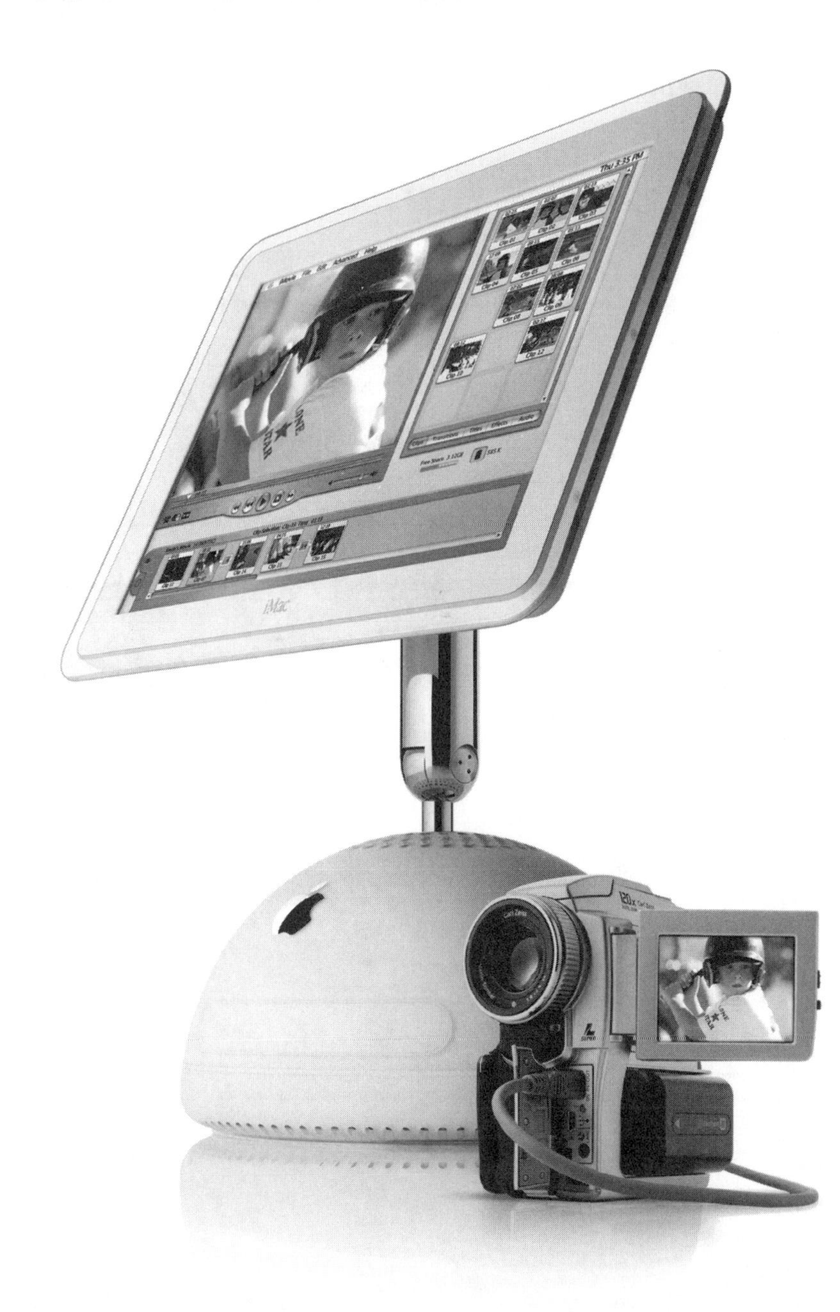

Chapter 1
Making iMovies that Work for You

Apple—iMovie http://www.apple.com/imovie/

iFilm http://www.ifilm.com/main.taf (see Figure B-1)

D.FILM Digital Film Festival http://www.dfilm.com/

FIGURE B-1 This site is dedicated to budding and independent film producers.

iMovieFest 2002 | Imagine http://imoviefest.cc.emory.edu/

Inside Reel http://www.insidereel.com/ (see Figure B-2)

Mac Filmmakers http://macfilmmakers.com/

Showing those Videos http://desktopvideo.about.com/cs/showingyourvideo/

The New Venue http://www.newvenue.com/

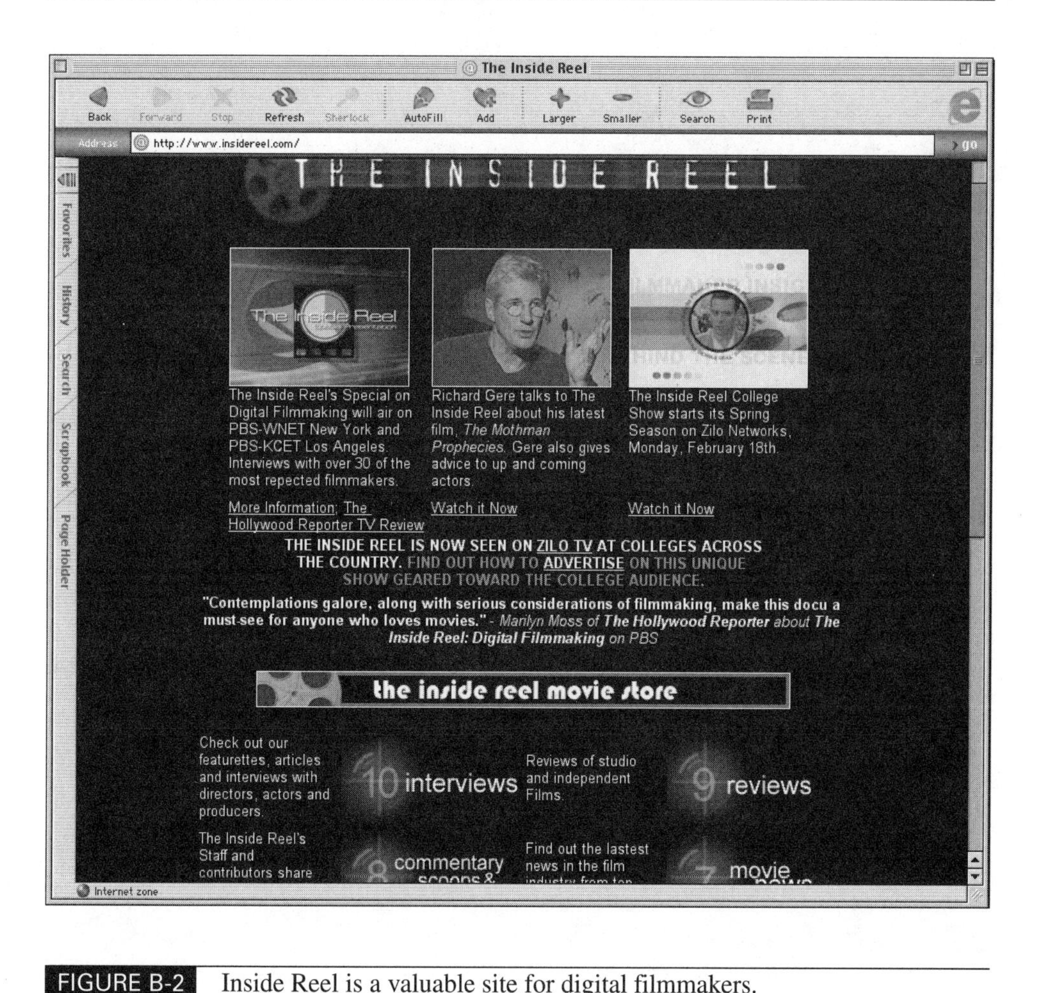

FIGURE B-2 Inside Reel is a valuable site for digital filmmakers.

Atom Films http://www.atomfilms.com (see Figure B-3)

Webcinema http://www.webcinema.org/

Welcome to Film.com Home Page http://www.film.com/

Welcome to MovieFlix http://www.movieflix.com/

FIGURE B-3 You can submit your film to this site and have it considered for commercial distribution.

Chapter 2
Setting Up Your DV Studio

AppleCare Knowledge Base http://kbase.info.apple.com/

Apple's FireWire Web Site http://www.apple.com/firewire/ (see Figure B-4)

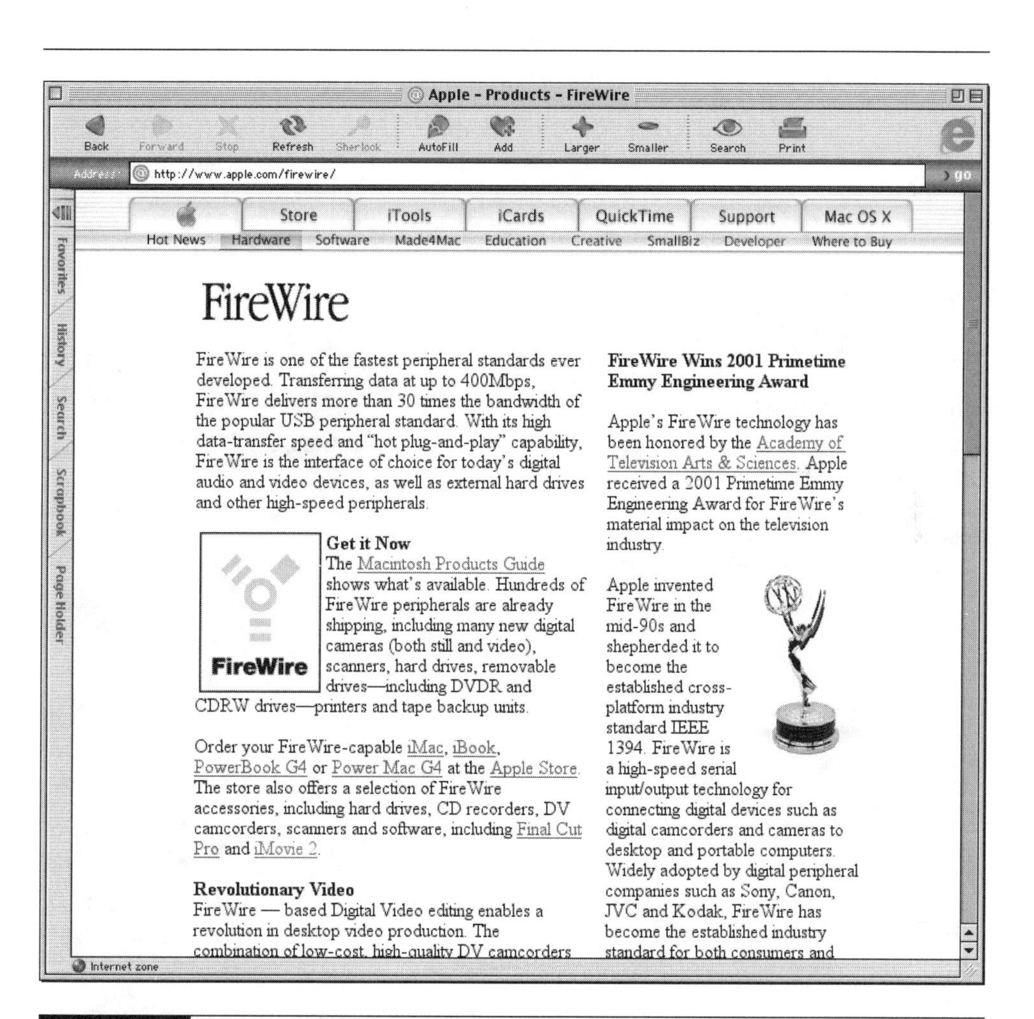

FIGURE B-4 The FireWire site lists products and offers technical information on Apple's award-winning technology.

FOLDOC—Computing Dictionary http://wombat.doc.ic.ac.uk/foldoc/index.html

iMovie FAQ http://www.danslagle.com/mac/iMovie/iMovieFAQ.html

Film Arts Foundation http://www.filmarts.org/ (see Figure B-5)

Memory Configurations http://www3.macdirectory.com/pages/Memory.html

Net Monitor Database http://www.griffintechnology.com/monitor.html

Tom's Hardware Guide: Digital Video Guide
http://www4.tomshardware.com/video/01q2/010515/index.html

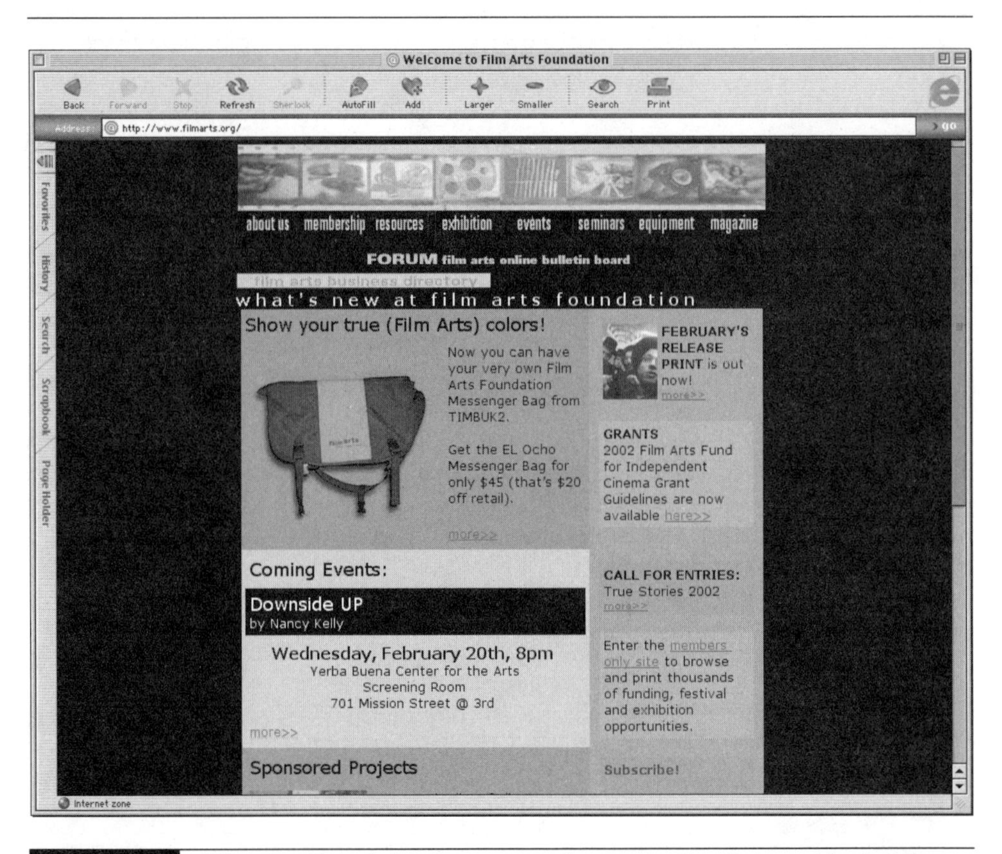

FIGURE B-5 Film Arts Foundation is a non-profit organization that provides training and information for filmmakers.

MacFixIt.com: Troubleshooting for your Mac http://www.macfixit.com/

The Mac Night Owl: Your Complete Mac Support Site
http://www.macnightowl.com (see Figure B-6)

VersionTracker.com—Macintosh Software Updates http://www.versiontracker.com

DV Magazine http://www.dv.com/ (see Figure B-7)

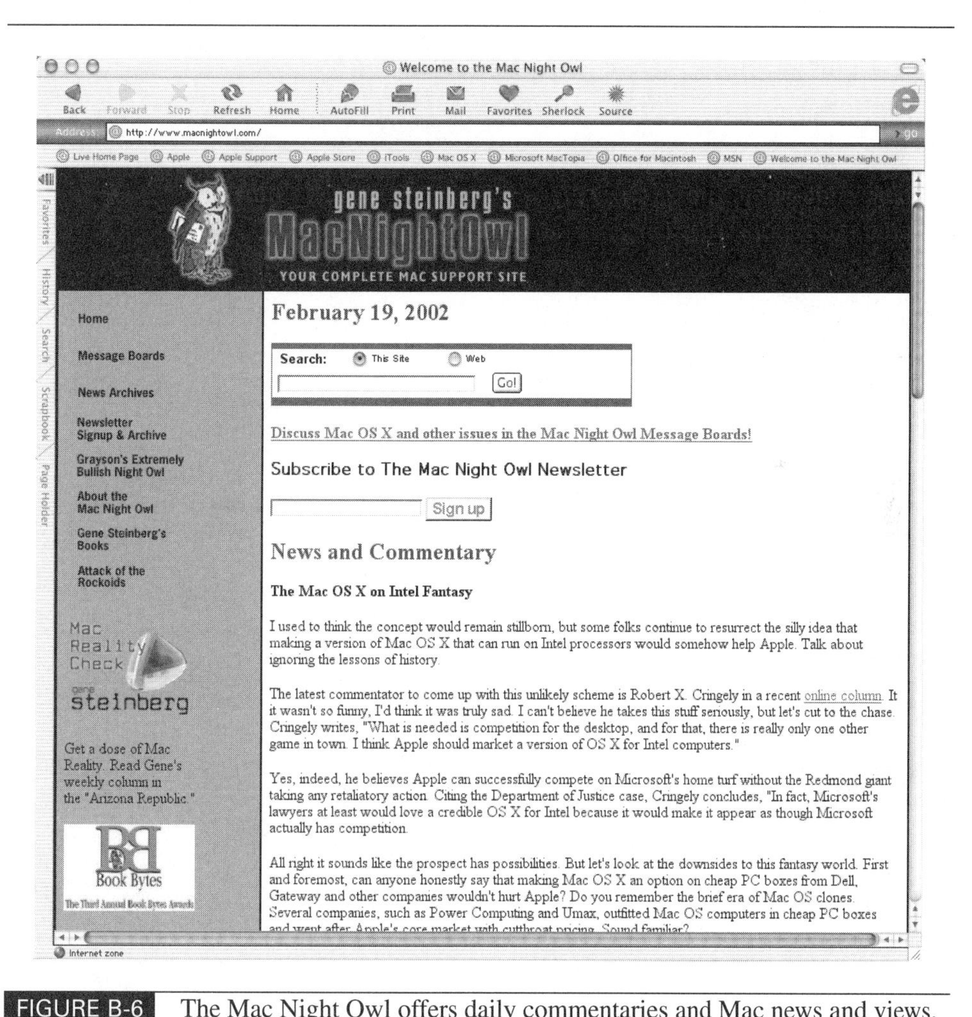

FIGURE B-6 The Mac Night Owl offers daily commentaries and Mac news and views.

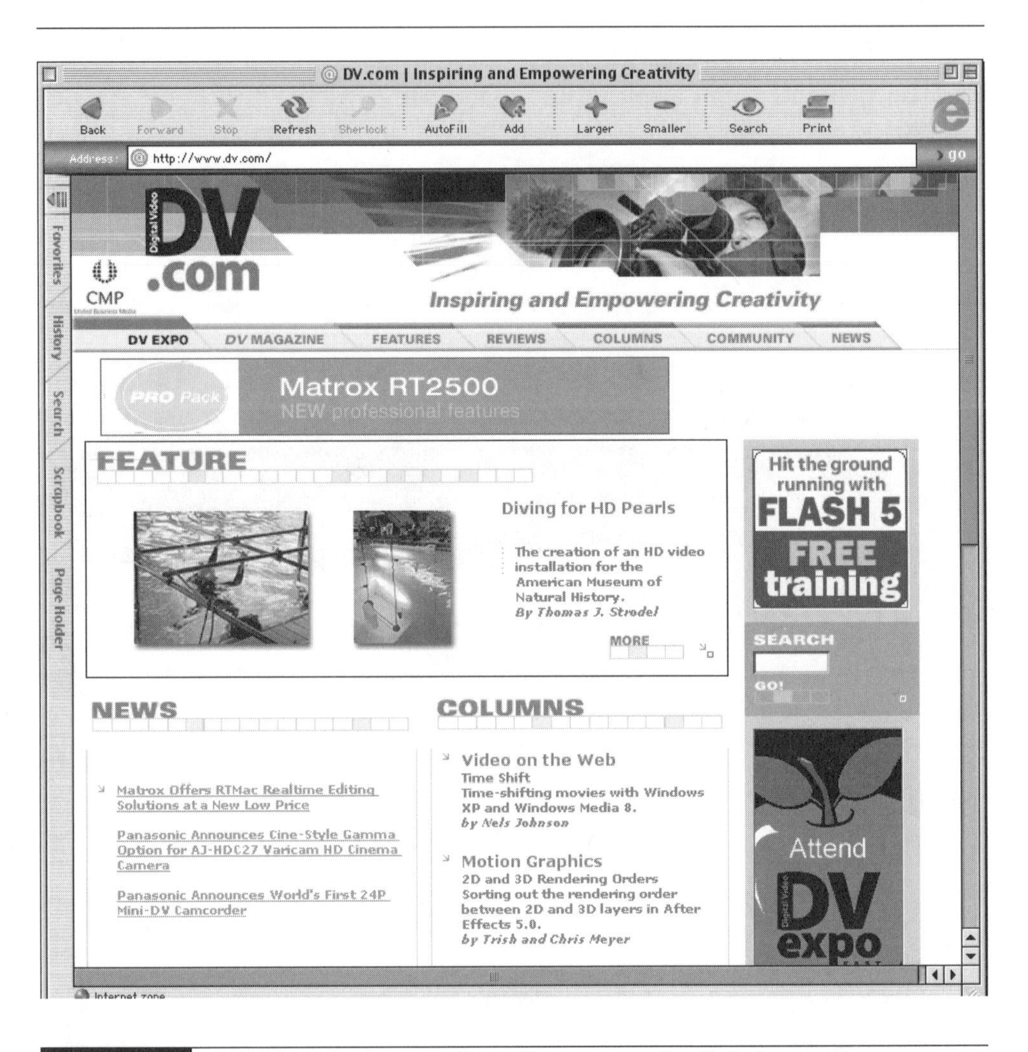

FIGURE B-7 DV Magazine is a popular online resource for digital content creators.

Chapter 3
Looking at Camcorders

Amazon.com—Camcorder Glossary
http://www.amazon.com/exec/obidos/tg/feature/-/94817/102-1860354-9420952

Camcorder and ComputerVideo Magazine http://www.candcv.com

The Digital Dimension—Glossary
http://www.powershot.com/powershot2/why/glossary.html

Sony Consumer Electronics Guide
http://www.sel.sony.com/SEL/consumer/ss5/generic/handycamrtmcamcorders/

American Society of Cinematographers http://www.cinematographer.com/
(see Figure B-8)

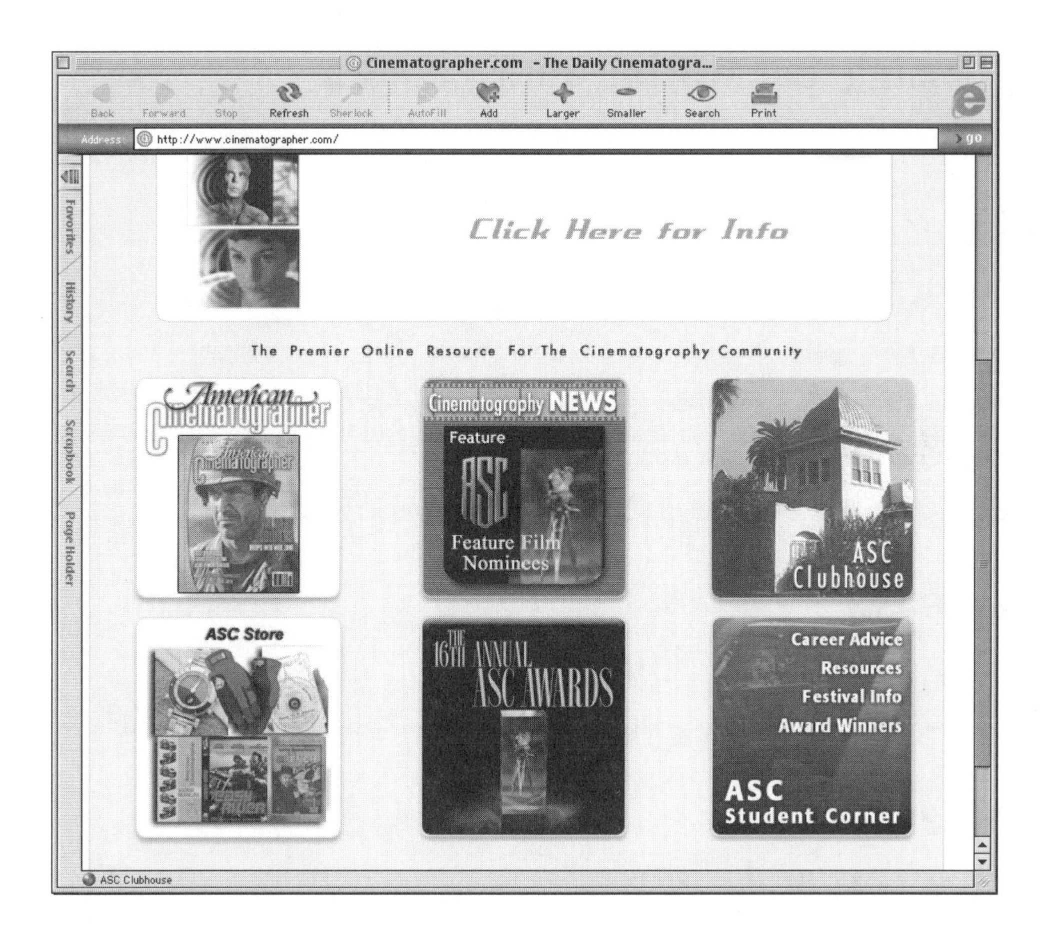

FIGURE B-8 American Society of Cinematographers is an online resource containing news, views and an online community for cinematographers.

Chapter 4
Planning, Plotting, and Producing

Final Draft 6.0—Carbonized for OS X http://www.finaldraft.com/

The Writers Guild's Registration Service (or Intellectual Property Registry) http://www.wga.org/registration/index.html

Chapter 5
Supporting and Moving Your Camera

Glidecam Industries, Inc. www.glidecam.com

Chapter 8
Recording Sound

Dream Escape—Live WebCast and Electronic Music http://www.dream-escape.org/

Sound Ideas www.sound-ideas.com (see Figure B-9)

Magix Entertainment www.magix.com

Wireless http://www.audio-technica.com/using/wireless/index.html

Chapter 12
Editing Video and Sound

Audio & Video Terminology http://www.cs.columbia.edu/~hgs/rtp/glossary.htm

Chapter 14
Adding Text and Titles

Digital Film Library www.artbeats.com

FIGURE B-9 Sound Ideas is an online resource for music and sound effects.

Chapter 15
Expanding Your Sources

DeWolfe Music Library http://www.dewolfemusic.com/

Groovemaker 2.0 www.groovemaker.com

Ulead Systems—Makers of Multimedia Software www.ulead.com

Hemera Technologies www.hemera.com

Chapter 16
Making Copies of Your iMovies

Dazzle Multimedia www.dazzle.com

Formac Electronic www.formac.com

Harman Multimedia http://www.harmanmultimedia.com/

JVC Corporation http://www.jvc.com/main.jsp

ViewSonic Corporation http://www.viewsonic.com/products/projectors.cfm

Chapter 17
Making iMovies for the Web

Cable Today—Engineer's Acronyms http://www.cabletoday.com/ct/acronyms.htm

Glossary of Internet Terms http://www.matisse.net/files/glossary.html

Streaming Cinema
http://www.thebitscreen.com/streaming_cinema/streaming_menu.html
(see Figure B-10)

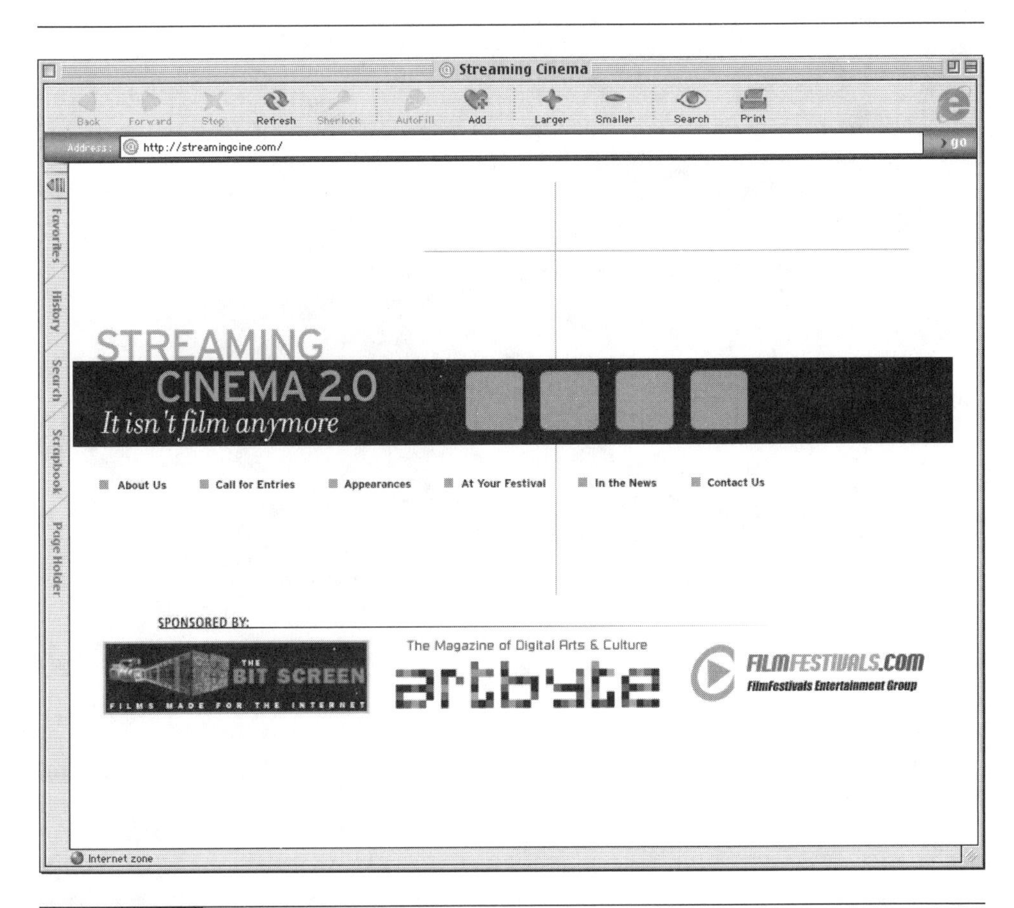

FIGURE B-10 Streaming Cinema is a magazine of digital arts and culture.

QuickTime Guide http://www.apple.com/quicktime/

RealPlayer Home Page http://www.real.com

Atom Shockwave Corp. http://www.shockwave.com/bin/shockwave/entry.jsp (see Figure B-11)

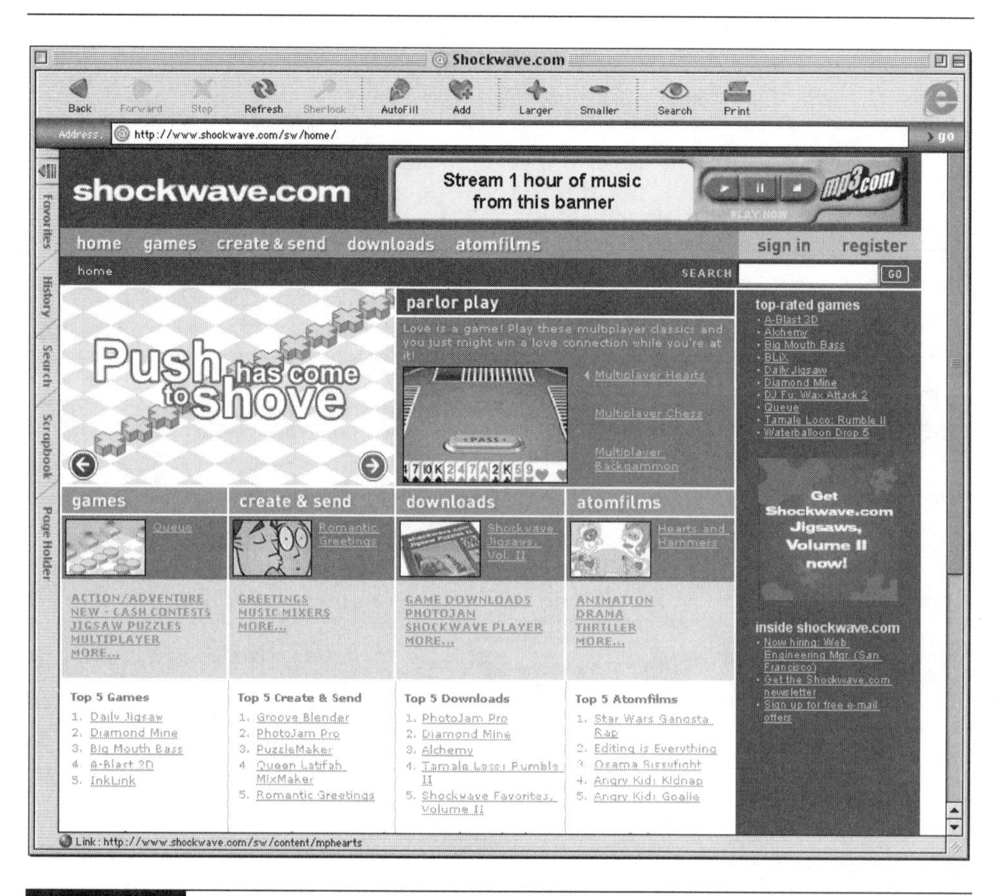

FIGURE B-11 Shockwave.com is another online resource from Atom Films.

Chapter 18
Transferring Your Videos to DVD with iDVD 2

Create DVDs on Your Desktop http://www.apple.com/idvd/

DVD Term Glossary http://www.dvdshop.com.au/jargon.html

Pioneer Electronics www.pioneerelectronics.com

Index

B

C

D

E

F

J

K

L

M

N

O

P

Q

R

S

T

U

V

W

Z

INTERNATIONAL CONTACT INFORMATION

AUSTRALIA
McGraw-Hill Book Company Australia Pty. Ltd.
TEL +61-2-9417-9899
FAX +61-2-9417-5687
http://www.mcgraw-hill.com.au
books-it_sydney@mcgraw-hill.com

CANADA
McGraw-Hill Ryerson Ltd.
TEL +905-430-5000
FAX +905-430-5020
http://www.mcgrawhill.ca

GREECE, MIDDLE EAST, NORTHERN AFRICA
McGraw-Hill Hellas
TEL +30-1-656-0990-3-4
FAX +30-1-654-5525

MEXICO (Also serving Latin America)
McGraw-Hill Interamericana Editores S.A. de C.V.
TEL +525-117-1583
FAX +525-117-1589
http://www.mcgraw-hill.com.mx
fernando_castellanos@mcgraw-hill.com

SINGAPORE (Serving Asia)
McGraw-Hill Book Company
TEL +65-863-1580
FAX +65-862-3354
http://www.mcgraw-hill.com.sg
mghasia@mcgraw-hill.com

SOUTH AFRICA
McGraw-Hill South Africa
TEL +27-11-622-7512
FAX +27-11-622-9045
robyn_swanepoel@mcgraw-hill.com

UNITED KINGDOM & EUROPE (Excluding Southern Europe)
McGraw-Hill Education Europe
TEL +44-1-628-502500
FAX +44-1-628-770224
http://www.mcgraw-hill.co.uk
computing_neurope@mcgraw-hill.com

ALL OTHER INQUIRIES Contact:
Osborne/McGraw-Hill
TEL +1-510-549-6600
FAX +1-510-883-7600
http://www.osborne.com
omg_international@mcgraw-hill.com